LAODICEA – one of the seven churches
From a sketch made on the spot.

THE WONDER BOOK

OF THE BIBLE

BOOKS IN THE BIBLE STUDY TEXTBOOK SERIES

THE WONDER BOOK
OF THE BIBLE

A Commentary On The
Book Of Revelation

Lee G. Tomlinson
A Servant Of The Lord Jesus Christ

Now unto Him that is able to keep you from falling, and to present you faultless before the presence of His glory with exceeding joy,

To the only wise God our Savior, be glory and majesty, dominion and power, both now and ever.

Jude 25

COLLEGE PRESS, Joplin, Missouri

DEDICATION

*Dedicated to the Truth
as it is in Christ Jesus*

CONTENTS

Opened—The Red Horse—Civil War in the Roman Empire—
The Barrack Emperors—The Significance of the Sword—The
Third Seal Opened—The Black Horse—The Significance of the
Balances—The Fourth Seal Opened—The Pale Horse—The Seal
of Death—Gibbon's Account of the Epoch of Death—The Fifth
Seal Opened—The Radical Change of Imagery—The Seal of
Persecution—Universal Persecution of Christians—Souls Under
the Altar—The Cry of the Martyrs—The Edict of Toleration—
The Opening of the Sixth Seal—The Striking Imagery—The
Meaning of the Symbols—A Study in Spiritual Astronomy—The
Earth shaking Changes under Constantine—His Acceptance of
Christianity—The decree concerning the First Day of the Week
—Abolition of Gladiatorial Combats—The First General Coun-
cil of the Church at Nicea—The Removal of the Capital from
Rome to Constantinople.

The parenthesis revealing the sealing of God's Servants—
The four Angels holding back the four winds—God's provision
for His own during time of political and religious revolution—
Significance of the numer twelve—Significance of the numbering—Both the Old Testament Israel of God and the New Testament Israel sealed—What tribulation is meant here—Summary.

The Seventh and Final Seal Opened—The First Trumpet—
The Second Trumpet—The Third Trumpet—The Star Falling
from Heaven—The Name of the Star is Called Wormwood—The
Fourth Trumpet.

The Sixth Trumpet—The Bottomless Pit—The Locusts—
Like Horses—Crowned with Gold—The Grass not Hurt—The
Five Months—The Sting in the Tails—Their King called Abad-
don, or Apollyon.

Second Parenthesis of First Division of Revelation—The
Open Book—Religious Renaissance—A Study in History—Sum-
mary of the Reformation Movement—The Seven Thunders—
Their Voice Sealed—The Little Book eaten—Sweet to Taste—
Bitter in Digestion—Word Taken to all Peoples.

of the Bride, the Lamb's Wife—John in the Spirit to View the Celestial City—Description of the City—Measurement of the City and of the Wall of the City—Twelve Occurrences of the Word "Twelve"—Why Were the Gates Made of Pearl?—No Temple in the City—All the Glory of the Nations brought Into the City—Nothing That Defiles Permitted to Enter.

Introduction—Blessedness of the Conditions Obtaining in the Holy City—The River of Life—The Tree of Life—Life, the Theme of the Closing Chapter—Introversion of the Theme—The Heavenly Diet—Leaves of the Tree of Life Banishes Disease—No More Curse—No Night There—End of Third Division of the Book of Revelation—The Epilogue—Blessedness for Reading and Keeping of the Sayings of Revelation—John Again Forbidden to Worship an Angel—Urgency for the "Uncovering" of the Sayings of This Book—Final Assurance of Christ's Return—Christ Makes it Clear That it is He Who Gave John These Revelations Through Angelic Ministrations—The Last of Christ's "I Am's"—Invitation of the Spirit and the Bride for Christ to Come—Gracious Invitation Extended By Them to All Who Have Heard the Promise to Join in the Invitation "Come"—Warning Against Adding to, or Taking From the Prophecy of this Book—John Bows His Head and Writes, "Amen, Even So Come, Lord Jesus."

INTRODUCTION TO REVELATION

AUTHORSHIP

There is no book of the New Testament to whose authorship the testimony of history is more definite. Within the space of a few, years after the death of John, the Apostle, it was being quoted and ascribed to John by writers who either knew him in person or who obtained their information from those who sat at his feet.

Papias

Our first witness is Papias. He was overseer of the church at Hierapolis, a city near Laodicea and Colosse. It was the last home and burial place of the Apostle Philip and two of his three daughters. Eusebius quotes Polycrates, elder in the church at Ephesus, saying, "Philip, one of the twelve apostles, who sleeps in Hierapolis, and his two virgin daughters." Another of his daughters, who lived in the Holy Spirit, rests at Ephesus." Eccles. Hist. 111 C. 31, V. 24.

He was the author of a work of five books entitled, "An Exposition of Oracles of the Lord." The whole work has perished, except a few quotations from it by early writers, chiefly Eusebius. Eusebius says that Papias talked with the daughters of Philip. "But we must now show how Papias, coming to them received a wonderful account from the daughters of Philip."—Eccles. Hist. 111 39.

Irenaeus says that Papias was a companion of Polycarp and a hearer of John.

"These things are borne witness to in writing by Papias, the hearer of John, and a companion of Polycarp, in his fourth book, for their are five books compiled by him."—Heresies V. 33.

Papias conversed with various persons who had been followers of the apostle and inquired of them what the apostle taught. He says: "But if I meet with one who has been a follower of the elders anywhere, I made it a point to inquire what were the declarations of the elders. What was said by Andrew, Peter, or Philip. What by Thomas, James, John or Matthew, or any other of the disciples of the Lord; for I do not think I derive so much benefit from books as from the living voice of those that are still surviving."—Eccles. Hist. 111 39.

Papias, as best we know, was born about A. D. 70 and Eusebius says Papias bore testimony to a number of the New Testament books.

1

Andrew of Caesarea, a Greek writer of the fifth century declares Papias bore testimony to the inspiration of the book of Revelation. The words of Andrew are as follows: "With regard to the inspiration of the Book (Revelation) we deem it superfluous to add another word; for the blessed Gregory, Cyril, and Theologus, and even some of still older date, Papias, Irenaeus, Methodius and Hippolytus, bore entirely satisfactory testimony to it."—Fragments of Papias VIII Anti-Nicene Library, Vol. 1.

Papias was a companion of Polycarp, who died February 23, A.D. 155. Polycarp declared at his martyrdom that he had served the Lord Jesus eighty-six years. The account reads: "Then the proconsul urging him and saying, 'Swear and I will set thee at liberty, reproach Christ;' Polycarp declared, 'Eighty and six years have I served him, and he never did me an injury, how then can I blaspheme my King, and my Savior?'"—Martyrdom of Polycarp C. IX Anti-Nicene Library, Vol. 1.

This dates his baptism as early as A. D. 70 the date of the destruction of Jerusalem. After his baptism he lived thirty years contempory with the apostle John. And as John spent the later part of his life at Ephesus, only fifty miles from Smyrna, where Polycarp was appointed overseer of the church by the apostles (so declared by Irenaeus) he must have seen and heard John.

Thus we see that Papias, being a companion of Polycarp, who was instructed by the apostle was in a position to know the facts when he declared the book of Revelation was written by inspiration by the Apostle, John.

Irenaeus

To Papias may be added Iranaeus born between A. D. 115 and A.D. 125, who tells us he was long a pupil of Polycarp. "But Polycarp was not only instructed by apostles, and conversed with many who had seen Christ, but was also by apostles in Asia appointed bishop of the church in Smyrna, whom I saw in my early youth, for he tarried a very long time, and, when a very old man, gloriously and most nobly suffering martyrdom, departed this life, having taught things which he had learned from the apostles, and which the church had handed down, and which alone are true."— Irenaeus, against Heresies 262, 263.

Of course, with such opportunities he certainly was not ignorant of what John had written, yet he declares explicitly that John is the author of the book of Revelation. He makes many quotations from the Apocalypse. He also states its approximate date, saying: "We will not, however, incur the risk of pronouncing positively as to the names of the Anti-christ; for if it were necessary that his name should be revealed at the present time, it would have been announced by him who beheld the apocalyptic vision. For that was seen not very long since, but almost in our day, toward the end of Domitian's reign."—Against Heresies Vol. 30,3.

Justin Martyr

He was a native of the ancient city of Shechem in Palestine, which was called Flavia Neapolis by the Romans, and is now called Nablus by the Arabs. His name, and that of his father, Priscus, and his grandfather, Bacchius, are Roman, indicating possible Roman lineage. The exact date of his birth is unknown, but he wrote about 150 years after Christ. He wrote two apologies, in the first of which he says, "Lest some should, without reason and for the perversion of what we teach, maintain that we say that Christ was born one-hundred and fifty years ago under Cyrenius, and subsequently, in the time of Pontius Pilate, taught what we say He taught; and should cry out against us as though all men who were born before him were irresponsible, let us anticipate and solve the difficulty."—First apology C. 46.

Justin Martyr quotes by name the apocalypse, or the book of Revelation and cites the name of the author. "There was a certain man with us whose name was John, one of the apostles of Christ, who prophesied by a revelation that was made to him that those who believed in our Christ should dwell a thousand years in Jerusalem and that thereafter the general and in short the eternal revelation and judgment of all men would likewise take place."—Dialogue 1 6.C.61.

Tertullian

The next witness is Tertullian, a famous Latin writer of Africa who was born in Carthage about A. D. 160 and died about A. D. 240. His knowledge of the New Testament books extended through the last quarter of the second century. He frequently quotes from Revelation, ascribing it to John.

3

"John in his apocalypse is commanded to chastise those who eat things sacrificed to idols and commit fornication." (Rev. 2:14)— Prescriptions against Heresies XXXIII 40.

Eusebius

Eusebius, called the father of Ecclesiastical History, because he wrote the first church history that has come down to our day, lived from A. D. 270 to A. D. 340. He was bishop of the church in Caesarea in Palestine. He lived through the persecution under the Emperor Diocletian which continued from A. D. 303 to 313 A. D. which he describes. He lived to see christianity established by law throughout the Roman Empire. He was commissioned by Constantine, the first Christian Emperor, to have transcribed fifty copies of the Bible for the use of the churches in Constantinople. He declares that John wrote the Apocalypse. "What shall we say of Him who reclined upon the breast of Jesus? I mean John, who has left one gospel, in which he confesses that he could write so many that the whole world could not contain them. He also wrote the apocalypse, commanded as he was to conceal and not write the voices of the seven thunders."—Eccles. Hist. VI, XXV, P. 246.

Muratorian Canon

We turn now from the evidence of the authorship of Revelation as given by the early church fathers, to the catalogues of the New Testament books.

The earliest formal catalogue of the New Testament books now extant, is a document called the Muratorian Canon. The manuscript of this document was found in 1740 A. D. in an old library in Milan, by an Italian named Muratori, whence the title Muratorian Canon. The manuscript belongs to the seventh or eighth century and is a Latin translation from a Greek original.

It claims to have been composed by a contempory of Pius, bishop of Rome, who died in the year 157. It could not be of a later date than A. D. 170. The existing manuscript is fragmentary having lost some lines from both the beginning and the end. It contains in the canon the book of Revelation.

Catalogue of Council of Carthage

Some of these catalogues are found in the acts of various ecclesiastical assemblies, which set forth the books of the Old and New Testaments.

The catalogue of the Council of Carthage names all of the canonical books of the Old Testament, included in our present Bible and then gives the New Testament books in the following order: "Four books of the gospels, one book of the acts of the apostles, thirteen of the Epistles of the Apostle Paul, one of the same to the Hebrews, two Epistles of the apostle Peter, three of John, one of James, one of Judas, one book of the apocalypse of John." It concludes: "We have received from our fathers that these are to be read in the churches."

This will conclude the evidence on the authorship of the apocalypse, or the book of Revelation.

DATE OF COMPOSITION

The ancient church assigned the date of writing the book of Revelation, near the end of the reign of Domitian, the Emperor of Rome. In our study of evidence of the authorship of the apolypse as presented by Irenaeus, we found he said that John "beheld the apocalyptic vision. For that was seen not very long since, but almost in our day, toward the end of Domitian's reign." This was in A. D. 96.

With this plain statement agree all the church fathers who speak of the subject, for the first three centuries. Beginning with the positive and definite statement of Irenaeus there is an unbroken agreement for nearly four centuries that the date of the writing of the book of Revelation belongs to the persecution of the reign of Domitian, some writers placing the exile in the fourteenth year of his reign, which extended from A. D. 81 to A. D. 96.

Clement of Rome

There is no book from an uninspired pen so highly prized by the early church as the Epistle of Clement to the Corinthians. Only three manuscripts of this Epistle are now extant. One of these, long believed to be the only one, is attached to the Alexandrian Manuscript of the New Testament, as if it were a part of the sacred volume. One was discovered in Constantinople in 1875. The third in Syriac Manuscript of the New Testament immediately following the catholic epistles viz. James, first and second Peter, first, second and third John and Jude.

"In 1875 critics and students were startled by the appearance of a careful and complete edition published in Constantinople from a manuscript discovered in the "library of the Holy Sepulchre", in that city. Its editor is Philotheos Bryennios, Metropolitan of Serrae.

Scarcely was this discovery realized when a Syrian Manuscript of the "Two Epistles was also found in 1876 in Paris."—Charteris, Canonicity Int. VIII, IX.

The epistle does not bear the name of Clement, but is written in the name of "the church of God which sojourns at Rome, to the Church of God sojourning at Corinth."

While Clement's name is not attached to the Epistle, Eusebius accredited it to him. "Of this Clement there is one epistle extant, acknowledged as genuine, of considerable length and of great merit, which he wrote in the name of the Church at Rome to that at Corinth, at the time when there was a discension in the latter. This we know to have been publically read for the common benefit in most of the churches, both in former times and in our own; and that at the time mentioned an edition did take place at Corinth, is abundantly attested by Hegesippus."—Eusebius Eccles. Hist. 111, 16.

The epistle was written, according to the opening statement of this epistle by Clement, after some "sudden and calamitous events" had just happened at Corinth. Such persecutions frequently occurred under the reign of Domitian, and the most probable date assigned to the epistle is A. D. 96 or 97.

Clement was old enough in the year 93 to be appointed bishop of a large church like Rome and thus it would seem he lived through all the period of the apostolic writings. The earliest of the New Testament books was I Thessalonians, which was written A. D. 52, just 41 years before Clements appointment to office. He had knowledge, then, of what writings had come from the pens of the apostles up to the date of his own epistle, seeing that his epistle was written before the death of John.

While he quotes from Matthew, Luke, Mark, Ephesians, Romans, Titus, Hebrews I and II Peter, he quotes nothing from John, for none of Johns' writings had gone into circulation, and

6

perhaps none of them had been written at the date of Clement's epistle. Then, this puts the date of the composition of Revelation close to the close of the first century.

INTERNAL EVIDENCE

The evidence necessary to confirm a document may be either external or internal. External evidence is that derived from other sources than the book itself, which has been the nature of the evidence we have already presented. Internal evidence is that found in the contents of the book itself. The proper method of procedure in this discussion is to first assume that the Book of Revelation is genuine, and then search its pages for evidence and reach our decision after this internal evidence is considered in connection with the external. We will consider only a few brief items.

First: An ecclesiastical organization reveals itself in the seven churches of the apocalypse which did not reveal itself until the very end of the first and the beginning of the second century. Note: Each church had an angel or man of the church through which the church is addressed. There is no evidence of an individual enjoying such a distinction before the last part of the first century.

Second: The expression "The Lord's Day" does not occur in the earlier apostolic writings. Rather, they always use the expression, "The first day of the week." (I Cor. 16:2) (Acts 20:7)

But the writers of the second century, even from its beginning use the phrase, "The Lord's Day."

This term then points to a period near the beginning of the second century.

Third: The expressions in Rev. 2:9 and 3:9 indicate a complete separation between the church and the synagogue. Such a separation did not finally take place until the time of the destruction of Jerusalem's down fall and the close of the first century.

Fourth: On the other hand, there is no internal evidence within the apocalypse against, either the genuineness of the book or the time of its writing at the end of the second century.

THE PLACE

The place where John received the apocalypse of future events is declared by the author himself. It is the universal testimony of the early church that John survived the destruction of Jerusalem, that when the holocaust of war fell upon that city, John in obedience to the Lord's warning (Matthew 24:16) fled from the approaching desolation and took up his residence in Ephesus. There he labored among the churches established by the apostle Paul.

This region was known as Asia. This constituted the peninsula lying between the Mediterranean and the Black Seas and bounded on the west by the Aegean.

In the latter part of the reign of Domitian he was banished to a rocky isle, about 20 miles from the coast of Asia. In the southern part of the Greek Archipelago is a tiny island called Patmo, or Patmos. John declares he was banished to this small island "for the Word of God and the testimony of Jesus Christ." It is only about a mile in diameter, by six or seven miles long.

CIRCUMSTANCES

A period of about sixty years had passed since the first church was founded in Jerusalem. All the other apostles had passed to their reward, receiving the crown of martyrdom, except John, concerning whom the Master had said, "If I will that he tarry till I come, what is that to thee?" (John 21:15-24).

Churches had been established in the principle cities of Asia and Europe, so much so that it aroused the fears and hatred of paganism.

Beginning with Nero, the church had undergone one persecution after another. The present persecution was that of Domitian. At this period, and for many generations after this, when the church is persecuted, the persecutor is always pagan Rome.

With this understanding, we need not wonder that the last of the apostles, fore-casting the future fortunes of the church should record the fortunes and misfortunes of the last great world empire, persecutor both of the Jews and the Church of Christ.

SYSTEMS OF INTERPRETATION

Before we begin the actual study of this wonderful book, it would be profitable to consider some of the systems of interpretation followed by men.

There is probably no other portion of the Scriptures concerning the meaning of which the interpreters have so widely differed. The differences are due to the different systems of interpretation employed. Of these are three principle ones, all containing some truth. Shall we consider the three principle systems.

The Preterist: According to the interpreters following this system, the apocalyptic visions of the book apply to events, chiefly in the history of the Jewish nation and of pagan Rome. They hold that these events have already occurred. They declare that the events took place before the visions were given and that there is no such thing as prediction in the book. Hence these interpreters are called Preterists. Most Catholic commentators hold this view.

The Futurists: Those who take this view hold that the predictions in the book apply to events still in the future and will be fulfilled in the future history of literal Israel. They assert that Israel will again occupy Palestine, that the temple will actually be rebuilt and that the Holy City will be trodden down for 1260 days by the Gentiles.

The Historical: This system holds that a succession of historical events, future when John penned of them, but now in part in the past, are portrayed by a series of visions. This system seems more nearly correct, BUT THE ERROR MUST BE AVOIDED of supposing that the book is continuously historical from beginning to end.

It must be born in mind that there is more than one series of visions; that when one series ends another follows which is synchronous, at least in part. By this we mean both series may describe events happening at the same time. These events have coincident periods.

It must ever be kept in mind that this book is definitely a book of prophecy. In the Old Testament we have a succession of prophets appearing and making their predictions. In Revelation, we have one prophet, John, proclaiming a succession of prophecies.

He was "shown the things which were shortly to come to pass." John recorded what he saw. The future was revealed to him in a series of visions. The pictures that appeared, in panoramic form before his eyes represents future events.

Thus we see that each is a symbolical representation of what was then future, but now may be past history. Symbolical pictures follow each other in rapid succession as the seals are opened and the trumpets sounded. A careful study of the scriptural meaning of these symbols is a necessary exercise to the proper interpretation of this mysterious book.

Divisions

We must ever keep in mind that there is more than one series of visions, and that these overlap each other, revealing different aspects and features of the same period.

There are two major divisions of the book.

First: The first division covers the first eleven chapters and is divided in turn into three parts.

1. The first covers chapters one through the third. This part deals with the introduction, the vision of the Son of Man and the letters to the seven churches.

2. The second part covers chapters four through the eleventh chapter and the eighteenth verse. This part opens with a vision of the throne, followed by a vision of a book sealed with seven seals in the hand of Him who sits on the throne and continues through the seals and trumpets.

The lamb of God prevails to open the seals. As each seal is opened a vision appears which presents a symbol representing a period of human history.

Six seals are opened in succession, followed by a pause before the opening of the seventh seal. When the seventh seal is opened it is discovered to embrace seven thunders and seven trumpets. The trumpets are blown in succession, each followed by great stirring events. When the last trumpet is blown the end comes when Christ is triumphant.

10

The seven seals, with the seven trumpets contained under the last seal, reach to the end of time.

Second: The second division covers the last eleven chapters of the book, and is divided in turn into three parts.

1. The first part chapters 12 to 18 opens with the vision of a woman, a symbol of the church, confronted by an enemy which appears as a sevenheaded and ten-horned beast. Later a false church, in contradistinction to the first woman—the true church, appears sitting on the seven-headed Beast. These opposing powers, under the symbolism of Babylon are finally overthrown.

2. The second part, chapters 19 and 20, describe the great victory over the Devil and his secular and religious organizations, the Millennial period and the final uprising and defeat of Satan.

3. The third part, chapters 21 and 22 describe the heavenly home of the Redeemed saints and ends with closing exhortations.

THE SCOPE OF REVELATION

The scope of Revelation is limited. It does not attempt to reveal all the everchanging history of all nations, races and kingdoms throughout the Gospel age. The question then arises: To what countries and accompaning events do the predictions and symbols apply?

If we turn to God's dealings with the Israel of God in the Old Testament as he spoke through a succession of prophets we will find a correct answer. There, we find, the central thought in all their predictions is the future history of the Old Testament People of God.

With this great divine purpose in mind, they predict the fate of the great gentile nations with whom the Jews come in contact, who affected their fortunes by aiding them or by becoming their conquerors. Hence Assyria, Babylon, Tyre, Egypt, Rome and Greece are made burdens of their prophecy.

Exactly, and by the same token, the same is true of the New Testament prophecies contained in the Book of Revelation. The prophecies deal with the future of the New Testament Israel of God, the church, and of necessity reveal much concerning the opposing powers and persecuting nations.

It was not Christ's purpose to give in Revelation the outline of all history, hence many nations are not mentioned, but to outline the fortunes, tribulations and triumphs of the church.

The church was, in the earlier centuries, almost wholly within the confines of the vast, persecuting empire of Pagan Rome, hence this opposing power presents itself often in the prophetic visions of Patmos.

Since later the mantle of the pagan empire, fell upon Papal Rome, we find that this new religious power plays a prominent part in the unfolding symbolic visions of Revelation. So we shall see that Revelation primarily outlines the history of the church, and in subordination of this primary purpose, it portrays the history of two great persecuting powers, Pagan and Papal Rome. Finally, it portrays the triumphant church and the glories of the New Jerusalem to be enjoyed by the overcoming saints.

Author's Foreword to the Reader

To write a book upon any subject is a task that calls forth the best that in a man lieth. To write a compendium on the Book of Revelation is the challenge supreme.

The writing of any book necessarily must be predicated upon some sound reason for such an engagement. The primus mobile of writing a dissertation upon the Apocalypse must be nothing short of a burning desire to magnify the sacredness, the authenticity and the inerrant accuracy of Divine prophecy.

To pen a text-book upon a secular subject enjoins a comprehensive knowledge of the best authorities on that subject, besides added individual research. To write a commentary on Revelation requires no less than the blessed guidance of the Holy Spirit whom Christ commissioned to show the things to come.

One must be impelled by the loftiest motivation in order to even begin such an effort so confronted with mountainous difficulties.

The interpretation of any book of the Bible is a challenging endeavor. To unfold the mysteries of a book written entirely in signs and symbols, such as characterize the Apocalypse, is an Herculean task to be assumed only under the directive of the inspired Word of God.

In the anticipation of such a project, the author must confess that he found himself in "a strait betwixt two". There was a great hesitancy to take up the pen to write when remembrance called to mind the fearful plagues promised as a wrathful visitation from God upon those who became guilty of adding to the things contained with'n the Apocalypse.

Again, the prospect of having his part in the book of life and of the holy city, taken away by taking from the words of the book of prophecy, also served as a strong deterrent for many years.

After a quarter of a century and more of contemplation of such a labor, the writer, by the grace of God, the love of Christ and the energizing of the Holy Spirit, began this work. I say began. Such a work can never be said to be finished.

The first determination to be made was, on the very face of things, that of method of interpretation. Three systems presented themselves.

First, there was the futuristic system. The proponents of this method of interpretation hold that everything described in the visions of this book is yet future to be fulfilled after the rapture of the saints. Obviously, the very first verse of this book of Revelation eliminates such a system. It reads:

"The Revelation of Jesus Christ, which God gave unto Him to show unto His servants *things which must shortly come to pass.*"

Second, there was the system, which for lack of better designation, I call the Spiritualistic. This is that method of interpretation which spiritualizes every thing away to where every symbol takes the meaning of each individual interpreter.

One verse of the Sacred Scriptures annihilates such an approach to the study of this great book:

"Knowing this first, that no prophecy of the Scripture is of any private interpretation" (11 Peter 1:20)

With the elimination of these two systems only one remained—the Historical. This system is based upon the primal declaration of the book itself, namely, that John was to "write the things which thou hast seen and the things which are, and the things which shall be hereafter." (Rev. 1:19)

But not only is the Historical view harmonious with the book's own declaration of its purpose, but history amply substantiates this viewpoint in that the events symbolized therein have either happened or are now coming to pass. So closely have the happenings of history paralleled the prophetic pronouncements of the Apocalypse that they cannot honestly be dismissed and rejected on the ground of coincidences.

When throughout the book one beholds the events of history fitting hand-in-glove with the succession of prophecies presented therein he must, like Thomas, come to believe with a like firmness of conviction.

This historical approach becomes all the more realistic when it is understood that the various visions given do not chronologically follow one another in point of time, although the events predicted in the vision itself are chronologically arranged. This leads logically to the second determination to be made—the starting point of each separate vision.

Like a surveyor cannot run his line without beginning at the Bench Mark, so each vision has an historical Bench Mark, or time and place of beginning. Having scripturally determined the true beginning the Spiritual surveyor is able to survey a true line of prophetic interpretation.

The visions may have the same starting point and take us over a segment of time already covered by a former vision, but this is in order to present things from a different angle, or events of a different sphere, yet all related to the life of the church throughout the gospel dispensation.

The third determination was an accurate interpretation of the meaning of the rich symbolism of the book. There has been a golden rule of interpretation, followed by lovers of God's Word, which declares:

"When the plain sense of the Scriptures makes common
sense, seek no other sense; therefore take every word at
its primary, ordinary, literal meaning unless the facts of
the context indicate clearly otherwise."

When one enters into the realm of Revelation, certainly the concluding clause of this Golden Rule of Interpretation becomes operative. "The facts of the context indicate clearly otherwise."

Revelation is pre-eminently a book of symbols, signs, wonders. The book is written not in common speech, like other books of the New Testament, but in sign language. "He sent and sign-i-fied it by His angel unto His servant John.

The interpretation of these symbols has proved to be a pitfall to many readers of the Apocalypse, although it should never have been.

If, as Peter says, "no prophecy of the Scripture is of any private interpretation," neither are the prophetic symbols to be privately interpreted.

14

Therefore, the author made, at the very outset, a fourth determination, namely, that every sign, symbol or figure is explained somewhere within the Bible itself. The Bible is its own, only and best interpreter. One may have to run the gamut of the entire Bible, but he will be richly repaid when in some "hidden corner" of God's Divine Library he discovers the meaning of some baffling symbol.

Added to the joy of a new discovery is the deep-down satisfaction of knowing God's mind in the matter.

The fifth and final determination was the naming of the book to be penned. At first no name presented itself with sufficient force to elicit lasting attention, but gradually and almost unconsciously an appropriate and scriptural title crossed and recrossed this stage of prophetic drama.

Since it was "the Revelation of Jesus Christ", it seemed altogether apropos to incorporate the name "Revelation" in whatever title was finally settled upon.

Again, since the Apocalypse was penned in a style nowhere universally characteristic of any other book of the Sacred Volume, that fact demanded consideration. Written, as it was, in the language of sign, symbol and wonder, why not call the book, "Revelation—the Wonder Book of the Bible"? And so the title was chosen.

John said, "Blessed is he that readeth and they that hear the words of this prophecy, and keep those things which are written therein, for the time is at hand." (Rev. 1:3)

The author's fervent prayer is that this book, launched upon a vast sea of books, may have so carefully charted its course by the Scriptural compass of Divine Interpretation, that its readers may land safely on that enchanted Isle of the Treasure Trove of Truth.

If it shall have afforded safe passage to one soul in reaching Heaven's Harbor of the Holy City, the labor shall not have been in vain.

Prayer

Oh Master of Wind and Wave we thank Thee gratefully that Thou hast enabled us to walk upon the waters of symbolic wonders.

CHAPTER I

INTRODUCTION

We are beginning the study of the final book of the Bible. It is, as it were, the climax of all the other books of the Holy Scriptures. So many other foolish vagaries and extravagant fancies have been published that many intelligent students of the Scriptures have turned away from the book of Revelation as a deep mystery that can not be understood. The book is not intended to be a puzzle, or an enigma which no one could solve. The writer expected his message to be understood by those who would spiritually discern its uncoverings.

Its very name signifies it can be understood; though all who approach its study must commit himself to a deeper delving into its truths, than any other book of the sacred volume requires. Here as in all other books, but in a greater degree, it is necessary that men shall have hearing ear and the understanding heart.

This book is called a "Revelation" of Jesus Christ of the things that must shortly come to pass. "The Greek word for the book is "Apocalypse", which means "uncovering". John used the word in the opening verse with the meaning that the covering is rolled off the future so that we may understand. So Revelation is not a sealed book, but the uncovering is done by the means of graphic symbolism. Doubtless, Christ resorted to symbolism to protect the book from destruction at the hands of the wicked institutions portrayed herein. Had such adversaries been called by their actual names they would have either destroyed the book, or declared the book of a later composition, because it named powers, religious and political, by names unknown until later centuries.

Again, symbolism was used that the true followers of Christ might know its mysteries, otherwise hidden to the worldling. Christ used this principle in speaking his parables. Upon one occasion as recorded in (Matthew 13:10-17) his disciples came asking "Why speakest thou unto them in parables?" He answered and said unto them, "Because it is given unto you to know the mysteries of the Kingdom of Heaven, but to them it is not given."

16

Why Men Have Blundered

There are several reasons why men have made grave mistakes in their attempts to understand the apocalypse.

First: Thy have stumbled at the symbolism. Indeed it is preeminently a book of symbols. There passed before John's eyes, like a panoramic picture, a great painting of scenes, made to move past the onlooker.

As Daniel by the river Ulai, and Ezekial by the river Chebar, saw series of visions in which were caused to pass before their minds a series of pictures portraying events of the future, so the apostle John on the Isle of Patmos, as the New Testament Prophet, beheld a panorama of the "things shortly to come to pass" as the future was unfolded to John by symbols which fitly represented the things signified, so his visions are filled with symbols.

As in all Old Testament prophecy it is necessary for us to interpret symbols according to the laws of symbolism, so we find the same need in the apocalypse.

These symbols aptly represent events that are to take place in the political and religious arenas of history, particularly as they affect the fortunes of the true church of Christ.

John simply records what he saw. A prophet is a fore-seer. John saw upon the sky, or upon the waters of the sea, or on the sands of Patmos, the exact events he describes symbolically. It is our province to examine the symbols and determine their meaning, by a careful comparison with history.

Second: The apocalypse has been misunderstood because we have failed to study it in the light of history. These events were future history to John when he wrote, but most of them have become history now. It is well to hold this book of prophecy in one hand and the books of history in the other. Who could ever understand Nebuchadnezzar's vision of the man with the head of gold, the breast and arms of silver, the belly and thighs of brass, the legs of iron with feet of part iron and part clay without studying the history of the kingdoms of Babylon, Media-Persia, Greece and Rome.

He who would approach the study of Revelation, must be versed in the history of the church, with her attendant perils from political and spiritual adversaries. Such a student will discover to his unending delight that secular history has unwittingly fortified the book of Revelation.

PROLOGUE 1:1-8

1 The Revelation of Jesus Christ, which God gave him to show unto his servants, even the things which must shortly come to pass: and he sent and signified it by his angel unto his servant John; 2 who bare witness of the word of God, and of the testimony of Jesus Christ, even of all things that he saw. 3 Blessed is he that readeth, and they that hear the words of the prophecy, and keep the things that are written therein: for the time is at hand.

4 John to the seven churches that are in Asia: Grace to you and peace, from him who is and who was and who is to come; and from the seven Spirits that are before his throne; 5 and from Jesus Christ, who is the faithful witness, the firstborn of the dead, and the ruler of the kings of the earth. Unto him that loveth us, and loosed us from our sins by his blood; 6 and he made us to be a kingdom, to be priests unto his God and Father; to him be the glory and the dominion for ever and ever. Amen. 7 Behold, he cometh with the clouds; and every eye shall see him, and they that pierced him; and all the tribes of the earth shall mourn over him. Even so, Amen.

8 I am the Alpha and the Omega, saith the Lord God, who is and who was and who is to come, the Almighty.

vs. 1 What a tender introduction is given by Christ to the church. This prologue runs through the first eight verses. This opening phrase could well read, *"The uncovering* by Jesus Christ, which God gave to show unto his servants." And the things shown were shortly to come to pass. The literal meaning is "to come to pass in quick succession." Christ sent and signified by his servant John or, he sent and sign-i-fied, uncovered the future in signs and symbols. He also signified by his angel. Throughout the apocalypse an angel appears to be employed in the task of unveiling the scenes that follow in successive order.

vs. 2 John bore record of all he saw and heard. A special emphasis is given here of his record because such world shattering events were revealed to him under such startling symbolism.

vs. 3 While the reading of any book of the Bible brings its blessing, it would seem that a special one is pronounced here upon the reader, the hearer and the faithful keeper of the "those things that are written therein." And it is an oft experienced fact that whether we can understand all that is written in this book or not yet it is always true that the book takes a peculiar hold upon the reader and hearer, as if to say, "stay by me, study me, search me." And this grip the apocalypse lays upon the one who studies its contents is further enhanced by the fact that "the time is at hand."

vs. 4 Now John begins to deliver the record of the visions given him to be in turn, given to the seven churches of Asia. The Asia of John's day did not refer to our Asia as we understand it today, but rather to the Roman province called Asia of which Ephesus was the capitol. All seven churches named in verse 11, were in that province. It would seem that seven, the perfect and sacred Scriptural number was chosen, because the seven were to refer not alone to the seven individual churches within the province, but symbolize the whole church of Christ throughout her history. This becomes patent when we keep in mind that John was to write of "the things which *thou hast seen*, and the *things which are*, and the things which *shall be hereafter*. (Rev. 1:19)

Again he addressed himself to more than the seven individual churches, because we know there were more than seven churches in the province of Asia at this time. The New Testament speaks also of Colosse, Meletus (Acts 20:17) and Hierapolis (Col. 4:13)

Even a casual study of the salutations and benedictions of each church of the seven demonstrates to us that these refer to seven great epochs or periods in the entire history of the church.

The benediction, like that in other New Testament Epistles, shows that Revelation is also classified by John as an epistle. While this epistle is addressed to seven individual churches, yet through them it is addressed to all the churches in every age.

Grace comes from the Holy Spirit, the numbers even indicating fullness, completeness, perfection. In (Rev. 3:1) we read "These things saith he that hath the seven Spirits of God." Christ, the speaker, has the fullness of the Spirit. Whereas, the apostles had the baptismal degree, others had a less measure conferred by the laying on of the apostle's hands, and those obedient to the gospel have the indwelling presence of the Holy Spirit, as a teacher, comforter, energizer. Christ had the spirit without measure. "For he whom God hath sent speaketh the Words of God: for God giveth not the Spirit by measure unto Him." (John 3:34) To give anything by measure indicates a partial, scanty bestowal. The Spirit of God, even in inspired prophets was but a partial and intermittent gift, but in Jesus, the Son of God, the Spirit of God dwelt fully and uninterruptedly. The present tense, "giveth" indicates a continuous communication of the Spirit. If Christ had received the Spirit "by measure", then his gift of the Spirit could become exhausted. Hence the fullness of the Spirit possessed by Christ, is presented by John as the seven Spirits of God. This benediction comes from the Christ in whom "dwelleth the fullness of the Godhead bodily." (Colossians 2:9)

vs. 5 We are loosed from our sins by the shedding of Christ's blood, which is applied to us when we are "baptized into his death," where He shed His blood. And through Christ's resurrection from the dead, life and immortality are brought to light for us all as we arise from baptism to walk in newness of life.

vs. 6 In Christ's church, or kingdom, each obedient baptized believer is a priest. No Christian needs a priest to offer up sacrifice for him, for he can go directly to the throne of grace, "by a new and living way, which He (Christ) hath consecrated for us through the veil, that is to say the flesh" (Hebrews 10:20) Peter, himself, said, "ye are a chosen generation, a royal *priesthood*, a holy nation, a peculiar people." (I Peter 2:9)

vs. 7 This refers to Christ's second advent when He shall return to judge all nations (Matthew 25:31-46). (Acts 1:9,11). The clouds always accompany Christ's heavenly presence. All shall see Him because He will judge all and Israel which pierced Him in the crucifixion shall see him. While all shall see Him in His return, they particularly are selected out because of what they did to Him in the flesh. John here quotes (Zech. 12:10). Consternation shall reign because it will be the time of judgment.

It cannot be too carefully noted that here, as in many other references to His return. Christ makes his second advent at the time of judgment and not before.

vs. 8 Alpha and Omega—the first and last letters of the Greek alphabet, hence also called "the beginning and the end." All begins with Him and He will ring down the curtain on the drama of human history.

This verse closes the introduction and the apocalypse proper begins with verse nine. Verse nine marks the beginning of Part 1, of Division 1, of Revelation.

BEGINNING OF APOCALYPSE

PART I

Text (1:9-20)

APOCALYPSE PROPER BEGINS

9 I John, your brother and partaker with you in the tribulation and kingdom and patience which are in Jesus, was in the isle that is called Patmos, for the word of God and the testimony of Jesus. 10 I was in the Spirit on the Lord's day, and I heard behind me a great voice, as of a trumpet 11 saying, What thou seest, write in a book and send it to the seven churches: unto Ephesus, and unto Smyrna, and unto Pergamum, and unto Thyatira, and unto Sardis, and unto Philadelphia, and unto Laodicea. 12 And I turned to see the voice that spake with me. And having turned I saw seven golden candlesticks; 13 and in the midst of the candlesticks one like unto a son of man, clothed with a garment down to the foot, and girt about at the breasts with a golden girdle. 14 And his head and his hair were white as white wool, white as snow; and his eyes were as a flame of fire; 15 and his feet like unto burnished brass, as if it had been refined in a furnace; and his voice as the voice of many waters. 16 And he had in his right hand seven stars: and out of his mouth proceeded a sharp two-edged sword: and his countenance was as the sun shineth in his strength. 17 And when I saw him, I fell at his feet as one dead. And he laid his right hand upon me, saying, Fear not; I am the first and the last, 18 and the Living one; and I was dead, and behold, I am alive for evermore, and I have the keys of death and of Hades. 19 Write therefore the things which thou sawest, and the things which are, and the things which shall come to pass hereafter; 20 the mystery of the seven stars which thou sawest in my right hand, and the seven golden candlesticks. The seven stars are the angels of the seven churches: and the seven candlesticks are seven churches.

vs. 9 John here names himself for the third time and twice again in Revelation he names himself by name (Rev. 21:2) and (Rev. 22:8).

He is an apostle, but walks as a brother not exalting himself above his brethren as men have done in later centuries who claim apostolic succession. He remembered Christ's injunction, "But be not ye called Rabbi for one is your Master, even Christ: and all ye are brethren." (Matthew 23:8).

He was a companion in tribulation because he was a partaker of the suffering of the church of Ephesus and of all the churches throughout the seven periods of history.

He was in the isle called Patmos. Our knowledge of the place of the revelation to John rests upon the testimony of John himself. It is a small island in the southern part of the Aegean Sea. Here he was in banishment under the reign of Domitian, because of his faithful witness for the Word of God.

vs. 10 He was absent from the saints assembled in Ephesus—a few miles across the sea—but he was "in the Spirit on the Lord's Day. The expression "The Lord's Day" does not occur in the earlier writings of the apostles; they always speak of this day as "the first day of the week", when Christians came together to commune (Acts 20:7) and to hear the preaching (Acts 20:7) and to "lay by in store as the Lord had prospered them (I Cor. 16:2). But we find the writers of the second century used the term "the Lord's Day." Epistles of Barnabas, Ignatius and Dionysius, written about this time, call the first day of the week, the Lord's Day and the name is of common occurrence from that time forward. Incidently, this term, then, points to a period near the beginning of the second century as the date of the writing of the apocalypse.

How natural to so refer to the day as the Lord's Day. On the Lord's day, or the first day of the week, the church was born on Pentecost—a first day of the week, which followed the seventh Sabbath after the one which fell in the Passover week. On this day the Holy Spirit came upon the apostles. On this day they preached the first gospel sermon, on this day began the adding to those being saved. Since the Lord's Day, or first day of the week was the day of worship under the Christian Dispensation, how fitting that the apocalypse should be given on that day.

vs. 11, 12 As John turned to see the speaker whose voice he had heard, his eyes rested upon a vision of surpassing glory. The first objects that drew his attention were seven golden candlesticks, which (Rev. 1:20) informs us are the seven churches, which in turn represent the seven great epochs in the history of the church.

And standing in the midst of the candlesticks he saw one "like unto the Son of Man",—not like the Son of Man John had seen in the day of his flesh when Christ walked among men, but more like the glorified Christ he had seen on the Mount of Transfiguration. Every manifestation the glory of Diety is accompanied with brilliant splendor.

Whether the burning bush of Horeb, the glory of Sinai, the Shekinah of the Holy of Holies, the Transfigured Christ on Hermon, the Son of man on Patmos, all indicate that where ever Diety manifests itself there is no darkness at all.

In the great intercessor prayer (17th Chapter of John) Christ had prayed "that they may behold my glory which Thou hast given me" and here is the beginning of the answer to that prayer when John beheld Him in all his heavenly splendor.

vs. 13 Moving amidst the seven golden candlesticks or the church in its sevenfold development, He was keeping his commission promise, "Lo I am with you always, even unto the end of the age." (Matthew 28:20)

He was dressed in the long robe of the High Priest and girt about with the girdle of a King. His voice was as the sound of surging waters. Here He is represented in His three-fold office, Prophet, Priest and King.

vs. 14 His white hair portrayed glorious purity. His eyes were as a flame of fire—fiery eyes with which to see everywhere, for all things and all lives are naked and open to Him.

vs. 15, 16 Out of His mouth went a sharp two-edged sword. This is a symbol of the Word by which Christ carries on his spiritual warfare and wins all conquests. The Christian soldier is to be armed with "the sword of the Spirit, which is the Word of God" (Eph. 6:17) and this sword, "the word of God is quick and powerful, and sharper than any two-edged sword, piercing even to the dividing asunder of soul and spirit, and of the joints and marrow, and is a discerner of the thoughts and intents of the heart" (Heb. 4:12)

This was the sword with which Christ should smite the nations (Rev. 19:15).

vs. 17 Though John had been familiar with the lowly Son of man, and had seen His glorious transfiguration, when he beheld the transcendent vision of Patmos, his heart failed him, and he fell at Christ's feet as one dead. But when the hand that held the seven stars was laid upon him it was with the same tender touch of the yesteryears. Then the Lord revealed the purpose of His appearing unto John, "Fear Not." How often in the days of His flesh had he said to His disciples, "Fear not!"

vs. 18 Christ here bears testimony to his own life, death and resurrection. He pronounces his own "Amen" to his declaration.

He said He had the keys of hell, or Hades and of Death. When Peter confessed Him in the coasts of Caesarea Philippi as the Christ the Son of the Living God, Christ had declared, "Upon this rock I will build my church and the gates of hell (Hades) shall not prevail against it." (Matt. 16:13-18). And on Pentecost, the birthday of the church of Christ, Peter proclaimed in the first gospel sermon the death, burial and resurrection of Christ and as he came to the climax of that message he said, "He seeing this before spoke of the Resurrection of Christ, that his soul was not left in hell (Hades), neither did his flesh see corruption." (Acts 2:31)

Christ proved the truth of Peter's confession of Him as the Christ, the Son of the Living God, by coming back from Hades, whose gates could not prevail against his diety. Not only was Christ triumphant over death, but the very gates of death and Hades are under His dominion. Hence, He was able to deliver John who had fallen as one dead, but all who love and obey Him from the bonds of death.

"Forasmuch then as the children are partakers of flesh and blood, he also himself likewise took part of the same, that through death he might destroy him that had the power of death, that is the devil; and deliver them, who through fear of death, were all their lifetime subject to bondage." (Hebrews 2:14-15)

vs. 19 Christ divided up the apocalyptic visions into three parts; viz. the past, the present, and the future. He was to write of the things he had seen during his life time, the things as they were at the time of the Patmos visions, and the things which would fall under the time denoted as "the hereafter."

vs. 20 Christ explains the mystery of the seven Stars and the seven candlesticks. The seven stars He declares are the angels of the seven churches, represented by the seven candlesticks.

The word angel means "a messenger" and is equally applicable to the messenger of God, as well as of man.

This last verse of the first chapter is of special signification in that it throws light upon the *Book as a whole,* giving us a clear understanding of the *principle upon which the Book is to be interpreted.*

In Mark 1:2 referring to John the Baptizer, Mark quotes from Malachi, "Behold I send my messenger before my face, which shall prepare thy way before thee."

It certainly holds the same meaning in this passage, for it is self evident these letters were not sent to the angels of God. The messengers were men filling some office in connection with the churches.

The term could not refer to a diocesan bishop, for such an office did not exist until the church apostatized from the New Testament pattern. The term can hardly refer to an elder for all the churches of the first century had a plurality of elders. It would seem more likely to refer to the preachers or evangelists of the churches. Particularly does this become so when we recall that each church represents a church epoch or period. This apocalyptic uncovering is entrusted to the preachers throughout the sevenfold history of the church. Christ was holding them in His hand to support and strengthen them throughout the gospel age.

CHAPTER II

LETTERS TO THE
SEVEN CHURCHES

INTRODUCTION

The letters to the seven churches of Asia were composed in accordance with an exact literary arrangement. Each one consists of the same parts: a salutation to the church addressed; a description of Christ from some particular aspect with direct relation to the spiritual condition of the church; a message of praise or censure; exhortations in keeping with the special need, a promise to him that overcometh and an admonition "He that hath an ear let him hear what the Spirit saith to the churches."

The only exception to this symmetry is in the matter of the last part—the admonition. In each of the first three letters it precedes the promise to the overcomer; in the last four letters it follows his promise.

The distinction makes two groups of letters, one of three and the other of four, just as the seven seals, the seven trumpets and the seven vials are divided into two groups each, of four and three. In this study of the seven letters see chart following page 41.

The Church in Ephesus
Text (2:1-7)

1 To the angel of the church in Ephesus write: These things saith he that holdeth the seven stars in his right hand, he that walketh in the midst of the seven golden candlesticks: 2 I know thy works, and thy toil and patience, and that thou canst not bear evil men, and

didst try them that call themselves apostles, and they are not, and didst find them false; 3 and thou hast patience and didst bear for my name's sake, and hast not grown weary. 4 But I have this against thee, that thou didst leave thy first love. 5 Remember therefore whence thou art fallen, and repent and do the first works; or else I come to thee, and will move thy candlestick out of its place, except thou repent. 6 But this thou hast, that thou hatest the works of the Nicolaitans, which I also hate. 7 He that hath an ear, let him hear what the Spirit saith to the churches. To him that overcometh, to him will I give to eat of the tree of life, which is in the Paradise of God.

vs. 1 It was perfectly natural that the first church addressed should be the one in Ephesus. The city was the capitol of the province and its chief religious and commercial center. It was called "The light of Asia". One of the seven wonders of the world, the temple of Diana, or Artemis, was located there. Here Paul founded the church and labored with it for more than three years, (Acts— chapter 18) and afterward addressed to it one of the New Testament epistles. Later he sent Timothy there and addressed two letters to him. Here, too, if early church tradition is to be accepted, John labored from about A. D. 70 until his death.

It was natural that the first message should be addressed to the church nearest to the apostle's heart.

"These things saith he that holdeth the seven stars in his right hand, who walketh in the midst of the golden candle sticks." By some such phrase each letter is linked to the divine Christ.

In Bible language, to have a thing in one's right hand means to have it under one's power. "Thy right hand, O Lord, is become glorious in power; thy right hand, O Lord, hath dashed in pieces the enemy. (Exodus 15:6)

The word "holdeth" in this verse is a stronger term than the "had" in (Revelation 1:16). In this salutation Christ assured the Ephesian church, which represented the infant church of the first century that he was not only walking among the churches but holding them in his strong right hand.

vs. 2 The patience of the church had been severely tried in its very inception, but Christ said, "I know thy works, and thy labor."

The church was not only to be praised for its work for Christ, but for the travail of labor in bringing the man-child, Christ, to the world.

The church also was commended for its utter abhorrence of those who were evil. This is all the more remarkable when we remember that these Ephesian Christians had but recently left the vileness of paganism. It puts the modern church, with its tolerance for all kinds of worldliness, to shame.

Again the church is commended for its rejection of false apostles. How well they had learned of John himself how such a test should be made. He had taught, "Beloved, believe not every spirit, but try the spirits whether they are of God; Every spirit that confesseth that Jesus Christ is come in the flesh is of God. And every spirit that confesseth not that Jesus Christ is come in the flesh is not of God: and this is that spirit of anti-christ, whereof ye have heard that it should come. And even now already is in the world." (I John 4:1-3)

There was no false softness in those first Christians; they found such to be plain liars.

vs. 3 For Christ's name sake the church had borne the labor of opposing those who would corrupt the gospel and had not grown weary, knowing in due season they would reap if they fainted not.

vs. 4 After these words of praise a stain on the church is pointed out. They had been loyal to the truth, orthodox in the faith and outstandingly clean in life, but they had not maintained the ardor and devotion of their first love. Nothing but the fervent love of the bride can satisfy the Bridegroom.

The church had fallen into the temptation to which contenders for the faith once and for all delivered to saints are peculiarly exposed, namely, that of censoriousness, suspicion, bitterness, factiousness and division over non-essentials. Zeal for pure doctrine easily degenerates into hatred for those who differ in their beliefs.

vs. 5 Christ's rebuke is sharp. If they fail to remember from whence they are fallen and repent and do the first works, he will come, and that quickly, and remove their candlestick out of its place.

He would not come in person, but in providence and judgment.

vs. 6 But here is another ground for commendation. "Thou hatest the deeds of the Nicolaitanes, which I also hate."

The exact origin of this sect and character of its beliefs are in dispute, but it is generally thought that the followers of Nicolas taught that Christian liberty meant licence. More will be given on this sect when it comes to full flower in the life of the Pergamos church.

vs. 7 "He hath an ear to hear, let him hear what the spirit saith unto the churches."

Since he addressed this injunction "unto the *churches*," it becomes evident that the epistle was not addressed to one local church alone, but to all the churches of the Ephesian period of church history.

This is a characteristic saying of the Lord. None other makes use of it. He employs it in connection with certain of His utterances in order to impress upon us their peculiar importance. It occurs eight times in the gospels, where in each case the plural "ears" is used. (Matt 11:15, 13:9, 43; Mark 4:9,23; 7:16; Luke 8:8; 14:35)

It occurs eight times in Revelation, in each of the seven letters, and again in Rev. 13:9, where the singular "ear" is used—in each case.

"To him that overcometh", is an expression peculiar to John. It occurs once in his gospel, six times in his epistles, I, II and III John, and sixteen times in Revelation, but only three times in all the remainder of the New Testament.

The reward to the overcomer is "to eat of the Tree of Life, which is in the midst of the Paradise of God". This tree is seen in the garden of Eden (Gen. 2:9; 3:22), then here in this letter to Ephesus and, finally, in the New Jerusalem. (Rev. 22:2)

The Tree of Life is seen in the garden of Eden and man was driven from it after he had sinned in eating of the Tree of Knowledge of Good and Evil, lest he should eat of the Tree of Life and live forever. Now in overcoming sin, of transgression, of omission and seduction to false teaching, he is given access to the Tree of Life that he may live forever sinless.

Thus we see the tree figures prominently in the sinless earth at first and then again it figures conspiciously in the vision of the glorified earth with which the book ends. It is a figure of eternal blessedness, eternal salvation in its fullest sense.

The Church in Smyrna
Text (2:8-11)

8 And to the angel of the church in Smyrna write: These things saith the first and the last, who was dead, and lived again: 9 I know thy tribulation, and thy poverty (but thou art rich), and the blasphemy of them that say they are Jews, and they are not, but are a synagogue of Satan. 10 Fear not the things which thou art about to

suffer: behold, the devil is about to cast some of you into prison, that ye may be tried; and ye shall have tribulation ten days. Be thou faithful unto death, and I will give thee the crown of life. 11 He that hath an ear, let him hear what the Spirit saith to the churches. He that overcometh shall not be hurt of the second death.

INTRODUCTION

"To the angel of the church of Smyrna write":

Following the letter to the church in Ephesus, it is quite natural that the church in Smyrna should be the next addressed. The city lay just forty miles north of Ephesus and still is second in importance. As Ephesus was called "The Light of Asia", Smyrna, because of its charming surroundings, was called "The Beauty of Asia."

The history of the planting of the church is unknown, but during the second century the church was quite prominent. Since the city had a large Jewish population, which was bitterly opposed to Christ and His church, it came to be known as "the suffering church", because of persecution.

vs. 8 To the church in Smyrna, Christ very fittingly presented himself as "the First and the Last, who was dead and is alive." To this martyr church came the cheering word that its head and Lord had triumphed over death and the grave.

It was well for the church now farther removed from Pentecost to be so saluted. He had been with the church from the beginning, as symbolized in the Ephesian epoch and he would be with the church through this church period, yea, even to the last one.

He wanted them to know that he was not dead, but alive. While he had given up His life, He had broken the shackles of death in the resurrected life. So if persecution should exact the extreme sacrifice of their lives He wanted them to hold fast to the promise, "For if the Spirit of Him that raised up Jesus from the dead dwell in you, He that raised up Christ from the dead shall also quicken your mortal bodies by His Spirit that dwelleth in you." (Romans 8:11)

vs. 9 He wanted them to understand that He knew of their works, which stirred up such persecution that they experienced great tribulation. Also He knew that their tribulation had produced their poverty.

The first century with its advantage of the newness of the gospel message has now passed and persecution sets in. Like Jesus enjoyed the period of popularity to be followed by that of opposition, so the Smyrnan church meets persecution.

But they were rich—rich in faith, hope and fruitful works.

Their witness for Christ was accompanied by vilification and slander. This form of blasphemy was attributed to Christ's old enemies, the Jews. They were experiencing what Paul earlier had experienced at Antioch of Pisidia where the Jews blasphemed and contradicted the preaching of Paul and Barnabas. (Acts 13:44-46)

While all this was true yet there is a deeper meaning here. These were claiming to be Jews in the sense that they claimed to be the true Israel of God in opposition to the rightful claim of the persecuted church to this designation.

Paul said, "For he is not a Jew, which is one outwardly; neither is that circumcision which is outward in the flesh; But he is a Jew, which is one inwardly; and circumcision is that of the heart, in the Spirit and not in the letter, whose praise is not of men, but of God." (Romans 2:28, 29)

This is further evidence by these Jews being called "the synagogue of Satan, who is called the devil in verse 10. This is the first mention in Revelation of the great adversary.

Christ here denies the right of these opposers to employ the term "Jews" in the sense of being God's chosen people.

Here in verse nine the reference is made to what might be called ecclesiastical activities of the adversary; for one of the most successful devices against the true church is the organization of religious societies in imitaton of the true church.

The pure primitive church was not an organization of government, but an organism of life, Christ being the head of his mystical, spiritual body. The church at Smyrna was opposed by such an organization. Those, who opposed the true church, professed to be "Jews", the symbolical name of God's people.

They set up substitute organizations for the church and declared they were just as good as those who refused to depart from the scriptural pattern. Christ calls this blasphemy. He stripped off their outward pretention and revealed them for what they were "the Synagogue of Satan."

Paul, the apostle likewise employs the name "Satan" in the same connection for in warning against false apostles who sought to pass themselves off as the apostles of Christ, he said, "And no marvel for Satan himself is transformed into an angel of light" (2 Cor. 11:13-15)

It is significant that the only other church, besides that at Smyrna, which received unqualified commendation from Christ (The Philadelphia church) was also opposed by them of the synagogue of Satan, which say they are Jews and are not, but do lie." (Rev. 3:9)

vs. 10 The church was to fear none of those things because of the reasons about to be presented. The activities of the adversary take the form of physical persecutions. He wanted them to know that back of their suffering, imprisonment and trials was none other than the devil, using men and institutions as his agents.

He declared, "Ye shall have tribulation ten days" The number "ten" in Bible symbology indicates a complete testing, or trial to the limit of human endurance. Thus Jacob complained that Laban had changed his wages "ten times". (Gen. 31:7,41). The plagues of Egypt were "ten" in number (Ex. Chapters 7,8,9,10,11,12,13) Israel was tested with ten commandments. (Ex. 20:1-19). God's patience had been tried to the limit. He said, they had tempted him now these "ten times". (Numbers 14:22) Daniel requested that he and his companions be tested "ten days". (Daniel 1:12-15).

So the church at Smyrna was to be fully tested, as the persecuted church.

He said, "Be thou faithful unto death" (unto martyrdom). For this they were to have, not a royal crown, but the garland crown of victory over death. (I Cor. 9:24,25) (II Timothy 4:8)

vs. 11 Again it is a call to be heeded, not only by the Smyrnan church but "the churches", which the one at Smyrna represented. "He that overcometh shall not be hurt of the second death." Those who win this incorruptible crown shall live forever. This corruptible shall put on incorruption (I Cor. 15:54,55). To die the second death is to me sent from the final julgment throne into hell (Rev. 20:14,15). They might suffer the death of the body, but not of the soul.

The Church in Pergamos
Text (2:12-17)

12 And to the angel of the church in Pergamum write: These things saith he that hath the sharp two-edged sword: 13 I know where thou dwellest, even where Satan's throne is; and thou holdest fast my name, and didst not deny my faith, even in the days of Antipas my witness, my faithful one, who was killed among you, where Satan dwelleth. 14 But I have a few things against thee, because thou hast there some that hold the teaching of Balaam, who taught Balak to cast a stumblingblock before the children of Israel, to eat things sacrificed to idols, and to commit fornication. 15 So hast thou also some that hold the teaching of the Nicolaitans in like manner. 16 Repent therefore; or else I come to thee quickly, and I will make war against them with the sword of my mouth. 17 He that hath an ear, let him hear what the Spirit saith to the churches. To him that overcometh, to him will I give of the hidden manna, and I will give him a white stone, and upon the stone a new name written, which no one knoweth but he that receiveth it.

INTRODUCTION

This church was the farthest north, geographically speaking, of the seven churches in Asia. The city was a great religious center. The temple of Aesculapius was located there, to which sufferers came for healing from the four corners of the empire. Here also were the temples of Zeus, or Jupiter, Dionyson or Apollo. It was a perfect pantheon of pagan dieties.

Here Polycarp, that great Christian martyr was burned alive.

vs. 12 The salutation. Christ here presents Himself as, "He that hath the sharp sword with two edges."

How appropriate this salutation! Owing to the fact that conditions were to be found in this church which called for refutation by the word of God it was altogether fitting that, the two-edged sword, which is the Word of God, should be the symbol under which Christ presented Himself to this church period.

The bearing of this is seen in verse 16, where speaking of those whom He had just reproved, He says, "Repent or else I will come quickly, and will fight against them with the sword of my mouth."

vs. 13 This verse contains strong commendation. "I know thy works, and where thou dwellest, even where Satan's seat is." "Seat" here signifies "throne". This church was in a place of peculiar danger, being directly exposed to the Adversary. "Satan's Seat" here;

some have supposed referred to the worship of Aesculapius, from the serpent being his characteristic emblem.

But there seems to be a deeper meaning here. It is called "Satan's seat" here because it was where Satan's authority was in some special way acknowledged.

It must be noted that his devices in this case did not take the form of either spurious Christianity, or of physical persecutions as at Smyrna, but were of the nature similar to the device employed by Baalam against Israel of old.

Of course, these epochs blend somewhat and we do find some faithful saint, named Antipas suffering martyrdom, and we also know Polycarp was burned alive, but the opposition took on a new dress here;—something more subtle and deceiving.

vs. 14 It will be profitable here to give a brief study of the doctrine of Baalam. Baalam taught Balak, the King of the Moabites, to cast a stumbling block before the children of Israel. Balak wanted the children of Israel cursed, but God would not permit Baalam to curse them as long as Israel was faithful to God's commandments.

So Baalam then taught Balak to induce the children of Israel to indulge in the heathen worship and orgies, and then, of course, they would fall under the curse of God. This was accomplished through the women of Moab, by whom the Israelites were seduced into to take part in idolatrous practices and to commit fornication (Numbers 25:1-3).

Evidently, here the true church, the Israel of God in the Christian dispensation, was enticed to commit spiritual fornication. The sin that answers to this on the part of the "Israel of God' 'today (Gal. 6:16) is their participation in the formal and ceremonial exercises of religious bodies, whose form of worship is not after the New Testament pattern.

And this is just what happened historically to the church in the Pergamos period. The church had just gone through the persecution under Diocletian A. D. 303 to A. D. 313. Myers describes that persecution:

> "Toward the end of his reign, Diocletian inaugurated against the Christians a persecution which continued until his abdication, and which was the severest, as it was the last, waged against the church by the pagan emperors......

For ten years, which, however, were broken by short periods of respite, the Christians were subjected to the fierce flames of persecution..It was during this and the various other persecutions that vexed the church in the second and third centuries that the Christians sought refuge in the catacombs."Pp. 522, 523 Myer's Ancient History. Revised Edition 1904

After the abdication of Diocletian, and the joint reign of Galerius and Constantine of only one year, Constantine was proclaimed emperor. In the now famous Battle of Milvian Bridge A. D. 312, Constantine's standard on this celebrated battle field was the Christian cross. And it was beneath this emblem that his soldiers marched to victory. This act constituted a turning point in the history of the Roman Empire, and especially the fortunes of the Church of Christ.

By a decree issued at Milan A. D. 313, the year after the battle of Milvian Bridge, the Edict of Toleration was issued and Constantine placed Christianity on an equal footing with the other religions of the empire. The Edict read as follows: "We grant to Christians and to all others full liberty of following the religion which each must choose." Hear Myers again:

"By subsequent edicts Constantine made Christianity in effect the state religion and extended to it a patronage which he withheld from the old pagan worship. By A. D. 321 he had granted the Christian societies the right to receive gifts and legacies, and he himself enriched the church with donations of money and grants of land. . . . From this moment can be traced the decay of its (the church's) primitive simplicity and a decline from its high moral standard. It is these deplorable results of the imperial patronage that Dante laments in his well-known lines!

Ah Constantine! of how much ill the mother,
Not by conversion, but that marriage dower
Which the first wealthy Father took from thee."
Inferno *XIX* 115-117
Myers Ancient History P. 526.

As Dante said, Constantine was not converted, but because he won the Battle of Milvian Bridge he embraced Christianity and made his soldiers and subjects Christian. Being a pagan, there were brought into the church many pagan practices.

Thus the doctrine of Baalam, the doctrine of Compromise characterized the Pergamos Period.

Constantine called the Council of Nicaea (A.D. 325) at Nicaea, a town of Asia Minor, and the first creed, or formula of faith was adopted, now known as the Nicene Creed. It was the fore-runner of all human creeds.

vs. 15 Here we read, "so hast thou also them that hold the doctrine of the Nicolaitanes which thing I hate."

This departure made its first appearance in the first church period—the Ephesian. There it was referred to as the "deeds" of the Nicolaitanes; here it is their "doctrine."

The clue to an explanation is found in the name itself, and this is worthy of consideration because we find support in the meaning of the name "Baalam", which occurs in the previous verse.

The name "Nicolas" which belonged to the person of whom these Nicolaitanes were followers, means "one who conquers," or "Lords it over" the people.

Now it can hardly be a coincidence in a book where names and numbers, as well as objects, are used as symbols, that the name "Baalam" in Hebrew has practically the same meaning as "Nicolas" in the Greek.

This would point to the conclusion that "Nicolaitanism" was some form of heresy having for its object that of bringing the Israel of God into some sort of spiritual bondage.

In this church period there did occur such a compromise as portrayed in the doctrine of Baalam. Also there occurred in the same epoch, and following closely on the doctrine of compromise, a lording it over of God's people.

How logical then that these Niclaitanes should first be mentioned in the first church epoch—the Ephesian! There Christ saw the beginning of such a departure.

How many times the Holy Spirit leaves some hidden door, which when discovered, makes proof of a truth crystal clear!

In (Acts 20:28-31), we have an account of Paul calling the elders of this same Ephesian church, which Christ used to symbolize the first church period, to meet him at Miletus. (Acts 20:17).

His conference with them was in the nature of a stern warning, "Take heed therefore unto yourselves, and to all the flock, over which the Holy Spirit had made you overseers, to feed the church of God." For I know this, that after my departing shall grevious wolves enter in among you not sparing the flock. Also *of your own selves* shall men arise speaking perverse things, to draw away disciples after them."

This clinches the proof of the nature of the Nicolaitane doctrine—the doctrine of overlordship. In the New Testament church, there was a *plurality of elders* over *one congregation,* but never was there one elder, or bishop over a plurality of congregations.

The departure from the primitive order of government began right in the eldership. The seed was dormant in the elders of Ephesus, but came to life and developed in the Ephesian period. And by the time we reach the Pergamos period, we find a bishop presiding over a group of congregations. This was the over-lordship of Nicolaitanes. And it was this very departure that changed the form of government of the first century church, and, the Nicolaitane government meeting in church councils, wrote the first human creed—the Nicene. This inaugurated the apostacy which produced bishops, arch bishops, prelates, cardinals and finally the papa, or pope.

It corrupted the church in government and substituted human creeds, catechisms, and human confessions of faith, for the Authority of the Word of God. No matter of wonder then, that Christ said of the Nicolaitanes in both the Ephesian and the Pergamos periods of church history "I hate this thing." No wonder, then this doctrine only in the embryonic stage in the Ephesian, but now in full flower in the Permagos period, was so hateful to Christ that He introduced Himself in the salutation to this Pergamos church, "These things saith He that hath the sharp sword with two edges." (Rev. 2:12)

Since the sharp sword with the two edges is the Word of God, His salutation becomes understandable. The only way to fight departures from the primitive order was to wield the sharp sword of the Spirit—the Word of God. Hence the call:

vs. 16 "Repent, or else I will come unto thee quickly, and will fight against them with the sword of my mouth."

From the wording of this warning it appears that we have here the case of a whole church being carried away with this evil doctrine, as the Ephesian church was charged with falling away from its first love. For Christ says, "I will come to thee and fight against them"—those who teach and practice this pernicious and hateful doctrine.

Yet the call to repent was to the whole church, which is, of course, responsible for the evils allowed to exist in its midst.

vs. 17 Finally, came the wonderful promises: "To him that overcometh will I give to eat of the hidden manna." This appears in contrast to eating things sacrificed to idols. (Rev. 2:14) In connection with the mention of Manna, Christ calls Himself the Bread of life. (John 6:48, 49). Christ is unseen walking among the churches, hence called the Hidden Manna. He is the bread from heaven. "And I will give him a white stone, and in the stone a new name written." Among the Greeks a white stone was a symbol of acquittal, as a black stone was one of guilt. The white stone speaks of justification and victory over this abominable doctrine of overlordship.

The gift of a new name carries with it some great blessing of high honor. Christ is to have a new name known only to Himself, (Rev. 19:12) and His faithful followers also have a new name known only to themselves.

While the order of symmetry is changed, Christ gives the admonition "He that hath an ear, let him hear what the Spirit saith unto the churches." Again it is not addressed to one church, but to *the churches,* proving again as in the two former church periods, the Pergamos church is symbolical of a period or epoch in church history.

Without this Nicolaitan apostasy of the Pergamos period, there could have been no following fruition of abomination in the succeeding Thyatira period.

The Church in Thyatira
Text (2:18-29)

18 And to the angel of the church in Thyatira write: These things saith the Son of God, who hath his eyes like a flame of fire, and his feet are like unto burnished brass: 19 I know thy works, and thy love and faith and ministry and patience, and that thy last works are more than the first. 20 But I have this against thee, that thou sufferest the woman Jezebel, who calleth herself a prophetess; and she teacheth and seduceth my servants to commit fornication; and to eat things sacrificed to idols. 21 And I gave her time that she should repent; and she willeth not to repent of her fornication. 22 Behold, I cast her into a bed, and them that commit adultery with her into

great tribulation, except they repent of her works. 23 And I will kill her children with death; and all the churches shall know that I am he that searcheth the reins and hearts: and I will give unto each one of you according to your works. 24 But to you I say, to the rest that are in Thyatira, as many as have not this teaching, who know not the deep things of Satan, as they are wont to say; I cast upon you none other burden. 25 Nevertheless that which ye have, hold fast till I come. 26 And he that overcometh, and he that keepeth my works unto the end, to him will I give authority over the nations: 27 and he shall rule them with a rod of iron, as the vessels of the potter are broken to shivers; as I also have received of my Father: 28 and I will give him the morning star. 29 He that hath an ear, let him hear what the Spirit saith to the churches.

INTRODUCTION

While we have no account of the establishing of the church in Thyatira, it is likely it began when Lydia and her household returned from Philippi, for certainly she was considered faithful by Paul. So she certainly would be expected to establish the church, in her home city Thyatira.

The Salutation

This is the longest of the seven letters. It reveals further the methods employed by the great Adversary, exposing the "depth of Satan."

vs. 18 In this salutation it is noteworthy as being the only time in the apocalypse that Christ is presented as "the Son of God." He, as the Son of God, is also described as He, "who hath his eyes like a flame of fire and his feet are like unto burnished brass."

The combination of these two symbols is very significant. The symbols strikingly present the Lord as the One whose eyes search out every evil deed, and whose feet trample in judgment upon the wicked deeds of men.

There is a special reason, why He introduces Himself to this church period as the "Son of God." It is because of the peculiar conditions found in the Thyatira period.

We must remember always that each of these seven churches is but a type of a succeeding church period, each revealing something in the affairs and history of the church through the ages.

Here in this letter we are given to see the inception of that masterpiece of Satan's deception, that monstrous heresy, which reached fruition in what we know today as Romanism.

vs. 19 Christ begins with the statement: "I know thy works and charity, and service, and faith and thy patience and thy works; and the last to be more than the first." All these are peculiarly characteristic of the Roman Church. But you will note that her works are mentioned twice. While works are mentioned of other church periods, this is the only double reference to works. There is a reason.

A prominent feature of Romanism is its insistence upon works, and works that are wholly unlike those required of the New Testament church.

The works of the Roman church are derived mainly from pagan sources. This is not surprising when we remember our study under the Pergamos period how Constantine, the pagan Roman Emperor, embraced Christianity, not because of conversion, but because of a victory at Milvian Bridge. The unregenerated pagan flooded the church with pagan ceremonies and practices. In proof of this we quote from the Externals of the Catholic Church," Her government, ceremonies, festivals, sacramentals, and devotions, by Rev. John F. Sullivan of the Diocese of Providence, second edition, Revised to conform to the new code of Canon Law. This is published by P. J. Kenedy & Sons New York 1918. It bears the approving names of Arthur J. Scanlan, S.I.D. Censor Librorum, and John Cardinal Farley, D. D. Archbishop of New York. March 27, 1918.

Just a few quotations to show the works of Romanism are pagan.

The Rosary—Page 186.

> The use of some means of counting prayers is not restricted to catholics. The Brahmin of India or Tibet has his long rosary which he uses to measure his eternal repetitions of the praise of Buddha. The Mohammedan votary has his chaplet of ninety-nine beads to count his fervent invocations of Allah."
>
> The use of the rosary "was established by St. Dominic, the famous founder of the order of Preachers, and he testifies in his writings that he acted under the direction of the Blessed Mother of God."

The Agnus Dei—Pages 204, 205, 206

> "In every form of religion, even in the grossest paganism, it has been customary to consider certain objects as holy and to use them as means of supposed protection from evil."

The origin of this sacramental is a matter of great obscurity. When the people of Italy and other countries had been converted from idolatry, they retained some of their belief in charms and amulets; and it is probable that the Agnus Dei was devised as a substitute for these relics of paganism. The church in many instances took the religious customs with which the people were familiar, and made these customs christian.

They were first used in Rome, and it is possible that they go back as far as the final overthrow of pagan worship in that city, about the fifth century. Indeed, there is some evidence that they were in use even a little earlier, for in the tomb of Maria Augusta, wife of the Emperor Honorius, who died in the fourth century, was found an object made of wax and much like our Agnus Deis of the present time."

Holy Water—Chapter 27 entitled Holy Water

"It is interesting to note how often our church has availed herself of practices which were in common use among pagans. The church and her clergy are all things to all men, that they may gain all for Christ, and she has often found that it is well to take what was praiseworthy in other forms of worship and adopt it to her own purposes, for the sanctification of her children. Thus it is true, in a certain sense, that some catholic rites and ceremonies are a reproduction of those of pagan creeds, but they are the taking of the best in paganism, etc."

Then follows a detailed description of the use of holy water.

Pilgrimages—Chapter LV

"The pious practice of making journeys to distant shrines, . . . is by no means exclusively catholic. The Romans had their shrines of Jupiter Capitolinus at Rome, of Apollo at Delphi, of Diana at Ephesus. To visit Mecca at least once in his lifetime is the ambition of the pius Mussulman. The great temples of India have their countless throngs of worshippers who have come to offer their homage to the Hindoo gods and to pray at the shrines of Buddha. In encouraging the making of pilgrimages our church has made use of a practice which has produced good results in other creeds." pp. 300, 302

These are only a few quotations of many that could be made.

vs. 20 The introduction of the name of Jezebel, as a symbol of evil seen by those flaming eyes, is very enlightening. Jezebel, a name meaning "unchaste" was the daughter of Ethbaal (with Baal). She became the wife of Ahab, King of Israel. Through her influence the pagan worship of Baal became the state religion of the ten tribes.

Baalism was a licentious religion; and hence it fitly symbolized that monstrous apostacy of the church, whose essential character istic is spiritual unfaithfulness to Christ.

In this church period the one great aim of this enemy of Christ, which is called "the depths of Satan" is to degrade the Lord Jesus Christ from his place as the Son of God.

As the Son of God He is presented in the Scriptures as the only way of access to the Father. He himself said: "I am the way, the turth, and the Life; no man cometh unto the Father, but by me! (John 14:6)

In complete opposition of this, though such opposition is cleverly disguised with almost diabolical cleverness, the Roman church systematically present Jesus Christ, not as the Son of God, but as the son of Mary.

In its doctrine, ceremonies, liturgy, pictures and images, this Jezebel church, with consumate and satanic craft, exalts Mary, making her the compassionate one, the efficacious intercessor in behalf of sinners, the mediatrix between God and man. Her devotees are led to put their trust in Mary instead of the "Son of God." You can see why He presents Himself, as to no other church period as "the Son of God."

Steadfastly, Mary is presented by the Roman Catholic church as the Mediatrix between God and man. The title given her is "Mary Mediatrix."

In the Marian Congress held in Ottawa in June, 1947, a one hundred foot statue of her was displayed in fireworks. She was pictured standing on a new moon, wearing a crown of stars, with a caption beneath the figure which read, "Ad Jesumper Marian" which translated reads: To Jesus through Mary.

This is pure paganism to present Mary as Mediatrix. In Babylon they had a goddess which bore the name Myletta, that is "The Mediatrix".

In accordance with this role of Mediatrix, she was called Aphrodite—that is the wraths of Douer—who by her charms could soothe the breast of angry Jove. In Athens she was called Amarusia, that is the mother of gracious acceptance! In Rome she was called 'Bona Dea,'—the 'good goddess!'

All this is sufficient to prove the pagan character which is ascribed to the Virgin Mary. It is an extraordinary thing that throughout history across the lives of the people of the pagan world is the figure of a woman which closely resembles the Virgin Mary of today. In ancient Babylon she was Semiramis; in Assyria she was Astarte; in Egypt, Isis, in Greece, Aphrodite; in Rome, Venus. Many of the titles which have been given to the Virgin Mary by the Roman Catholic church have been taken directly from paganism. Hesiod, one of the earliest Greek writers describes her as "the mother of the gods." Catholics call Mary "the mother of God!"

"And this introduction of rank paganism traced back to the Thyatira period of church history which began in the fourth century.

Nestorius, Patriarch of Constantinople set himself against this. Quoting him, "Has God," said he, "a mother?" Then is paganism to be pardoned for introducing a mother of the gods, and St. Paul is a liar, who said in speaking of Christ's god-head that it is without father or mother or descent. Let us cease to call Mary, her who bore God, that we be not tempted to become pagans." At this point the sermon was interrupted by the shout "That is atheisam!"

From third chapter, 2nd volume of his "Handbook to the Controversy with Rome" by Karl Von Hase, professor of Theology in the University of Jena for 53 years, 1830 to 1883.

And this in the light of Mary's declaration (Luke 1:47) that she needed a savior! If she needed a Savior, how could she become a savior? Also this in the light of Paul's statement, "For there is one God, and one Mediator between God and men, the Man Jesus Christ." (1 Timothy 2:5). How then can Mary be called "Mediatrix?"

Not until 1854 was she declared Immaculate, on December 8th of that year. After the question had been considered by a special commission of cardinals and theologians, and after consulting with the entire college of cardinals, Pope Pius IX solemnly declared the dogma in Peter's church in Rome in the presence of more than two hundred cardinals, bishops and others, who had been invited to the assembly. After mass and singing he read as follows:

"That the most blessed Virgin Mary, in the first moment of her conception, by a special grace and privilege of Almighty God, in virtue of the merits of Christ, was preserved immaculate from all stain of original sin."

He decreed this to be a divinely revealed fact and dogma which must be believed constantly and firmly by the faithful. Those who refuse to accept it must be cut off from the church.

It was not until the end of the so called holy year of 1950 did the present pope declare the doctrine of her assumption. This then reached the fullness of paganism to deify her as ascending directly to heaven in bodily form. No wonder Christ spoke of the Thyatira church as "the depths of Satan."

In Biblical symbology, and particularly in the apocalypse, a woman is the symbol of an elaborate religious system. In this instance Jezebel stands for a system of doctrine, in that she is referred to as "a prophetess" one who taught Christ's servants to commit fornication—spiritual unchastity.

vs. 21 She was given time to repent for this spiritual fornication but she refused to repent. History has shown how she has only grown worse.

vs. 22 Sickness and a bed are scriptural symbols of affliction and punishment. Even today we have a saying; "He made his own bed, let him lie in it."

Her adultery was like the adultery of Israel. (Jer. 3:6-11) (Ezek. 16:23-42)

vs. 23 The words, "I will kill her children with death is significant as she teaches that she is the mother of all churches. Rome delights in the name "mother."

Her children are her adherents and Christ said he would kill them with death. This visitation of judgment would cause all the churches to know that Christ searcheth the reins and hearts of men and will reward every man according to his works. This word "works" calls up the idolatrous works of the Thyatira church, into which Christ looks with "eyes like unto flames of fire." (Rev. 2:18)

43

vs. 24 Evidently not all in Thyatira were involved in this paganism, because Christ has a special word of encouragement for them, "the rest in Thyatira (as many as have not this doctrine, and which have not known the depths of satan, as they speak), I will put upon you none other burden.

vs. 25 The only burden he would lay upon them was "to hold fast until I come."

vs. 26 A prominent feature of Romanism is its settled purpose, from which it has never deviated in all the centuries of existence, to exercise "power over the nations." She has always advocated union of church and state and the power to crown and uncrown kings.

How appropriate, then, is this promise to those of Thyatira who overcome this pagan doctrine—the depths of satan. "I will give him power over the nations!" In the coming period when Christ shall rule all kingdoms the saints which have endured shall reign with him.

vs. 27 A sceptre of iron means a firm and enduring power. The word "rule" in the original meas "to rule as a shepherd." It will not be the cruel rule of a dictator, but the gentle guardianship of a shepherd, even Christ, the good shepherd, who laid down his life for the sheep.

Christ will break the nations in pieces and all shall become one under the rule of Him.

vs. 28. The promise of the Morning Star points to the possession of Christ in some special way. It is one of the titles of Christ. In Rev. 22:16 He says of Himself, "I AM the root and the offspring of David, the bright and morning star." Christ will give to those who overcome "the depths of satan," a fellowship with Himself in that they shall share his dominion.

Summary Thus we have traced Paul's "mystery of iniquity (which) doth already work" (2 Thess. 2:7), called in the Ephesian period, "the deeds of the Nicolaitanes;" in the Smyrna period, "the synagogue of satan; in the Pergamos period, "the doctrine of the Nicolaitanes," "where Satan's seat is," and in the Thyatira period, "the doctrine of Jezebel," "the depths of satan."

Here in the Thyatira period the doctrine of the Nicolaitanes— the doctrine of overlordship—reached "the depths of satan."

We traced briefly in the Pergamos period how the simplicity of the policy of the New Testament church was surplanted by a rising ecclesiastical hierarchy in the elevation of men in authority over the churches. "The depths of Satan" was reached in the Thyatira period when the bishop of Rome—called "papa" or "pope" gradually assumed supreme authority over the churches.

There began the growth of an empire within an empire. Quoting from Myer's Ancient History, pages 582, 583 we read:

"Long before the fall of Rome there had begun to grow up within the Roman Empire an ecclesiastical state, which was shaping itself into the imperial model. This spiritual empire, like the secular one, possessed a hierarchy of officers, of which deacons, priests or presbyters, and bishops were the most important. These bishops collectively formed what is known as the Episcopate. There were four grades of bishops, metropolitans or archbishops, and patriarchs." At the end of the fourth century there were five patriarchs, that is, regions ruled by patriarchs. These centered in the great cities of Rome, Constantinople, Alexandria, Antioch and Jerusalem.

Among the patriarchs, the patriarchs of Rome were accorded almost universally a precedence in honor and dignity. They claimed further a precedence in authority and jurisdiction. Before the close of the eighth century there was firmly established over a great part of christendom what we may call an ecclesiastical monarchy."

This ecclesiastical monarchy reached the "depths of satan" when, after centuries of argument, the doctrice of the infallibility of the pope was made a canon law in the year 1870 A. D. by the council called for that purpose by Pius IX.

With the growth of the papal state spiritually there was also a parallel development of the temporal power of the popes.

"In the dispute about the use of images in worship, known in history as the "war of the Iconoclasts," which broke out in the eighth century between the Greek churches of the East and the Latin churches of the West, drew after it far-reaching consequences as respects the growing power of the Roman Pontiffs. In this quarrel with the Eastern Emperors the Roman bishops formed an alliance with the Frankish princes of the Carolingian house. The popes consecrated the Frankish

chieftians as kings and emperors; the grateful Frankish kings defended the popes against all their enemies . . . Such in broad outline was the way in which grew up the papacy."
Myers Ancient History pages 585, 586.

Thus for centuries we behold union of church and state until July 2, 1871 when Victor Emmanuel entered Rome and took up his residence there.

"The occupation of Rome by the Italian government marked the end of the temporal power of the pope, and the end of an ecclesiastical state, the last in Europe, which from long before Charlemagne had held a place among the temporal powers of Europe . . . the papal troops, with the exception of a few guardsmen, were disbanded. . . . By a statute known as the Law of the papal guarantees (1871), the pope was assured in the exercise of his spiritual functions."

Thus, finally, as a result of the reformation the doctrine of the Nicoliatanes, "which thing I hate" said Christ, was refuted, both in its spiritual and temporal functions. However, it must be said in the interest of truth that the doctrine still holds sway, spiritually, in the overlordship of the papacy over the Roman church, and, temporally, in the eternal struggle of the pope to regain his power over the nations.

In these letters we have revealed or uncovered to us those tactics the great adversary, the devil, employs against the church of Christ.

vs. 29 Again we meet with the statement which indicates that Thyatira, like the three churches before it, represents not just one church, but the churches of a period. "He that hath an ear, let him hear what the Spirit saith to the *Churches.*

CHAPTER III

THE SALUTATION
THE SARDIS CHURCH
Text (3:1-6)

3 And to the angel of the church in Sardis write: These things saith he that hath the seven Spirits of God, and the seven stars: I know thy works, that thou hast a name that thou livest, and thou art dead.

SEVEN-FOLD ARRANGEMENT of the SEVEN LETTERS

	Chapters I & II				Chapter III		
	EPHESUS Verse	SMYRNA Verse	PERGAMOS Verse	THYATIRA Verse	SARDIS Verse	PHILADELPHIA Verse	LAODICEA Verse
• SALUTATION	1	8	12	18	1	7	14
• DECLARATION OF WORKS	2	9	13	19	1,2	8	15
• PRAISE OR CENSURE	3	9	13	20	2	9,10	15a
• REPROOF	4,6	None	14	21,22	3	None	16,17
• EXHORTATION	5	10	16	23-25	4	11	18
• ADMONITION	7	11	17	Promise 26-28	5	12	21
PROMISE	7	11	17	Admonition 29	6	13	22
APPROXIMATE TIME	Pentecost	A.D. 100	313 A.D. to	533 A.D. to	1517 A.D. to	1809 A.D. to	1909 to
OF CHURCH PERIODS	to A.D. 100	to 313 A.D.	533 A.D.	1517 A.D.	1809 A.D.	1909 A.D.	End.
CHARACTERISTICS	Doctrinally Right	Persecuted	Compromised	Apostacized	Denominational	Restored	Lukewarm
CHURCH IN HISTORY	The First Church	Church of 2nd, 3rd. Centuries	Church of 4th, 5th Centuries	Catholic	Denominational	Church of Christ	Present Church

2 Be thou watchful, and establish the things that remain, which were ready to die: for I have found no works of thine perfected before my God. 3 Remember therefore how thou hast received and didst hear; and keep it, and repent. If therefore thou shalt not watch, I will come as a thief, and thou shalt not know what hour I will come upon thee. 4 But thou hast a few names in Sardis that did not defile their garments: and they shall walk with me in white; for they are worthy. 5 He that overcometh shall thus be arrayed in white garments; and I will in no wise blot his name out of the book of life, and I will confess his name before my Father, and before his angels. 6 He that hath an ear, let him hear what the Spirit saith to the churches.

The character of the last three messages to the churches is definitely different from the four preceding.

In the first four church periods we are given the uncovering of the development of an abominable doctrine which progressed through the stages from "the deeds of the Nicolaitanes," "the synagogue of Satan," "the seat of Satan," until it reached "the depths of Satan" in the fourth church period.

Beginning with Sardis we find, not the rise and progress of a system of satanic wickedness, but a state of decline and decay, dying out of spirituality and love for the truth.

While one church period blends into and intermingles with the preceding and succeeding periods, yet each epoch has an individual entity of its own.

Following the great, and longest period of Thyatira, or the Roman Catholic epoch, we know from history that there followed the weaker and declining period of denominationalism. The Sardis church ushers in the days of the Reformation. The preceding dark ages had left the church spiritually dead and decadent. After the reformation begun by Zwingli, Luther, Calvin and Knox, the church era was marked by multiple divisions, declining weakness and diminishing spirituality. This decline became so marked that the Wesleys spent their lives in an effort to restore some spirituality to a dying and decadent Christendom.

vs. 1 Hitherto, Christ has begun each letter with words of commendation, but here he commences with words of condemnation.

He presents Himself as "He that hath the seven spirits of God, and the seven stars. As already pointed out the "seven spirits" symbolize the fullness of the One Spirit. Upon Christ, the divine spirit abides in all the perfection of his operation and power. The seven stars represent the entire sweep of the life of the church from

Pentecost to the end of the age. He is asserting his complete authority over the church in all the Christian dispensation. He is able to impart spiritual life—the life that was lacking in this church period addressed. *"I know thy works,"* says the Christ. The denominational period has had a reputation for feverish activity. Services well attended and carefully conducted, with working committees and many social activities. This period has been characterized by great financial drives, building programs and world-encirclng movements. *"Thou has a name that thou livest."* How appropriate!

Perhaps nothing has so characterized the denominational epoch as the wearing and stressing of human names. Men have gloried in this name or that—names that gave no honor to the Christ, or his church, but rather have divided the followers of Christ into competing sects.

Since an outstanding trait of this church was its weakness, it is altogether logical that denominational names should be worn.

The word comes from the same root from which we get the word "denominator," which means fractional, or below par. The wearing of a denominational name is an unconscious confession of being fractional and below par excellence. It cannot be too well noted that God has never permitted a church, which did not take the Scripture for full and final authority for its rule of practice, to wear the Scriptural name. Proclaiming part truth, they ever wear an unscriptural and below par, fractional, or denominational name.

So it is looked upon, by Christ, as dead.

vs. 2 But to this church period Christ makes a patient and gracious appeal. "Be watchful and strengthen the things which remain, that are ready to die."

The denominational period has thrown off much of the doctrine of Baalam and the overlordship of the Nicolaitanes. Pagan practices borrowed from heathenism by the Thyatira church, have been expunged.

But there are still traces of compromising with error, setting up of ecclesiastical establishments to govern the beliefs and practices of its adherents.

Yet over against this there has been an awakening after the passing of the dark ages and the spiritual Renaissance which followed. The Bible has been loosed from the cloister pale, and translated and printed in over a thousand languages and dialects.

However, in spite of this noble endeavor, there has been a tendency to chain the Bible, not to a book shelf of the monastery, but to the prejudiced interpretation of denominational bias.

He declares, "I have not found thy works perfect before God," but be watchful and strengthen the things that remain.

vs. 3 To stimulate the church of this period to action, He makes an appeal to remember the better days. It shows that they had now heard His word, because they are to "remember how thou hast received and heard."

Church history discloses how the church of the Sardis, or denominational period, has lost its fervor for the Word of God and has turned to humanism, modernism, skepticism, and even outright doubt and infidelity. If they do not watch He says, "I will come on thee as a thief in the night."

While He is not announcing his immediate return, yet here seems to be the beginning of the calling to the church's attention that the return must be kept in mind. How significant! The denominational period of the church has throughout its days stressed, with increasing tempo, the return of Christ.

While a few misguided souls have set dates, Christ both in His ministry, through the voice of His apostles and here in his apocalypse, declared His coming would be "as a thief in the night." (Matthew 24:36-51) (1 Thess. 5:2) (2 Peter 3:10) (Rev. 16:15) The coming of Chirst is a blessed hope to the watchful and ready, but to the unprepared it will be an event of surprise and terror.

vs. 4 But there were a few who had kept pure, both in faithfulness to God's Word and in life. "Thou hast a few names in Sardis which have not defiled their garments."

How true it is that throughout denominationalism there are to be found those who, though wearing a fractional name, are living beyond the teaching of their particular group. They have outstripped their church in a return to New Testament belief, practice and living.

There are fine folk who have thrown off human creedalism, infant baptism, papal sprinkling (a practice authorized by the pope in the Council of Revenna in A.D. 1311), closed communion, human ecclesiasticism and many other unscriptural practices in order to stand free in Christ. These things need to be strengthened.

A few have not defiled their garments, either doctrinally or spiritually. These shall be clothed in white because they walk with the Lord. Their belief and practice kept step with Christ's commands. How well did Amos write, "Can two walk together except they be agreed?" (Amos 3:3)

White is often appplied to divine and heavenly things. The garments of the bride are to be "fine linen, clean and white."

On the earth, man is the only one of God's countless species of living creatures that has no natural clothing. Sin stripped him of his garments of glory and beauty, wherein he stood in the likeness of God. So he is the most shabbily dressed creature in the whole world.

But the worthy of Sardis are promised to one day walk with Him, dressed in the whiteness of the purity of His righteousness. (1 Cor. 1:30)

vs. 5 "I will not blot his name out of the Book of Life."

The book of Life is prominent in the last chapters of Revelation (Rev. 13:8; 17:8; 20:12, 15; 21:27; 22:19). The mention of it in the letters to the Sardis period is very appropriate in view of the fact that life and death are the main theme of the letter.

Among all denominations of this period there have been rare souls, who have not defiled their garments either doctrinally, or ecclesiastically, having obeyed the gospel and by that obedience and subsequent faithfulness have their names upon the book of life.

The final clause of this verse of promise recalls Christ's promise recorded in (Matt. 10:32, 33).

vs. 6 Then comes the final admonition, as in all seven letters. "He that hath an ear, let him hear what the Spirit saith unto the churches." This regularly repeated injunction emphasizes the truth that each message is addressed to more than an individual church, but to many churches, represented in successive periods of church history.

The Salutation
The Phiadephia Church
Text (3:7-13)

7 And to the angel of the church in Philadelphia write: These things saith he that is holy, he that is true, he that hath the key of David, he that openeth and none shall shut, and that shutteth and none openeth: 8 I know thy works (behold, I have set before thee a door opened, which none can shut), that thou hast a little power, and didst keep my word, and didst not deny my name. 9 Behold, I give of the synagogue of Satan, of them that say they are Jews, and they are not, but do lie; behold, I will make them to come and worship before thy feet, and to know that I have loved thee. 10 Because thou didst keep the word of my patience, I also will keep thee from the hour of trial, that hour which is to come upon the whole world, to try them that dwell upon the earth. 11 I come quickly: hold fast that which thou hast, that no one take thy crown. 12 He that overcometh, I will make him a pillar in the temple of my God, and he shall go out thence no more: and I will write upon him the name of my God, and the name of the city of my God, the new Jerusalem, which cometh down out of heaven from my God, and mine own new name. 13 He that hath an ear, let him hear what the Spirit saith to the churches.

INTRODUCTION

The Salutation—Christ does not present Himself to this church in characters taken from the sevenfold description of Him in chapter one.

To the other churches He addressed himself as holding the seven stars in his right hand, walking amidst the golden candelsticks, as the first and the last, as He which hath the sharp sword with two edges, as "He who hath his eyes like a flame of fire and feet like fine brass, etc.

Here, he uses an entirely new set of symbols of himself in this salutation to Philadelphia.

In each letter Christ reveals himself in a character that is in keeping with the condition of that particular church.

Since the conditions in Philadelphia are quite different from that of every other church, we find He presents Himself in an entirely different manner.

vs. 7 "These things saith He that is Holy."

There is no reference here to the eyes of flame or the feet of brass, nor the sword of His mouth. The very words indicate that the church in Philadelphia is in such a state of spirituality and harmony with God's will as to know Him who is holy, and who is true. Here Christ makes a strong assertion of His diety, for only

51

God can say, "I AM HOLY." "Because it is written, Be ye holy, for I am holy" (1 Peter 1:16). "For thus saith the High and Lofty One that inhabiteth eternity, whose name is holy." Isaiah 57:15.

"These things saith He that is true."

These words, "He that is true" take us to John 17:3, where He says, "And this is life eternal, that they might know Thee, the only True God." "And we know that the Son of God is come, and hath given us an understanding that we may know Him *THAT IS TRUE*, and we are in HIM THAT IS TRUE, even in His Son, Jesus Christ." (John 5:20)

"These things saith "He that hath the key of David."

The study of this key becomes intensely interesting when we remind ourselves that these seven churches represent seven church periods. The period following the denominational period represented by "Sardis" which had the name it lived, is the Restoration period, in which there appeared again on earth the church restoring the practices of the first century.

As the first period of the church was marked by the first love, the restoration period is marked by the name, Philadelphia, meaning "brotherly love." Love had again been restored in the church. The Ephesian period was marked by leaving its first love, the Restoration period is one in which love is restored.

As the first church was given the keys (Matt 16:16-19)so here the keys are being restored.

The first use of the key to indicate restoration was in Isaiah 22:22 "And it shall come to pass in that day that I will call my servant Eliakim . . . And the key of the house of David will I lay upon his shoulder, so he shall open and none shall shut; and he shall shut and none shall open." The key was laid upon Eliakim's shoulders in that he was given the key of government, or authority, so in the Restoration period, God is again setting up the kingdom, restoring it in that he is reigning in the church instead of the rule of church councils, presbyteries, synods, conference, etc. Christ's authority is again being restored.

Eliakim means "God will set up" and as in Eliakim's day, so the Restoration period, God is setting up or restoring the kingdom.

In Eliakim's case none could shut when he had opened nor open when he had shut, so it is in the Restoration period.

The key was given to Eliakim when there were breeches in the walls of Jerusalem (Isa. 22:9), and the key was restored in the

Philadelphia or Restoration period when there were breeches in the spiritual Jerusalem, caused by denominational division.

A lock on a door has a combination and a key must have the same combination as the lock in order to open the door.

When Jesus was about to leave His apostles He gave His commission under which they were to labor in opening up the Kingdom to the sinner.

This commission is found near the end of what are called the "synoptic" gospels, namely, Matthew, Mark and Luke. They are so called because they have a common or similar view. The commission, according to these three records of the gospel, reads as follows:

"Go ye therefore, and teach all nations, baptizing them in the name of the Father, and of the Son, and of the Holy Spirit." Teaching them to observe all things whatsoever I have commanded you: and, lo, I am with you alway, even unto the end of the world."—Matthew 28;19, 20)

"And He said unto them, go ye into all the world, and preach the gospel to every creature.

He that believeth and is baptized shall be saved; but he that believeth not shall be damned." (Mark 16:15, 16)

"And said unto them, Thus it is written, and thus it behoved Christ to suffer and to rise from the dead the third day: And that repentance and remission of sins should be preached in his name among all nations, beginning at Jerusalem. And ye are witnesses of these things."—(Luke 24:46-48)

This commission is predicated upon all the right of absolute authority, and all the force of absolute power. Shall we present a breakdown of these three records.

Matthew mentions *going, teaching, baptizing* into the name of the Father, and of the Son, and of the Holy Spirit and *teaching* the baptized hearers to *observe all things whatsoever* I have commanded you, or in other words to continue in the things heard.

Mark mentions *going, preaching* the *gospel* (which consists of three facts—the death, burial and resurrection of Christ I Cor. 15:1-4, *believing,* being *baptized* and *salvation.*

Luke mentions the facts of the gospel *repentance* and *remission* of sins, or *salvation.*

Putting all these elements together we have: *Going, teaching* or *preaching, believing, repentance, salvation or remission* of sins and *continuing.*

Having now ascertained the elements of the commission we are ready to consider the combination or order of these elements.

Naturally, the matter of "going" comes *first. Second,* the object of going is to *teach,* so teaching is the next in order. *Third,* hearing would be the next in order because the object of teaching is to get men to hear. *Fourth,* the result of hearing is *faith,* because Paul said, "How then shall they call on Him in whom they have not believed? and how shall they believe in Him of whom they have not heard? and how shall they hear without a preacher?. . . . So then faith cometh by hearing and hearing by the Word of God." (Rom. 10:14-17) So the fourth in order is faith. The next or fifth would be *repentance,* because until we believe we will not obey Christ's command to repent. The *sixth* in order is *Baptism,* because all repentant believers were commanded to be baptized. This is not only the scriptural order, but, likewise the logical order. Faith changes our mind: repentance changes our will and baptism changes our state, translating us from the kingdom of darkness into the kingdom of God's dear Son.

Baptism is for the remission of sins because Peter so declared in Acts 2:38 "Repent and be baptized every one of you in the name of the Lord Jesus Christ for the remission of sins."

Our sins are remitted in baptism because Paul declares that in being baptized we are baptized into the death of Christ. It was in Christ's death that the only blood which could remit sins was shed. Baptism puts us into the death of Christ, or under the atoning blood.

Now shall we hear Paul on this:

"How shall we that are dead to sin, live any longer therein? Know ye not, that so many of us as were baptized into Jesus Christ were *baptized into His death?* Therefore, we are buried with Him by baptism into death: that like as Christ was raised up from the dead by the glory of the Father, even so we also should walk in newness of life. (Rom. 6:2-4)

Therefore, since remission of sins is the result of the repentant believer being baptized into the death of Christ, it naturally is the *seventh* in divine order.

But while baptism remits or blots out our past "just as if I'd" never sinned, the sinner must continue to the end to be saved, or to obtain salvaiton. Jesus said, "And ye shall be hated of all men for my name's sake: but he that endureth to the end shall be saved." (Matt. 10:22)

He repeated the promise of salvation to the enduring or continuing one. In Matthew 24:13, we read:

"But he that shall endure unto the end, the same shall be *saved*." So salvation is the eighth and final element in the order of the key combination of the commission. Briefly stated they are:

1. Going
2. Teaching
3. Hearing
4. Believing
5. Repenting
6. Being baptized
7. Continuing
8. Salvation

The order as Practiced by the New Testament Churches.

To Peter as well as to all the apostles was given the keys to the opening of the kingdom on Pentecost, the birthday of the church.

"And I say also unto thee that thou art Peter, and I will give unto thee the keys of the kingdom of heaven; and whatsoever thou shalt bind on earth shall be bound in heaven: and whatsoever thou shalt loose on earth shall be loosed in heaven" (Matt. 16:18, 19).

This same power was given to the other apostles also. In John 20:23 we read, "Whose soever sins ye remit, they are remitted unto them; and whose soever sins ye retain, they are retained."

As the spokesman on the Day of Pentecost Peter, filled with the Holy Spirit, using the divine combination, opened the door and all the divine elements are then either mentioned or implied.

1. There was a going—to the one place (Acts 2:1)
2. There was preaching—"But Peter standing up with the eleven, *lifted up his voice* and said unto them" (Acts 2:14)
3. There was a hearing, for we read, "Now when they *heard* this, they were pricked in their hearts. (Acts 2:37)
4. While faith is not mentioned, the very fact that they were pricked in their hearts and said, "men and brethren what shall we do?" And that they gladly received his word shows they believed. (Acts 2:37)
5. They were told to repent. (Acts 2:38)
6. They were baptized. (Acts 2:41)

7. They continued steadfast. (Acts 2:42)
8. They were recipients of salvation because "The Lord added to the church daily such as should be saved." (Acts 2:47)

This, then is the combination of the Key, and the order of that combination as used by the first church of Christ of the New Testament pattern.

The Changing of the Combination

But what a change the centuries have brought. When through a gradual apostacy the Roman Catholic church came into being they changed the order.

Instead of going, they brought little babies and performed upon them what they called baptism for their salvation. Then, when the child reached the age of twelve put him in a confirmation class and taught him.

Their order is a departure from the New Testament order and runs as follows:

Teaching, hearing, believing, repenting, continuing.

The denominational churches that spring from the Catholic church, called Pedo-Baptists, because they practice the baptism of infants, also follow the same order, perverting the combination by bringing babies to be baptized for their salvation and later teaching them.

It can not be said too forcibly that never was a person ever baptized by the New Testament church who did not first hear by being taught or being preached to. Jesus said, "Go teach, preach, he that *believeth* and is baptized *shall be saved*."

The Baptists have restored the order of going, teaching and hearing, but have also changed the order by putting repentance before faith. They base their action on Mark 1:15, which reads:

"And saying, the time is fulfilled, and the kingdom of God is at hand: repent ye, and *believe* the gospel."

At first reading this would seem to substantiate their practice, but further and more careful consideration does not. Rather it reveals their order to be unscriptural.

Paul commanded us to: "Study to show thyself approved unto God, a workman that needeth not to be ashamed, rightly dividing the Word of truth." (2 Timothy 2:15)

The reason for the Baptist putting repentance before faith and basing it on Mark 1:15, is that they do not rightly divide God's Word. Mark 1:15 refers to a time before the cross, before the gospel had come into its fulness in the death, burial and resurrection of Christ. Since the facts of the gospel had not been fulfilled at the time referred to in Mark 1:15, all that could be said was, "Repent and believe the gospel when it comes in its fullness."

After the cross, after the death, burial and resurrection of Christ, the order of the New Testament church was to believe the gospel and then repent.

Then another change in the order or combination was made by the Baptists in that they teach that you are saved before you are baptized, declaring that you are baptized *because* you are saved. If this were true then the commission should have read, "He that believeth and is saved, shall be baptized." But it reads "He that believeth and is baptized *shall* be saved."

Salvation, according to the commission of Christ is predicated upon both believing and being baptized. Shall we diagram the sentence:

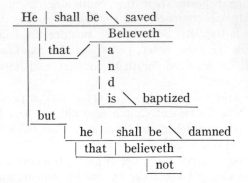

Thus it is manifestly clear that salvation does not precede baptism, but rather it follows baptism.

Since this is true then salvation is based upon a penitent baptized believer who must continue faithfully to the end. And it is not scripturally true that one who is "once saved is always saved," or "he who is once in grace is always in grace," or that he can never fall.

Yet Christ taught we must endure to the end to be saved. Paul said:

"But I keep under my body, and bring it into subjection; lest that by any means, when I have preached to others, I myself should be a castaway." (1 Cor. 9:27)

Again Paul said: "Work out your own salvation with fear and trembling. (Phil. 2:12)

Peter said: "If ye do these things, ye shall never *fall.*" (2 Peter 1:10)

The escape from falling is conditioned on the principle "If" ye do these things.

There remains a brief consideration of the Church of Christ. In 1809 there began a movement to restore the Church of the first century by discarding human creeds, confessions of faith, books of discipline, and decrees of church councils, synods, presbyteries and religious conferences.

This came to be known as the Restoration movement. Among the many things restored after the New Testament pattern was the return to the divine order and scriptural combination of the use of the Key of the Kingdom. A study of the accompanying chart will give a graphic presentation of the restored order.

The Economy of the Gospel

Note:

On the chart on page 59A are listed the eight conversions recorded in the book of Acts. Under each conversion is listed only the numbers of the acts of obedience actually mentioned in each case. It will be seen that only number six, or baptism is mentioned in all eight records of conversion.

However, all were taught or preached to, even though, in some cases such teaching or preaching was not specifically mentioned. Since all were taught, it naturally and logically follows that all heard, although hearing is only actually mentioned in the cases of the Pentecostians, Cornelius, Lydia and the Corinthians. And so the other items not mentioned might be so considered.

Does this mean that each one was saved in a different manner? Positively not. God is not the author of confusion. There is being demonstrated to us here the Economy of the Gospel.

Each hearer was only told to do, that which he had not already done. What he had done, in complying with the whole range of required obedience, was not mentioned. All compiled with the same requirements to be saved. There was a uniform pattern of obedience.

The same law of obedience is still binding on us today. Christ has neither changed the items, nor the order of scriptural obedience to the gospel.

The chart presents the principle departures from the divine order of obedience as practiced by certain groups in Christendom and the restoration of that divine order by the church of the Philadelphia, or Restoration Period.

vs. 8 "I know thy works." Their works were so pleasing to Christ that, even though they had a little strength, he had set before the church an open door that no man could shut.

The Restoration movement has not had the wealth and strength of ecclesiastical power that the denominational world, but because they have kept his words they have an open door.

"Thou hast kept my word." The Restoration movement has stressed as its motto, "Where the Bible speaks, we speak, and where the Bible is silent, we are silent." They have discarded all human creeds and books of discipline and taken the Bible as the only rule of faith and practice.

"Thou hast not denied my name." The Restoration movement threw away all denominational names and called the church, "The Church of Christ" and the individual followers of Christ "Christian," because that was speaking according to God's Word.

This church and the church of Smyrna are the only churches for which there is no reproof.

vs. 3:9 Then follows a word of encouragement and exhortation.

"Behold, I will make them of the synagogue of Satan, which say they are Jews, and are not, but do lie, behold, I will make them to come and worship at thy feet, and to know that I have loved thee."

The Restoration movement has constantly faced the claim of the denominational world that they, too, are Jews." Note the word "Jew" refers to those who are the elect of God.

Like the other church without reproof, the church of Smyrna, we find two conditions that are repeated in Philadelphia.

First, they in Smyrna were opposed and persecuted by false brethren, who said they were "Jews," but in reality were "the synagogue of Satan."

Second, they were about to have great tribulation (tribulation ten days). This second condition is found in Philadelphia also,

Scriptural Record	The Gospel—God's Power unto Salvation (Rom. 1:16)	Effect on Hearer	Conditions Met by Man	God's Offer of Grace
Acts 2, The Jews on Pentecost	Peter preached Christ 1. God approved (22) 2. Crucified (23) 3. Raised (32)	Many "pricked in their heart" asked, "What shall we do?" (37)	Must "Repent and be baptized" (38)	1. Remission of sins (38) 2. Gift of the Holy Spirit (38)
Acts 3, Other Jews in Jerusalem	Peter preached Christ 1. Rejected of men (13, 14) 2. Raised (15) 3. Prophecy fulfilled (18)	Recognition of guilt implied by response	Must "Repent and turn" or "be converted" (19)	1. Blot out sins (19) 2. Seasons of refreshing (19)
Acts 8, the Samaritans	Philip preached Christ (5) and "Things concerning the kingdom of "God"" (12)	"	1. They believed (12) 2. They were baptized (12)	The blessings extended to all penitent, baptized believers (Cf. Acts 2: 38)
Acts 8, The Ethiopian	Philip preached Jesus (35)	"	1. Confessed his faith (37) 2. Was baptized (38)	1. Blessings of Acts 2: 38 or 3: 19 2. Joy (8: 39)
Acts 9, 22 and 24, Saul of Tarsus	Christ gave proof of his deity (4, 5)	Recognition of guilt demonstrated by response (22: 10)	1. Confessed Jesus (22: 10) 2. Fasted and prayed 3. Repented (22: 10) 4. Was baptized (22:16)	1. Blessings of Acts 2: 38 2. Peace (9: 19; Rom. 5: 1)
Acts 10 and 11, Cornelius	Peter preached "Peace by Jesus Christ" (10: 31ff.)	Recognition of guilt implied by response	"Baptized in the name of Jesus Christ" (10:48)	Blessings of Acts 2: 38 or 3: 19
Acts 16, Lydia	Paul preached Christ to her (14) (Cf. 1 Cor. 2: 2)	Recognition of guilt implied by response	1. Attended to things heard (14) 2. Was baptized (15)	Blessings of Acts 2: 38 or 3: 19
Acts 16, The Jailer of Philippi	Paul preached the word of the Lord (31, 32)	Recognized guilt by washing stripes of Paul and Silas and in obedience to the word (33)	Was baptized (33)	Blessings of Acts 2: 38 or 3: 19

for verse 10 reads, "Because thou hast kept the word of my patience, I also will keep thee from the hour of temptation, which shall come upon all the world, to try them that dwell upon the earth."

But there is the great difference. Those in Smyrna were to suffer "unto death," therefore the promise to the overcomers was that they "should not be hurt of the second death." There was no open door of escape for them.

But the church in Philadelphia, was to be kept from the impending trial, whatever the nature of it.

vs. 11 "Behold I come quickly." This great announcement explains how this church will enjoy exemption from the coming tribulation.

Since there is only one more church period to come, He directs this church's attention to his second advent. This solemn call prepares the church for the final call, "Behold I stand at the door and knock," the benediction given the church of Laodicea.

"Hold fast that which thou hast that no man take thy crown."

This again takes us back to (Isaiah 22:22). There Shebna and Eliakim are the characters. Shebna had the "crown," he was "over the House," and wore the "robe" and "girdle" of office; but God said "I will clothe Eliakim with thy robe, and strengthen him with thy girdle, and I will commit the government into his hands (Isa. 22:15, 20-22). Thus Shebna's crown was taken by another. So the Philadelphia church is warned lest some one take her crown. This crown was not the crown of royalty (Diadema in the Greek), but the garland crown (Stephanos) given as a reward. In Greek, a garland or crown was a wreath or chaplet. It formed the prize at the Greek games. Hence it became a symbol of victory. This reminds us of Paul's exhortation: "Know ye not that they which run in a race run all, but one receive the prize? So run that ye may obtain. And every man that striveth for the mastery is temperate in all things. Now they do it to obtain a corruptible crown, but we an incorruptible," etc. (I Cor. 9:24-27).

vs. 12 "Becoming a pillar" is a term implying strength, permanence and honor. This speaks of finality, as the Bible does not speak of men as being pillars in His temple while on earth.

"He shall go no more out; and I will write upon him the

name of My God, and the name of the city of my God, which is New Jerusalem, which cometh down out of heaven from My God, and I will write upon him my new name."

These promises are great beyond the power of words to express.

Since the key of David and David, himself, comes into prominence in this church period, we are reminded of his longing for the House of God. (Psa. 23:6) and the one thing he desired and sought after was that he might "Dwell" in the house of the Lord all the days of his life. (Psa. 27:4)

The promise to become a pillar in the temple, refers not to any material temple, but in heaven. The New Jerusalem has no temple in it, because it is all temple.

The promise "I will write upon him" is interesting when we remember that as one enters the church the spiritual temple below, three names are recorded in the baptismal formula—the Father, Son and Holy Spirit. When he enters the kingdom above, three names are again written upon him, the name of God, of the heavenly city, and Christ's heavenly name.

The promise of the new name is again connected with that city in the last chapter of Revelation "The throne of God and of the Lamb shall be in it; and His servants shall serve Him; and they shall see His face; and His name shall be on their foreheads." (Rev. 22:3-4)

vs. 13 Again he uncovers to us the fact that He is not addressing just one local congregation, but taking the church at Philadelphia as a symbol of an entire period of church history, which we have found corresponds to the restoration period that followed immediately after the denominational epoch called Sardis.

The Laodicean Church
Text (3:14-22)

14 And to the angel of the church in Laodicea write: These things saith the Amen, the faithful and true witness, the beginning of the creation of God: 15 I know thy works, that thou are neither cold nor hot: I would thou wert cold or hot. 16 So because thou art lukewarm, and neither hot nor cold, I will spew thee out of my mouth. 17 Because thou sayest, I am rich, and have gotten riches, and have need of nothing; and knowest not that thou art the wretched one and miserable and poor and blind and naked: 18 I counsel thee to buy of me gold refined by fire, that thou mayest become rich; and white garments, that thou mayest clothe thyself, and that the shame of thy nakedness be not made manifest; and eye-salve to anoint thine eyes, that thou mayest see. 19 As many as I love, I reprove and chasten:

be zealous therefore, and repent. 20 Behold, I stand at the door and knock: if any man hear my voice and open the door, I will come in to him, and will sup with him, and he with me. 21 He that overcometh, I will give to him to sit down with me in my throne, as I also overcame, and sat down with my Father in his throne. 22 He that hath an ear, let him hear what the Spirit saith to the churches.

INTRODUCTION

While in the first four churches, we are given to see the development of a positive evil within the church, ranging from the "deeds of the Nicolaitanes" in Ephesus, "the synagogue of Satan" in Smyrna, "the doctrine of the Nicolaitanes" and "the doctrine of Baalam" in Pergamos, the "depths of Satan" in Thyatira; so with the Sardis church we have revealed to us the development of a state of decline, beginning with Sardis, "having a name and are dead," and reaching the final state in Laodicea in which the church is so lukewarm that "it is wretched and miserable, and poor, and blind, and naked."

vs. 14, 15 The Lord here presents Himself as "The Amen, the Faithful and true Witness, the Beginning of the Creation of God."

These characters are not taken from the seven-fold description of Chapter 1:13-16, but they are taken from other revelations of the Lord Jesus Christ found in that chapter. There He is presented as the "Alpha and Omega," the "Beginning and the ending" (vs. 8), and also as "The faithful Witness." (vs. 5)

Here Christ calls himself by one of the names of God. It is a remarkable name. It is found in Isaiah 65:16. It is found in the midst of a prophecy of the overwhelming judgments that are to fall upon apostate Israel.

So here in the last church period, Christ uses the name of God when judgment is to be meted out. In Isaiah 65:17, he says, "For behold, I create a new heaven and a new earth." So following the Laodecean there is to be a new creation.

Again this title "The Amen," describes God as the One who accomplishes all His purposes and all His promises. The Lord is this God, the Amen. "For all the promises of God in Him are yea, and in Him Amen!" (II Cor. 1:20) And most appropriately he presents Himself as "The Amen" in the closing period of church history. The very use of this title, gives us the cue of this being the seventh and final stage of the history of the church in the closing days of the gospel age. God is about to ring down the curtain in the history of the church.

He presents Himself as the "Faithful and True Witness." The witness of the church had been dimmed by her departure into compromise, paganism, division of denominationalism and, after a brief return to adherence to His Word and name in the Restoration period, gone into total eclipse in the lukewarmness of the final epoch.

Therefore He wants the church to know He is keeping the witness clear, by introducing Himself as the "Faithful and true Witness."

"The beginning of the Creation of God." Here He presents Himself, not as a part of the creation, but the uncreated principle of creation from whom it (creation) took form.

Nay there is also here the added and deeper thought, that He is the beginning of the new creation in His redemptive work of bringing many sons into glory. (Heb. 2:10) He is the first born among many breathren. (Romans 8:29)

"*I know thy works.*" In every letter we have, without exception, this soul-searching declaration. Christ not only knows the works of each individual congregation, but here he is declaring he knows the works of the last church period. This is because He knows all things from the beginning. He looked down the ages and saw this last age of the gospel dispensation and saw the paralyzing effects of lukewarmness.

The loss of first love, of the Ephesian period, reaches its ultimate end in the awful lukewarmness of the last and final age of this dispensation.

vs. 16, 17 The Sharp word of reproof. Usually, in the other letters, the third division of the seven-fold division of the letters, is a word of commendation, followed by the word of reproof. But in this letter the reproof comes before the commendation. It would seem that Christ is so displeased with the final stage of the church that he hastens to the reproof.

Thou art neither hot nor cold; I would thou were cold or hot, so because thou art lukewarm, and neither hot nor cold, I will spew thee out of my mouth.

Tepid religion is nauseating to Christ. He looked with loathing on the Pharisees of the days of His flesh, who looked upon themselves as religious paragons while their hearts were not right with God, either spiritually or doctrinally.

63

The Laodiceans were not warm in their affection for Christ, they were not burning with zeal in His cause; nor yet were they cold and altogether heartless. If they had been outright cold, it would have been easier for Him to deal with them, and there would have been a greater likelihood of their discovering their condition.

Ignorance of its true condition was to be a characteristic of the last church period. How true this has become in our day and how completely fulfilled. The mass of people today do not realize their lost condition. They live in the midst of delusion about their lost estate. Thinking itself rich when in reality it was poor; thinking itself well supplied with all that a church of Christ should have, when in reality it was destitute of the most essential things.

This church is just the opposite of that in Smyrna, which was seemingly in poverty and tribulation, but in reality was rich. There was no tribulation in Laodicea, no persecution, no synagogue of Satan to molest them. They were having a very easy and comfortable time.

How true of this age. The church has fine buildings, up-to-date facilities, the services are carried out in the best approved form. But it is hard to get this kind of church today to realize their low estate, spiritually speaking.

vs. 18 But Christ does not abandon them, but says, "I councel thee." He calls them to repent, coupling that call with a most tender word of exhortation. He had declared them "poor, blind and naked," but immediately offers to supply them with "gold" that they might be rich and white raiment that they might be suitably clad, and with eye salve, that they might see. He offers them:

"Gold tried in the fire" In Psa. 19:7-11, David declares the value of the Word of God—"More to be desired are they than gold, yea, than much fine gold." But the church today is generally uninterested in the gold of God's word. Modernist preachers stand in the pulpit preaching platitudes and the hearers take dross for gold, and pewter for silver. Hence the appalling spiritual poverty.

"White raiment that thou mayest be clothed." Rev. 19:8 explains that the fine linen, clean and white, represents the righteousness of saints. In the last age when so many are rejecting blood atonement, no wonder he speaks of them as being naked.

"Eye-salve, that thou mayest see." The advice to "anoint thine eyes with eye-salve" suggests that the church of the last period is destitute of the gifts of the Holy Spirit, for John speaks of the

Holy Spirit as the Unction (or anointing) from Christ, the Holy One. (I John 2:20)

vs. 19 Sharp as had been His rebuke to this lukewarm church, his rebuke was a proof of his unfailing love.

He calls them to be zealous, instead of lukewarm. He calls them to repent. He adds a final word. (Rev. 3:20)

vs. 20 This marvelous invitation needs consideration. First, it is not that Christ is outside that chiefly impresses us, but that He is so near, even at the very door, and not only so, but is ready to enter instantly it is opened. "Just outside the door," but the lukewarmness of the church fails to invite Him in. This is the only church of the seven that keeps Christ outside. The self-satisfied church is "inside," the door is closed, and Christ is knocking for admission.

The second thing that impresses us is that this invitation indicates this is the last church period and Christ is about to return and he "stands at the door and knocks." He is about to come in his second advent. Note: He wants to come in and sup with the saints. When Christ returns we are to sup with him at the wedding feast. (Luke 12:35-40) (Rev. 19:7-9)

There is no real commendation in this letter. There was nothing to commend a lukewarm church.

Next comes a word of encouragement. The message is that it has a special word to the individual—"If any man."

In Thyatira the Lord recognizes a remnant of faithful ones, "the rest in Thyatira, as many as have not this doctrine;" and in Sardis, "there are a few names which have not defiled their garments," but in Laodicea there is a word of strong encouragement to the individual who, amidst general indifference to the things of God, longs for personal fellowship with the Lord.

It would seem that the indifference of lukewarmness of this last period would be so widespread that his encouragement would have to be given to the individual instead to the entire church.

vs. 21 Next comes the greatest of all the promises to any church.

To him that overcometh will I grant to sit with me in my throne, even as I also overcame and am set down with my Father in His Throne." How significant this statement becomes since it is the closing promise!

65

Since He is about to return—stands even at the door and knocks—He promises them who overcome to sit down and reign with Him, since at His return the kingdoms of this world become the kingdom of our Lord and His Christ.

The devil had promised Him the kingdoms of this world in the temptation, but Christ rejected it, for the price of that glory was the worship of the devil.

Christ refused the offer from the devil, that He might wait for this glorious hour when He, as an overcomer, with all the overcomers, should have earned the right to reign.

Paul said, "If we suffer with Him, we shall also reign with Him." (II Tim. 2:12)

Lastly, we hear the final urgent call. "He that hath an ear, let him hear what the Spirit," etc. Like the declaration, "I know thy works," this call is found in all the seven letters. It is a stirring call to the churches of this Laodicean period. Seven times He repeats this injunction, lest we lose sight of the history of the whole church throughout the seven periods of her life from Pentecost to the end.

Thus we have seen that these letters foretold the main developments and principle eras of the church down through the gospel age.

Also they were written to admonish, encourage, warn, guide, reprove, and call us to heed, to the end that we may pass the time of our sojourn here working out our salvation with fear and trembling, having respect to the "recompense of the reward."

As each of Jacob's sons had different personalities and these personalities pictured the characteristics of the tribes descending from them, so do these seven churches, through their local conditions, symbolize the conditions in each of the seven great church periods.

PART II

CHAPTER IV

THE VISION OF THE THRONE

Text (4:1-11)

1 After these things I saw, and behold, a door opened in heaven, and the first voice that I heard, a voice as of a trumpet speaking

66

with me, one saying, Come up hither, and I will show thee the things which must come to pass hereafter. 2 Straightaway I was in the Spirit: and behold, there was a throne set in heaven, and one sitting upon the throne; 3 and he that sat was to look upon like a jasper stone and a sardius: and there was a rainbow round about the throne, like an emerald to look upon. 4 And round about the throne were four and twenty thrones: and upon the thrones I saw four and twenty elders sitting, arrayed in white garments; and on their heads crowns of gold. 5 And out of the throne proceed lightnings and voices and thunders. And there were seven lamps of fire burning before the throne, which are the seven Spirits of God; 6 and before the throne, as it were a sea of glass like unto crystal; and in the midst of the throne, and round about the throne, four living creatures full of eyes before and behind. 7 And the first creature was like a lion, and the second creature like a calf, and the third creature had a face as of a man, and the fourth creature was like a flying eagle. 8 And the four living creatures, having each one of them six wings, are full of eyes round about and within: and they have no rest day and night, saying, Holy, holy, holy, is the Lord God, the Almighty, who was and who is and who is to come. 9 And when the living creatures shall give glory and honor and thanks to him that sitteth on the throne, to him that liveth for ever and ever, 10 the four and twenty elders shall fall down before him that sitteth on the throne, and shall worship him that liveth for ever and ever, and shall cast their crowns before the throne, saying, 11 Worthy art thou, our Lord and our God, to receive the glory and the honor and the power: for thou didst create all things, and because of thy will they were, and were created.

INTRODUCTION

Beginning with this chapter we meet a tremendous change in the nature of the "unfolding" of the apocalypse. The chapter is filled with imagery of the most striking nature. The scene has changed entirely.

No longer does John see the Christ walking among the candlesticks, but in spirit he is permitted to look through a door opened in heaven and behold a throne! The throne is the central object of this scene, with all symbolism taking its place and significance with reference to that throne.

The entire symbolism here makes it very evident that the main purpose of this vision given John was to reveal the ascended and glorified Christ in the act of occupying His throne, at His Father's right hand.

It was of this enthronement which Peter spoke on the day of Pentecost: "This Jesus hath God raised up, whereof we all are witnesses. Therefore, being by the right hand of God exalted, and having received of the Father the promise of the Holy Spirit, he hath shed forth this which ye now see and hear. For David is not ascended into the heavens: but he saith himself, The Lord said unto my Lord, *sit thou on my right hand,* until I make thy foes thy footstool. Therefore let all the house of Israel know assuredly that God hath made that same Jesus, whom ye have crucified, both Lord and Christ. (Acts 2:32-36)

Beyond the shadow of a doubt, then, we have the "uncovering" of the transcendently glorious event fulfilling the prophecy, "The Lord said unto my Lord, sit thou at my right hand, until I make thine enemies Thy footstool," (Psalsm 110:1),—the event which the Spirit-endowed Peter proclaimed in his first sermon on the birthday of the church and later declared in his epistle, "Who is gone into heaven, and is on the right hand of God, angels and authorities and powers being made subject unto Him. (I Peter 3:22)

To this Paul adds his Spirit-filled testimony, "and what is the exceeding greatness of his power to us-ward who believe, according to the working of his mighty power, which he wrought in Christ, when he raised him from the dead, *and set him at his own right hand* in the heavenly places, far above all principality and power, and might, and dominion, and every name that is named, not only in this world, but also in that which is to come." (Ephesians 1:19-21)

In the light of these scriptures it is crystal clear that the group of visions beginning here in the fourth chapter, and embracing the entire program of the seals and trumpets, has for its starting point the ascension of the risen Christ into heaven and His occupation of the throne, of which He only could be worthy, at the right hand of the majesty in the heavens.

This group of visions has then, to do with those events which began to occur from his coronation at Pentecost.

In the interpretation of the Book of Revelation, very much depends upon where we locate this vision of the throne and the book.

By the references we have mentioned, it is impossible therefore, without setting aside the plainest declarations of the scripture, to place the occupying by Christ of His throne on God's right hand at any other time than upon His ascension into heaven.

Christ, himself connects this vision with the one preceding. In His letter to the church of the Laodicean period He said, "Even as I also *overcame* and am *set down* with my Father in His throne." (Rev. 3:21) The past tenses of the verbs used in this verse declare plainly that His occupation of His Father's throne had already taken place when He appeared unto John in the vision on the isle of Patmos.

vs. 1 "After this," or "these things," as in the Revised version, means, after the letters addressed to the seven churches, this new and startingly different vision was given to John. While the fourth chapter begins a second prophetic portion, it is not itself prophetic, but introductory.

"The first voice which I heard was as it were of a trumpet talking to me," seems to be the same voice of which we read in (Rev. 1:10) "I was in the Spirit on the Lord's Day, and heard behind me a great voice, as of a trumpet."

That voice now summons John, evidently to pass through the open door, by saying, "Come up hither, and I will show thee things which must be hereafter."

But John, in the flesh, could not obey such a summons, so we read:

vs. 2 "And immediately, I was in the Spirit." Since the first vision of the seven-fold portrait of Christ came to John in the Spirit (Rev. 1:10-18) so this second vision of Christ, portrayed as now sitting on the throne, could only come to John "in the Spirit."

The voice called to John to leave the realm of the natural man and enter the region of the supernatural. These words indicate that, between the first vision and the present series of visions, there was an interval in the which John was in his natural state.

This experience of John recalls such an experience by the apostle Paul. (In II Corinthians 12:1-5) "It is not expedient for me doubtless to glory. I will come to *visions* and *revelations* of the Lord. I knew a man in Christ above fourteen years ago (whether in the body, I cannot tell, or whether out of the body, I cannot tell: God knoweth); such an one caught up to the third heaven.

And I knew such a man, (whether in the body, or out of the body, I cannot tell: God knoweth). How that he was caught up into paradise, and heard unspeakable words, which it is not lawful for a man to utter. Of such an one will I glory, yet of myself I will not glory, but in mine infirmities."

We must note this fact very carefully, that John, after his first vision left the spirit and reverted to his natural state and the second series of visions could not be given until he was caught up, as it were "in the Spirit" a second time.

We can never arrive at a true understanding of Revelation until we realize that the book does not give a regularly progressive unfolding of the future, but is divided into a number of visions, each complete in itself, and each beginning, not where the last one left off, but at some starting point, best suited to the series of events "uncovered" in that particular vision.

"Behold a throne!" introduces the special object of attention in this vision of the door opened in heaven. Truly, the throne is the central object of this scene. This becomes all the more evident when we note that in chapters four and five, the word "throne" occurs no less than seventeen times!

Thus, this rebellious earth has revealed to it, through the apocalypse, that there is a throne in heaven and that all things, both in heaven and on the earth are under Christ's authority. Did not Christ declare upon His departure to occupy this throne, "All power hath been given unto me in heaven and in earth"? (Matthew 28:18)

Truly we must ever remind ourselves that this book is a revelation, or "uncovering" of Jesus Christ. His participation in the government of the universe is but dimly seen by the eyes of men. This fact is known, and can only be known by the medium of revelation.

The ministry of the Holy Spirit is to reveal the Christ. Christ, in the days of His flesh said, "Howbeit when he, the Spirit of truth is come, he will guide you into all truth: for he shall not speak of himself; but whatsoever he shall hear, that shall he speak: and he will show you things to come. He shall glorify me: for he shall receive of mine, and shall show it unto you." (John 16:13-14)

So John had to be caught up in the Spirit to have this revealing, by the Spirit, of the coronated Christ.

Christ has given us here a symbolic presentation of his twofold work of creation and recreation or redemption. The symbolism of this vision reveals that redemption has been provided by the payment of the ransom price—"the blood of Christ" hence He is presented as the Lamb that was slain in the fifth chapter, and "by His own blood, He entered in once into the Holy place, having obtained eternal redemption." (Heb. 9:12)

But there still remained many things to be accomplished before "the redemption of the purchased possession. (Eph. 1:14) Unto this day of redemption we have been sealed, said Paul, by the Holy Spirit of God. (Eph. 4:30)

Between those two phases of His work of redemption—the payment of the purchase price by the Lamb of God who has shed His blood, and the taking of possession of the whole redeemed creation, is to be found the entire history of the dispensation of the Holy Spirit.

Revelation is the uncovering of the events between these two phases.

vs. 3 Just as John had given us a seven-fold description of Christ walking among the candlesticks, before he uncovered the history of the seven church periods, so here he describes the Christ sitting upon the right hand of God, before he proceeds to uncover the events contained in the seven seals, and the seven trumpets.

He said, "And he that sat was to look upon like a jasper and a sardine stone: and there was a rainbow round about the throne, in sight like unto an emerald."

The three stones mentioned here are, of course symbols. Doubtless their meaning is found in their colors.

The jasper stone is mentioned again in Revelation 21:11 where it is described as a stone most precious and of dazzling brightness, clear as crystal. It portrayed the wondrous light of the Holy Jerusalem, and that light it declares "is the glory of God." Evidently that is its meaning here. The jasper represented the glory of God.

The sardius is a dark red stone. Orpheus speaks of "the blood colored sardius." How appropriate, since Christ is presented in the fifth chapter as "the Lamb as it had been slain," that the blood-red sardius should appear in relation to the throne.

Since the rainbow is green in color "like unto an emerald," it may indicate that the events that are about to be "uncovered" have to do with the earth, since green is the color of earth, as blue is the color heaven.

"There was a rainbow round about the throne."

Much prominence is given to the rainbow by John. He was impressed by the fact that it was a complete circle. The rainbow we see on the storm cloud is incomplete—a half circle. This half rainbow is a token of the covenant God made with Noah and his sons, as well as with every living creature. (Gen. 9:8-17) This lengthy description in a book like Genesis noted for its brevity, testifies to its importance as a symbol.

The half circle rainbow was a token that the storm had already passed over the place where the beholders stand.

The complete, full-circle rainbow which encircles the throne

71

of God is visible to those over whom the spiritual storms have passed, because the onlookers had the blood of their passover Lamb upon them. The storm of God's judgment had already passed over the place where the redeemed stand and can never come again.

This complete rainbow is a token of Christ's covenant made with every redeemed Christian.

vs. 4, 5 John saw twenty-four seats, or literally "thrones." The central throne was encompassed by twenty-four lesser thrones. And upon these thrones he saw twenty-four elders sitting. Since these are so closely associated with the four living creatures, their identity will be better considered after an explanation of these four living creatures is given in verse six.

That they were clothed with white raiment speaks of their ineffable purity. In the fact that they were seated upon thrones and had on their heads crowns of gold, indicate they share the reign of Him whose throne they encircle. Since incense is a type of the "prayers of saints" (Rev. 5:8), it would seem that they are divine agents through whom the prayers of the saints reach God.

Such a function of divine being can be better understood when we recall that Daniel had his prayer delayed twenty-one days by the prince of the Kingdom of Persia. We read in (Daniel 10:12-13) "Then said he unto me, Fear not, Daniel: for from the first day that thou didst set thine heart to understand and to chasten thyself before thy God, thy words were heard, and I am *come for thy* words.

But the prince of the Kingdom of Persia withstood me one and twenty days, but, lo, Michael, one of the chief princes, came to help me."

This brings to our minds Paul's declaration, "For we wrestle not against the rulers of the darkness of this world, against spiritual wickedness in high places." (Eph. 6:12)

Evidently these are heavenly princes who have power with God in respect to our prayers. When Jacob wrestled successfully with the heavenly visitor until the breaking of day, the latter said unto Jacob, "Thy name shall be called no more Jacob, but Israel: for as a *prince* hast thou power with God and with men and hath prevailed." (Genesis 32:28)

So these princes in John's vision had power with God.

They undoubtedly belonged to the same class of heavenly intelligence as the four living creatures for the following reasons:

First, when the four living creatures gave glory to Him that sat on the throne, the twenty-four elders also worship Him. (Rev. 4:9, 10)

Second, They have harps and vials full of odors the same as the four living creatures.

Third, When the four living creatures say, "Amen," the twenty-four elders worship Him who is on the throne.

Fourth, When an innumerable company of the redeemed, praise God for salvation, the angels, elders and four living creatures are above the throne and not counted among the redeemed. (Rev. 7:9-12)

Fifth, They do not praise God for their own redemption. Lange on Revelation, Page 152, says the "us" of Rev. 5:9 is an interpolation. It has been found that the oldest Greek manuscripts give an entirely different meaning than the authorized version.

Tischendorf, Alford and Lange translate as follows:

"Thou wast slain, and hast redeemed to God by thy blood,
out of every kindred, and tongue, and people, and nation,
and hast made them unto our God kings and priests, and
they shall reign on the earth."

They do not praise the Lamb for their own redemption, but for the redemption of the world.

Sixth, In Revelation, 14th Chapter, the Lamb has one hundred and forty and four thousand saints about Him, who sing a new song *before* the throne, and *before* the four living creatures, and the elders. (Rev. 14:1-3) Only the redeemed could sing that new song; the elders did not join in the singing.

So we see they are about the throne, associated with the angels, but not with the martyrs. They are always separated from those who praise God for redemption.

This distinction reveals their character. They belong to the heavenly intelligences, to the same class as the cherubim. They are princes of heaven, and not of men.

The number twenty-four is probably associated with the twenty-four courses of the priests of the temple, which was a pattern of things in the heavens. Here in this vision we are looking at the heavenly things themselves (Hebrew 9:23) which no natural eye could behold.

The number twenty-four is the result of multiplying the factors of twelve and two. The spiritual theocracy of God is represented in the Old Testament by the heads or elders of the twelve tribes of Israel, and in the New Testament the Christocracy of the Kingdom is headed by the twelve apostles.

We are not looking at objects that bear any physical resemblance whatsoever to the heavenly things. For instance, there could be no physical likeness between the glorified Christ and "A Lamb having seven horns and seven eyes."

What we are trying to do is to decipher a description *written in hieroglyphics.*

The seven lamps of fire are said to be the seven Spirits of God, which we found in the study of this symbol in the first chapter, represents the fullness of the Spirit as manifested in Christ.

vs. 6, 7 John saw four beasts, or to be exact, "four living creatures." The term "beasts" applied to these beings is incorrect, particularly in view of the fact that the same term is used to portray the monsters of iniquity as seen in chapters thirteen, seventeen and nineteen. The Greek word in the thirteenth chapter of Revelation is a different term. The Greek word for "beasts" is entirely different.

The word used for the four creatures is "Zoa," meaning "living forms," or "living ones."

We are now ready to decipher the heiroglyphic of "Living Creatures." Shall we let the Bible be its own interpreter.

In the first chapter of Ezekial, we find that the exiled prophet of the Old Testament dispensation saw, by the river Chebar of Babylon, the same beings that John portrayed in Revelation. While there were minor differences, the general features are identical. Both prophets, Ezekial and John saw (1) four living creatures; both saw (2) four faces, like those of a man, a lion, an ox or calf, and a flying eagle. The living creatures, described by each prophet, are full of eyes, (3) each are winged. There are minor differences in the wings: John saw six wings, Ezekial saw four wings and a pair of hands under the wings, making six members. Also the Seraphim of Isaiah sixth chapter had six wings. Finally, the same Greek term is used to represent the four living creatures of both Ezekial and John. It follows then that if we can ascertain the meaning of the symbols beheld by Ezekial and Isaiah, we shall thereby "uncover" the meaning of the same symbol in Revelation.

In the tenth chapter of Ezekial, the prophet speaking of the heavenly beings that he beheld the second time, says in verse 22, "and the likeness of their faces was the same faces which I saw by the river Chebar, their appearances and themselves." In verse 15, he also says these are "the living creatures I saw by the river Chebar." In verse twenty, he says, "I knew they were Cherubim."

Isaiah says they were seraphim. It is also interesting to note that in Isaiah's description he also saw the throne in heaven and Him that sat thereon, and above the throne were the seraphim, and he also mentions the door. (Isaiah 6:1-4)

Therefore, we know positively that these four living creatures are cherubim, or seraphim, the highest order of the angelic hosts. We know very little about them, but they are always near the throne of God.

The cherubim were first seen at the gate of the garden of Eden (Gen. 3:24), guarding the way to the tree of life with a flaming sword.

In the tabernacle cherubim hovered over the mercy seat and were embroidered on the curtains. God is addressed in (I Samuel 4:4) as the one who dwells between the cherubim. His Shekinah glory, in the Holy of Holies, was manifested from between the cherubim on the Ark of the Covenant. In Ezekial the brightness of the Lord is represented as attending the cherubim. In Rev. 5:6, the Lamb stands "in the midst of the throne and of the four living creatures.

The forms seen by Ezekial and John have a symbolic significance. It may be they have to do with both the material creation and the final redemption. (Rev. 4:7) Their combined make up embraces the resemblance of the man, the lion (chief of wild beasts), the ox (chief of tame beasts) and the eagle (chief of the air).

They indicate possibly, that the whole creation groaneth and travaileth in pain together until now . . . waiting for the adoption to wit, the redemption of our body." (Romans 8:22, 23)

vs. 8-10 They were "full of eyes before and behind" in order to be able to see all things, their wings were always in motion, indicating tireless activity and like Isaiah's four living creatures, so John's four creatures utter the same "Holy, Holy, Holy, Lord God Almighty."

They praise Him as the one "which was, and is, and is to come." They proclaim Him as the self existant one—the I AM, and Rev. 4:9. They praise him as the eternal One.

vs. 11 They ascribe all glory to Him as the Creator.

While the authorized version reads: "And for thy pleasure they are and were created," the Revised Version says, "Because of thy will they are, and were created." His will was the creative cause.

This well may be called the "Oratorio of Creation."

CHAPTER V

THE BOOK WITH SEVEN SEALS

Text (5:1-14)

Introduction

1 And I saw in the right hand of him that sat on the throne a book written within and on the back, close sealed with seven seals. 2 And I saw a strong angel proclaiming with a great voice, Who is worthy to open the book, and to loose the seals thereof? 3 And no one in the heaven, or on the earth, or under the earth, was able to open the book, or to look thereon. 4 And I wept much, because no one was found worthy to open the book, or to look thereon: 5 and one of the elders saith unto me, Weep not; behold, the Lion that is of the tribe of Judah, the Root of David, hath overcome to open the book and the seven seals thereof. 6 And I saw in the midst of the throne and of the four living creatures, and in the midst of the elders, a Lamb standing, as though it had been slain, having seven horns, and seven eyes, which are the seven Spirits of God, sent forth into all the earth. 7 And he came, and he taketh it out of the right hand of him that sat on the throne. 8 And when he had taken the book, the four living creatures and the four and twenty elders fell down before the Lamb, having each one a harp, and golden bowls full of incense, which are the prayers of the saints. 9 And they sing a new song, saying, Worthy art thou to take the book, and to open the seals thereof: for thou wast slain, and didst purchase unto God with thy blood men of every tribe, and tongue, and people, and nation, 10 and madest them to be unto our God a kingdom and priests; and they reign upon the earth. 11 And I saw, and I heard a voice of many angels round about the throne and the living creatures and the elders; and the number of them was ten thousand times ten thousand, and thousands of thousands; 12 saying with a great voice, Worthy is the Lamb that hath been slain to receive the power, and riches, and wisdom, and might, and honor, and glory, and blessing. 13 And every created thing which is in the heaven, and on the earth, and under the earth, and on the sea, and all things that are in them, heard I saying, Unto him that sitteth on the throne, and unto the Lamb, be the blessing, and the honor, and the glory, and the dominion, for ever and ever. 14 And the four living creatures said, Amen. And the elders fell down and worshipped.

The last chapter which we have just studied centers its symbolism around the throne in the "way of the Holiest of all," where the crucified and risen Christ sits on God's right hand.

While in the earthly tabernacle there were the altar of burnt offering, the lavar and the holy place, with its furniture, consisting of the seven-armed candlestick, the table of show bread and its altar of incense, here in the vision of the most Holy Place, or heaven itself, these aforementioned pieces of furniture and the veil are gone. Paul tells us in (Hebrews 9:8) that the veil in the tabernacle and, later the temple on earth were to pass. "The Holy Spirit thus signifying that the way into the Holiest of all was not yet made manifest, while as yet the first tabernacle was yet standing."

Furthermore Paul declared this veil before the Holiest of all represented the prepared body of Jesus Christ. (Heb. 10:5) He added, "Having therefore, brethren, boldness to enter into the Holiest by the blood of Jesus, by a new and living way, which he hath consecrated for us through the veil, that is to say His flesh; and having a high priest over the house of God, let us draw near with a true heart in full assurance of faith," et. (Heb. 10:19-22)

When Christ was crucified, and yielded up the spirit as a ransom for sin, the veil was rent in twain from top to bottom. So in this vision there is no veil. We are looking into heaven itself "Whither the forerunner is for us entered, even Jesus, made a high priest for ever after the order of Melchisedec." (Heb. 6:20)

"For Christ is not entered into the holy place made with hands, which are the figures of the true, but into heaven itself, now to appear in the presence of God for us." (Heb. 9:24) So the first part of the vision reveals Christ seated at the right hand of God.

In the fourth chapter, which covers the first part of the vision, the only activity is the worship of the four living creatures, and the four and twenty elders, or princes of God. The theme of their worship is "Creation," as revealed by their anthem:

"Thou art worthy, O Lord, to receive glory and honor and power; for Thou hast *created* all things and because of thy will they are and were created." (Rev. 4:11)

If we had no other proof that these are heavenly intelligences and not redeemed men, this anthem would establish it. They sang not of redemption, for no redemption was ever needed by an obedient angel and no fallen angel was ever promised it. As created beings, higher than man, they sang of the glory of God's creation.

While the first part of this great vision of a door opened in heaven is centered around the throne and the worshipping angels, in the second part the attention is directed to "a book," or scroll (such being the form of books in that day). This scroll is seen in "the right hand of him that sat upon the throne." It was written within and in the backside and sealed with seven seals.

The very atmosphere of this part of the vision assures us that this scroll represents something of transcendent importance. This sealed scroll being a book containing the hidden mysteries of the future, was unrevealed to both angels and men.

vs. 1, 2 But the contents were of such grave import that a strong angel proclaimed with a loud voice: "Who is worthy to open the book, and to loose the seals thereof?"

The angel's interest in having the book opened reminds us of what Peter said concerning the desire of angels to look into man's salvation: "Which things the angels desire to look into." (I Peter 1:12)

vs. 3 John records that no man in heaven, nor in earth was able to open the scroll, neither to look therein." The word "man" does not occur in the Greek. Literally it reads, "no one" was found, either among angels, or among men.

This recalls Christ's own statement while in the flesh, "But of that day and hour knoweth no man (again the word man is not in the Greek) no, not the angels of heaven, but my Father only." (Matt. 24:36)

Again in (Acts 1:7), while addressing His apostles He said, "It is not for you to know the times or the seasons, which the Father hath put in his own power."

vs. 4 This caused John not only to weep, but to weep much. His distress shows that the finding of one worthy to open the book was a matter of greatest consequence.

What a revelation of John's interest in the future of the church, to which he had given so many years of labor and of which he was the last apostle! He was now old and about ready to depart. His intense anxiety to be able to penetrate the secrets of the future, as it related to the fortunes of the church which he loved better than life itself, is understandable.

His burdened spirit implores with a flood of tears that some one might be found worthy to open and read the scroll. And the longing of his loving heart is answered.

vs. 5 And one of the elders (one of the twenty-four) said unto him, "Weep not: behold, the lion of the tribe of Judah, the root of David, hath prevailed to open the book, and to lose the seals thereof."

One of the twenty-four elders, or one of the heavenly princes, so speaking to John makes clear that the duty of instructing a prophet in things pertaining to spiritual matters has never been laid upon a human being under either the old or the new Testament Covenants. Such a duty marks out these elders as being heavenly beings.

vs. 6 The prophet turns to see the Lion of the Tribe of Judah, and to his amazement, the Christ, who is the Lion of the Tribe of Judah, now is "the Lamb of God that taketh away the sins of the world." (John 1:29)

At Christ's second coming He will return as the victorious Sovereign—the Lion of the Tribe of Judah, but in the mediatorial reign John saw Him as "the Lamb that was slain."

This Lamb had seven horns. A horn is ever a symbol of power—a symbol of kings, kingdoms or power. Seven horns here, then symbolize power without limitation, since seven is the symbol of perfection.

"The seven eyes" he says "are the seven Spirits of God." We have already, in the study of chapter one, learned that the seven Spirits symbolize the fullness of the Spirit without measure which Christ possessed. The sending of this Holy Spirit to the earth (John here says "sent forth into all the earth), Christ promised just before His departure.

"Nevertheless, I tell you the truth; it is expedient for you that I go away: for if I go not away, the Comforter will not come unto you, but if I depart, I will send him unto you. And when He is come, he will reprove the world of sin and of judgment." (John 16:7, 8)

The Christ makes known His wisdom through the Holy Spirit. "Howbeit when he, the spirit of truth is come, he will guide you into all truth." (John 16:13)

So we see "the seven horns," signified the perfection of sovereign power, and the "seven eyes," or "seven spirits of God" signified perfection of wisdom. The combined symbols represented what Paul said of Christ: "Christ the power of God and the wisdom of God." (I Cor. 1:24)

79

vs. 7, 8 John saw the Lamb take the book out of the right hand of Him who sat on the throne." This, truly, was the investiture of the King. This proclaimed His right to rule and control the unfolding events of the age to come.

Upon Christ taking the Book, the twenty-four angelic princes fell down before the Lamb, having golden harps and vials full of odors, which are the prayers of the saints.

This angelic function was dealt with in the fourth chapter. They are here represented as presenting the prayers of the saints on the earth, before the throne. What a comforting thought that our petitions are presented before the throne of grace by none other than these princes of God! What heavenly import and dignity are given our prayers.

The Heavenly Doxologies
Text (5:9-14)

These elders sang a new song; new, because it is in praise of a new triumph of Christ, who has been found worthy to open the seals which are to "uncover" the events of the future.

Whereas, in the fourth chapter, we hear the angelic princes singing the "Oratorio of Creation," here there is being sung the "Oratorio of Redemption."

Music lovers will understand that an oratorio is a musical composition in which solos and choruses are sung in accompaniment to instruments. Here we see Cherubim and Seraphim and angelic princes, with their golden harps, together constituting a heavenly choir, chanting celestial music.

Note the arrangement and order of these musical numbers.

The oratorio begins with a quartet, the four living creatures, singing the seraph's song. "Holy, holy, holy Lord God Almighty, which was, and is, and is to come." (Rev. 4:8)

This is followed by the massed singing and playing of the twenty-four princes.

"Thou art worthy, O Lord, to receive glory and honor,
and power, for Thou hast created all things, and for thy
pleasure they are and were created." (Rev. 4:11)

Thus we see the first part of the oratorio is devoted to the subject of the creation. The created angelic intelligences, having never needed nor experienced redemption, could sing only in praise of their creator.

Following the singing of creation there is heard a solo voice of
a strong angel;

"Who is worthy to open the book, and to loose the seals thereof?"
(Rev. 5:2)

Then follows the gladsome response by one of the elders:

"Weep not: behold the Lion of the Tribe of Judah, the
Root of David, hath prevailed (or overcome) to open the
book and to loose the seven seals thereof." (Rev. 5:5)

When the Lamb takes the book out of the hand of the Creator,
the quartet and the choir of heavenly princes break forth in
unison, singing the new song.

"Thou art worthy to take the book, and to open the seals
thereof: for thou wast slain, and didst purchase unto
God with thy blood men of every kindred, and tongue,
and people, and nation, and hast made them to be unto
our God kings and priests: and they shall reign on the
earth." (Rev. 5:9, 10)

Then the entire angelic choir, consisting of ten thousand times
ten thousand and thousand of thousands bursts forth in majestic
chorus, which must have reverberated throughout the corridors of
glory. They sang perfectly as one voice and with a loud voice:

"Worthy is the Lamb that was slain to receive power and
riches, and wisdom, and strength, and honor, and glory,
and blessing."

Then comes the grand finale of this stirring oratorio as it comes to
a swelling crescendo. In this concluding epilogue of this transcendently glorious oratorio the "four living creatures," or seraphim
and cherubim; the elders, or angelic princes; the myriads of angels,
heavenly creatures a little higher creation than man (Hebrews
2:6, 7); and every created thing which is in heaven and on earth, and
under the earth, and such as are in the sea, and all that are in
them join in mighty chorus in praising both Creator and Redeemer:

"Blessing and honor, and glory, and power, be unto Him
that sitteth upon the throne (the Creator) and unto the Lamb
(the Redeemer), for ever and ever." (Rev. 5:13)

Then as the heavenly oratorio, like the sound of many waters,
dies away, there is heard the sound of a great and grand "Amen.'"
It is chanted by the "four living creatures," or the highest range
of God's angelic intelligences, the cherubim and seraphim.

Then there seems to fall a great hush and breathless silence as the twenty-four heavenly princes fall down to worship Him who liveth forever and ever.

Truly we have been listening through the open door to the oratorio of the Choir Invisible!

This instrumented Heavenly choir has prepared us for the opening of the seals. How fitting this should be:

The prophets of old prophesied to the tune of instrumental music:

> "Thou shall meet a company of prophets coming down
> from the high place with a psaltery, and a tabret, and a
> pipe, and a harp before them; and they shall prophecy."
> (I Samuel 10:5)

The hand of the Lord came upon Elisha when the minstrel played.

> "But now bring me a minstrel. And it came to pass, when
> the minstrel played, that the hand of the Lord came upon
> him." (II Kings 3:15)

The sons of Asaph, Heman and Jeduthun prophesied with harp, psalteries and cymbals (I Chron. 25:3-6)

And Habakkuk closed his prophesies with instructions "to the chief singer on my stringed instruments." (Habakkuk 3:19)

As the prophets of old spoke to the accompaniment of instrumental music so the opening of the seals was preceeded by the massed choirs of heaven and earth singing this wondrously soul-inspiring oratorio.

No wonder Christ in the model prayer taught them to pray, "Thy will be done, on earth as it is in heaven." (Matthew 6:10) It is His Divine will that singing, and with instruments shall be done by choirs on both sides of the veil—heaven and earth.

CHAPTER VI

THE OPENING OF THE SEALS

Text (6:1-17)

INTRODUCTION

1 And I saw when the Lamb opened one of the seven seals, and I heard one of the four living creatures saying as with a voice of thunder, Come. 2 And I saw, and behold, a white horse, and he that sat

thereon had a bow; and there was given unto him a crown: and he came forth conquering, and to conquer.

3 And when he opened the second seal, I heard the second living creature saying, Come. 4 And another horse came forth, a red horse: and to him that sat thereon it was given to take peace from the earth, and that they should slay one another: and there was given unto him a great sword.

5 And when he opened the third seal, I heard the third living creature saying, Come. And I saw, and behold, a black horse; and he that sat thereon had a balance in his hand. 6 And I heard as it were a voice in the midst of the four living creatures saying, A measure of wheat for a shilling, and three measures of barley for a shilling; and the oil and the wine hurt thou not.

7 And when he opened the fourth seal, I heard the voice of the fourth living creature saying, Come. 8 And I saw, and behold, a pale horse: and he that sat upon him, his name was Death; and Hades followed with him. And there was given unto them authority over the fourth part of the earth, to kill with sword, and with famine, and with death, and by the wild beasts of the earth.

9 And when he opened the fifth seal, I saw underneath the altar the souls of them that had been slain for the word of God, and for the testimony which they held: 10 and they cried with a great voice, saying, How long, O Master, the holy and true, dost thou not judge and avenge our blood on them that dwell on the earth? 11 And there was given them to each one a white robe; and it was said unto them, that they should rest yet for a little time, until their fellow-servants also and their brethren, who should be killed even as they were, should have fulfilled their course.

12 And I saw when he opened the sixth seal, and there was a great earthquake; and the sun became black as sackcloth of hair, and the whole moon became as blood; 13 and the stars of the heaven fell unto the earth, as a fig tree casteth her unripe figs when she is shaken of a great wind. 14 And the heaven was removed as a scroll when it is rolled up; and every mountain and island were moved out of their places. 15 And the kings of the earth, and the princes, and the chief captains, and the rich, and the strong, and every bondman and freeman, hid themselves in the caves and in the rocks of the mountains; 16 and they say to the mountains and to the rocks, Fall on us, and hide us from the face of him that sitteth on the throne, and from the wrath of the Lamb: 17 for the great day of their wrath is come; and who is able to stand?

In this chapter it is given to us to see how the Redeemer proceeds to exercise the power or authority bestowed upon Him. He opens six seals in succession, after which the dramatic action is interrupted by a separate vision of the four angels standing on the four corners of the earth (Rev. 7:1). The seventh seal is not discribed until the eight chapter is reached.

Since this book was in scroll form, which was a long strip of parchment rolled up and sealed with seven seals, our understanding is that Christ breaks the first seal, thus revealing the words written in the scroll as far as the second seal. He then opens the second seal and further unrolls the scroll. This He continues until the scroll is completely unrolled.

The unrolling of the scroll has these effects: First, it uncovers to view the hidden purposes of God, and second, it reveals the successive events whereby His purposes are accomplished.

We must constantly keep in mind the scope of Revelation, that it is limited. It does not attempt to reveal the future history of all nations, but deals with future history of the church and those opposing powers that affected the fortunes of the Bride of Christ.

Since the church, at the starting point of this vision—the enthronement of Christ at the right hand of God—is wholly within the confines of the vast persecuting empire of pagan Rome, we logically and rightfully understand the events of these seals begin in the Roman empire nearest to the starting point of time and continue through the seventh seal where the remotest events are chronicled.

We must ever remember there was being revealed "things which shortly must come to pass." Therefore, the events of this vision do not refer to things somewhere in the distant future. Also John was to "write the things which thou hast seen, and the things which are, and the things which shall be hereafter."

And these things are recorded in the Book of Revelation—a book which is written in the language of signs. He sent and "signified" it —Sign-i-fied it, that is communicated it by *signs* to His servant John.

Thus we must move slowly in the "uncovering" of the symbols contained in the seven seals. In determining the meaning of this series of prophetic symbols, protraying events which follow successively, it is of supreme importance to correctly interpret the first seal. A wrong start will lead us astray throughout the unrolling of this scroll.

Certainly we are not to spiritualize these visions because John, as we have seen already, was to write the things he had seen, the things which are and the things which shall be hereafter. If language means any thing, then these are *actual, historical events*.

These seals uncover a series of events affecting the fortunes of the church, but also immediately connected with the vast Roman empire in whose confines the church lived and moved and had her being.

These are visions of peace and war, of famine and death, of the persecution of the church and the judgments with which this age will end.

The First Seal

vs. 1, 2 As this first seal is broken, John heard the voice of one of the four living creatures saying with a voice of thunder, "Come and see."

Beginning with the breaking of this first seal we note that the first living creature speaks, and with the opening of each suceeding seal another one of the four living creatures speak.

With the opening of this first seal, as well as the next three seals, the contents of the book are not read, but its messages are translated into action.

In response to the invitation to come and see, immediately John beholds "a white horse and he that sat thereon had a bow, and a crown was given him and he went forth conguering and to conquer.

There are a number of features to this vision.

First, our attention is called to a horse. We are to remember that this is a symbol and the Bible must be consulted to interpret its meaning. The horse is a symbol of war. He was never used by either the Jews or the orientals as a beast of burden; the ox and the ass were used for that purpose. The horse was always reserved for war.

Shall we turn to the Old Testament for our interpretation of this symbol, for the horse is not mentioned in the New Testament, except in Revelation. We discover that the horse is first of all the symbol of strength of a certain kind; not strength for labor like the ox, or for the mastery of enemies, like the lion, but a symbol of might or conquest. Especially does it typify strength and courage for conflict.

In (Job 39:19-23) the description of a horse pertains to qualities that have to do with war. God in addressing Job said, "Hast thou given the horse strength? Hast thou clothed his neck with thunder? Canst thou make him *afraid* as a grasshopper? The glory of his nostrils is terrible. He paweth in the valley and rejoiceth in his *strength*. He goeth on to meet the *armed* men . . . neither turneth he back from the sword."

In the 25th verse of this same chapter we read, "He saith among the trumpets Ha, Ha; and he smelleth the battle afar off, the thunder of his captains, and the shouting."

In the song of Moses on the far side of the Red Sea, we read, "I will sing unto the Lord, for He hath triumphed gloriously: the horse and his rider hath He thrown into the sea." (Ex. 15:1)

From this we learn that the horse represents the progress of some great force or cause backed by strong military power.

Bearing in mind the significance of the horse as a Bible symbol, this first horse, as well as the remaining three are prophetic pictures of mighty military forces and campaigns beginning with the time of the enthroning of Christ on the right hand of God and continuing one after the other.

Second, "A white horse." Since there are three more horses in the three remaining seals, each of different colors, each color must hold some very significant meaning.

The white horse here must have an altogether different significa- tion from the red, black or pale colorations. White was, then in the arena of war a symbol of victory, prosperity and joy. It was a symbol of triumphant war.

When a Roman general returned from victorious campaigns in the far-flung frontiers of the empire he halted with out the city walls of Rome until the senate voted the manner of his entry. If that body voted that the general was entitled to a triumphantal entry, snowy white horses were hitched to his chariot and drawn through the streets of the imperial city, followed by a long line of captive generals, slaves and spoils of war.

Third, the armed warrior. We know this was a military figure be- cause he carried a bow, a weapon of war. The symbolism here points to a period of triumphant war.

Fourth, the bow. There were bowmen in all ancient armies, but the prominence given the bow here would seem to point to a partic- ular race of people.

Fifth ,"A crown was given Him." The crown upon this rider indi- cates that he shall be a crowned monarch. And note carefully that he is not crowned *because* of his *conquests,* but it was given him before these victories.

Sixth, His mission. "He went forth conquering and to conquer."

Having now determined the meaning of these symbols it now is our task to discover if "shortly" after John wrote, history records events which correspond to these symbols.

At the time John penned this "uncovering" of things he had seen, which are, and which are to come to pass shortly, a great Roman general was successfully extending the borders of the empire to its greatest bounds. He truly "went forth conquering, and to conquer. Hear Myers on this:

"To Trajan belongs the distinction of having extended the boundaries to the most distant points to which Roman ambition and prowess were ever able to push them."—Myers Ancient History—Page 506.

A grateful emperor erected a memorial to Trajan's achievements in what came to be known as Trajan's Forum, a splendid marble shaft called Trajan's Column. The stately pillar is almost as perfect today as when reared nineteen centuries ago.

Trajan's reign marked not only an age of conquest and victory, symbolized by the white horse and his rider, but also an age of internal peace and prosperity. I have before me Volume I of Gibbon's Rome edited by Milman. On Pages 95, 96 we read:

"If a man were called to fix the period in the history of the world, during which the condition of the human race was most happy and prosperous, he would without hesitation, name that which elapsed from the death of Domitian to the accession of Commodus. The vast extent of the Roman empire was governed by absolute power, under the guidance of virtue and wisdom. The armies were restrained by the firm but gentle hand of four successive emperors, whose characters and authority commanded involuntary respect. The forms of civil adminstration were carefully preserved by Nerva, Tragan, Hadrian, and the Antonines, who delighted in the image of liberty."

Of these four, Trajan, who ascended the throne four years after the death of Domitian, is the most outstanding. The symbols of this first seal are strikingly fulfilled in this epoch of Roman history. It furnished one of the greatest conquerors of the Roman Empire, and, at a time which fits into this vision on Patmos. Trajan was a crowned conqueror, as revealed in this vision and went forth conquering and to conquer. Since the scope of John's prophecy falls within the Roman empire, all events of this epoch correspond to the divine revelation.

Particularly, one feature of this vision is significantly fitting. The rider of this white horse—the symbol of military conquest—was armed with a *BOW!* At first this would seem contradictoy evidence, for the bow was not a Roman weapon. Rome ever conquered with the sword, carrying into battle the javelin for longer range fighting, but the sword to be used in close quarters. There were bowmen in the Roman legions, but they were not Romans. The use of the bow as a symbol is quite enlightening.

There were two nations on the earth at the time of this revelation who were renowned as users of the bow. The bow was the military weapon of the Parthians beyond the Euphrates, and of the Cretans, dwellers of the island of Crete. Cretan bowmen were constantly featured in Grecian history.

So the bow, the weapon carried by this first rider, must signify some one whose ancestry was rooted in Crete. How amazingly accurate this symbol is to history! If a Roman had been symbolized in this rider, he would not be represented armed with a bow. The bow points us to some one of another nation rather than that of Rome. And history supplies us with the answer.

Beginning with Julius Caesar, the twelve Caesars who reigned over the Roman empire were all of pure Roman blood. Domitian, the one who exiled John to Patmos, was the last of the twelve Caesars. He was followed on the throne by Nerva, the founder of a line that supplied five Caesars in succession.

The five "good emperors" as they came to be known, were Nerva, Trajan, Hadrian and the two Antonines—Aurelius Antoninus and Marcus Aurelius. They reigned from A.D. 96 to A.D. 180.

Nerva, the first of this new line of emperors was not of Roman blood. Cassius, a historian of that day declares that Nerva was a Greek and Aurelius Victor, another Roman Historian says that Nerva's family came from the Grecian island of Crete.

Already we know that *the national weapon of the Cretans was the bow*. The Cretans were as famous for their skill with the bow as the Rhodians were for their use of the sling, or the Romans with the javelin and short sword.

We cannot note to carefully that the founder of this new family of emperors, was an alien—the first to ever rule Rome. His family was of Cretan blood and the national weapon of the islanders of Crete was the *bow!*

The Second Seal

vs. 3, 4 "And when he had opened the second seal, I heard the second living creature say, "come and see" The second cherubim repeats the command of the first living creature, "Come and see."

vs. 4 At once the first vision makes way for a second, "And there went out another horse that was *red.*" This horse, also representing some great military force, naturally symbolizes, chronologically, the next series of events following those of the first seal.

But the horse is no longer white, but red. The horse is the symbol of war, but the changed color points to the fact that the conditions of war are entirely changed. It would seem to indicate that now the stage of the conflict has brought blood shed within the empire. Whereas the white horse symbolized peace, prosperity and victory within the Roman empire, now blood shed invades her borders.

It is a fact in history that during the period of the first seal—through the reigns of "the five good emperors"—the Roman Empire never saw the forces of an invading army. All conquests were waged in the countries of her enemies, for Rome was *going forth conquering and to conquer.*

Under the strong but mild rule of Trajan, Hadrian and the Antonies, every man dwelled safely under his own vine and fig tree. No hostile invasion or internal upheavals ever troubled the tiller of the soil or the artisan of trade. The first seal was a period of triumphant war, but of internal peace.

The second seal indicates from its very opening the continued existence of war. Internal peace has vanished. The first and second horsemen are strikingly contrasted. The first horsemen represents peace though there was outside war, but the second horse symbolizes civil war and bloodshed.

This is all the more emphasized because this is a blood-red horse.

"And power was given unto him that sat thereon to take peace from the earth." The earth spoken of by John would be the Roman Empire, for the empire was the last great world empire as seen by Daniel, and the scope of Revelation always contemplates this world power.

In this epoch, peace is taken from the empire and we know this peace has been lost through civil war by the phrase, "That they should kill one another." This is in as plain language as symbolism can speak.

As the first seal of peace was substantiated by corroborating history, so we may expect to find further events of history correspond'ng to the symbolism of this second seal. This we find to be abundantly true.

At the close of the reign of Commodus we find the end of peace in the Roman empire. Commodus was slain. As son of Marcus Aurelius, the last of the Antonines, he proved to be a most unworthy successor of his illustrous father. For three years he reigned well, but an unsuccessful attempt against his life, three years after his ascension to the throne seemed suddenly to kindle all the dormant passions of a Nero. The remaining ten years of his reign were marked by the perpetration of all manner of cruelties and the staining of the imperial purple with the most detestable debaucheries and crimes.

The empire was finally relieved of this insane tyrant by some members of the royal household who put him to death. This began a reign of civil war. Hear Myers on this:

"For nearly a century after the death of Commodus (192 to 284 A.D.) the emperors were elected by the army, and hence the rulers of this period have been called, "The Barrack Emperors." Upon the death of Commodus, Pertinax, a distinguished senator, was placed on the throne; but his efforts to enforce discipline among the praetorians aroused their anger, and he was slain by them after a short reign of only three months. The soldiers then gave out notice that they would sell the empire to the highest bidder. It was accordingly set up for sale at the praetorian camp and struck off to Didius Julianus, a wealthy senator, who promised twenty-five thousand sesterces to each of the twelve thousand soldiers at this time composing the guard. So the price of the empire was three hundred million sesterces (about $12,000,000).—Myers Ancient history P. 515.

This gives us a preview of what lay in store for the empire. During this period of the national history thirty-two emperors, and twenty-seven pretenders alternately hurled each other from the throne. Hear Sismondi:

"With Commodus commenced the third and most calamitous period. It lasted ninety-two years, from 192 to 284. During that period thirty-two emperors, and twenty-seven pretenders alternately hurled each other from the throne by *incessant civil warfare*. Ninety-two years of almost incessant civil warfare taught the world on what a frail foundation the virtue of the Antonines had placed the felicity of the empire."—Sismondi's Fall of the Roman Empire Vol. 1, P. 36.

Gibbon in the first volume of his Decline and Fall of the Roman Empire devotes two hundred pages to the description of this "Red Horse" period of civil strife and rapine.

Of these thirty-two emperors, besides the pretenders only two died natural deaths; Severus, who died 211 A.D. and Volusion who died 253 A.D. All others died violent deaths.

What could more fittingly represent a period of fratricidal bloodshed and rapine, of constant civil war, than a *red* horse and its rider "to whom was given a great sword, and the power to take away peace, that men should kill one another?"

We wish to further consider the giving of that "great sword." The bow is gone now, which was the emblem of an alien, and a sword, the national weapon of Rome, replaces it.

This sword marks some special feature of the fulfillment of the events of the seal. It points to an epoch when the jealous ambitions of men of the sword drove them to brutality and murder.

There were stationed at Rome an army corps which outranked all others. We have already referred to them as the Praetorian guards and recounted their sale of the empire to Didius Julianius. It was an order in which the Praetorian Perfect was inducted into office by the public investment *with a sword*. It was the Praelorian Perfect and his guard that inaugurated this century of bloodshed.

What could more fittingly describe such a period, as portrayed under the second seal, than the giving of a great sword, the military emblem, to the *figure* that *rides the red* horse of John's prophecy?

The Third Seal

vs. 5, 6 Famine always follows war, and particularly civil war with its internal devastation of men, materials, industry and food production.

Therefore, it is only natural that we should read when the third seal was opened: "I heard the third living creature say, come and see. And I beheld, and lo a black horse; and he that sat on him had a pair of balances in his hand. And I heard a voice in the midst of the four living creatures say, a measure of wheat for a penny: and see thou hurt not the oil and the wine."

How natural that the period of civil war, indicated by the *red horse,* a period of bloodshed and anarchy should produce events symbolized by a *black horse.*

The horse, whatever his color, is a symbol of war, the change in color only signifies a changed aspect of that war. Black would indicate that the empire is still torn by calamitous war, but war that brought mourning and despair. Black has ever been the color of mourning in Scriptural usage. Jeremiah said: "Because of the drought Judah mourneth, and the gate thereof languish; they are in deep mourning (literally black) for the land." (Jer. 14:2)

After noting the color of the horse, recognition is given to the fact that "he that sat on him had a pair of balances in his hand." If the balances were presented alone, we might see in them a symbol of justice, but in the hands of the rider of the black horse, and in connection with the weighing of grain that follows, they undoubtedly indicate a period characterized by scarcity of food.

The significance of balances in relation to food is made clear in the Scriptures. "And when I have broken the staff of your bread, the women shall bake your bread in one oven, and they shall deliver your bread again by *weight*s and ye shall eat and not be satisfied" (Lev. 26:26)

"Moreover he said unto me, son of man, behold, I will break the staff of bread in Jerusalem: and they shall eat bread by *weight*, and with care; and they shall drink water by *measure* and with astonishment: That they may want bread and water and be astonished with one another, and consume away for their iniquity." (Ezek. 4:16, 17)

The prices quoted here for wheat and barley are famine prices. The "measure" spoken of here was, roughly speaking, the equivolent of our quart, and the word rendered "penny" is the Greek "denarius," which equals about fourteen cents in our money. A bushel of wheat, at the price designated would be nearly five dollars, and a bushel of barley one dollar and fifty cents.

A denarius was the usual rate for one day's labor. In our money, considering the rate of exchange, that would mean a bushel of wheat cost about twenty dollars and a bushel of barley shows that rich and poor alike were affected, because wheat was the grain of the rich and barley the staff of the poor.

Since oil and wine were common articles of food for the people, the prohibition of their use, taken in connection with the context would seem to imply that at this time these items were no longer used by the common people.

But balances were also, in that day, employed in taxation. A portion of the production of the land was a part of the taxes extorted by the Roman empire. The balances then would symbolize a period of excessive taxation, as well as scarcity.

This heavy taxation began even in the days of the second seal period when Caracalla granted Roman citizenship to multitudes in his empire in order to tax the more persons.

"Caracalla's sole political act of real importance was the bestowal of citizenship upon all the free inhabitants of the empire; and this he did, not to give them a just privilege, but that he might collect from them certain special taxes which only Roman citizens had to pay."—Myers Ancient History P. 517

But with the death of the last emperor of the third seal period, Carinus in 284, a new type of government was inaugurated by Diocletain. The change was marked by Diocletian's assumption of the titles of Asiatic royalty and court ceremonials. Ostentation and extravagance marked all the appointments of the palace. He also inaugurated a new administrative system.

"The century of anarchy which preceded the ascension of Diocletian; had made manifest the need of a system which would discourage assassination and provide a regular mode of succession to the throne. Diocletian devised a system the aim of which was to compass both ends. First, he chose as a colleague a companion ruler, Maximian, who, like himself, bore the title of Augustus. Then each of the co-emperors associated with himself an assistant, who took the title of Caesar and was considered the son of the Emperor. There were thus two Augusti and two Caesars. (From the number of rulers, this government has received the name of Tetrarchy) . . . a most serious drawback to this system was the heavy expense involved in the maintenance of four courts with their endless retinue of officers and dependents. It was complained that the number of those who received the revenues of the state was greater than those that contributed to them. *The burden of taxation grew unendurable. Husbandry in some regions ceased* and great numbers were reduced to beggary or driven into brigandage . . . it was this vicious system of taxation which more than any other one cause. after slavery, contributed to the depopulation, improverishment and final downfall of the nation." Myers' Ancient History Pages 521, 522.

This feature of taxation is peculiar to the third seal. A quotation or two will suffice. This taxation began even in the second seal, but reached such ruinous proportions in the third seal as to render it an outstanding feature of that epoch. Gibbon speaks of the beginning of such taxation under Caracalla. (A.D. 211-217)

"Nor was the rapacious son of Severus (Caracalla) contented

with such a measure of taxation as had appeared sufficient to his moderate predecessors. Instead of a twentieth, he exacted a tenth of all legacies and inheritances, and during his reign he crushed alike every part of the empire under the weight of his iron scepter."—Gibbon's Decline and Fall of Rome Vol. , P. 95.

Lactantius, an historian of the fourth century recorded:

"Swarms of exactors sent into the provinces, filled them with agitation and terror, as though a conquering enemy were leading them into captivity. The fields were separately measured, the trees and vines, the flocks and herds were numbered, and an examination made of men . . . the sick and the weak were borne to the place of inscription, a reckoning was made of the age of each, years were added to the young and subtracted from the old, in order to subject them to the higher taxation the law imposed. The whole scene was filled with *wailing and sadness."*
—Lactantius.

Surely, no more impressive or expressive symbol, than a black horse, indicating *mourning,* and its rider holding a pair of balances in his hand, indicative of famine, could have properly described the epoch covered by the third seal.

The Fourth Seal

vs. 7, 8 "And when he had opened the fourth seal, I heard the voice of the fourth living creature say, "Come and see." And I looked, and behold a pale horse: and his name that sat on him was Death, and Hell followed with him. And power was given unto them over the fourth part of the earth, to kill with sword, and with hunger, and with death, and with beasts of the earth."

The conditions under the fourth seal reach the worst. The color of the fourth horse is pale. Remembering the horse is ever a symbol of war, whatever its color, we are by the continued use of the symbol of the horse reminded that it is still a time of war. The color of the horse now being "pale"—the bloodless color of death—pictures such conditions that the rider of this pale horse appropriately is called "Death."

Behind him Hades, the abode of the dead, follows close upon Death's heels, to swallow up the dead in his awful maws.

Death and Hades accomplish their task by the employment of four familiar and fearful instruments:

1. The sword, or war. 2. Hunger, or famine. 3. Death, or pestilence, for the word here used is often so translated, and such is its signification here, and 4. Finally, destruction caused by wild beasts.

The conditions described under the fourth seal are the logical result of the events which transpired under the three preceding seals.

When we recall that thirty-two military governors, and twenty-seven pretenders alternately hurled each other from the throne in a period of nienty-two years, and that of the thirty-two military governors all died violent deaths but two, we can better understand how Death and Hades took such a toll of human life by civil war, famine, pestilence and wild beasts which would increase as the provinces became depopulated.

Shall we turn to the most authentic Roman historian which we have, even Gibbon:

"But a long and general famine was a calamity of a more serious kind. It was the inevitable consequence of rapine and opppression, which extripated the produce of the present, and the future harvests. Famine is almost always followed by epidemical diseases, the effect of scanty and unwholesome food. Other causes must, however, have contributed to the furious plague, which, from the years two-hundred fifty to the year two-hundred sixty-five, raged without interruption in every province, every city, and almost every family of the Roman Empire. During some time five thousand persons died daily in Rome; and many towns, that had escaped the hands of the barbarians, were entirely depopulated . . . about half the people of Alexandria perished." Volume 1, pages 328, 329.

No wonder it was said that power was given Death and Hades to destroy one fourth part of the earth.

Summarizing, we have found that:

1. The first seal was the *seal of conquest*.

2. The second seal was the *seal of civil war*.

3. The third seal was the *seal of want or famine*.

4. The fourth seal was the *seal of Death*.

The seals on the one hand collectively, say, "Here is the future in symbolism." History, on the other hand, says, "Here is the fulfillment."

How faithfully they agree! At the mouth of two or three witnesses a thing is established.

The Fifth Seal

vs. 9-11 With the opening of the fifth seal the scene changes completely. It is obvious, from the radical change of imagery, that the subject of the prophetic vision is completely different. No longer is the horse, the symbol of war, present. With the passing of the horses, the armed riders are gone. The fifth seal gives us a vision of the suffering saints.

The vision implies the peril and persecution of the church on earth. This is to be expected when we consider that Revelation is the "uncovering" of the future as it relates to the church, or the Israel of God under the Gospel Dispensation.

"And when he had opened the fifth seal I saw under the altar the souls of them that were slain for the Word of God, and for the testimony which they held. And they cried with a loud voice, saying, How long, O Lord, holy and true, dost thou not judge and avenge our blood on them that dwell on the earth?"

And white robes were given unto every one of them; and it was said unto them that they should rest yet for a little season, until their fellow-servants also and their brethren that should be killed as they were, should be fulfilled."

Since this calls our attention to something happening under the altar, which was a piece of furniture in the temple, it would indicate that this vision refers to the martyrs of the church. This is not an oratorio of praise, but a chant of suffering, coming from the souls of those who had been slain.

The fifth seal is the *Seal of Persecution* and it evidently refers to some period in the history of the church when a war of extermination was waged against the early Christians.

Since the first four seals cover conditions through the terrible events from Pentecost to nearly the close of the third century, we naturally look to see if conditions following these seals correspond to the symbolism of the fifth seal.

At the death of Commodus, a very notable, but cruel ruler came to the throne of the Roman Empire. He was Diocletian, who reigned from 284 A.D., to 305 A.D. Myers says:

"The ascension of Diocletian marks an important era in the history of the Roman Empire. The two matters of chief importance connected with his reign are the changes he effected in the government and his persecution of the Christians."

Myers Ancient History P. 520.

While the church had suffered persecution before, beginning with that perpetrated by the Jews of the Apostles' day, and with the beginning of Gentile persecution under Nero, no persecution had ever before been so universal, so long continued and so brutal. Diocletian determined to wipe the name "Christian" from the earth. Says Myers:

"Toward the end of his reign, Diocletian inaugurated against the Christians a persecution which continued long after his abdication, and which was the severest, as it was the last, waged against the church by the pagan emperors.

The imperial decrees ordered that their churches be torn down; that the property of the new societies should be confiscated; that the writings of the sect should be burned; and that the Christians themselves, unless they should join in the sacrifices to the gods of the state, should be pursued to death as outlaw. For ten years, which, however were broken by short periods of respite, the Christians were subjected to the fierce flames of persecution. . . . It was during this and various other persecutions that vexed the church in the second and third centuries that the Christians sought refuge in the Catacombs, those vast subterranean galleries and chambers under the city of Rome."—Gibbon's Decline and Fall of Rome, pages 522, 523.

To Myers we add that of the ancient historian Gibbon. He writes of the persecution inaugurated by Diocletian as follows:

"The resentment, or the fears of Diocletian, at length transported him beyond all bounds of moderation, which he had hitherto preserved, and he declared, in a series of cruel edicts, *his intention* of abolishing the *Christian name*. By the first of these edicts, the governors of the provinces were directed to apprehend all persons of the ecclesiastical order; and the prisons, destined for the vilest criminals, were soon filled with a multitude of bishops, presbyters, deacons, readers and exhortists. By a second edict, the magistrates were commanded to employ every method of severity, which might reclaim them from their odious superstition, and oblige them to return to the established worship of gods. This rigorous order was extended, by a subsequent edict, to the whole body of Christians, who were exposed to a violent and general persecution."
—Gibbons Decline and Fall of the Roman Empire, Volume 11, page 69.

Diocletian's persecution certainly would inaugurate conditions as symbolized under the fifth seal.

Other persecutions had been local, this was general. Others were for a little season, Diocletian's persecution raged for ten years; others were designed to stay the progress of Christianity, the prime purpose of this was "to abolish the Christian name from the earth."

No wonder the bleeding, mangled church cried, 'O Lord, how long dost Thou not judge and avenge our blood on them that dwell on the earth?"

These martyred Christians called for judgment and retribution. The answer to this cry is worthy of our notice. Three things are featured.

First, it is said that they must await the great judgment, which would not occur until another distinct group of martyrs should be slain. The group of the fifth seal had been slain by pagan Rome, the second group referred to evidently were to be those martyred by Papal Rome, which succeeded the pagan empire.

Second, they must wait "a little season." Of course such a season must be measured by God's standard of measurement, to whom "one day is as a thousand years, and a thousand years as one day." (II Peter 3:8)

Third, they were to be given white robes. White robes are a symbol of justification and victory. In the marriage of the Lamb, to his wife is "to be granted that she should be arrayed in fine linen, clean and white: for the fine linen is the righteousness of saints." (Rev. 19:7-8)

Another startling factor in this promise to the martyrs is this: These souls were not in the Holy of Holies, a type of heaven itself (Heb. 9:24) but under the altar of the outer court—a type of the world.

These white robes—symbols of justification and victory—then imply the justification and triumph of the church on earth. And thus everything did come to pass.

At the close of this persecution symbolized in the fifth seal, Constantine, by a decree issued at Milan A.D. 313, the year of the Battle at the Milvian Bridge, declared, and here are the words of that decree:

"We grant to Christians and to all others full liberty of following that religion which each may choose."

The Sixth Seal

vs. 12-17 The opening of the sixth seal is described in six verses of rare majesty and power. The scenes portrayed are calculated to fill the heart with awe and consternation.

The earth with mighty convulsions reels with a terrific earthquake that shakes mountains and islands from their places. There are also heavenly demonstrations. The sun becomes black as sackcloth; the moon turns red as blood, stars fall and the heavens themselves are rolled away as a scroll. The inhabitants of earth are so terror stricken at the sight they call for the mountains to fall upon them.

The imagery here is very striking, but we must remember that these are not literal earthquakes, falling stars, moving islands or mountains. These are symbols, so we look not for literal fulfillment of such *physical phenomenon*, but for *historical* events which correspond to these symbolical pictures.

Before, we search out the fulfillment in historical events, we must first ascertain the meaning of these symbols which are used. These symbols are borrowed from the mightiest agencies and powers in nature.

A Study of these Symbols

First, we take up the meaning of an *earthquake* when used symbolically. As John's "earth" constantly refers to the Roman Empire, this earthquake refers to political and religious upheavals within its borders. The earthquake is used by the prophets of the old Testament as a symbol of political and religious agitation. In Haggai 2:6, 7, we read:

"Yet once, it is a little time, and I will shake the heavens, and the earth, and the sea, and the dry land, and I will shake all nations, and the desire of all nations shall come."

Second, the sun, moon and stars are used in the Scriptures to represent earthly potentates and dignitaries and great lights in political and religious realms. To illustrate: In the dream of Joseph which turned his brothers against him, these physical symbols were employed to represent people.

"And he dreamed yet another dream, and told it to his brothers, and said, Behold, I have dreamed a dream more; and, behold,

99

the sun and the moon, and the eleven stars made obeisance to me." "And he told it to his father, and to his brethren; and his father rebuked him, and said unto him, what is this dream that thou hast dreamed? Shall I and thy mother and thy brethren indeed come to bow down ourselves to thee to the earth?" (Gen. 37:9, 10)

Orientals often referred to the king as a sun, and princes and lesser rulers to stars. In Daniel, as he describes the world kingdoms we read:

"And it (the little horn) waxed great, even to the host of heaven: and it cast down some of the host of the *stars to the ground* and stamped upon them." (Daniel 8:10)

Again in Ezekial 32:1-15 we have a prophecy which will help us in the imagery of divine symbolism of the sixth seal. The prophet is predicting the violent overthrow of Egypt at the hands of Nebuchadnezzar. This national overthrow is described in the following symbols:

"And when I shall put thee out (or extinguish thee), I will cover the heaven, and make the *stars* thereof dark; I will cover the *sun* with a cloud, and the *moon* shall not give her light." (Ezekial 32:7)

Again in Joel 3:15, we read:

"The *sun* and *moon* shall be darkened, and the stars shall withdraw their shining. The Lord also shall roar out of Zion, and utter His voice from Jerusalem, and the heavens and the earth *shall shake*."

In the above quoted passages we see that the overthrowing of a nation was described in the imagery of the sun being blackened, the stars becoming dark and the earth being shaken.

Isaiah, also, furnishes us with a passage which is closely related in thought and verbiage to that of the sixth seal. The prophet is speaking of the time when "the indignation of the Lord shall be upon the nations."

"And all the host of heaven shall be dissolved, and the heavens shall be *rolled together* as a *scroll*; and their *host shall fall* down, as the leaf falleth off the vine, and as a *falling fig* from the *fig tree*." (Isa. 34:2-4)

How similar this language to Johns' who said, "The stars of heaven fell unto the earth, even as a fig tree casteth her untimely figs."

We are not studying physical astronomy in the Book of Revelation. That is where so many folk have been in error. They have tried to associate these symbols with actual physical earthquakes, falling material stars and darkening of the sun.

We are studying spiritual astronomy here and these symbols portray human events in the which great dignitaries in the political arena are said to fall and governmental systems are shaken.

Third, the *mountain* and *island* are used to denote earthly kingdoms. *Mountains* in the scriptures stand for conspicuous nationalities. In Jeremiah's prophecy against Babylon, he says:

"Behold, I am against thee, O Destroying Mountain, saith the Lord, which destroyeth all the earth: and I will stretch out mine hand upon thee, and roll thee down from the rocks, and will make thee a *burnt mountain.*" (Jeremiah 51:25)

The island symbolizes lesser powers. In his prophecy of Christ, he said, "He (that is Christ) shall not fail nor be discouraged, till he have set judgment in the earth: and the isles shall wait for his law." (Isaiah 42:4)

This imagery is most appropriate to express a complete breaking up and removal of the whole system of human government.

With this clarification of the symbols, it is not difficult to discover that the sixth seal is a period of great and startling revolutions, not in the heavens, but upon the earth. All this symbolism foreshadows a violent, bloody upheaval of governmental systems, rulers and the establishment of a new order on the earth.

And since "earth" to the mind of John is the Roman Empire, it naturally is within its boundaries that we must search for the fulfillment.

We shall look for events in political, social and religious spheres, which are pictured here in terms of physical things.

There are some stirring convultions in history immediately following the persecution under the fifth seal. As the fifth seal was the seal of *Persecution,* the sixth seal can be designated, "the seal of *Revolution.*"

Having considered the meaning of the symbols, we are now ready to search out the time of this seal.

The Time of this Seal

We found that the fifth seal closed with the Edict of Toleration issued by Constantine in A. D. 313, so then these events naturally follow that epoch.

We note that one of the characteristics of this sixth seal is that the time will be one of mourning. The mourners now are not the souls under the altar, but the falling stars, or great of earth, who opposed the One who sat on His Throne. They cry out and say to the mountains: "Fall on us, and hide us from the face of Him that sitteth on the throne, and from the wrath of the Lamb." (Rev. 6:16)

Then taking a brief look forward to the next chapter—the seventh—we observe there follows a period of great joy and prosperity experienced by the people of God.

Holding this sixth seal and its symbolism in one hand and a book of history in the other, do we find a time in which the unbelieving world on the one hand is in mourning, and the church, on the other hand enjoying a time of victory and prosperity?

Hear Myers on this:

"Galerius and Constantine, who became Augusti on the abdication of Diocletian and Maximian, had reigned together only one year when the latter died at York, in Britain. His soldiers, disregarding the rule of succession is determined by the system of Diocletian, proclaimed his son Constantine emperor. Six competitors for the throne arose in different quarters. For eighteen years Constantine fought to gain the supremacy."
—Myer's Ancient History, page 524.

Also hear Gibbon on this matter:

"The abdication of Diocletian and Maximian was succeeded by eighteen years of discord and confusion. The empire was afflicted by five civil wars; and the remainder of the time was not so much a state of tranquility as a suspension of arms between several hostile monarchs, who viewing each other with an eye of fear and hatred, strove to increase their respective forces at the expense of their subjects."—Gibbons Decline and Fall of Rome, page 451.

In passing we may say that Gibbon devoted fifty pages (small print) to the description of the evils of this time. Surely, we have here a time of death and mourning when kings and pretenders fell like stars and great mourning resulted from one civil war following after a preceding one. This was a time when kingdoms, indicated by mountains and islands, were moved out of their places.

The forces of paganism had rolled around the enemies of Constantine. When he was crowned in triumph upon the wreck of six imperial thrones and their royal claimants, there was great mourning on the part of the enemies of the Lamb and the cross. For when Constantine, after the battle of Milvian Bridge, granted amnesty to all Christians, paganism went into deep mourning.

Shall we enumerate a few of the outstanding earth-shaking, heaven-removed-as-a-scroll, results of all this change. Not only was paganism shaken but Christianity waited with bated breath. The church watched Constantine progress with singular interest. While Constantine had not embraced Christianity before Milvian Bridge, yet his mother, Helena, was a Christian and it was generally believed he was friendly toward his mother's faith. After his embracing of the Christian faith these earthquake like results followed:

1. In 313 A.D. Constantine issued the decree at Milan placing Christianity on an equal footing with the other religions of the empire.

2. In 319 A.D. he decreed his mother's religion should be the acknowledged faith of the empire.

3. In 321 A.D. he decreed that Sunday, the day of worship of Christians, since Pentecost, should be observed in all the cities by a cessation of labor.

4. In 325 A.D. he abolished by royal decree the bloody gladiatorial combats, against which the Christians had objected. The far reaching impact of this can better be grasped when we remember this Roman institution had existed for one whole millennium.

5. In 325 A.D. he called the first general council of the church at Nicea, a town in Asia Minor, Arianism was denounced, and a formula of Christian faith adopted, which became known as the Nicene creed—the mother of all human creeds.

6. In 331 A.D. he decreed that the pagan religion should no longer exist and ordered the destruction of all heathen temples.

7. He completely reorganized the government by laying out the

empire into four divisions called perfectures, which were sub-divided into thirteen dioceses, and there again into one hundred and sixteen provinces. Truly, the old heavens were being moved away as a school and the Roman earth was being shaken like a mighty earthquake.

8. But the greatest earth-shaking change is yet to be described. Constantine did not seem to be satisfied with the destroying pagan faith, changing Roman customs and laws, he aimed his greatest blow at the imperial city itself. For over one thousand years Rome had been the seat of the empire, growing from a tiny village to the capitol of the world. In 330 he determined to shake the Roman world from center to circumference, by removing the capitol from Italy to a new city on the banks of the Hellespont, and to call it after his own name—Constantine. Surely, the mighty mountain of the west was moved from its place.

Hear Myers on this:

"After the recognition of Chirstianity, the most important act of Constantine was the selection of Byzantium on the Bosporus, as the new capitol of the empire. There were many and weighty reasons urging Constantine to establish a new capitol in the east.

First, there were urgent military reasons for making the change. The most dangerous enemies of the empire now were the barbarians behind the Danube and the kings of the recently restored Persian monarchy. This condition of things rendered almost necessary the establishment in the east of a new and permanent basis for military operations.

Second, there were also commercial reasons for the transfer of the capitol. Rome had long before this ceased to be in any sense the commercial center of the state, as it was in early times. Through the Roman conquest of Greece and Asia, the center of the population, wealth and commerce of the empire had shifted eastward. Now of all the cities in the east, Byzantium was the one most favorably situated to become the commercial metropolis of the enlarged state.

Third, there were religious motives. The priests of the pagan shrines particularly resented the action of Constantine in espousing the new and rated religion, and regarded him as an apostate. It was the existence of these sentiments and feelings among the inhabitants of Rome, which, for one thing, led Constantine to seek elsewhere a new center and seat of his court and government.

But far outweighing all other reasons for the removal of the capitol were the political motives. Constantine, like Diocletian, wished to establish a system of government modeled upon the despotic monarchy of the east . . .

In honor of the emperor the name was changed to Constantinople, the "city of Constantine."—Myers Ancient History, pages 527, 528.

These historical events, forming the most remarkable revolution that the world has ever seen, constitute an exact fulfilment of the symbolism of the sixth seal. Sun and moon are darkened and stars fall, mountains and islands are removed out of their places.

With the blasting of pagan hopes by the victories of Constantine and his subsequent embracing of Christianity, accompanied by his decree to destroy all heathen temples, more than one imperial champion of paganism called out in distress.

Some of the pagan writers almost used the very language of Revelation in their description of this particular period of history:

"As a dreadful and amazing prodigy, which covered the earth with darkness, and restored the ancient dominion of chaos and night."

We have styled the sixth seal as "the seal of Revolution," both in the political and religious realms.

CHAPTER VII

SEALING OF GOD'S SERVANTS

Text (7:1-17)

1 After this I saw four angels standing at the four corners of the earth, holding the four winds of the earth, that no wind should blow on the earth, or on the sea, or upon any tree. 2 And I saw another angel ascend from the sunrising, having the seal of the living God: and he cried with a great voice to the four angels to whom it was

given to hurt the earth and the sea, 3 saying, Hurt not the earth, neither the sea, nor the trees, till we shall have sealed the servants of our God on their foreheads. 4 And I heard the number of them that were sealed, a hundred and forty and four thousand, sealed out of every tribe of the children of Israel: 5 Of the tribe of Judah were sealed twelve thousand; of the tribe of Reuben twelve thousand; of the tribe of Gad twelve thousand; 6 Of the tribe of Asher twelve thousand; of the tribe of Naphtali twelve thousand; of the tribe of Manasseh twelve thousand; 7 Of the tribe of Simeon twelve thousand; of the tribe of Levi twelve thousand; of the tribe of Issachar twelve thousand; 8 Of the tribe of Zebulun twelve thousand; of the tribe of Joseph twelve thousand; of the tribe of Benjamin were sealed twelve thousand.

9 After these things I saw, and behold, a great multitude, which no man could number, out of every nation and of all tribes and peoples and tongues, standing before the throne and before the Lamb, arrayed in white robes, and palms in their hands; 10 and they cry with a great voice, saying, Salvation unto our God who sitteth on the throne, and unto the Lamb. 11 And all the angels were standing round about the throne, and about the elders and the four living creatures; and they fell before the throne on their faces, and worshipped God, 12 saying, Amen: Blessing, and glory, and wisdom, and thanksgiving, and honor, and power, and might, be unto our God for ever and ever. Amen. 13 And one of the elders answered, saying unto me, These that are arrayed in the white robes, who are they, and whence came they? 14 And I say unto him, My lord, thou knowest. And he said to me, These are they that come out of the great tribulation, and they washed their robes, and made them white in the blood of the Lamb. 15 Therefore are they before the throne of God; and they serve him day and night in his temple: and he that sitteth on the throne shall spread his tabernacle over them. 16 They shall hunger no more, neither thirst any more; neither shall the sun strike upon them, nor any heat: 17 for the Lamb that is in the midst of the throne shall be their shepherd, and shall guide them unto fountains of waters of life: and God shall wipe away every tear from their eyes.

vs. 1 After the cry of the panic-stricken kings and potentates resulting from the political and religious upheaval symbolized in the sixth seal, we would naturally expect the seventh seal to be opened at once, and the unfolding events described therein to follow immediately.

But this is not the case. Rather the first of two parenthesis of the first division of Revelation is thrown in to reveal the sealing of God's servants.

Here in this parenthesis a scene of a very different character is presented.

"And after these things I saw four angels standing on the four corners of earth, holding the four winds of earth, that the wind should not blow on the earth, nor on the sea, nor on any tree.

And I saw another angel ascending from the east, having the seal of the living God; and he cried with a loud voice to the four angels, to whom it was given to hurt the earth and the sea, saying, hurt not the earth, neither the sea, nor the trees, till we have sealed the servants of our God in their foreheads." (Rev. 7:1-3)

Why, we might ask, is this particular vision, occupying the entire seventh chapter, introduced at this time? The answer is obvious. The preceding visions of the seals "uncover" how things were to go, during that time in history, with men in general. The need now was that a vision should be given to show what provision God had made for His own during this time of political and religious revolution.

The company of sealed servants of God is in direct contrast to that of the panic stricken opponents of the Lamb of God.

We must remember that we are still under the sixth seal and will be until the seventh seal is opened in (Rev. 8:1).

"And after these things" (Rev. 7:1) refers to the events described under the seals of the sixth chapter. Now the sealing of the saints follows "after these things."

John saw four angels standing on the four corners of the earth, holding the four winds. These four angels undoubtedly represent four hurtful agencies which are to perform their works of destruction.

The wind in the Scriptures is used as a symbol of divine visitation using human instrumentality to accomplish God's purpose. We read in (Jeremiah 51:1)

"Thus saith the Lord, Behold, I will raise up against Babylon and against them that dwell in the midst of them that rise up against me, a destroying wind."

Again in Jeremiah 49:36, the divine judgments coming in from every quarter are spoken of as the *four winds*.

"And upon Elam will I bring the *four winds* from the four quarters of heaven."

In Daniel 7:2 we read, "Daniel spoke and said, I saw in my vision by night, and, behold, the four winds of the heaven strove upon the great sea."

These scriptures not only define the symbol of "wind" as a divine visitation using some human instrument of force, but they give us a strong hint that armies of powerful and cruel nations play a signifiicant part in this last stage of the sixth seal.

These four powerful angels seen by John were observed holding back for a time these four destroying powers.

vs. 2 and John says, "I saw another angel ascending from the east, having the seal of God, and he cried with a loud voice to the four angels . . . saying, "Hurt not the earth, neither the sea, nor the trees till we have sealed the servants of our God in their foreheads."

What this sealing in the foreheads was is not revealed, but it certainly has to do with their eternal safety. In a similar impending temporal judgment on the population of Jerusalem, Ezekial saw a vision of God's glory, and heard a command given to one clothed in linen to go through the city and set a mark on the foreheads of those who sighed and cried because of the abominations thereof. (Ezekial 9:3, 4) This man had an inkhorn by his side, and while it is not said that he used this inkhorn, yet the implication is that he did use it in marking the foreheads.

vs. 3 In Rev. 22:4 we read, "And they shall see His face and His name shall be on their foreheads." The servants of Christ dwelling in the place of Christ has gone to prepare will have His name on their foreheads. Here in Rev. 7:5 it would seem the mark in the forehead refers to an open profession of obedient belief in the Lamb, as the mark in the hand would indicate service. The seal is the mark of God, as the seal of a state is the mark of that state.

vs. 4 John heard the number of them that were sealed. It was one hundred and forty-four thousand of the tribes of the children of Israel. John, in this vision of the sixth seal, saw two companies of sealed saints. He saw first a vast company of Abraham's descendants in the blood line, and then he saw another company so vast in host that no man could number them. Since the gospel, as Paul said, is the power of God unto salvation to every one that believeth, to the Jew first, and also to the Greek" (Rom. 1:16), so the Jewish Christians are likewise mentioned first here.

The number of the tribes of Israel mentioned here is one hundred forty-four thousand and twelve thousand from each of the twelve tribes of Israel.

Significance of the Number Given

These numbers are hardly to be taken literally, since we must ever keep in mind that we are still in the realm of symbolism, and studying in a book sign-i-fied" or written in symbols. They signify a great number. But there seems to be a profounder meaning than this. The number signifies "totality," that is to say, the complete and perfect number of God's servants out of the old Israel of God.

The meaning is intensified by the fact that of each tribe the number sealed is given as precisely twelve thousand. In the total, the number twelve is multiplied by itself and then by one thousand. This makes a square of twelve multiplied by the number of enlargement and totality—a thousand.

In Exodus 30:12-15 we have God's original directions for numbering His Israel of God in that day.

"When thou takest the sum of the children of Israel, them that are to be numbered then shall they give every man a ransom for his soul unto the Lord, when thou numberest them. This they shall give, every one that passeth among them that are numbered, half a shekel after the shekel of the sanctuary . . . the rich shall not give more than a half shekel, when they give an offering to the Lord to *make an atonement for your souls.*"

This presents these glowing facts that every man who is numbered has been ransomed, for whom atonement has been made, and that all men stand on the same level with God, who is no respector of persons. All require precisely the same ransom, for there is no difference between Jew and Gentile, for "both have been proved under sin." (Romans 3:9, 222, 23)

When the people were numbered by Moses, the number came out *unequal,* signifying incompleteness, "for the law made nothing perfect." But in this final enumeration of those for whom Christ "gave Himself as a ransom" (1 Tim. 2:6) the result is perfection.

The number "twelve" not only symbolizes completeness, but it also symbolizes the perfection of the final abode of the ransomed. We shall deal with this when we come to the description of that eternal city which has twelve gates, twelve angels at the gates, and twelve foundations, and the names of the twelve tribes of Israel, etc.

There is some difficulty in reference to the naming of the twelve tribes of Israel in the vision John saw. Of the tribes, Ephraim appears under the name of Joseph and the tribe of Dan is omitted altogether. The number twelve is preserved by naming Manassas, Joseph's first born son in the place of Dan. Dan's name may have been dropped because he fell away into idolatry, but this is only a surmise.

vs. 9 "After this I beheld, and, lo, a great multitude," which no man could number, of all nations, and kindreds, and people and tongues."

Here we find an innumerable multitude which no man could number. They were from every nation.

This second multitude represented the saved of all the nations—the Gentiles, in other words.

In the first part of this vision, which had to do with Abraham's descendants being sealed, John said he *heard* the number of them. Here he is given to *see* the vast throng of sealed from every nation.

Christ spoke of this Gentile multitude, "and I say unto you that many shall come from the east and west and sit down with Abraham, Isaac and Jacob in the kingdom of heaven." (Matt. 8:10, 11) John here sees the fulfillment of Christ's prediction, when this host of Gentiles is incorporated into the Israel of God today.

These "stood before the throne, and before the Lamb clothed with white robes." This is ever the garb of the redeemed. They have washed their robes and made them white in the blood of the Lamb.

"And palms in their hands." This declares them to be sharers of Christ's victory.

vs. 10-12 "And cried with a loud voice, saying salvation to our God which sitteth upon the throne, and unto the Lamb."

This multitude, "of all nations, and kindreds, and people, and tongues," are by their singing of salvation identified with the company John heard singing the new song in Rev. 5:9, for that was a preview of this. The theme of the song here entitled "Salvation" is given in fuller detail in the vision of the seals, where we have the words, "For thou wast slain, and has redeemed us to God by thy blood, out of every kindred, and tongue and people and nation."

This is the "great salvation" whereof Peter speaks in (I Peter 1:9-12), which things the angels desire to look into," for the next words of the scripture here are,

The Seven-Fold Doxology

And all the angels stood round about the throne, and about the elders, and the four living creatures, and fell down before the throne on their faces, and worshipped God, saying, Amen: Blessing and glory, and wisdom, and thanksgiving, and honor, and power and might, be unto our God for ever and ever, Amen."

It is interesting to compare this seven-fold doxology with that of Chapter 5:12. They are identical in six of the seven items (for "strength" in Rev. 5:12 is the same in the original as "might" in Rev. 7:12). The only difference in terms being that in this later song the expression "thanksgiving" takes the place of "riches" in the former song. This is understandable in that here is the fulfillment historically of that in prospect in Rev. 5:12. They were singing "thanksgiving" for the "riches of His grace."

vs. 13, 14 As if to call especial attention to this singing multitude, one of the elders, or angelic princes, answered (we wonder if this is in response to an unrecorded question of John's) saying unto John, "What are these which are arrayed in white robes? and whence came they?

vs. 14 John confesses his inability to answer either question by saying," Sir, thou knowest." whereupon the elder replies: "These are they which come out (literally "are coming out") of the great tribulation." While the authorized version reads "great tribulation" there is an article in the Greek,—literally "those who are coming out of the great tribulation."

What Tribulation is Meant Here?

Some expositors teach this "great tribulation" to be the same spoken of by Christ in (Matt. 24:21) "And then shall be great tribulation, such as was not since the beginning of the world to this time, no nor even shall be." They make it a period of tribulation yet future, a period *immediately* following the return of the Lord to raise the dead and transform the living saints. These of the "Futurist" school teach there is to be a "great tribulation" after the rapture of the saints.

But this cannot be because the elder expressly said of those John saw, that they were *then,* at that very time, *coming* out of the great tribulation. This forever forbids postponing the tribulation mentioned here to some future dispensation after Christ's return.

Another identifying feature of the time of this tribulation is a fact that we must not overlook. This opening of the sixth seal corresponds historically with the beginning of the *Pergamos period,* in which the doctrine of compromise in writing of human creeds (Council of Nicea called by Constantine) and the doctrine of the Nicolaitanes

111

(Elevation of bishops to lord it over God's heritage) lead to the "depths of satan" in the Thyatira Period. *And it was in the Thyatira Period* that we read of the apostate church, called Jezebel, but known historically as the Catholic church, in (Rev. 2:22)

"Behold, I will cast her into a bed, and them that commit adultery with her *into great tribulation,* except they repent."

This "tribulation" in the vision of the seven churches, coincides with that of the parenthesis between the sixth and seventh seals. In the Thyatira church there is mentioned the *cause* of the tribulation and in Rev. 7:14, we see those who have repented and *are coming out of the great tribulation.*

vs. 15-17 Because they have stood the trial and remained true, "Keeping his words unto the end" (Rev. 2:26), they are permitted to be before the throne to serve God constantly and experience the unspeakable joy of having God's presence among them. They shall neither hunger or thirst any more and all tears shall be wiped from their eyes. The "Man of Sorrows" shall banish all sorrow.

Summary

Thus we bring to a close the discussion of the parenthesis between the sixth and seventh seals by presenting a summary of the chapter.

The theme has been the sealing of the servants of God, both of the Jews and the Gentiles. But while we have been absorbed in this task we must not lose sight of the fact that four destructive agencies were being withheld until this sealing was completed.

These powers were restrained until some great work of the church could be accomplished. The eighth chapter continues with the opening of the seventh and last seal, in the first division of which, this quartet of destruction is let loose under the symbolism of the blowing of four trumpets in succession. We shall find that these first four trumpets heralded the four tides of invasion which swept over the western half of the Roman Empire.

But before these great catastrophes fell upon the western part of the empire, did the church experience a great triumph? Let us remember this is a book of great symbolism and this is a symbolic picture of great historical events connected with the welfare of the saints.

We have already learned under the sixth seal that Constantine had embraced Christianity and by decree in A.D. 331 ordered the destruction of pagan temples and the abolishing of pagan worship in the empire.

Thus we see that the church of Christ had grappled with the ancient pagan religions and, after centuries of trial and untold suffering, had won a glorious victory. The temples of Jupiter, Mercury and Mars were closed and their idol worship forbidden. If a person today could have visited Rome in the end of the second century he would have beheld a pagan world. Had they visited the eternal city in the latter portion of the fourth century he could have hardly believed his eyes, for he would have looked upon an empire blessed with churches filled with followers of the Christ.

Until this sealing of the saints, was completed, the four winds of destruction were held back. It was a definite act of God to see that they were restrained from their missions of destruction until Christianity had captured the empire.

Had these four destructive agencies done their work before this great victory of the church in the sowing of the seed of the kingdom everywhere, Christianity could never have survived the wreck of the empire and the passing of a civilization hoary with age.

Christ indwelling in the hearts of converted Romans helped them to rise above the ruins of the past. The invading hordes from the north laid aside their paganism and embraced the Christian belief from those whom they had vanquished.

We are now ready to consider the events accompanying the opening of the seventh seal.

CHAPTER VIII
THE SEVENTH SEAL OPENED

Text (8:1-13)

1 And when he opened the seventh seal, there followed a silence in heaven about the space of half an hour. 2 And I saw the seven angels that stand before God; and there were given unto them seven trumpets.

3 And another angel came and stood over the altar, having a golden censer; and there was given unto him much incense, that he should add it unto the prayers of all the saints upon the golden altar which was before the throne. 4 And the smoke of the incense, with the prayers of the saints, went up before God out of the angel's hand. 5 And the angel taketh the censer; and he filled it with the fire of the altar, and cast it upon the earth: and there followed thunders, and voices, and lightnings, and an earthquake.

6 And the seven angels that had the seven trumpets prepared themselves to sound.

7 And the first sounded, and there followed hail and fire, mingled with blood, and they were cast upon the earth: and the third part of

113

the earth was burnt up, and the third part of the trees were burnt up, and all green grass was burnt up.

8 And the second angel sounded, and as it were a great mountain burning with fire was cast into the sea: and the third part of the sea became blood; 9 and there died the third part of the creatures which were in the sea, even they that had life; and the third part of the ships was destroyed.

10 And the third angel sounded, and there fell from heaven a great star, burning as a torch, and it fell upon the third part of the rivers, and upon the fountains of the waters; 11 and the name of the star is called Wormwood: and the third part of the waters became wormwood; and many men died of the waters, because they were made bitter.

12 And the fourth angel sounded, and the third part of the sun was smitten, and the third part of the moon, and the third part of the stars; that the third part of them should be darkened, and the day should not shine for the third part of it, and the night in like manner.

13 And I saw, and I heard an eagle, flying in mid heaven, saying with a great voice, Woe, woe, woe, for them that dwell on the earth, by reason of the other voices of the trumpet of the three angels, who are yet to sound.

INTRODUCTION

We have now arrived at the beginning of a new period in the history of the Roman Empire, the arena in which the history of the church is also unfolded. The saints having been sealed, the four agencies of destruction could no longer be held back. Let us say, in passing, there is nothing mysterious to be attached to this sealing of the saints. What Paul said of the Ephesians, could just as truthfully be said of the saints of this parenthetical period of time:

"In whom ye also trusted, after that ye heard the word of truth, the gospel of your salvation: in whom also after that ye believed, *ye were sealed* with that Holy Spirit, which is the earnest of our inheritance until the redemption of the purchased possession, unto the praise of His glory." (Ephesians 1:13,14)

After the sealing of the saints, the seventh seal is opened and we read,

vs. 1 "There was silence in heaven about the space of half an hour."

This silence comes as a sudden surprise. This comes in marked contrast with the *rejoicings* in heaven at the beginning of this series of visions, when the Lamb that was slain "came and took the book out of the right hand of Him that sat upon the throne." (Rev. 5:7).

This silence is too startling to be given over to conjecture in interpretation. Shall we let the scriptures help us. In Habakkuk 2:20, we read, "The Lord is in His Holy Temple; let all the earth *keep silence* before Him."

These words are spoken in connection with the going forth of Almighty God in judgment. Hence, when He is about to visit the earth (the Roman Empire, as understood by John), with the awful judgments of the seventh seal, nothing could be more fitting than that heaven itself should stand breathless, awaiting the blowing of the seven trumpets of the seventh seal.

Another passage will suffice. In Zephaniah 1:7, in a passage which incorporates the judgments of God Almighty, we read these significant words: *"Hold thy peace* at the presence of the Lord God; for *the day of the Lord is at hand."*

The word, "Hold thy peace" here is identically the same as that rendered "Keep silence" in (Hab. 2:20).

In the light of these passages, it can be clearly seen the appropriateness of introducing the fearful judgments to follow with a half hour silence in heaven.

It is, as it were, the hush before the march of events about to begin; the calm before the storms of judgment break.

It doubtless, also is designed to give great emphasis to the events that follow.

vs. 2, 3 "I saw the seven angels which stood before God". It seems that among angels there are ranks, degrees, dominions, powers. These are "the seven who stand before God." In Matthew 18:10, we learn that those who believe in Christ have angels who stand before God and behold His face:

> "Take heed that ye despise not one of these little ones, (In Matt. 18:6, Christ identifies 'one of these little ones' as, 'one of these little ones which believe in me') for I say unto you, that in heaven their angels do always behold the face of my Father which is in heaven."

We even know the name of one of these angels, "And the angel answering said unto him (Zacharias), I am Gabriel, that stand in the presence of God, and am sent to speak unto thee, and to show thee these glad things. (Luke 1:19).

"And to them were given seven trumpets." The fact that the trumpets are committed to angels of the highest order indicates the importance in God's sight of these trumpet judgments.

But before the first trumpet is sounded, "Another angel came and stood at the altar." (Rev. 8:3). The scene is borrowed from the service of the Old Testament tabernacle. In the Holy Place, before the second veil, stood the golden altar . . . Morning and evening, fire was placed upon it from the altar of sacrifice, and upon the fire was poured the sacred incense. The incense that Moses was commanded to make was a most hallowed thing—so hallowed that if any one should even attempt to imitate the fragrance, he was to be 'cut off from his people.' (Exodus 30:34-38).

The cloud of perfume which rose and filled the sanctuary, was a symbol of prayer.

To this ministering angel was given "A golden censor and there was given to him much incense." We have found that incense, in the Bible, is a symbol of prayer.

Here, however, another feature is added, or rather included. He was given *much incense*" that he should offer it with the prayers of all saints, upon the golden altar which is before the throne."

Two things present themselves here. First, a ministering angel matches the prayers of petitioning saints. The more we pray, the more is prayer offered from the heavenlies. Yea, more, *much* incense was given him, as if to say, heaven more than matches the volume of earthly prayers.

Second. It would seem that the prayers of the saints become acceptable only when there is added to them the incense of the prayers of heaven, or in other words, there must be added the intercession of Christ and the effects of his atoning work.

116

This brings to our mind the inspired statement of Paul, "Likewise the Spirit also helpeth our infirmities: for we know not what we should pray for as we ought: but the Spirit itself maketh intercession for us with groanings which cannot be uttered."

And he that searcheth the hearts knoweth what is the mind of the Spirit, because he maketh intercession for the saints according to the will of God." (Romans 8:26,27).

vs. 4 "And the smoke of the incense which came with the prayers of the saints, ascended up before God out of the angel's hand."

What a comforting thought! We can be sure that our prayers are acceptable to God, because of the added incense of the ministering angel. This gives us another insight of the work of angels. Paul said of them, "Are they not all ministering spirits, sent forth to minister for them who shall be heirs of salvation?" (Hebrews 1:14).

But the symbolism suddenly changes. Rev. 8:5: "And the angel took the censer, and filled it with fire of the altar, and cast it into the earth." We have a similar instance in Ezekial 10:2. "And he spoke unto the man clothed with linen, and said, go in between the wheels, even under the cherub and fill thine hand with coals of fire from between the cherubim, and scatter them over the city."

As here in Ezekial, so in Revelation, the fire of God, like coals from the altar, is cast upon the earth.

"And there were voices, and thunderings, and lightnings, and an earthquake," These symbolize the terrible things that will happen in the scenes to follow when the seven angels sound their trumpets. All things are now ready for the blast of the first trumpet.

CHAPTER IX

THE SEVEN TRUMPETS

Text (9:1-12)

The Division of the Trumpet Series

1 And the fifth angel sounded, and I saw a star from heaven fallen unto the earth: and there was given to him the key of the pit of the abyss. 2 And he opened the pit of the abyss; and there went up a smoke out of the pit, as the smoke of a great furnace; and the sun and the air were darkened by reason of the smoke of the pit. 3 And out of the smoke came forth locusts upon the earth; and power was given them, as the scorpions of the earth have power. 4 And it was said unto them that they should not hurt the grass of the earth, neither any green thing, neither any tree, but only such men as have not the seal of God on their foreheads. 5 And it was given them that they should not kill them, but that they should be tormented five months: and their torment was as the torment of a scorpion, when it striketh a man. 6 And in those days men shall seek death, and shall in no wise find it; and they shall desire to die, and death fleeth from them. 7 And the shapes of the locusts were like unto horses prepared for war; and upon their heads as it were crowns like unto gold, and their faces were as men's faces. 8 And they had hair as the hair of women, and their teeth were as the teeth of lions. 9 And they had breastplates, as it were breastplates of iron; and the sound of their wings was as the sound of chariots, of many horses rushing to war. 10 And they have tails like unto scorpions, and stings; and in their tails is their power to hurt men five months. 11 They have over them as king the angel of the abyss: his name in Hebrew is Abaddon, and in the Greek tongue he hath the name Apollyon.
12 The first Woe is past: behold, there come yet two Woes hereafter.

However, before we begin the actual "unfolding" of the symbolism of the seven trumpets, it is well that we take a long view of this division of the trumpet series, in order to get a proper perspective.

As with the vision of the seals, which were divided into two parts, so in the trumpet series, likewise is divided into two groupings; first, a group of four, followed by a group of three.

This is evidenced by the fact that after the sounding of the fourth trumpet (Rev. 8:12), the action is interrupted and John sees an angel flying in the midst of heaven, saying, with a loud voice, "Woe, woe, woe, to the inhabiters of the earth, by reason of the other voices of the trumpet of the three angels which are yet to sound." (Rev. 8:13).

118

We shall find, also, there is a further interruption after the sixth trumpet, where another parenthesis, the second in Revelation, is introduced, and the vision of the mighty angel with the little book is described.

Shall we recall that, in our previous study, Constantine in 330 A.D., moved the capital to Byzantium on the Bosporus and renamed the city after himself, calling it "the city of Constantine", or Constantinople.

This resulted in the Empire being divided into two divisions, with Rome the most important city of the Western part of the Empire and Constantinople capital of the whole empire, and the most important city of the eastern section of the Empire.

It was upon the western half of the Empire we shall find that forces of invasion struck and brought that portion to desolation. These forces are symbolized by the four trumpets, the blowing of each, marking a new invading army overrunning the Western Empire.

In the east, however, there remained, after the desolution of the west, the Eastern Empire. Two of the last three trumpets, we shall find have to do with the invasion of the eastern division of the Empire. These last three trumpets are called the "woe trumpets", because of the severity of their judgments. They stand out all to themselves, being preceeded by a special threefold announcement of woe; therefore designated as the three *woe* trumpets.

Significance of the Trumpets

The trumpet was used to give a signal. With the peal of trumpets, God descended upon Mt. Sinai. At the blast of trumpets the camp of Israel rose up to continue the journey to the promised land. At the sounding of the trumpets of ram's horns, the walls of Jericho fell. Trumpets announced the inauguration of Solomon's reign. The seventh month, the month of atonement was ushered in by trumpets. Trumpets heralded the dawn of the year of Jubilee.

Many times it implied the march of armies. The sounding of trumpets summoned men to battle. A passage will suffice to substantiate this last use of the trumpet:

"Again the word of the Lord came unto me saying, Son of Man, speak to the children of thy people, and say unto them, when I bring the sword upon a land, if the people of the land take a man of their coasts, set him for their watchman. If when he seeth the sword come upon the land, he blow the trumpet, and warn the people, then whosoever heareth the sound of the trumpet, and taketh not warning; if the sword come, and take him away, his blood shall be upon his own head. But if the watchman see the sword come, and blow not the trumpet, and the people be not warned, if the sword come, and take any person from among them—his blood will I require at the watchman's hand. (Ezekiel 33:1-6)

That the sounding of these trumpets severally mark distinct events or eras of time in the history of the world, is indicated by the seventh angel, "*in the days* of the voice of the seventh angel, when he shall begin to sound, the mystery of God shall be finished." (Rev. 10:7).

The First Trumpet (8:7)

vs. 7 "The first angel sounded and there followed hail and fire mingled with blood."

The symbols of destruction are here enumerated as hail, fire and blood. These form a combination of destructive forces entirely outside the realm of nature. We find in another instance that hail and fire were co-mingled in the seventh of the ten plagues visited upon Egypt.

"And Moses stretched forth his rod toward heaven; and the Lord sent thunder and hail, and the fire ran along upon the ground, and the Lord rained hail upon the land of Egypt. And the hail smote throughtout all the land of Egypt all that was in the field, both man and beast; and the hail smote every herb of the field, and broke every tree of the field." (Ex. 9:23,25).

But in this trumpet scene we have another element added, that of blood. Therefore, fire and hail are symbols most suitable to represent destructive agencies, and the third symbol, *blood,* fittingly represents the terrible loss of life. John has presented a mingling of blood with the symbols of fire and hail, that he might point out great destruction and slaughter.

120

Remembering we are still walking in the realm of symbolism. "A third part of the trees was burnt up."

"Trees", are a familiar figure in Scripture for human greatness.

In Jeremiah 17:8, the man that trusts in God is likened to a tree. "For he shall be as a tree planted by the waters."

In Ezekiel 31:3, we read, "Behold, the Assyrian was a cedar in Lebanon with fair branches, and his tip was among the thick boughs." There follows a lengthy description and the continued comparison to him as a tree. See Ezekiel (31:4-9).

In Daniel 4:20-22, Daniel in interpreting the dream of Nebuchadnezzar, likened him to a tree:

"The tree which thou sawest, which grew and was strong, whose height reached unto heaven, and the sight thereof to all the earth . . . it is thou, O King, that thou art grown and become strong . . . and reacheth unto heaven, and thy dominion to the end of the earth."

The burning up of a "third part of the trees", would, therefore, indicate that portion of the leading men of the earth (the Roman Empire) being consumed. Later, we will describe more fully concerning the expression, "the third part."

The expression "and all the green grass was burnt up," would point to the destruction of national and earthly property.

And how the history of the Roman Empire, at this exact time fulfills this symbolism! It would seem that Gibbon in his, "Decline and Fall of the Roman Empire," had the words of this first trumpet symbolism before him, as he wrote. This infidel historian actually uses the very language of Revelation to describe the events of this first trumpet period. As this period opens with the sound of a trumpet, in his 31st chapter, Volume 3, page 282, he describes the invasion of Rome, as follows:

"At the hour of midnight, the Salarian Gate was silently opened, and the inhabitants were awakened by the tremendous sound of the Gothic *trumpet*."

121

Again he says, "at the first sound of the *trumpet,* the Goths left their farms and rushed to the invasion."

Again he says, "The Goth's *conflagration* consumed the Empire. He, here is describing the pillaging of the Western Empire and the sacking of Rome.

On page 271, same volume and chapter, in describing the attitude of the rulers of Rome at Alaric's attack of the city, he records, they said, "If Alaric refused them a fair and honorable capitulation, he might *sound his trumpets,* and prepare to give battle to an innumerable people, exercised in arms and animated by despair."

In this same chapter, page 249, he describes the wealth of the Roman nobles and then procedes, from page 249 to 268, to give in much detail the glory of the public and private buildings of the city and the indescribable wealth contained in the city, suming up at the end as follows: "Such was the state of Rome under the reign of Honorius, at the time when the Gothic army forced the seige, or rather the blockade of the city." Page 268, Vol. 3. His summation of this seige reads as follows:

"Eleven hundred and sixty-three years after the foundation of Rome, the Imperial City, which had subdued and civilized so considerable a part of mankind, was delivered to the licentious fury of the tribes of Germany and Scythia." Vol. 3, Page 282.

So great was the pillaging of the incredulous wealth of Rome, that he says, "the clergy, were sometimes tempted to confound the destruction of the capital and the destruction of the globe." Vol. 3, page 289.

He uses the next eight pages in an attempt to describe the six day stripping of the wealth of the city.

How many pages would be required to describe the pillaging of the whole of the Western Empire!

Thousands of leading citizens were taken captive or killed. Thus, a third of the trees were destroyed and the wealth, as symbolized in the words, "green grass was burnt up."

Myers describes the sack of Rome by Alaric, in these words:

"Alaric turned upon the city, resolved upon its sack and plunder. The barbarians broke into the city by night "and the inhabitants were awakened by the tremendous *sound of Gothic trumpet*". Precisely eight hundred years had passed since its sack by the Gauls. During that time the Imperial City had carried it's victorious standards over three continents and had gathered within the temples of it's Gods and the palaces of it's nobles, the plunder of the world. Now it was given over for a spoil to the fierce tribes from beyond the Danube.

For six days and nights the rough barbarians trooped through the streets of the city on their mission of pillage. Their wagons were heaped with costly furniture, the rich plate, and the silken garments stripped from the palaces of the Caesars and wealthy patricians. Amidst the license of the sack, the barbarian instincts of the robbers broke loose from all restraint, and the streets of the city were wet with blood, while the nights were lighted by burning buildings."—Myers Ancient History. page 540.

The Third Part

No less than twelve times do we find in Revelation the expression, "the third part." Under the first trumpet, we read, "One third part of the trees were burned up." As we have already discovered that the "earth" meant the Roman Empire, then this would indicate that one third of that empire was burned. The "third part" of the sea became blood when the second trumpet was sounded. At the blast of the third trumpet, a burning star fell upon a "third part" of the rivers, and a "third part" of the waters became wormwood. Under the fourth trumpet, a "third part" of the sun, moon and stars was smitten.

After a careful reading and consideration of these occurances, it appears that these four "third parts" refer to the same third part of the Roman Empire. The first occurance refers to the scourging of one third of the land; the second, to one third of the sea; the third, to one third of the rivers, and the fourth, to one third of the heavens.

All combined, would indicate the devastation of one third part of the earth, or the Roman Empire. The first four trumpets announce the scourging, by land, sea, rivers and air, of one third of the earth. This is understandable when we recall that the Roman Empire, or earth of John's day, was divided into three divisions.

Said Gibbon, Vol. 5, page 364:

> "From the age of Charlemagne to that of the Crusades, the world (for I overlook the remote monarchy of China) was occupied and disputed by three great nations of the Greeks, the Saracens, and the Franks."

The Greeks and Arabians called the nations of the west, "Franks." The Franks were the Latins.

Harris, in his Philological Inquiries, Part 3, Chapter 1, speaks of the world being divided into three parts or divisions from the fifth to the fifteenth centuries.

> "Three classes of men during that interval are conspicuous, the Saracens or Arabians, the Latins or Franks, inhabitants of Western Europe, and Byzantine Greeks."

It then becomes a fact that during a period of a millennium—the time period of John's vision of the trumpets—the Empire, or earth was divided into three parts. And history records the destruction by three separate forces, the three divisions of the earth.

The four invasions from the north destroyed the Latin, or western portion of the earth, or Empire. The fifth angel looses the Saracen invasion on the Arabian third of the Empire, and under the sixth trumpet, the "four angels which were bound in the great river Euphrates", pour forth their teeming multitudes to over run and devastate the Greek third of the Empire.

The Second Trumpet (8:8-9)

8:8,9 "And the second trumpet sounded, and as it were a great mountain burning with fire was cast in to the sea: and a third part of the sea became blood; and the third part of the creatures which were in the sea, and had life, died, and the third part of the ships were destroyed."

The Apostle sees a great burning mountain cast into the sea and there follows a destruction of one third of the ships and inhabitants of the sea. The trumpet, the blood and the destruction of one third of the ships, all speak of war and the arena of activity is the sea. Since this is against the Latin or Western third of the Empire, the warfare will be naval and on the Western half of the Mediterranian.

An outstanding feature of this second trumpet is the prominence given the symbol of a burning mountain cast into the sea.

A mountain is a Biblical synonym for a nation. In Jeremiah 5:25, Babylon is called a mountain:

"Behold, I am against thee, O destroying mountain, saith the Lord, which destroyest all the earth; and I will stretch out mine hand upon thee, and roll thee down from the rocks, and will make thee a *burnt* mountain."

In Zechariah 4:7, we read:

"Who art thou, O great mountain? before Zerubbabel thou shall become a plain."

This great mountain before Zerubbabel was the Persian Kingdom which had set itself against the building of the temple.

This "mountain burning with fire", indicates a great nation or power. It symbolizes a raging volcanic 'mountain' of fire smiting the sea. History corroborates this.

Shall we catch up the thread of history. After the sack of Rome, Alaric, the leader of the Gothic invasion, led his soldiers to the extreme southern end of Italy. Hear Myers:

"Alaric led his soldiers to the extreme southern point of Italy, intending to cross the straits of Messina, into Sicily, and then to carry his conquests into the Provinces of Africa. His designs were frustrated by his death which occurred A.D. 410."—Myers Ancient History, page 541.

Let Gibbon take up the account at this point:

"The ferocious character of the Barbarians was displayed in the funeral of a hero whose valor and fortune they celebrated with mournful applause. By the labor of a captive multitude, they

125

forcibly diverted the course of the Busentinus, a small river that washes the walls of Consentia. The royal sepulchre, adorned with the splendid spoils and trophies of Rome, was constructed in the vacant bed; the waters were then restored to their natural channel; and the secret spot, where the remains of Alaric had been deposited, was forever concealed by the inhuman massacre of the prisoners, who had been employed to execute the work."

His followers recrossed the Alps and settled in the south of Gaul and the north part of Spain and came to be known as the Kingdom of the Visigoths or West Goths.

While these Goths were thus setting up their Kingdom, about A.D. 422, another mighty horde poured down from the north and were so destructive, they gave a new word to our vocabulary. The principle tribe of this vast horde was known as the Vandals. From their ruthlessness, we get our word, "Vandalism." Moving from their seat in Pannonia, they crossed the Pyrenees, where they occupied a large section of the present country of Spain. This region is now known by the name of Andalusia, preserving the memory of these barbarians.

From here, about A.D. 439, they crossed the Straits of Gibraltar and overthrew the Roman Empire in all northern Africa, making Carthage the seat of a short-lived, but dreaded Corsair empire. Hear Myers on this:

"The Kings of the Vandal Empire in Northern Africa had acquired as perfect a supremacy in the Western Mediterranean, as Carthage ever enjoyed in the days of her commercial pride. Vandal Corsairs swept the seas and harassed the coasts of Sicily and Italy, and even plundered the maritime towns of the provinces of the Roman Empire in the East. In the year 455 A.D., a Vandal fleet led by the dread Geiseric (Genseric) sailed up the Tiber.

Leo, (the bishop of Rome) went forth to intercede in the name of Christ, for the Imperial city. Geiseric granted the pious bishop the lives of the citizens, but said the movable property of the capital belonged to his warriors. For fourteen days and nights the city was given over to the ruthless barbarians. The ships of the Vandals, which almost hid with their number, the waters of the Tiber, were piled, as had been the wagons of the Goths before them, with the rich and weighty spoils of the capital. From the Capitoline sanctuary were borne off the golden candlestick and other sacred articles that Titus had stolen from the temple in Jerusalem.

The greed of the barbarians was sated at last, and they were ready to withdraw. The Vandal fleet sailed for Carthage, bearing, besides the plunder of the city, more than thirty thousand of the inhabitants as slaves."—Myers Ancient History, page 545.

Thus we see how, by building ships, they crossed the Mediterranean and struggled with the Roman Empire for the mastery of that sea. For six hundred years Rome had ruled the waves of this almost land locked sea. But the fleet of the Vandals drove the Roman ships from the seas, destroying them and reddening the sea with the blood of the slain. After thirty years, since the sea battles began, the Vandals invaded Italy and beseiged and sacked the city of Rome. Thus we see the second of the four winds, which were held back until the sealing of the saints in the interlude between the sixth and seventh seals, has been released in the blowing of the second trumpet.

Rome is hurt upon the sea, but not totally conquered. In a few months Genseric, the Vandal King is dead and Rome is freed from the tramp of the second invaders.

A feature to be noted here, is that this great disaster Rome suffers, comes from the sea and the seas of a third part of the Roman Empire are conquered.

The Third Trumpet (8:10, 11)

vs. 10, 11 "And the third angel sounded, and there fell a great star from heaven, burning as it were a lamp, and it fell upon a third part of the rivers, and upon the fountain of waters; and the name of the star is called Wormwood; and the third part of the waters became wormwood; and many men died of the waters, because they were made bitter."

A different angel each time sounds the trumpet—the signal for new conquests. In our study thus far, we have found that the sounding of each of the first two trumpets opened a new phase of the gradual overthrow of the Roman Empire of the west, by some new invasion lead by some great leader.

We have found in the explanation of symbols, under the sixth seal, that a star is used in the Scriptures to represent earthly potentates and leaders. A "star", we have discovered, is a notable person. In this third trumpet period, he is likened to a "burning star", burning as a lamp or torch and that "it fell upon a third part of the rivers".

Where it falls upon the rivers and fountains of waters, they become bitter as wormwood. This manifestly points our attention to a time when great calamities should fall upon the Rivers of the Roman Empire. This "Star" or mighty chieftan would center his activities upon the headwaters and river systems of the Western Roman Empire. Again shall we turn to history for corroboration. Surely, since John was to write "of the things which are and the things which must be hereafter," we must constantly hold this Book of symbolism in one hand and a history book in the other. Myers gives a vivid description of the third invasion of Western Rome. While they do, at times, overlap a little, nevertheless, they were distinct invasions of the Empire of the West. He dates the beginning of this new thrust in A.D. 451:

> "The barbarians (Goths and Vandals), that were thus overrunning and parceling out the inheritance of the dying empire were now in turn, pressed upon and terrified by a foe *more hideous and dreadful* in their eyes than were they in the sight of the peoples among whom they had thrust themselves. These were the non-Aryan Huns, of whom we have already caught a glimpse as they drove the panic-stricken Goths across the Danube.

> At this time, their leader was Attila, whom the affrighted inhabitants of Europe called the *"Scourge of God."* It was Attila's boast that the grass never grew again where once the hoof of his horse had trod . . .

> Finally he turned westward, and, at the head of a host numbering, it is asserted, seven hundred thousand warriors, crossed the

Rhine into Gaul, purposing first to ravage that province and then traverse Italy, with *fire* and *sword,* in order to destroy the last of the Roman power.

The Romans and their German conquerors united to make common cause against the common enemy. The Visigoths were rallied by their King, Theodoric; the Italians, the Franks, the Burgundians, flocked to the standard of the able Roman general, Aetius.

Attila drew up his mighty hosts upon the plain of Chalons, in the north of Gaul. The conflict was long and terrible. Theodoric was slain; but at last fortune turned against the barbarians. The loss of the Huns is variously estimated at from one hundred thousand, to three thousand warriors. Attila succeeded in escaping from the field and retreated with his shattered hosts across the Rhine." Myers Ancient History, pages 543, 544.

But Attila was not one to give up. We again quote from Myers:

"The year after his defeat at Chalons, Attila crossed the Alps and *burned* and plundered all the important cities of Northern Italy."

How minutely this fulfills John's symbolic prophesy of this "falling star," falling "upon the fountains of waters." An examination of a map of Italy will show how the rivers have their fountain heads in the northern section of the country.

And here *a notable thing happened which emphasized the fact that the theater of this third invasion was to be upon the rivers and, particularly their head-waters.*

Hear Myers again:

"The barbarians threatened Rome, but Leo the Great, bishop of the capital, went with an embassy to the camp of Attila and pleaded for the city. He recalled to the mind of Attila how death had overtaken the impious Alaric, soon after he had given the Imperial city as a spoil to his warriors, and warned him not to call down upon himself the like judgment of heaven. To the admonitions of the Christian bishop was added the persuasion of a bribe from the Emperor, Valentinian; and Attila *was induced to spare southern Italy and to lead his warriors back beyond the Alps*. Shortly after he had crossed the Danube, he died suddenly in his camp, and like Alaric was buried secretly".— Myers Ancient History, page 544.

Gibbon says:

"Neither the spirit, nor the forces, nor the *reputation,* of Attila were impared by the failure of the Gallic expedition. In the ensuing spring, he repeated his demand of the Princess Hororia and her patrimonial treasures. The demand was rejected . . . and immediately the indignant loser took to the field, passed the Alps, invaded Italy and besieged Aquileia . . . the seige was prosecuted with fresh vigor . . . the Huns mounted the assault with irrestible fury; and the succeeding generation could scarcely discover the ruins of Aquileia."

After this dreadful chastisement, Attila pursued his march, and as he passed, the cities of Attinum, Concordia, and Padau were reduced into heaps of stones and ashes. The inland towns; Vicenza, Verona, and Bergamo, were exposed to the *rapacious cruelty* of the Huns . . . Attila spread his ravages over the rich plains of modern Lombardy; which are divided by the *Po,* and bounded by the Alps and Apennine." Gibbons Decline and Fall of the Roman Empire. Vol 3, pages 443, 444, 445.

Thus, we see how Attila's campaigns were carried on upon the headwaters of the rivers, and along the rivers of Northern Italy.

Then, Gibbon proceeds to relate how Leo interceded successfully with Attila to spare Rome itself. His description of Attila's death is too lengthy to give here, but this will suffice:

"The remains of Attila were enclosed within three coffins, of gold, of silver and of iron, and privately buried at night; the spoils of a nation were thrown into his grave; the captives who had opened the ground, were inhumanely massacred." Gibbons Decline and Fall of the Roman Empire, Vol. 3, page 452.

The exact place of burial is unknown. but it is believed they lie under the waters of the Danube and there they remain—the bones of the star called, "Wormwood", that fell upon the rivers.

Recapitulation

The Roman Empire of the west weakened, and ready to topple to ruin has suffered the blasts of three trumpets and now, awaits the blast of the fourth trumpet.

The first trumpet heralded the invasion of Alaric, the Goth who sacked Rome in 410 A.D. The Second trumpet sounded the Vandal conquest of the Mediterranean, and the second sack of Rome by the Vandals, under Genseric. The third trumpet introduced the rush of Attila, the Scourge of God, and his Huns, upon the rivers of the Rhine, Marne of Gaul, and the river system of Northern Italy. No wonder Attila, called *"the scourge of God,"* in history and *"wormwood,"* in Scriptures, was likened to a *"burning star,"* when we recall that in just three short years from his first appearance on the borders of the Roman Empire, he had run his brilliant, but bitter course, and was dead!

Now, only one of the hurtful forces of the four, which had been withheld until the sealing of the saints of the sixth seal, remains to blast the Western Empire.

Rome, now weakened and toppling to her fall reminds us of Daniel's vision of that very empire. The feet of iron as seen in Nebuchadnezzar's vision, are now become weak as miry clay. (Daniel 2:42). Now, there was needed only the rush of the fourth wind to blast the empire into helpless ruin.

The Fourth Trumpet (8:12)

> *vs. 12* "And the fourth angel sounded, and the third part of the sun was smitten, and the third part of the moon, and the third part of the stars, so the third part of them were darkened, and the day shone not for the third part of it."

As the fourth angel sounds, the fourth wind, which had been re-

131

strained until the sealing of the saints, was loosed. The result is darkness. A third part of the sun, moon and stars were smitten.

We have already deciphered the symbolism of the sun, moon and stars, and found they are symbols of kings, dignitaries, princes and great men of the earth.

The creative work of the fourth day of the first chapter of Genesis was the appointing of the sun, moon, and stars to their respective duties in respect to the earth. The sun was to *rule* the day, and the moon to *rule* the night, "and the stars also".

Thus we see the fourth day is, definitely, associated with the function of government, and the sun, moon and stars have ever been symbols of governmental authority, powers and functions.

Therefore, these symbols, collectively, represent the whole governmental system of the earth, or the Roman Empire, as John understood it.

Paul said, "the powers that be are ordained of God." (Rom. 13:1). So, just as in the physical heavens, God has set the sun, moon and stars with their authorities and power, he has set in the political heavens; some rulers with the power and authority of the sun; some with that of the moon, which gives a reflected light of the sun, or represents delegated authority and power; and some with the function of a star.

The blowing of the fourth trumpet, then, heralds a new war of invasion on the tottering Roman Empire of the west. And in this war, one of the rulers was to become subservient to other authority, or, in other words, be darkened.

This is just what we find to have happened in the closing events of the history of the western division of the Empire.

Hear Myers again:

> "Only the shadow of the Empire in the west remained. All the provinces, Illyricum, Gaul, Britian, Spain and Africa, were in the hands of the Goths, the Vandals, the Franks, the Burgundians, the Angles and Saxons, and Various other intruding tribes . . Myers Ancient History, page 546.

Says Gibbon, Vol. 3, Page 513.

"In the space of twenty years since the death of Valentinian, nine emperors had successively disappeared; and the son of Orestes, a youth recommended only by his beauty, would be the least entitled to the notice of posterity, if his reign, which was marked by the extinction of the Roman Empire in the west, did not leave a memorable era in the history of mankind."

"During the years from A.D. 456 to 472, the real ruler in Italy was a Sueve, named Count Ricimer."—Myers Ancient History, page 546.

Says Gibbon:

"During that period, the government was in the hands of Ricimer alone, and, although the modest barbarian disclaimed the name of king, he accumulated treasures, formed a separate army, negotiated private alliances, and ruled Italy with the same independent and despotic authority, which was afterwards exercised by Odoacer and Theodoric."—Gibbon's Decline and Fall of the Roman Empire. Vol. 3, page 484.

Continuing from Myers:

"He, (Count Ricimer) set up four emperors. Upon his death, a Pannonian, by the name of Orestes deposed the emperor then on the throne and placed the emperial crown upon the head of his own son, a child of six years.

By what has been called a freak of fortune, this boy-soverign bore the name of Romulus Augustus, thus uniting, in the name of the last Roman emperor of the west, the names of the founder of Rome and the establisher of the empire. He reigned only one year, when Odoacer, the leader of the Heruli, a small, but formidable German tribe, having demanded *one third of the lands of Italy* to divide among his followers, for their services rendered the empire, and having been refused, put Orestes to death and dethroned the child emperor.

The Roman senate now sent to Constantinople an embassy to

represent to the Eastern Emperor, Zeno, that the West was willing to give up its claim to an emperor of its own, and to request the German chief, with the title of "patrician," might rule Italy as his viceroy. This was granted; and Italy now became in effect, a province of the Emperor of the East."—Myers Ancient History, page 546.

Thus Romulus Augustus, who became known as Augustulus, "the little Augustus," was dethroned by Odoacer, the Roman senate that had sat for twelve hundred and twenty-eight years, was driven from the senate chambers and the mighty fabric of the empire fell to pieces. Great men were humbled. Thus, the sun, moon and stars lost their authority and power and ceased to give light.

"Odoacer, in 476 A.D. assumed authority in the west and was the first barbarian," says Gibbon, Vol. 3, Page 615," who reigned in Italy, over a people who had asserted their just superiority above the rest of mankind."

Gibbon continues on Page 518, Vol. 3. "*One third of those ample estates*, to which the ruin of Italy is originally imputed, was extorted for the use of the conquerors."

The emperors, with less dignataries and landed owners of great estates,—one third of the sun, moon and stars were darkened!

Thus, in the overthrow of the Empire of the West, ends the work of the four hurtful angels, held back for a season, but released under the blast of the first four trumpets.

There now remain three angels, the "woe" angels, to blow their trumpets.

The Fifth Trumpet

Turning back to the seventh chapter and the last verse, we observe a pause before the sixth angel sounded his trumpet.

We have already seen how the trumpet series of seven angels sounding their trumpets is divided into two groups. Like the seven church periods, and the seven seals, so the trumpets are divided into two groups, one of four and the second of three periods. We have considered the first group of four trumpets; there remain three trumpets termed the "other three voices of the trumpet of the three angels which are yet to sound." (Rev. 8:13).

Thus we see there is a pause after the sounding of the trumpet of the fourth angel. The action is interrupted at that point by the vision of "an angel, flying in the midst of heaven, saying with a loud voice, woe, woe, woe, to the inhabiters of earth, by reason of the other voices of the trumpet of the three angels, which are yet to sound." (Rev. 8:13).

It is clear that the destructive work of the first four angels has been finished and that the remaining three angels perform another and distinctively different work of devastation. This is to cause great woe upon the inhabiters of the earth. Remembering that the "earth" to John meant the Roman Empire, and, also, the fact that the destructive work of the first four angels was done in the western half of the empire; the last three "woe" angels operate in the Eastern half of the Roman Empire.

Though Rome itself had fallen, the eastern half of the empire still remained. How natural, then, that the further history of the Roman Empire, now centered in the east, with Constantinople as its capital, should be the burden of revelations symbolized in the last three "woe trumpets."

It is quite clear that the scene has been transferred from the west to the east, and all the symbolism points with unerring precision and definiteness to one country, which so far has not, before this "uncovering" of the things that shall be hereafter, appeared in divine history. We shall find that country to be Arabia.

Recalling, too, that the last of the four invasions was under Odoacer, in 476 A.D., then the events of the fifth trumpet must, of necessity, be after that date.

The Era of Justinian

It seems altogether fitting that we should give here a brief sketch of events which transpired in the Eastern Empire during the interval between the fourth and fifth trumpets. Said Myers:

135

"During the half century immediately following the fall of Rome, the Eastern emperors struggled hard and sometimes doubtfully to withstand the waves of barbarious inundation which constantly threatened Constantinople with the same awful calamities that had befallen the Imperial City of the west . . .

Fortunately, in the year 527, there ascended the Eastern throne, a prince of unusual ability, to whom fortune gave a general of such rare genius that his name has been allotted a place in the short list of great commanders of the world. Justinian was the name of the prince, and Belisarius, that of the soldier. The sovereign has given name to the period, which is called after him, the "Era of Justinian."—Myers ncient History. page 592.

His reign was marked by two outstanding accomplishments. First, he restored to the Empire, Africa, from the Vandals. Italy was next recovered from the Goths. But the second, and most outstanding achievement of his era, was the collection and publication by him, of the Corpus Juris Civilis, the "Body of the Roman Law." By this publication, Justinian earned the title of "the Lawgiver of Civilization."

His reign was followed by a half century of unimportance until we come to the reign of Heraclius. For many years he struggled heroically to maintain the integrity of the empire.

This brings us up to the time of the fifth trumpet and the Saracen invasion of the empire.

This period covered by the fifth trumpet is manifestly of great importance, because of the space given it. It is also quite evident that this epoch, referred to as "those days" is one of considerable length; because it is described as a period of suffering and woe which would last "five months," or one-hundred and fifty days. A day in prophetic history is equivalent to one year in actual history. Shall we pause in our present train of thought to consider this.

Back in the book of Ezekiel, that prophet received a command to graphically demonstrate how the city of Jerusalem should be besieged, of which demonstration it was said, "This shall be a *sign* to the house of Israel. So like the Book of Revelation, we are *moving in the realm of signs or symbols*. With this understanding shall we read:

> "Lie thou also upon thy left side, and lay the iniquity of the house of Israel upon it: *according to the number of the days* that thou shalt lie upon it thou shalt bear their iniquity.

> For I have laid upon thee the *years of their iniquity,* according to the *number of days,* three hundred and ninety days, so shalt thou bear the iniquity of the house of Israel.

> And when thou hast accomplished them, lie again on thy right side, and thou shalt bear the iniquity of the house of Judah *forty days; I have appointed thee each day for a year."* (Ezekiel 4:4-6).

That a day in prophetic history denotes a year is further revealed to us in the prophesy of the time interval between the commandment to restore and build Jerusalem and the coming of Christ, the Messiah. In Daniel 9:25.

> "Know therefore and understand, that from the going forth to restore and to build Jerusalem unto the Messiah, the Prince, shall be seven weeks, and threescore and two weeks: The street shall be built again, and the wall, even in troublous times."

It was 483 years from the going forth of the command to rebuild Jerusalem until Christ came to the Jordan and was immersed of John and there became the Annointed One, in that he was annointed with the descent of the Holy Spirit like a dove upon him.

So here again a day stands for a year in prophetic parlance. At the mouth of two witnesses, the Scripture declares, a matter is established.

Thus we see that this epoch was one of great length.

Shall we now hear the blast of the fifth angel: "And the fifth angel sounded, and I saw a star fall from heaven into the earth."

The first action that follows the blast of the trumpet is the fall of a star from heaven to earth. We have already discovered in earlier studies of symbolism, that a star represents a leader. Attila, "the scourge of God," you will remember was symbolized by a burning star. That a man, and not a literal star is referred to, is made clear by the next words, "and to *him*", *definitely a person, was given the* Key to the bottomless pit. And *he* opened the bottomless pit.

The fact that the star had fallen would indicate that at the time the Key was given to him, he did not possess the pre-eminence he once enjoyed. We shall find this to be true, historically, when we uncover the identity of this great leader.

When this great fallen star, or leader was given the Key, he opened the bottomless pit and out of it poured a dense smoke, "as the smoke of a great furnace."

Clearly this smoke that arose is a symbol of some spiritual force, for it affects "the sun," or power of government "we have found the sun represents great dignitaries over a government," and "the air," or spiritual realm. Paul said:

"Wherein in times past ye walked according to the course of this world, according to the prince of the power of the *air,* the spirit that now worketh in the children of disobedience." (Eph. 2:2).

This proves that the "air" represents the spiritual realm. So this leader was to influence both earthly government and spiritual affairs. Shall we keep this important fact in mind.

"And there came out of the *smoke,* (this spiritual activity) locusts upon the earth."

But they are not such locusts as men know. They do not feed upon vegetation; they attack men, but only those men who have not the seal of God upon their foreheads. They do not kill—they torment with a torment as scorpions, so that men would desire death rather than endure such suffering. These, then, are a symbol and a chilling one at that.

Since we are ever in the realm of symbols, our next task is to unravel the meaning of the symbol of a locust.

Turning to the Scriptures as our unerring and infallible guide, in the interpretation of symbolism, we find in the Book of Joel, that the armies of Assyria which were to overthrow the land of Palestine, were likened to locusts, as in the passage before us in Revelation. Shall we note the similarities:

1. First, both were likened to *locusts*.
   "And that which the palmerworm (a different stage of development of the locust) hath left hath the *locust* eaten, and that which the *locust* hath left hath the cankerworm eaten." (Joel 1:4)

   And there came out of the smoke locusts upon the earth." (Rev. 9:3)

2. Both had *teeth of a lion*.
   "For a nation is *come up* (like Revelation's *locusts* arising out of "the bottomless pit") upon the land, strong and without number, whose teeth are the teeth of a lion, and he hath the cheek teeth of a great lion. (Joel 1:6).
   "Their teeth were as the teeth of lions." (Rev. 9:8)

3. A *trumpet* is sounded before each army of locusts invade.
   "Blow ye the *trumpet* in Zion, and sound an alarm in my holy mountain." (Joel 2:1).
   "And the fifth *trumpet* angel sounded." (Rev. 9:1)

4. Both of them had the appearance of horsemen.
   "The appearance of them is as the appearance of *horses;* and as *horsemen,* so shall they run." (Joel 2:4).
   "And the shapes of the locusts were like unto *horses* prepared for battle." (Rev. 9:7)

5. Both represented a nation.
   "For a nation is come upon my land strong and without number." (Joel 1:6)
   "The locusts of Revelation are said to have a King over them, "And they had a king over them, which is the angel of the bottomless pit." (Rev. 9:11)

Thus again the Bible clearly interprets the symbolism for us. It is plain that the locusts are conquering armies, sweeping over the earth (the Roman Empire) in great numbers. The locusts were not insects, because they hurt no green thing, but were men because they were to hurt only men, who had not the seal of God in their foreheads. (Rev. 9:4)

But this conquering people was to be unlike the Assyrians, the *locusts* of Joel's vision, in that the *locusts* of Revelation were to be a people that had *spiritual power* as well as *physical power*. In fact, it is quite evident that their *spiritual* power was to far exceed their *physical* force, although their physical power was to be very great.

The repeated reference to "scorpions" in verses 3, 5, 10, emphasizes the predominance of the spiritual over the physical, especially when we consider verse 10. "And they had tails like scorpions, and there "were *stings in their tails*."

Shall we read in connection with this passage one from Isaiah 9:15: "And the *prophet* that *teaches lies,* he is the *tail*."

The "tail" is used symbolically to represent the deadly power of *false prophesy.* Shall we keep this fact in mind for future illumination.

This fatal sting in this spiritual power, likened to scorpions, because of its deadly poison, was in their tails. Since a false prophet who teaches lies is likened to a tail, then this deadly sting lay in the spiritual poison which was to be spread over the earth by some false prophet—a fallen star—and his hosts of armed false religionists.

Again we wish to call attention to the statement that these armies of locusts "had a king over them *which is the angel of the bottomless pit,* whose name in the Hebrew tongue is Abaddon, but in the Greek tongue hath his name Apollyon." (Rev. 9:11)

1. First, he is a King, and a King of spiritual forces, as well as of physical. Jesus spoke of the devil as being the prince of this world (John 14:30), and Paul considered the realm of satan as a kingdom, for he declared, "Who hath delivered us from the power of darkness and hath translated us into the Kingdom of his dear son." (Col. 1:13).

2. Second, he is called an angel. In Daniel 10:13, 20, we read;

"But the prince of the kingdom of Persia withstood me one and twenty days, but, lo, Michael, one of the chief princes, came to help me; and I remained there with the Kings of Persia. Then said he, knowest thou wherefore I come unto thee? And now will I return to fight with the Prince of Persia: and when I am gone forth, lo, the Prince of Grecia shall come."

From these verses, it appears that the great empires of earth have each a presiding or ruling angel over them. This vision in the apocalypse, then, reveals to us a mighty nation, having a supernatural origin, rising from some obscure region, spreading its forces, both physical and spiritual over the earth, (or Roman Empire). These armies were to be largely horsemen and the head of this nation was to come out of the bottomless pit and be called Abaddon and Apollyon.

This is quite revealing since in Rev. 20:1, 2, we discover that the bottomless pit is the home of the devil:

"And I saw an angel come down from heaven, having the Key to the bottomless pit and a great chain in his hand. And he laid hold on the dragon, that old serpent, which is the devil and satan and bound him a thousand years, and *cast him into the bottomless pit.*"

By this we learn that these locusts, or armies carrying on a conquest, both physical and spiritual, were led by a leader motivated by the devil himself. No wonder he is called Abaddon, which in the Hebrew tongue means, "destruction;" and Apollyon, which in the Hebrew tongue means, "one who exterminates."

Of the devil, said Jesus:

"Fear not them which kill the body, but are not able to kill the soul; but rather fear *him* which is able to destroy both body and soul in hell." (Matt. 10:28)

So this Abaddon was able to destroy the body and this Apollyon could exterminate the very soul, the body, by conquest of war, the soul, by false teaching.

It would seem that both Hebrew and Greek names were used

to warn both the Hebrew Christians and the Greek, or Gentile Christians, of his destructive and exterminating power.

Having interpreted the symbolism in the ninth chapter, we now turn to history to identify the leader, the locust army, and the physical and spiritual warriors.

The locust, the ground work of all this symbolism, is peculiarly Arabic. It was an east wind that swept from Arabia, that brought the plague of locusts at the time of the exodus of the children of Israel from Egypt. Syria was often invaded by locusts which came from Arabia.

These locusts had the shape of horses. Arabia is famous as the home of the horse. From time immemorial, Arabia has produced the most famous horses of the world. The Arabian horse is sought by men of all nations. Says Gibbon, in his Decline and Fall of the Roman Empire, Vol. 5, pages 78, 79:

"Arabia, in the opinion of the naturalist, is the genuine and original country of the *horse*; the climate most propitious, not indeed to the size, but to the spirit and swiftness, of that generous animal . . . these horses are educated in tents, among the children of the Arabs, with a tender familiarity, which trains them in the habits of gentleness and attachment . . . their powers are reserved for the moments of flight and pursuit; but no sooner do they feel the touch of the hand or the stirrup, than they dart away with the swiftness of the wind."

Truly, the zoology of the symbolism points, beyond the least doubt, to the land of Arabia.

Again, the locusts "were like horses prepared for battle." The Arabians unlike the four invaders of the Western, or Latin portion of the Empire, namely Goths, Vandals, Huns and Heruli, were horsemen, and moved over the landscape with the swiftness of the locust. There was not a foot soldier among them, whereas the invaders of the Western Roman Empire were pre-eminently foot soldiers.

The vision of the flying angel in (Rev. 8:13), not only serves to

set off the first four trumpets in a distinct group from the remaining three "woe" trumpets, but also to show that the events in
the first group are separated by a substantial interval of time,
possibly quite a long one from the events pictured in the "voices
of the trumpet of the three angels which are yet to sound."

This we find to be manifestly true. The armies which invaded
the Greek, or eastern half of the Roman Empire in 622 A.D., a
century and a half after Odoacer conquered Rome in 476 A.D.,
were from Arabia, and horsemen that wore turbans which would
give the impression of crowns being worn. The historians of that
period often speak of these people as "the turbaned Arabs."

The Sabeans, were a tribe of the Arabians and in the Old Testament we read of them as follows:

"The Sabeans of the wilderness who wore bracelets upon
their hands and beautiful crowns upon their heads." (Ezek.
23:42).

We can readily see how yellow turbaned horsemen would resemble men wearing crowns of gold as John beheld them in the
vision of the fifth trumpet.

We found that the locusts had faces of men, but to this description was added the female adornment of long hair.

The Arabs of this date, the sixth century, wore long hair. Pliny,
(Nat. History 7:28), speaks of the turbaned Arabs with their un-
cut hair. Ammianus Marcellinus, in the fourth century speaks of
the long haired Arabs, as also did Jerome, in the fifth century.

In this vision John sees the riders flash by with long hair
streaming backward in their swift flight.

These horsemen also had breastplates of iron. The chroniclers of
the Arabian wars often speak of the iron coats of mail worn by
them. I have before me Gibbon's History, Vol. 5, page 132, and
there he says, in part:

The resentment of the public and private loss stimulated

143

Abu Saphian to collect a body of three thousand men, seven hundred of whom were armed with cuirasses."

I have the Koran before me and in it I read, "God hath given you coats of mail to defend you in your wars."

By these quotations, and an array of evidence, we know this invasion comes from Arabia. Before six hundreds A.D., the Arabs were little known as they lived in the trackless sands of the desert, safe from outside nations by virtue of the nature of their habitat. But in the first part of the seventh century, they poured out of their desert wilderness and spilled out upon the Roman Empire, with a fury unparalled in the annals of warfare.

Said Myers: "We have seen the German barbarians of the north descend upon and wrest from the Roman Empire, all its provinces in the west. We are now to watch a similar attack made upon the empire, by the Arabs of the south, and to see wrested from the Emperors of the East, a large part of the lands still remaining under their rule." Myers Ancient History, page 595.

This startling invasion was inspired by a fanatical religious leader, by the name of Mohammed. Hear a brief history of this man by Myers;

"Mohammed, the great Prophet of the Arabs, was born in the Holy City of Mecca probably in the year 570 A.D. He sprang from the distinguished tribe of the Koreish, the custodians of the sacred shrine of the Koaba, (so named from it's having the shape of a cube). In his early years, he was a shepherd and a watcher of flocks by night, as the great religious teachers Moses and David had been before him. Later, he became a merchant and a camel driver.

He declared that he had visions, in which the angel Gabriel appeared to him and made to him revelations which he was commanded to make known to his fellow men. The essence of the new faith which he was to teach was this: There is but one God, and Mohammed is his Prophet.

The teachings of Mohammed at last aroused the anger of a powerful party among the Koreiah, who feared that they, as the guardians of the national idols of the Koaba, would be compromised in the eyes of the other tribes, by allowing such heresy to be openly taught by one of their number, and accordingly they began to persecute Mohammed and his followers.

To escape these persecutions, Mohammed fled to the neighboring city of Medina. This *"Hegira"* or flight," as the word signifies, occurred 622 A.D. and was considered by the Moslems as such an important event, in the history of their religion, that they adopted it as the beginning of a new era, and from it still continue to reckon historical dates."

Myers Continues:

"His cause being warmly espoused by the inhabitants of Medina, Mohammed, now, assumed along with the character of a lawgiver, and moral teacher, that of a warrior."—Myers Ancient History, pages 596, 597.

The year following the Hegira, he and his followers began to attack and plunder the adjacent cities. The flame of sacred war was soon kindled. Their recklessness was intensified by his teaching that death met in fighting the infidels (as all non-Mohammedians were termed) guaranteed the martyr instant entrance into the joys of paradise.

Mohammed died ten years after the beginning of a religious war that was destined to conquer Persia, Syria, Egypt, North Africa, Spain and France. Hear Myers again:

In the year 732 A.D., just one hundred years after the death of the Prophet, the Franks, under their leader, Charles Martel, and their allies, met the Moslems upon the plains of Tours, in the center of Gaul. The Arabs suffered an over whelming defeat and soon withdrew behind the Pyrenees."—Myers Ancient History, Page 600.

Here we have read the brief history of a movement that began like a whirlwind out of the desert and conducted a war that was

both carnal and religious, in which Mohammed—the fallen star
—and a religious prophet, scorched much of the empire, and particularly the eastern section. To extend his religion, he resorted
to the sword. They went forth like scorpions with sting in their
tails, to poison the earth with their lies of the false prophet—
Mohammed. A like period of conquest is unknown in the annals of
history.

This had all the fatalism, fanaticism and fierceness of a holy
war, whose motivation sprang from the bottomless pit.

The term translated *"Pit"* is used in (Ezek. 31:17), and
(Luke 8:31) and (Rev. 20:1), with the thought of "Hell," or
abode of that prince of darkness. That is evidently the meaning
here, indicating that the fallen star would employ hellish means
to further his work of Abaddon, or destruction. This could only be
fulfilled by such a system of imposture and false religion. Out of
the smoke of the new fanatical faith they rushed upon the earth to
torment, to sting and to darken the minds of men.

These "locusts" did not destroy any green thing of the earth.
They destroyed the bodies and souls of men. Said Abubeker, the
successor to the prophet, after Mohammed's death:

> "When you fight the battles of the Lord, acquit yourselves
> like men . . . destroy no palm trees, nor burn any fields of corn,
> cut down no fruit trees, nor do any mischief to cattle, only
> such as you kill to eat."—Gibbons Decline and Fall of the
Roman Empire, Vol. 5, P. 189.

Thus, we see that the policy of the Saracens was in sharp contrast
to that of the Goths. The Goths destroyed "the trees of one third
of the earth, and every green thing." The Arabs coming out of the
treeless deserts of Arabia, looked upon the tree almost with veneration. How remarkable that the Book of Revelation should emphasize the diverse actions of the armies of the first and fifth
trumpets! How exactly did history corroborate the difference
noted by John!

Another amazing feature of this vision is not only the command "not to hurt any green thing," but they *were to hurt,*

"only those men which have not the seal of God in their foreheads." "And to them it was given that *they should not kill* them but that they should be tormented five months and their torment was as the torment of a scorpion, when he striketh a man." (Rev. 9:4, 5)

While atrocities did occur and it was a war of the sword, yet it is remarkable that they went forth not so much to slay. They went forth as missionaries of the false prophet. They fought the enemy on the battlefield, but upon cessation of hostilities, they converted the vanquished. This is just the opposite of the western spectacle. There the invaders conquered, but were converted *by* the vanquished. A part of the marching orders given by Abubeker, successor to Mohammed, were as follows:

"As you go on, you will find some religious persons who live retired in monasteries, and propose to themselves to serve God that way: Let them alone, and neither kill them nor destroy their monasteries. (See note at bottom of page)

And you will find another sort of people, that belong *to the synagogue of Satan,* who have shaven crowns, be sure you cleave their skulls, and give them no quarter till they either turn Mohametans or pay "tribute."—Gibbon's Decline and Fall of the Roman Empire, Vol. 5, Pages 189, 190.

Note how Gibbon refers to those of the synagogue of Satan! In our study of the seven churches, the false teachers of the Smyrnan period were referred to as the synagogue of Satan. This finally developed into "the depths of Satan," in the Thyratira period—the Roman Catholic period. The invasion of the Eastern Roman Empire by the Saracens, or Arabs, met with the monks who represented the syangogue of Satan, which reached its full fruition in the depths of Satan, before the Thyratira period, roughly 400 A.D. to 1500 A.D., came to its fulness of fulfillment.

These fanatical missionaries of Mohammed were to torment the earth (those who did not have the seal of God), for five months. This period we have already found to be one-hundred and fifty years—five months being one hundred and fifty days, or one hundred and fifty years—a day in prophetic history being one year.

And was this period of torment fulfilled?

(Note: "M. Pauu (Recherches sur les Egyptiens, Tom. 11, P. 192, Edition Lausame) represents the Bedoweens as the implacable enemies of the Christian monks."

In 632 A.D., the Arabs broke forth in their religious war upon the nations. In 722 A.D., exactly a century after they emerged from their desert fortresses, they were defeated by Martel in the Battle of Tours, in Gaul, and driven back over the Pyrenees. In 750, the vast dominion of the Caliphs, was rent with discention. Hear Myers:

> "At the close of the first century of the Hegira, the Caliphs were the most potent and absolute monarchs of the globe.

> But in a short time the extended empire, through the quarrels of sectaries and the ambitions of rival aspirants for the honors of the Caliphate, was broken in fragments, and from three capitals—from Bagdad, upon the Tigris, from Cairo, upon the Nile, and from Cordova, upon the Guadalquiver— were issued the commands of three rival Caliphs, each of whom was regarded by his adherents as the sole rightful spiritual and civil successor of Mohammed. All however, held the great Prophet in the same reverence, all maintained, with equal zeal the sacred character of the Koran, and all prayed with their faces turned toward the holy city of Mecca."— Myers Ancient History, Page 600.

After this division, the Saracens gradually gave up their designs of universal conquest and began to seek the ways of peace.

By the last quarter of the eighth century, they reached what has been called the golden age of Saracen power. Bagdad was called "the City of Peace." This was the age of "the Arabian Nights."

In the second year of Haroun Al Rashids' reign (782 A.D.), we find him engaged in friendly correspondence with the Christian rulers of the empire. From that time forward, the Saracens ceased their efforts to force Mohammedanism upon the earth. They had fulfilled their mission as portrayed in the days of the fifth trumpet. And how long it had been since the beginning of this torment? It is now A.D. 782. The holy war of the false prophet began in 632. That is one hundred and fifty years, or five months! And John said, "And to them it was given that they should not kill them,"—those sealed of God, "but that they should be tormented five months!"

So, we close the exposition of this fifth trumpet period with secular history substantiating and corroborating inspired symbolic predictions of that period. Verily, the Word of God is yea and amen!

The Sixth Trumpet

Text (9:13-21)

13 And the sixth angel sounded, and I heard a voice from the horns of the golden altar which is before God, 14 one saying to the sixth angel that had the trumpet, Loose the four angels that are bound at the great river Euphrates. 15 And the four angels were loosed, that had been prepared for the hour and day and month and year, that they should kill the third part of men. 16 And the number of the armies of the horsemen was twice ten thousand times ten thousand: I heard the number of them. 17 And thus I saw the horses in the vision, and them that sat on them, having breastplates as of fire and of hyacinth and of brimstone: and the heads of the horses are as the heads of lions; and out of their mouths proceeded fire and smoke and brimstone. 18 By these three plagues was the third part of men killed, by the fire and the smoke and the brimstone, which proceeded out of their mouths. 19 For the power of the horses is in their mouth, and in their tails: for their tails are like unto serpents, and have heads; and with them they hurt. 20 And the rest of mankind, who were not killed with these plagues, repented not of the works of their hands, that they should not worship demons, and the idols of gold, and of silver, and of brass, and of stone, and of wood; which can neither see, nor hear, nor walk: 21 and they repented not of their murders, nor of their sorceries, nor of their fornication, nor of their thefts.

In the study of the fifth trumpet, we have reviewed the rise and conquest of the religion of Islam, beginning under the leadership of the false prophet, Mohammed, and reaching its zenith under the reign of the Caliphs. The termination of that period, we found, came when Rashid, in 782 A.D., just one hundred and fifty years after the death of Mohammed in 632 A.D., brought the holy war to a close.

149

But a very startling, as well as illuminating fact in the history of the religion of Islam, is that there were two distinct stages. First, its phase in the Saracen invasion, dated from the death of Mohammed in 632 A.D. But this period came to an abrupt crest in the defeat of the Mohammedans in the Battle of Tours, A.D. 732. There followed a long period of stagnation, but it had a wonderful recrudescence and revival under the invasion of the Ottoman Turks.

Strangely, these were not Mohammedians at all, but began their triumphant march against the Mohammedans. Later the Turks became Mohammedans, largely for political advantages, for much the same reason that Constantine embraced the Christian faith, after the Battle of Milvian Bridge.

And the fifth and sixth trumpets present, in the language of symbolism, this two-fold stage or phase of the march of the religion of Islam. While separated from the four preceeding trumpets, these two trumpets are closely linked together, leaving the seventh trumpet to follow, standing all by itself.

It should be noted, too, that the fifth and sixth trumpets are blown without any intervening symbolism, again showing their close affinity. Since the fifth trumpet introduced the mighty Mohammedan movement, it logically follows that the sixth trumpet heralds another tide of invasion which will overrun the decaying and disintegrating Eastern Empire. Shall we begin the consideration of the sixth trumpet:

vs. 13 "And the sixth angel sounded, and I heard a voice from the four horns of the golden altar which is before God." John does not say who spoke, but only records what he heard. The voice is addressed to the angel that has the sixth trumpet. The voice said:

vs. 14 "Loose the four angels which are bound in the great river Euphrates."

Shall we note that whereas the authorized, or King James version here reads, "'Bound *in* the great river Euphrates," the Greek preposition is not *"en,"* but "epi," which means, "upon," "at," or "by." The four angels were bound, not *"in,"* but *"at"* or *"by,'* this great river. Then, we know this second "woe" must come from the region beyond the Euphrates River. It is a fact, in history, that the Turks did make their sudden appearance from that quarter of the world.

Their exact origin is still a mystery, but a few years before A.D. 1000, a fierce Tartar race, characterized by their great numbers and brave ferocity, burst forth from their habitat, east of the Caspian Sea, and moved in a southwesterly direction, until they reached the Euphrates River. By their conquests a vast territory, consisting of Persia and part of India, east of the Euphrates, fell under their sway of dominion. But as if bound "by" this river, they remained for some years on the eastern banks.

Though originally idolaters, they embraced the beliefs of Islam, the faith of the conquered. After a half century, in A.D. 1055, they conquered Bagdad. In 1057, the Caliph of that city commissioned them to carry the Koran and the faith of Islam westward. In that same year, they crossed the Euphrates and invaded the Eastern Roman Empire. Now we come to the meaning of the four angels which had for sixty years bound them at the Euphrates River.

The four angels which stood upon the four corners of earth, in the seventh chapter, were symbols of the four barbarian powers which overran the Western Empire. Likewise, these four angels bound at the River Euphrates, represent four powers. On page 523, Volume 5 of Gibbon's Decline and Fall of the Roman Empire, we find that at the death of Malek Shah, the Turkoman Kingdom was divided into four divisions. Says Gibbon:

"The greatness and unity of the Turkish Empire expired in the person of Malek Shah. His vacant throne was disputed by his brother and his four sons; and after a series of civil wars, the treaty which reconciled the surviving candidates confirmed a lasting separation in the Persian Dynasty, the eldest and principle branch of the house of Seljuk. The three younger Dynasties were those of Kerman, of Syria, and of Roum."

The four divisions, we see, were Persia, Kerman or India, Syria, and Roum, or Asia Minor. These are the four powers symbolized by the four angels bound by the Euphrates River.

vs. 15 "And the four angels were loosed, which were prepared for an hour, and a day, and a month, and a year, to slay the third part of men."

The term here used for "year," is not "kairos," the prophetic year of twelve months, or three-hundred and sixty days, but "eniantos," the word for a regular solar year, which is three-hundred sixty five and one-fourth days. Putting all the time elements of an hour, a day, a month and a year together, we have a total of three hundred and ninety-six years and four months. 365 ¼ plus 30 plus 1 plus 1/12 equals 396 and 4/12 days, or in years, 396 years and four months.

We shall pass by the fulfillment of this prophesy until we reach the latter part of this chapter. Shall we continue with the description of these armies.

vs. 16 "And the number of the army of horsemen were two hundred thousand thousand, and I heard the number of them." In other words, countless numbers are indicated.

Literally, in the original, it reads: *"Two myriads of myriads."* This would signify a number too astronomical to compute. No wonder John says, "I *heard* the number of them," or else he could never have counted them.

Gibbon says of this great host of horsemen:

> "The myriads of Turkish horsemen overspread a frontier of six hundred miles, from Tauris to Arzeroum, and the blood of one hundred and thirty thousand Christians was a grateful sacrifice to the Arabian prophet. Gibbon's Decline and Fall of the Roman Empire, Vol. 5, page 512.

Again, same Volume, page 515, we read:

> "Again the report of this bold invasion, which threatened his hereditary dominions, Alp Arslan flew to the scene of action, at the head of thirty thousand horse. His rapid and skilful evolutions distressed and dismayed the superior numbers of the Greeks."

Again, on page 525, same Volume 5, we read:

> "Soliman accepted the royal standard, which gave him the free
> conquest and hereditary command of the provinces of the
> Roman Empire, from Arzeroum to Constantinople, and the
> unknown regions of the west. Accompanied by four brothers,
> he passed the Euphrates. The Turkish camp was soon seated
> in the neighborhood of Kutaieh in Phrygia; as his flying cav-
> alry laid waste the country as far as the Hellespont and the
> Black Sea. Since the decline of the Empire, the peninsula
> of Asia Minor had been exposed to the transient, though de-
> structive inroads of the Persians and Saracens, but the fruits
> of a lasting conquest were reserved for the Turkish Sultan."

Surely, it cannot be mere coincidence that the Turkish armies
of horsemen were counted, not by thousands, but by "myriads,"
and the infidel historian, Gibbon, used the very language of Revelation to denote the great numbers of horsemen invading the
Eastern Empire from across the Euphrates River.

And note the next verse in Revelation:

vs. 17 "And thus I saw the horses in the vision, and them that
sat on them, having breastplates of fire, and of jacinth, and
brimstone. And the heads of the horses were as heads of lions:
and out of their mouths issued fire and smoke and brimstone."

Here is expressed the conquering power of lions. Said Gibbon,
Vol. 5, page 512, as he describes the leader of this host of horsemen:

> "The name of Alp Arslan, the Valiant *lion*, is expressive of the
> popular idea of the perfection of *man*; and the successor of
> Togrul displayed the fierceness and generosity of the royal
> animal."

There is also presented here the swiftness of *horses* and the
destructive agencies of *fire, smoke* and *brimstone.*

The breastplates worn, were likened to fire, jacinth, and brimstone, or colors of red, blue and yellow. These were until recently,
when the Turkish uniforms were modernized, the colors of Turkish

battle uniforms. Doubtless, these colors were on the breastplates of the horsemen of John's vision.

But John saw fire and smoke and brimstone belching out of the horses mouths. This symbolism is again in wonderful agreement with the actual history of the Turkoman invasion from across the Euphrates.

Gunpowder was unknown to the Romans and was never used by either the invading Goths, Vandals, Huns or Hernli of the four invasions of the Western Empire. Neither was it employed by the Saracens in the invasion of the Eastern Empire under the fifth Trumpet.

But not so with the Turkish invasion, of the second "woe" trumpet. Gibbon, the best known authority on the History of the Decline and Fall of the Rmoan Empire informs us of a new and revolutionary weapon used by the Turks. He writes of the use of gunpowder by the Turkish Sultan sacking Constantinople.

"Among the implements of destruction, he studied with peculiar care the recent and tremendous discovery of the Latins; and his artillery surpassed whatever had yet appeared in the world. A founder of cannon, a Dane (or Dacian) or Hungarian, who had been almost starved in the Greek service, deserted to the Moslems, and was liberally entertained by the Turkish sultan. Mahomet was satisfied with the answer of his first question, which he eagerly pressed on the artist, "Am I able to cast a cannon capable of throwing a ball or stone of sufficient size to batter the walls of Constantinople? I am not ignorant of their strength; but were they more solid than those of Babylon, I could oppose an engine of superior power; the position and management of that engine must be left to your engineers." Gibbon's Decline and Fall of the Roman Empire, Volume 6, Pages 379, 380.

On pages 388 and 389, of the same volume, we read:

"The great cannon of Mahomet has been separately noticed; *an important and visible object in the history of the times:*

but that enormous engine was flanked by two fellows almost of equal magnitude; the long order of the Turkish artillery was pointed against the walls; fourteen batteries thundered at once on the most accessible places; and of one of these it was ambiguously expressed, and it was mounted with one hundred and thirty guns, or that it discharged one hundred and thirty bullets. Yet in the power and activity of the Sultan, we may discern the infancy of the new science."

Thus we see why the symbolism of fire, smoke and brimstone was used. It fittingly represented the use of fire arms and gunpowder in the war of invasion.

vs. 18, 19 "By these three was the third part of men killed, by the fire and by the smoke and by the brimstone, which issued out their mouths."

While the new use of firearms may be a part of this symbolism, since the two invasions were primarily punishments of God upon the apostate Eastern Empire, it would seem there is also a deeper signification. Shall we study the meaning of these three symbols.

1. *Fire* is a token of persecution. Christ said: "I am come to send fire upon the earth and what will I if it be already kindled." (Luke 12:49). Also, fire stands for God's wrath, its effects being war.

"There went up a smoke out of his nostrils, and *fire out of* his *mouth*. (Psa. 18:8).

"A fire shall come forth out of Hesbbon and a flame from the midst of Sihon." (Jer. 48:45).

2. *Smoke* is a symbol of the anger and wrath of God. This we read in (Psa. 18:8).

In Revelation 14:11, we read of "the smoke of their torment ascending up."

3. *Brimstone* is a symbol of the judgments of God as evidenced by the destruction of the cities of Sodom and Gomorrah.

155

In Psalms 11:6, we read: "Upon the wicked he shall rain snares (or quick burning coals), *fire* and *brimstone*."

"And I will call for a sword against him (Gog) throughout all my holy mountains, saith the Lord God . . . and I will rain upon him and upon his bands, and upon the many peoples that are with him, an overflowing rain, and great hailstones, *fire* and *brimstone*." (Ezek. 38:21, 22)

So we see that fire (persecution), smoke (God's wrath) and brimstone (His judgments) were thus symbolized as the invading Turks meted out the wraths and judgments of God upon those who were not sealed in their foreheads.

As to the power resident in the tails, we have already dealt with that under the fifth trumpet and found it to be lies of the false prophet. The added symbolism "their tails were like serpents", reminds us that the source of all lies and false teaching is that old serpent, called the devil and satan. (Rev. 12:9). Jesus said of him:

"Ye are of your father the devil, and the lusts of your father will ye do. He was a murderer from the beginning, and *abode not in the truth,* because there is no truth in him. When he speaketh a *lie,* he speaketh of his own: for he is a *liar,* and the father of it." (John 8:44)

This supernatural power to enflame multitudes, even stern, fierce and blood-thirsty men with such a degree of religious fanaticism, rising at times to the highest pitch of frenzy, is without parallel in human history. Nothing but smoke rising out of the bottomless pit, the final abode of the devil, could properly symbolize this.

All these symbols are so largely a repetition of those of the fifth trumpet, that although a different invading force is indicated, the same motivating force of the false teaching of the bottomless pit is behind it all.

The history of Islam agrees in startling detail with the meaning of these symbols. We can draw no other conclusion than the most logical one, that we find the fulfillment of prophecy is proved by the coming to pass of the thing prophesied.

"And by these three was the third of men killed."

In the comments under Rev. 9:15, we found that the length of the time of this trumpet was to be "an hour, and a day, and a month, and a year," or a period of three hundred and ninety-six years and four months.

Early in January 1057, the Turkomen marched out of Bagded under the commission of the Caliph, to begin their long conquest. On May 29th, 1453, they sacked Constantinople, ending the Eastern Empire, just *three-hundred and ninety-six years and four months,* lacking a few days, from the time they crossed the Euphrates! Again history and Apocalyptic symbolism march hand in hand. One predicts; the other fulfills!

Again we note that they were to destroy the third part of the earth (or to John's understanding, the Roman Empire).

We have already found that the earth, or the Roman Empire, was divided into three divisions.

The Goths and Vandals subjugated one "third part" of the Western Empire, described prophetically under the first four trumpets. The Saracens conquered a second "third part," known from that time as the Empire of the Caliphs, and the third "Third part," or the Grecian portion of the Eastern Empire, was overrun by the Turks, of the sixth trumpet.

Reasons For These Punishments

The remaining verses in this chapter plainly and startlingly give the reasons why these scorching punishments of the invading Saracens and Turks were brought upon the dying Empire. Shall we consider these reasons:

> *vs. 20* "And the rest of the men which were not killed by these plagues yet repented not of the *works of their hands.*"

First, that they should not worship devils, or demons. A demon is the spirit of a departed man. The saint worship of the great Pagan-Catholic Apostasy is demon worship. Listen to an infidel historian's account of the practices of that age. Says Gibbon, Vol. 5, Pages 1, 2 and 3.

"I have reviewed, with diligence and pleasure, the objects of ecclesiastical history by which the decline and fall of the Roman Empire were materially affected, the propagation of Christianity, the constitution of the Catholic Church, and the ruin of paganism. . . . At the head of this class, we may justly rank the worship of images, so fiercely disputed in the eighth and ninth centuries. (Note: he refers here to the war of the Iconoclasts-Image Breakers); since a question of popular superstition produced the revolt of Italy, the temporal power of the popes, and the restoration of the Roman Empire in the west.

The primitive Christians were possessed with an unconquerable repugnance to the use and abuse of images . . . the Mosaic law had severely proscribed all representations of the Diety . . . the wit of the Christian apologists was pointed against the foolish idolaters, who bowed before *the workmanship of their own hands,* the images of brass and marble . . . the first introduction of a symbolic worship was in the veneration of the cross, and of relics. The saints and martyrs, whose intercession was implored, were seated on the right hand of God; but the gracious and often supernatural favors, which in the popular belief, were showered round their tomb, conveyed an unquestionable sanction of the devout pilgrims, who visited and touched, and kissed these lifeless remains, the memorials of their merits and sufferings. But a memorial, more interesting than the skull or the sandals of a departed worthy, is the faithful copy of his person and features, delineated by the arts of painting and sculpture."

Second, that they should worship idols of gold, and silver, and brass, and stone, and of wood: "which neither can see, nor hear, nor walk."

To the passages already quoted from Gibbon on idol worship, we add from the same Volume 5, page 37, which gives the record of the proceedings of the Second General Council of Nice, held in 787, on the question of using icons or images.

"No more than eighteen days were allowed for the consummation of this important work: the iconoclasts (image breakers) appeared, not as judges, but as criminals or penitents: the scene was decorated by the legates of Pope Adrian and the Eastern patriarchs, the decrees were framed by the president Taracius, and ratified by the acclamations and subscriptions of three hundred and fifty bishops. They unanimously pronounced, that worship of images is agreeable to the Scriptures and reason, to the fathers and councils of the church; but they hesitate whether that worship be relative or direct, whether the Godhead, and the figure of Christ, be entitled to the same mode of adoration."

How dumb a person is to worship images, either directly or relatively is declared by the Scriptures. In Psalms 115:2-8, we read:

"Wherefore should the heathen say, where is now their God? But our God is in the heavens: he hath done whatever he pleased.

Their idols are silver and gold, the work of men's hands. They have mouths but they speak not; eyes have they, but they see not: They have ears, but they hear not: noses have they, but they smell not: feet have they, but they walk not: neither speak they through their throat.

They that make them *are like unto them, so is everyone that trusteth in them."*

That describes how dumb one is to bow down, or kneel before images, which are helpless to do anything, while the God in heaven whom we worship, the Psalmist says: "He hath done whatsoever He hath pleased!"

Third, "Neither repented they their *murders."* (Rev. 9:21)

One only has to read the history of the crusade against the Albigenses, those Christians who rejected the heathen abominations of the Church of Rome, began in 1209, to ascertain whether murders have been committed. Myers, in his Mideaval and Modern History, pages 142, 143, gives the beginning of this crusade against them:

"In the south of France was a sect of Christians, called Albigenses, (from the name of a city and district in which their tenants prevailed), who had departed so far from the orthodox faith that Pope Innocent 3, declared them to be, "more wicked than Saracens." He therefore, after a vain endeavor to turn them from their errors, called upon the French King, Philip 2nd, and his nobles to lead a crusade against the heretics and their rich and powerful patron, Raymond, 6th, Count of Toulouse. . . . a great number of his nobles responded eagerly to the call of the church. The leader of the first Crusade (1209-1213), was Simon de Monfort, a man cruel, callous, and relentless beyond belief. A great part of Languedoc, the beautiful country of the Albigenses, was made a desert, the *inhabitants being slaughtered and the cities burned.*

In 1229, the fury of a fresh crusade burst upon the Albigenses . . . the Albigensian heresy was soon totally extirpated by the tribunal of the Inquisition, which was set up in the country."

Fourth. "Nor of their sorceries." A sorcerer is one who deceives followers by tricks. A Scriptural example is Simon the Sorcerer. The papacy in every age has permitted the palming off upon the credulous, all kinds of pretended miracles. Statues of the Virgin weep, children see apparitions of the Virgin Mary, miraculous cures are claimed.

This has been going on since paganism apostitzed the church.

Fifth. "Neither repented they of their fornication. I quote from Gibbon, Vol. 5, page 38:

"I shall only notice the judgment of the bishops on the comparative merit of image worship and morality. A monk had concluded a truce with a demon of fornication, on condition of interrupting his daily prayers to a picture hung in his cell. His scruples prompted him to consult the Abbot. "Rather than abstain from adoring Christ and his mother in holy images, it would be better for you," replied the casuist, "to enter every brothel, and visit every prostitute in the city."

Sixth. "neither repented they of their *thefts.*"

Every cent an apostate church extorts from a gulible people by false pretense, is theft. That the disastrous sacking of Constantinople, in 1453, did not cause the church to repent of thefts, is evidenced by the fact that a Dominican friar, by the name of Tetzel, was selling indulgences to commit sin through Germany, in 1516, which led to Martin Luther's tacking his 95 theses on the door of the Castle Church in Wittenburg, in protestation. This set aflame the fires of the Reformation.

Thus, we see the destructive agency of the Turks, in the sixth trumpet period, was God's punishment inflicted upon an impenitent apostate church and her people.

How amazing is the corroboration of Apocalyptic symbolism and history!

CHAPTER X

THE MIGHTY ANGEL AND
THE LITTLE BOOK

Text (10:1-11)

1 And I saw another strong angel coming down out of heaven, arrayed with a cloud; and the rainbow was upon his head, and his face was as the sun, and his feet as pillars of fire; 2 and he had in his hand a little book open: and he set his right foot upon the sea, and his left upon the earth; 3 and he cried with a great voice, as a lion roareth: and when he cried, the seven thunders uttered their voices. 4 And when the seven thunders uttered *their voices*, I was about to write: and I heard a voice from heaven saying, Seal up the things which the seven thunders uttered, and write them not. 5 And the angel that I saw standing upon the sea and upon the earth lifted up his right hand to heaven, 6 and sware by him that liveth for ever and ever, who created the heaven and the things that are therein, and the earth and the things that are therein, and the sea and the things that are therein, that there shall be delay no longer: 7 but in the days of the voice of the seventh angel, when he is about to sound, then is finished the mystery of God, according to the good tidings which he declared to his servants the prophets. 8 And the voice which I heard from heaven, I heard it again speaking with me, and saying, Go, take the book which is open in the hand of the angel that standeth upon the sea and upon the earth. 9 And I went unto the angel, saying unto him that he should give me the little book. And he saith unto me, Take it, and eat it up; and it shall make thy belly bitter, but in thy mouth it shall be sweet as honey. 10 And I took the little book out of the angel's hand, and

ate it up; and it was in my mouth sweet as honey: and when I had eaten it, my belly was made bitter. 11 And they say unto me, Thou must prophesy again over many peoples and nations and tongues and kings.

As an interlude or parenthesis was introduced between sixth and seventh seals, so here between the sixth and seventh trumpet we come to the second parenthesis. Both of these interruptions were designed to bring comfort and blessing to the people of God.

Between the sixth trumpet, or second woe, and the seventh trumpet, or third woe, a parenthetical vision of the mighty angel with the little Book is given.

This vision, however, differs from the message of comfort found between the sixth and seventh seals. That vision emphasized the safety of the persecuted saints of God. This vision describes a mingling of the sweet and the bitter.

This vision belongs to the period of the sixth trumpet as evidenced by two facts:

1. *First,* the end of the sixth period is plainly stated in (Rev. 11:14)
   "The second woe is past; behold, the third woe cometh quickly."

2. *Second,* the mighty angel of this vision says, "But in the days of the voice of the seventh angel when he shall begin to sound." This plainly indicates the time of the sounding to the seventh angel to yet be future.

These two facts make it clear that this parenthetical vision belongs to the time of the sixth trumpet. We feel it is of utmost importance that we take cognizance of this fact.

The scenes of the first and second woe trumpets had to do with the earth (or Roman Empire) at large; and in beholding the Saracen and Turkoman invasions the question naturally arises, "How did it fare, in the fifth and sixth trumpet periods with the saints of God?" As the action in the happenings of the Roman Empire was arrested between the sixth and seventh seals in order that we might see the state of God's people in that day, so here again comes an interruption for the same reason.

Correspondences of this kind bear testimony to the Divine methodical plan that manifests itself throughout this marvelous book.

As to the time, or point of beginning of this vision of the little Book of the tenth chapter, we have found that the events of the preceeding chapter culminated with the sack of Constantinople in 1453 A.D. and the eventual overthrow of the Eastern Roman Empire. Therefore the symbols of the tenth and eleventh chapters must logically be subsequent, or follow that date.

vs. 1, 2 "And I saw another mighty angel come down from heaven, clothed with a cloud, and a rainbow was upon his head, and his face was as it were the sun, and his feet as pillars of fire.

The first thing we note here is that this angel is not one of the seven trumpet angels, but "*another* strong angel."

Nor would this be the Christ, as some have taught. He remains the Lamb of God that was slain, as we found Him in the vision of chapters four and five, at the right hand of God, who sat upon the throne. In that vision John saw "a *strong* angel proclaiming with a *loud* voice, "Who is worthy to open the book, and to loose the seals thereof?" (Rev. 5:2)

In the vision here in the tenth chapter John sees a "strong angel come down from heaven" (Rev. 10:1), who also "cried with a *loud* voice, as when a lion roareth. (Rev. 10:3) While the vision of the fourth chapter did not describe this strong or mighty angel, as did the vision in the tenth chapter, yet all evidence of circumstances points to the fact that they are one and the same angel. The word "another" refers to another angel other than the seventh trumpet angel.

In the former vision this strong angel appears at the opening of the seven sealed book, in the latter one the strong angel reappears at the giving of the *Little Open Book*. The former scroll *was to be opened by Christ*, the slain Lamb, the latter little book *was already open*, and it *was to be eaten* and digested *by John*. So we have here contrasted the *little open book*, with the *relatively large* (completely sealed—seven—scaled—number of completeness) book of chapter five.

The description of this mighty angel is so similar to that of the Son of Man in the first chapter, that it would seem to signify or symbolize some great movement in the which Christ is the moving cause. It implies that the whole action of this parenthetical vision is animated by the spirit of Christ.

The "rainbow upon His head" speaks of the covenant protection and promise vouch-saved to those having a part in this movement. Being "clothed with a cloud" and coming down from heaven indicates a mission of divine or heavenly character, coming to the earth or the Roman Empire. "His face as it were the sun" signifies the bringing of the light of the gospel of Christ again to the earth. This recalls to our minds the statement of Paul:

> "But if our gospel be hid, it is hid to them that are lost. In whom the god of this world hath blinded the minds of them which believe not, lest the light of the glorious gospel of Christ, who is the image of God, should shine unto them." (II Cor. 4:4)

The mention of "his feet as pillars of fire" is significant. The feet carry the messenger of God as he spreads the gospel over the earth. Again we quote Paul:

> "How beautiful are the feet of them that preach the gospel of peace and bring glad tidings of good things!" (Romans 10:15)

Remembering as we must that this vision corresponds to the time when the world was religiously and intellectually coming out of the "Dark Ages" and entering into the time of the "Renaissance"— that transitional movement in Europe between the fourteenth and fifteenth centuries,—the shining of the face and feet indicates a spreading of light and intelligence throughout the earth.

His having in his hand a little book sharply directs our attention to the source of this awakening, especially spiritually.

Remembering that in the closing verses of the second woe period (Rev. 9:20-21) we have the description of the great Roman Catholic apostacy, in which the worship of saints, idols of gold, silver, brass and stone, murders, sorceries, fornication and thefts are delineated, it would be both natural and logical that this movement described in the tenth and eleventh chapters has to do with the destruction of this apostacy by the instrumentality of a *little book*.

A Study in History

Shall we take a brief journey into history? Was there a movement at this time in the annals of the world in which a little book was the heart, center and soul? Indeed there was such a movement.

JOHN WYCLIFFE It began in the fourteenth century under the leadership of John Wycliffe, who was called "the morning star of the Reformation." He was the first man to begin a systematic translation of the Bible into English. I quote from the World Book Encyclopedia, Volume XII, pages 7902 and 3:

"He, Wycliffe, made systematic attacks on the established order of the church, and laid special emphasis on numerous vulnerable points, principally the right of the secular power to control the activities of the church.

More and more definitely, his ideas began to take form, and by 1375 he developed the thought which became the guilding principle of all his acts: that each individual Christian may claim immediate dependence upon God, without intervention of clergy, each individual having the right to take *the Bible* and reason as the foundations of his belief. In 1373 Pope Gregory XI issued *five bulls* against him."

JOHN HUSS Following Wcyliffe came John Huss (1373-1415) a Boehmian religious reformer and martyr. Again I turn to The World Book Encyclopedia, Volume VI, page 3299.

"To whom (John Huss) it was given to transmit from John Wycliffe to Martin Luther the torch when kindled the fires of the Protestant Reformation. In 1401 he was ordained a priest, becoming a popular preacher and confessor to the Queen of Bohemia. By this time the teachings of the English reformer Wycliffe made a profound impression upon him, and his translations of Wycliffe writings and spirited defense of his opinions stirred up the opposition of the university authorities, who forbade him to discuss the new doctrines. Neither this prohibition nor the bull issued by Pope Alexander V in 1409 against Wycliffe's teachings, nor the decree of excommunication directed against him and his disciples the following year seemed to turn Huss. Affairs moved rapidly to a crisis. In 1414 he was summoned to appear before the Council of Constance to answer charges of heresy. On his arrival in Constance, Huss was arrested and cast into Prison. On June 5, 1415, his case came to trial. The Council found him guilty of heresy and he was delivered over to the civil authorities to be burned at the stake. The sentence was carried out July 6th, and on the day of his execution his ashes were thrown into the waters of the Rhine."

JEROME OF PRAGUE He was a staunch companion and champion of John Huss and his defense of Huss's principles cost him his life. He was burned at stake May 30, 1416, and his ashes thrown into the River Rhine.

The movements, centered around "the Little Book," Ta Biblica —the Book, beginning in the fourteenth and fifteenth centuries reached maturity in the sixteenth century, about sixty-five years after the fall of Constantiople in 1453 A.D. This leads us to the great reformer, called the founder of Protestantism—Martin Luther (1483-1546 A.D.)

MARTIN LUTHER He entered the monastery of the Augustine order at Erfurt and in 1507 was ordained a priest. Then came the fateful year of 1517. I quote from Vol. VII, The World Book Encyclopedia, page 4158.

"In the year 1517, Johann Tetzel, a Dominican priest, appeared in the vicinity of Wittenburg (where Luther held the chair of Philosophy at the university; as a messenger of Pope Leo X, asking the people to secure indulgences. The proceeds of this sale were to go toward the building of Saint Peter's church in Rome."

Luther opposed these sales and made public his objections by nailing to the door of all Saints church in Wittenburg a protest which has become celebrated as the "ninety-five thesis." This lead to the breaking away from the Roman Catholic church and the empire-shattering movement known as the Reformation. Luther in 1519 publically, at Wittemburg, burned a copy of a Papal Bull threatening him with excommunication.

Summoned before the Diet of Worms in 1521, convened by the Emperor Charles V to demand Luther retract his statements, Luther replied:

"I cannot and I will not retract anything, unless what I have written shall be shown contrary to the *Holy Scriptures,* or to plain reason, for to act against conscience is neither safe nor upright." He closed with these words: "Here I stand. I cannot do otherwise. God help me. Amen."

Placed under the ban of the Empire he started home, but while passing through a valley near Eisenach, he was seized by a band of masked horsemen and carried to the Castle of Wartburg. This was done by order of his good friend, Frederich, elector or Saxony, who feared for his safety.

During nearly a year of sojourn there Luther made a translation of the New Testament from the original Greek into the German. His translation did for the German what Wycliffe's translation did for the English language and literature.

Summary

Thus we see that the Reformation came at the right time signified by the parenthesis between the sixth and seventh trumpets following the fall of Constantinople. It was the mightiest movement since the inauguration of the church on Pentecost and the carrying of the open book to the Roman World in Apostolic days and two centuries following. If the apostacy of the church is a subject of inspired prophesy, we need experience no surprise that the movement to throw off the shackels of that religious apostacy should be revealed to John on Patmos.

It would be almost impossible to employ any imagery of symbolism which could so fittingly portray this earth shattering movement, centered around "A BOOK."

The "book" in the angel's hand is an "open book," unsealed and unrolled that it could be read. It was unrolled out of the dead language and put in the vernacular of the common people. The conspicuous place of prominance given the "Little Book" most assuredly is a symbol of a great prophecy. It is given that "he who runs may read." The Reformation was the *Work* of a *Book,* the *Bible.*

The translation of the Bible by Wycliffe, Tyndale and Coverdale, out of the Latin—a dead language-into English; the translation of the Bible out of the Greek into German by Luther brought on the Reformation. "Indebted for its origin to the "book," it made it an *open book* to the world.

Today the Bible, in whole or in part, has been translated into nearly 1100 languages and dialects. This great accomplishment is most certainly best symbolized by "an book open" in the hands of a radiant angel!

Returning to the latter part of verse 2, in chapter ten, we read of this radiant angel, "which had in his hand a little book open, and he set his right foot upon the sea, and his left foot upon the land." This planting of the feet indicates the world wide scope of this movement of "the little Book."

Again the original commission of the Christ was being obeyed.
"Go ye, therefore, and teach all nations, baptizing them in the name of the Father, and of the Son, and of the Holy Spirit. Teaching them to observe all things whatsoever I have commanded you, and, lo, I am with you always, even unto the end of the world." (Matthew 19-20)

And again: "Go ye into all the world, and preach the gospel to every creature. He that believeth and is baptized shall be saved; but he that believeth not shall be damned." (Mark 16:15-16)

vs. 3 "He cried with a loud voice, as when a lion roareth." The angel cried with a loud voice, so loud that it was likened to the deafening roar of a lion. While we do not have revealed what he said, yet there is the implication that the angel wished to call the attention of the inhabitants of earth and sea, upon which he had placed his left and right foot, to the book he held in his hand. Since this book was to play the leading role in the spiritual drama he wanted all to take note of the book he held.

"When he cried *seven* thunders uttered their voices." Shall we pause to consider these seven thunders. While we are not told what they said, and we do not wish to be wise above that which is written, perhaps we can arrive at the reason why John was not permitted to write what they said. John was commanded by a voice from heaven to "seal up those things which the thunders uttered, and write them not." However much we would like to know what they said, their pronouncements were not to be permitted to divert our attention from the little book the angel held, and from what the angel had to say. So we will only digress a brief span to ascertain what these thunders were, and the reason for their utterances being withheld.

The Voice of the Seven Thunders

First, we would call attention to the article "the." The definite article "the" precedes the "seven thunders" in all three of the instances in which it ocurs. (Rev. 10:3-4) We have no allusions to these thunders, either before or after their brief mention. Perhaps a comparison will help us here. We speak of the mayor, the governor, the president, even if they have not been mentioned before. Why? Because they are so well known to everyone. Perhaps that is the reason why the definite article "the" is used here, because these thunders were such well known facts in history.

A few pages previous to this we spoke of Wycliffe, "the Morning Star of the Reformation." Le Bas, in his life of Wycliffe, page 198, says:

"The thunders which shook the world when they issued *from* the *seven hills,* sent forth an uncertain sound, comparatively faint and powerless, when launched from a region of less devoted sanctity."

These thunders of the ecclesiasticism were all powerful *because* they originated from the seven-hilled city. Rome has ever been known in history as the city resting upon the seven Palatine Hills, the names of which are:

(1) Quirinal   (2) Capitoline   (3) Viminal   (4) Esquiline
(5) Palatine   (6) Aventine   and   (7) Caelian

How appropriately should the bulls and anathemas hurled from the Roman see, situated on these seven hills be called *"the seven thunders!"*

Here we are viewing a scene where "the little book" is the center of attention and that little book exposed the spiritual corruption and scriptural apostacy of the Roman church. As, in symbolism, the angel with the book in his hand, cried with a loud voice, and he was instantly answered by the voice of the seven thunders; so in history, the instant men with the translated word of God began to speak from the little book, Rome thundered her bulls and anathemas.

It was so with Wycliffe. Quoting from our previous quotation, "He (Wycliffe) developed the thought which became the guiding principle of all his acts: that each individual Christian may claim immediate dependence upon God, without intervention of clergy; each individual having the right to take *the Bible* and reason as the foundations of his belief." In answer to this use of "the Little Book," Pope Gregory XI, in 1373, issued *five bulls* against Wycliffe!

As was the experience of "the Morning Star" of the Reformation, so, likewise Luther, the Founder of the Reformation. Hear Myers on this:

"It was six years after Luther's visit to Rome when Tetzel began in the neighborhood of Wittenburg, where Luther was, the preaching of indulgences. The people were running in great crowds after the preacher of indulgences. Luther was greatly distressed. Not being able to get any one in authority to intervene to put a stop to the scandal, he resolved to take hold of the matter himself. Accordingly he drew up ninety-five theses bearing on indulgences and nailed them upon the door of the castle church at Wittenburg. By means of the press the theses were spread broadcast. They were eagerly read and commented upon by all classes, particularly in Germany. Tetzel issued counter-propositions. . . . At first Pope Leo had been inclined to make light of the whole matter, declaring that it was "a mere squabble of monks," but at length he felt constrained to take decisive measures against Luther. The monk was to be silenced by *a papal bull.* . . .

At length a copy of the papal bull came into Luther's hands. Luther took a startling determination. He resolved to *burn the bull.* A fire was kindled outside one of the gates of Wittenburg, and in the presence of a great throng of doctors, students, and citizens, Luther cast *the bull,* together with the papal decretals and some books of his opponents, into the flames.

The audacious proceeding raised a terrible storm, which raged "high as the heavens, wide as the earth! Luther wrote a friend that he believed the tempest could never be stilled before the day of judgment."—Myers Mediaeval and Modern History, page 302, 303, 304.

So we see that the "Little Book open" which began the Reformation, called forth the "seven thunders that uttered their voices." The papal pronouncements that had for so long shaken the revived Roman empire, in the form of ecclesiastical power, were hurled at the translators of the Bible and the early leaders of the great reformation movement.

The pope, claiming to be the vicar of Christ, hurled his anathemas in the voice of the *seven thunders* coming from the city of the seven Palatine hills.

Shall we now go back to the Scriptures.

vs. 4 John was about to write but we read "I heard a voice from heaven saying unto me, seal up those things which the seven thunders uttered, and write them not." Why? Because the pronouncements of an apostate church, and its claimed vice-regent of God, have not the same authority as the Word of God, and must not be considered or treated on the same level with the Scriptures contained in the little Book.

The "Voice from heaven" commanded him to seal up what the voice of the seven thunders uttered. It was to have no lot or portion in the words recorded by divine sanction. The voice from the seven hills have no divine standing or authority and are consigned to oblivion! That is heaven's estimate of the worthlessness of the papal pronouncements. Would to God "the will of God," "might be done on earth as it is in heaven." John was not to record these seven thunders as the Word of God. This symbolism of the voice of the seven thunders simply represents what did happen to those who used the little book that was open.

In 1518 Luther wrote the pope defending his course in attackimg Tetzel, but declared, "I will acknowledge thy voice as the voice of Christ!" Like John, who was about to write the voice of the seven thunders into the scriptures, so Luther and the other reformers were at first disposed to receive them as of divine authority. And, again like John, when he had heard the voice from heaven which said, "seal up those things which the seven thunders uttered, and write them not," did not include these utterances in the book of Revelation, so these reformers, when they too, heard the voice of divine authority from heaven, rejected the thunders from the seven hills.

vs. 5, 6, 7 "And the angel which I saw stand upon the sea and upon the land, lifted up his hand to heaven, and sware by him that liveth forever and ever, who created heaven, and the things that therein are, and the earth, and the things that therein are, and the sea, and the things which are therein, that there should be time no longer."

Here we discover a marvelous parallel. In Rev. 6:11, the suffering saints, martyrs of pagan Roman persecution were told that they should rest for a little season (CHRONOS) until their fellowservants also, and their brethren, that should be killed as they were, should be fulfilled."

171

This second group of martyrs, here referred to, we see are those who suffered at the hands of Papal Rome. To these come the assurance "that there should be time (CHRONOS,—the same word used in Rev. 6:11) should be no longer" or literally time, or *delay* no longer, but that "in the days of the voice of the seventh angel, when he shall begin to sound, the mystery of God should be finished, as he hath declared to his servants the prophets." (Rev. 10:7) Note: the word "declared" here literally means "preached the glad tidings."

The martyrs of Roman paganism cry "O Lord, how long," here to the second body of martyrs is given assurance that events are hastening to an end.

The mystery of God in this instance is the mystery of his long delay to exercise divine authority, as against puesdo papal authority, and to open the Scriptures to reveal the apostacy of the then existing corrupt church.

We must note carefully that the angel does not declare that time shall not end until the seventh trumpet has been blown, but rather that the days of tribulation are drawing to a close and its end shall not be long delayed.

Then shall the mystery of God, of his creative work, his redemptive labor and his preparation of a place for the redeemed, be completed and fully understood.

vs. 8-10 "And the voice which I heard from heaven spake unto me again, and said, go and take the little book which is open in the hand of the angel which standeth upon the sea and upon the earth. And I went unto the angel, and said unto him, give me the little book. And he said unto me, take it, and eat it up; and it shall make thy belly bitter, but it shall be in thy mouth sweet as honey."

"And I took the little book out of the angel's hand, and ate it up; and it was in my mouth sweet as honey: and as soon as I had eaten it, my belly was bitter."

Shall we go back to the book of Ezekial which has aided us so much in the interpretation of symbolism. Here the Old Testament prophet receives a commission concerning the rebellious house of Israel.

"But thou, son of man, hear what I say unto thee; be not thou rebellious like that rebellious house: open thy mouth, and eat that I give thee. And when I looked, behold, an hand was sent unto me: and, lo, a roll of a book was therein and he spread it before me; and it was written within and without, and there was written therein lamentations, and mourning and woe." (Ezek. 2:8-10)

Like John, this roll was sweet to the prophet's mouth, but it became bitter because it was full of "lamentations, mournings and woe."

Ezekial was commissioned to speak against Jerusalem and the temple, and in John's vision, a city and a temple appear in symbols in the eleventh chapter. So these two visions, one of the Old Testament and the other in Revelation are in close affinity.

John did eat the book and found it sweet to the taste, in his mouth. The psalmist said, of God's word, or commandments and judgments, "More to be desired are they than gold, yea than much fine gold, sweeter also than honey and the honey comb." (Psalsm 19:10)

But in the belly, John found the book he had devoured something bitter. Shall we note that the word "belly" is used rather than "stomach." The stomach is a storage place for food; but it is in the belly where digestion takes place. The word of God is sweet as honey in the eating, but bitter when digested and assimilated.

John here symbolically experiences what the reformers and their followers actually found out in digesting this little book. While they ate the book with great enjoyment, the results that followed were bitter indeed.

The Roman Catholic church had hidden their ceremonies in ritualistic formalities and their services in Latin, a dead language. They had hidden the Bible in the dust of the monasteries and buried it under the accumulating debris of ecclesiasticism, tradition, and papal decrees.

While today a gesture is made to indicate their acceptance of the Bible, there is the black record of centuries of opposition to the distribution of God's word with countless instances of burning it publicly. In many countries the Bible was a forbidden book and those who read and followed it were subjected to the bitterest sort of persecution. To cover up this stigma, the Roman church claims it preserved the Bible. The only grain of truth in that pronouncement is that it was a preservation by utter neglect and not one of printing, reading and practicing its teaching.

All, even today who read this "little book," find it sweet to the taste but to digest it in practice brings great bitterness.

vs. 11 "And he said unto me, thou must prophesy again before many peoples and nations, and tongues and kings."

Here we see another result of eating this book. The word prophesy not only means "to predict" but also "to teach and declare" the word of God.

This message of the gospel had been originally declared by the apostles, both in person and through those who had faithfully preached the apostles' doctrine, or teaching. For centuries before this vision the preaching of the word had almost ceased. Now with the eating of this little book brought back to the people by translation and the recently invented printing press, there was experienced a great revival of apostolic preaching.

This word was to be declared to "many peoples, and nations and tongues," and even "to kings in high places."

In closing this chapter we leave a final thought. This book is to be devoured, *in whole* and *not in part*. We are not to eat some choice portions of it—that which is pleasant and agreeable to us, but we are to digest all of it even though the resultant effect is a great bitterness.

CHAPTER XI

THE MEASUREMENT OF THE TEMPLE

Text (11:1-18)

1 And there was given me a reed like unto a rod: and one said, Rise, and measure the temple of God, and the altar, and them that worship therein. 2 And the court which is without the temple leave without, and measure it not; for it hath been given unto the nations: and the holy city shall they tread under foot forty and two months. 3 And I will give unto my two witnesses, and they shall prophesy a thousand two hundred and threescore days, clothed in sackcloth. 4 These are the two olive trees and the two candlesticks, standing before the Lord of the earth. 5 And if any man desireth to hurt them, fire proceedeth out of their mouth and devoureth their enemies; and if any man shall desire to hurt them, in this manner must he be killed. 6 These have the power to shut the heaven, that it rain not during the days of their prophecy: and they have power over the waters to turn them into blood, and to smite the earth with every plague, as often as they shall desire. 7 And when they shall have finished their testimony, the beast that cometh up out of the abyss shall make war with them, and overcome them, and kill them. 8 And their dead bodies lie in the street of the great city, which spiritually is called Sodom and Egypt, where also their Lord was crucified. 9 And from among the peoples and tribes and tongues and nations do men look upon their dead bodies three days and a half, and suffer not their dead bodies to be laid in a tomb. 10 And they that dwell on the earth rejoice over them, and make merry; and they shall send gifts one to another; because these two prophets tormented them that dwell on the earth. 11 And after the three days and a half the breath of life from God entered into them, and they stood upon their feet; and great fear fell upon them that beheld them. 12 And they heard a great voice from heaven saying unto them, Come up hither. And they went up into heaven in the cloud; and their enemies beheld them. 13 And in that hour there was a great earthquake, and the tenth part of the city fell; and there were killed in the earthquake seven thousand persons: and the rest were affrighted, and gave glory to the God of heaven.

14 The second Woe is past: behold, the third Woe cometh quickly. 15 And the seventh angel sounded; and there followed great voices in heaven, and they said,

The kingdom of the world is become the kingdom of our Lord,
and of his Christ: and he shall reign for ever and ever.

16 And four and twenty elders, who sit before God on their thrones, fell upon their faces and worshipped God, 17 saying, We give thee thanks, O Lord God, the Almighty, who art and who wast; because thou has taken they great power, and didst reign. 18 and the nations were wroth, and thy wrath came, and the time of the dead to be judged, and the time to give their reward to thy servants the prophets, and to the saints, and to them that fear thy name, the small and the great; and to destroy them that destroy the earth.

Our attention is drawn in this chapter to the measuring of the temple, or the church as we shall find this temple to be.

vs. 1 "And there was given me a reed like unto a rod: and the angel stood, saying, Rise, and measure the temple of God, and the altar, and them that worship therein."

This passage reminds us of a parallel one in the Old Testament, in the book that has been called the Apocalypse of the Old Testament. The parallel is found in (Zechariah 2:1-2) Zechariah was a prophet to the remnant which returned out of Babylon after the seventy years captivity. The prophet sees a man with a measuring line in his hand, who upon being asked, "wh'ther goest thou?" replied, "To *measure* Jerusalem and to see what is the breadth thereof, and what is the length thereof."

The significance of this parallel lies in the fact that Jerusalem was being rebuilt after its destruction. Likewise in the New Testament revelation the spiritual Jerusalem was being rebuilt after its destruction by the apostacy.

The spiritual Jerusalem of the New Testament is the church. Paul said, "But Jerusalem which is above is free, which is the mother of us all." (Gal. 4:26) There in the apocalypse of the Old Testament, Zion (Zech. 2:10) is being separated from everything not according to God's word (or Babylon) and in the New Testament Apocalypse God's people or Zion is being called out of the Babylon of confusion of apostacy.

As the temple in Zechariah was being made ready for God's occupancy "I will dwell in the midst of thee"—so in the apocalypse of the New Testament, the living church, the temple of God (I Cor. 3:16 "Know ye not that ye are the temple of God") or Zion—(the city of the Living God, "But ye are come to mount Zion, and into the city of the Living God" (Heb. 12:22) is being rebuilt again and made ready for God's occupancy and use.

In the Old Testament apocalypse we read, "And many nations shall be joined to the Lord in that day, and shall be my people," and in the last verse of the tenth chapter of Revelation, just before the beginning of the measurement of the temple, we read, "Thou must prophesy, or teach, again before many peoples and nations and tongues and kings."

Shall we carefully analyze this verse. We note:

1. *First* Who does this measuring.

It is not an angel who does the measuring but an apostle, even John himself. John is the sole remaining representative of the twelve apostles. In the giving of this little book in the beginning we read, that the church "continued steadfastly in the apostles' teaching" (Acts 2:42). The apostles, in the beginning did the measuring of the church. Now after the long and terrible apostacy when the little book is again given to the world through the work of translation, John, an apostle measures the temple.

The church for centuries, during the dark ages, had been measured, not by the word of God, but by the decrees of church councils and the pronouncements of the popes. The measurement is committed to a representive of the apostolic group. Originally in the day of regeneration beginning at Pentecost. Jesus said of this body:

"Verily, I say unto you, that ye which have followed me, in the regeneration (greek-palingenesio. or "re-creation," "making new" - the word occurs again in Titus 3:5 "not but works of righteousness which we have done, by his own mercy he hath saves us, by the washing of regeneration" etc.)

When the Son of man shall sit in the throne of his glory, ye also shall sit upon twelve thrones, judging the twelve tribes of Israel." (Matt. 19:28)

Now, again, in the regeneration after the apostacy, they, the apostles, shall measure the church of Christ.

2. *Second* shall we consider what measure is used. It is called a reed like unto a rod." A rod is often used as a symbol of correction.

"Thou shalt break them with a rod of iron" (Psalms 2:9)

"I will visit their transgression with a rod." (Psalms 89:32)

"A rod is for the back of him that is void of understanding." (Proverbs 10:13)

"A rod for the fool's back" (Proverbs 26:3)

"Foolishness is bound in the heart of a child; but the rod of correction shall drive it far from him." (Prov. 22:15)

"And he shall smite the earth with the rod of his mouth." (Isa. 11:4)

So in correcting the departures from the truth a measure was *given* John by which he should measure the temple. The measure then is not a human standard, because it was given John. John did not make or choose this rod, nor did any of the apostolic body. The reed was given him. Therefore, it is a divine measure. A divine standard of measurement was given the apostles by Christ. That measure, or reed was the New Testament.

"He that rejecteth me, and receiveth not my words, hath one that judgeth him: the word that I have spoken, the same shall judge him in the last day." (John 12:48)

The New Testament, written by the apostles, given to them by the inspiration through the Holy Spirit, "who" shall teach you all things and bring all things to your remembrance whatsoever I have said unto you," (John 14:26), is the only divine standard with which the church, her worshippers, and her worship is to be measured.

3. *Third,* shall we consider what is measured. He was to measure the temple. This could not have been the Jewish temple in Jerusalem because it had been destroyed under Titus and his Roman legions in A.D. 70. So this refers, not to a material temple, (because we are still in the realm of symbolism) but a spiritual temple. We have already heard Paul in (1 Cor. 3:16) declare that obedient believers are "the temple of the Living God."

In Ezekiel the fourteenth chapter, (which is too long to quote in its entirety here), the prophet sees a vision (he, too, is in the realm of symbolism) in which an angel was measuring with a reed a temple unlike any earthly, or material temple. The whole temple itself is exactly *equal to* the *measurement of the reed,* and each of its many chambers of which it is composed is also *exactly equal to the measurement of the reed.*

This strange and mysterious symbolism, representing what is apparently impossible perfectly symbolized the true church of Chirst when it attains unto the fullness of the divine measure.

The whole temple is exactly the size, being neither larger nor smaller than the reed. So the true church of Christ corresponds minutely with the divine measurements of the New Testament description of that glorious institution. In other words, the New Testament church, "Speaks where the New Testament speaks, and is silent where the New Testament is silent." It neither adds to where there is silence, nor subtracts from that which is spoken.

Again, as the temple in Ezekiel's vision was made up of many chambers, each of which was the same size of the reed, or of the whole temple itself, so the church of Christ is composed of a multitude of congregations, or called out assemblies, each of which corresponds exactly to the reed of divine measurement, the New Testament.

The individual congregations should all speak the same things, said the apostle Paul. They should not differ in name, creed, worship and observance of the ordinances of Christ as do the denomination-alism of the Sardis period.

Paul gives us the perfect seven of the divine pattern of the New Testament church. (Eph. 4:4-6) He says, "There is—
1 - One body - one organism, the church (Eph. 1:22-23; Col. 1:18);
2 - One Spirit - life animating the one body, even the Holy Spirit. (John 14:26) (1 John 4:1-3);
3 - One Hope - the certainty of Life eternal (Acts 23:6; 1 Cor. 15:19; Heb. 6:18-20)
4 - One Lord - one authority (Matt. 28:18 - Luke 2:11 - Acts 2:25 - Acts 10:36);
5 - One Faith - one confession that Jesus is the Christ, the Son of the Living God. (Matt. 16:16-18 - John 11:27 - 20:31 Acts 8:37 - 10:43)
6 - One Baptism - one common practice, water immersion into the name of the Father and of the Son and of the Holy Spirit. (Matt. 28:19)
7 - One God and Father of all - God by creation and Father by recreation. Father of his one and only begotten Son (John 3:16) and of all baptized believers by adoption (Rom. 8:15 - Gal. 4:6-7)

We must also take note that not only were the temple and its worshippers measured, but its altar. It was on the altar that the sacrifice was offered, so the churches belief in the one atonement made by Christ is to be measured. This is very significant. The apostate church had taught the resacrifice of the Christ in the mass as conducted at the altar, though they claim it is unbloody. If it is a bloodless sacrifice it is entirely without efficacy, because "without the shedding of blood there is no remission of sins" (Hebrews 9:22)

Neither was Christ to be re-sacrificed, because we read:
"Nor yet that he should offer himself often, as the high priest entereth into the holy place every year with the blood of others. For then must he often have suffered since the foundation of the world: but now *once* in the end of the world hath he appeared to put away sin by the *sacrifice* of *himself*. . . . . So Christ was once offered to bear the sins of many, and unto them that look for him shall he appear the *second* time without sin unto salvation." (Heb. 9:25-28)

So we see He only returns once, so He could not return in every mass conducted. The Lord's supper is the *"remembrance"* of a *"finished"* sacrifice. Only one absent needs to be remembered.

And does history record such a measurement? The most cursory examination of history will acquaint us with such a measurement. In the last chapter, the tenth, we found that the little Book, the Bible, was given to the world through the translation by the reformers, Wycliffe, Huss, Coverdale, Tyndale and Luther.

These reformers brushed aside the voice of the papacy, the writings of the fathers, tradition and decrees of various church councils as false reeds of measurement and accepted the Bible as the only rule of faith and practice.

Of course history also records that these reformers many times failed to continue to use this divine reed of measurement.

Luther substituted the Augsburg Confession and used it as a measuring reed. John Calvin resorted to the Westminster Confession of Faith; the Wesley's to the Book of Discipline, the church of England and Episcopalianism to the Thirty-Nine articles. But the principle survived and from all these groups there emerged in the dawn of the nineteenth century a movement of Restoration, which took as its divine reed of measurement "Where the Bible speaks, we speak; and where the Bible is silent we are silent." These Christians of the

Restoration movement understood what is involved in the symbol of measuring a building. They well understood that its limits are fixed in every direction. *All that belonged to the church,* as patterned after the New Testament model, was included; and *whatsoever did not belong* to *that spiritual edifice* was *'excluded'.*

Thus we, today are looking back upon a continued searching of the "little Book" for the old landmarks long obscured by the accumulation of the ecclesiastical debris of the centuries.

In this latter movement to restore the church in all her pristine glory and apostolic pattern there has been a seeking after the old paths and the whole church of that movement, as well as the thousands of individual "call-out-assemblies" are all one, each equal to the measurement of the divine reed.

vs. 2. "But the *court* which is *without the temple* leave (or "cast out" margin) and measure it not; for it is given to the Gentiles."
Note the word "cast out", not leave out as in the King James version, is very forceful.

Those within by implication are "Jews". We have already found in this book the word "Jew" is used to designate the true people of God, who are 'within'. By the same token, and in contradistinction, the "gentile" world symbolizes those who are said to be "without". In Rev. 22:15 those that are excluded are spoken of as "without are dogs",—that being the appellation applied to the Gentiles by the Jews, since dogs were ceremonially unclean animals.

In the physical temple of Jesus' day the court without the temple was for the Gentiles, though they had precious little opportunity to enter to worship for the priests filled it with bleeting sheep, cooing doves and the barking of venders, accompanied by the jingle of the money changers!

The court without was not to be measured. Here is meant the court of the Gentiles which surrounded the temple itself. This is symbolical of the world, and since the court without is not to be measured then the world with its unregenerate sinners, of which the court was a type, was not to be measured, because it did not and could not come up to the divine standard of measurement.

181

"And the holy city shall they tread under foot forty and two months." We will not go into the symbolism of the "forty and two months" at this time, but later. Five times this period is referred to in Scriptures.

The "Holy City" is a type of the true church, which is the city of the Living God (Heb. 12:22) and it is to be trodden down or oppressed for a period of forty and two months, or twelve hundred and sixty days. Since a day in prophetic symbolism represents one year, then this time period is one of twelve hundred and sixty years.

The Two Witnesses

vs. 3, 4 "And I will give power unto my two witnesses and they shall prophecy a thousand two hundred and three score days, clothed in sackcloth".

By this verse and the context in which we find it we are evidently to understand these two witnesses are to testify concurrently during the same period of time that the Holy City is trodden under foot, and since they are to testify in sackcloth, they are to be in great tribulation during that length of time.

We may well pause to ask, "Why two witnesses?" Since we are living in a book of symbolism, the number 'two" like other numbers found in this book must be symbolical.

Two, we may say, is the number of *divine sufficiency* in *God's testimony*. Christ said, "But if he will not hear thee, then take with thee one or two more, that in the mouth of two or three witnesses every word may be established" (Matt. 18:16)

Christ sent his disciples, who went forth witnessing, in pairs. Pairs are frequently encountered in the Scriptures. Moses and Aaron labored before all Israel; Joshua and Caleb brought back a favorable report concerning the land and together declared that "We are more than able to go up and take the land;" Haggai and Zechariah were twin prophets of the time of the rebuilding of the temple. On the missionary journeys Paul took another with him, sometimes Barnabas, at other times Silas and again Timothy.

On the evil side of things we meet with Jannes and Jambres.

182

Paul declared: "Wherein God, willing more abundantly to show unto the heirs of promise the immutability of his council, confirmed it by an oath: that by *two* immutable things, in which it was impossible for God to lie, we might have strong consolation." (Heb. 6: 17-18)

We learn from this verse that they are God's witnesses, so what they speak must be by divine inspiration.

The Two Olive Trees and Two Candlesticks

Furthermore we learn that these two witnesses are the two olive-trees and the two candlesticks.

The purpose of a candlestick is to give light and that light is supplied by the burning of oil; evidently in this case, olive oil. The olive tree furnishes the oil required of the lamp to continue to burn and give light.

This reference to the two olive trees and two candlesticks harks back again to the apocalypse of the Old Testament, the book of Zechariah. They both are mentioned in the fourth chapter. Zechariah saw them, likewise in a vision where symbolism is the order of things. The angel asked Zechariah, "knowest thou not what these be? and I said, no, my lord. Then said he, these are the two annointed ones (literally sons of oil) that stand by the Lord of the whole earth" (Zech. 4:13, 14)

This declares that God's two witnesses are furnished continuously with the outpouring of the Holy Spirit as typified by the constant flow of the golden oil through the golden pipes (Zech. 4:12)

I think we have enough information before us to identify the two witnesses. The "little Book" or the Bible is divided into two divisions or the Old and New Testaments. Here then, we have *two* testaments. The word *testament* signifies a "witness." It is derived from the Latin word, "testor", which means, "I testify". The two testaments, then, are the two *witnesses*.

And both *testaments,* or *witnesses* are inspired by the Holy Spirit, the oil of the olive trees. Peter said of the Old Testament prophesy,

"For the prophesy came not in old time by the will of men; but holy men of God spake as moved by the Holy Spirit." (II Peter 1:21)

Again he declared in II Pet. 3:1-2:

"This second epistle, beloved, I now write unto you, in both which I stir up your pure minds by way of remembrance. That ye may be mindful of the words which were spoken before by the holy prophets and of the commandment of us the apostles of the Lord and Savior."

Paul said: "The household of God is "built upon the foundation of the apostles and prophets, Jesus Christ himself being the chief cornerstone." (Eph. 2:20)

These two witnesses, the Old and New Testaments, testify of Christ. Jesus said of the Old Testament Scriptures "Search the Scriptures, for in them ye think ye have eternal life and they are they which testify of me." (John 5:39)

In the new Testament, John, the author of Apocolypse said in (John 20:31) "These things are written that you might believe that Jesus is the Christ, the Son of God; and that believing ye might have life in his name."

One of the witnesses - the Old Testament - testifies of the Lord in type and shadow, and prophesy; the other - the New Testament - witness of the Christ in fact and fulfillment. These two witnesses are the Lord's.

And to them He gives divine power to testify, because they are fed with the oil of inspiration, which is the Holy Spirit, one of whose names is the Comforter, or one who energizes—gives power. Reading on:

vs. 5 "And if any man will hurt them, fire proceedeth out of their mouth, and devoureth their enemies; and if any man hurt them, he must in this manner be killed."

They speak as one, for we read "fire proceedeth out of *their*

184

mouth." Jeremiah likens the word of God to a fire, and it is quite startling to learn that the fire of God's *anger* is particularly directed against the prophets that speak and claim for their own utterances the authority of God, by saying, "He saith." Hear Jeremiah:

"Is not my word like as a fire? saith the Lord; and like a hammer that breaketh the rock in pieces" Therefore, behold, I am against the prophets, saith the Lord, that steal my words every one from his neighbor.

Behold I am against the prophets, saith the Lord, that use their tongues, and say, He saith." (Jeremiah 23:29-31)

Again the Lord said to Jeremiah: "Behold, I will make my words in thy mouth *fire,* and this people wood, and it shall *devour* them."

He here uses the same word "devour" as Revelation employed in describing the destructive power of the fire of His word, or the two witnesses.

Paul says "Every man's work shall be made manifest; for the day shall declare it because it shall be revealed by fire; and the fire shall try every man's work of what sort it is." (I Cor. 3:13)

So God's word shall try every teacher or prophet and every mans work, whether it be true or false.

Christ, you remember, fought against the teaching of compromise in the Bergamos period with the sword of His mouth, so it is significant that this destroying fire of his two witnesses is said to proceed from the mouth. And it is true that the word of God can both save and destroy. It can both justify and condemn. At the judgment bar of God the fate of all men will be decided by the word. Jesus said in His commission:

"Go ye into all the world and preach the gospel to every creature. He that believeth and is baptized shall be saved; but he that believeth not shall be damned." (Mark 16:15-16)

vs. 6 "These have power to shut heaven, that it rain not in the days of their prophecy: and have power over waters to turn them into blood, and to smite the earth with all plagues, as often as they will."

In other words, while this is symbolic language, these two witnesses have the characteristics of Elijah, the prophet and Moses, the lawgiver. Like the former they have "power to shut heaven that it rain not in the days of their prophecy, and power like the latter over waters to turn them into blood, and to smite the earth with plagues."

They two, collectively, have the power to do both.

vs. 7 "And when they shall have finished their testimony" the thought here is, "when they shall have made their testimony complete." This does not mean when they have ended testifying, but when it is complete or full.

"The beast that ascendeth out of the bottomless pit shall make war against them, and kill them." Where ever the word is fully, or completely proclaimed the beast will make war against the word to kill it. Did not Jesus tell his followers, "When anyone heareth the word of the Kingdom, and understandeth it not, then cometh the wicked one, and catcheth away that which was sown in his heart." (Matt. 13:19)

A beast in Revelation is a symbol of a temporal power. The power that comes from the bottomless pit or the abyss we have already found to be Satanic, (Rev. 9:2-11). The beast then represents some devilish power or influence. This era, we shall find represents the great beast government upon which ecclesiastical dominion rides to great heights of power and dominion. According to the symbolism of this book, then, we are to understand that God's two witnesses will be suppressed for a brief time by governmental authority, under the sway of Satan.

vs. 8 "The scene of their being overcome is next given: "And their dead bodies shall lie in the street of the great city, which *spiritually* is called Sodom and Egypt where also our Lord was crucified."

The last six words of this verse have caused some to think it refers to Jerusalem in Palestine, but this is not so, because we read, "which *spiritually* is called Sodom and Egypt. So the physical Jerusalem is positively not indicated here.

186

This term is used eight times in Revelation and is never used referring to the physical Jerusalem. It is used in contrast to the Holy City. Since the Holy City, we have found symbolizes the church, a wicked city would signify an apostate church and a corrupted religion.

The designations *"Sodom"* and *"Egypt"* are significant. Sodom with it sins and sorceries is a type of this apostate church, or city. Egypt, the house of bondage, typifies the followers of apostasy, in bondage to false teaching of that great city. Sodom speaks of moral and spiritual corruption, Egypt speaks of spiritual bondage and darkness, as well as cruelty and oppression.

"Where our Lord was crucified" is worthy of special attention. Later on in Revelation, we shall find that the apostate church is likened to a city resting on seven mountains. It is this city church which crucified our Lord!

The outstanding characteristic of the Roman church, whose seat of authority is the city resting on the seven Palatine Hills, is her innumerable crucifixions of our Lord. While she has crucified Him with the apostacy of false teaching and practice, we must ever remember that the heart and center of her worship, both of the living worshippers, the ministration of her priests, and the burial of her dead is the "Mass."

And in the mass, under the false doctrine of transubstantiation, which claims the bread and wine are the literal body and blood of the Lord, she has Christ crucified millions, yes billions, of times. How well is it then designated, "Where also our Lord was crucified." How much is written in this symbolic expression.

But since the next verse reveals how long these witnesses were to lie unburied, it now becomes the proper and logical time to interpret the expression which signifies how long these two witnesses shall prophesy before they are slain.

Back in Rev. 11:3, these two witnesses were to prophesy in sackcloth for a period of a thousand two hundred and three score days.

The Twelve Hundred and Sixty Days

Sackcloth was in John's day a garment of mourning. It was a symbol of sorrow and tribulation. So we are informed then that the two witnesses, or the Word of God, shall testify in times of mourning

187

and deep tribulation. There were to be oppositions, hinderances, restraints and efforts to stifle their testimony. Does history bear this out? Let him who runs also read.

The Roman Catholic church buried the manuscripts of the Word in the dust of neglect of its monasteries. Copies that were not thus lost were burned. Tischendorf found a monk at the convent of St. Catherine, as late as 1859 in the act of preparing to burn a manuscript which proved to be one of the three best preserved copies of the Bible. He induced the Czar of Russia to buy it and later it was sold to the British Museum for a quarter of a million dollars, where it now resides.

Besides neglect and destruction the Roman church took the Bible out of the hands of the common people and made it a crime for any one to possess a copy of it. Many martyrs died at the hands of the apostate church because of having read it and daring to preach its truths. Among such, a few names stand like mountain peaks above the plain of common humanity; namely John Huss, Wycliffe, Jerome, Savonarola, Latimer, Ridley etc.

Thousands were consigned to the stake for no greater crime than that of having in their possession the Holy Scriptures.

Then, besides all this, the Bible was buried in Latin, a dead language, which few understood. Even the masses were said in Latin. It has been a standing policy of the Papcy to refuse to circulate the "two witnesses" in the common vernacular. Truthfully, the witnesses did prophesy in sackcloth.

And this period of mourning was to be twelve-hundred and sixty days. This span of time is spoken of under various figures of speech, but all refer to the same length of years. In Daniel 7:25, the horn which arose out of the ten hors was "to wear out the saints of the most High for a period of 'a time and times and half a time'." This is generally understood to be a period of three years and a half years, or forty-two months, or 1260 days. Since a day in prophetic symbolism stands for a year, this would mean 1260 years.

In Rev. 11:2, the outer court was to be trodden down by the gentiles for forty-two months, or 1260 days, or years. In Rev. 11:3 the two witnesses were to prophesy a thousand two hundred and three score days. The woman was fed of God in the wilderness for 1260 days, or 1260 years (Rev. 12:6). She is said to be nourished there for a time, and times and half a time, (Rev. 12:14) or three and one half years, or 1260 days or years. The same phraseology as used in Daniel.

So here we have five different passages in the Scriptures and all cover the same period of time in the history of the church, and all pertain to a long period of time of bitter persecution.

Since a day in prophetic symbolism represents a year, then horn referred to by Daniel will speak great words against the Most High for 1260 years. For 1260 years the Gentiles, or a world empire shall tread the church under foot. For 1260 years the Bible shall testify in sackcloth and, the woman—a type of the true church—, shall flee into the wilderness, or be in hiding, where God shall feed her for that length of time.

Can we identify this period? History again is our right hand companion. The church suffered at the hands of two great powers, first, of Pagan Rome and second, of papal Rome, which came to preeminence and power upon the decline and fall of pagan Rome.

If the misfortunes of the Empire tended to inhance the prestege and power of the ecclesiastical government seated in Rome, much more did the final downfall of the Empire hasten that religious domination to fruition.

With the removal of the Emperor the bishop of Rome became ecclesiastical and temporal sovereign. The development, while gradual was none the less sure and irresistible. Paul in his time saw the mystery of iniquity already at work. Hear the apostle on this very beginning of departure from the faith once and for all delivered unto the saints and the rise of the man of sin:

"For the mystery of iniquity doth already work: only there is one that restraineth now until he be taken out of the way. And then shall be revealed the lawless one, whom the Lord shall slay with the breath of His mouth, and bring to naught by the manifestation of his coming, even he whose coming is according to the working of Satan with all power and signs and lying wonders." (II Thess. 2:7-9)

Since the development is so imperceptible it is difficult to arrive at the exact year in the growth of papal power, which would be the beginning of the 1260 year period.

Earlier in this discussion of the apocalypse we briefly reviewed the life of Justinian who ascended the eastern throne in 527. He was a man of unusual ability, so much so that the time of his sovereignity became known as the "Era of Justinian." He became the Restorer of the Empire by conquest, and the law given to civilization by his collection and publication of the "Body of the

189

Roman Law." But his activities did not end here. He took a strong hand in the affairs of the church also. Says Gibbon:

"The reign of Justinian was a uniform yet various scene of persecution: and he appears to have surpassed his indolent predecessors, both in the contrivance of his laws and the rigor of their execution. The insufficient term of these months was assigned for the conversion or exile of all heretics; and if he still connived at their precarious stay, they were deprived under his iron yoke, not only of the benefits of society but of the common birthright of men and Christians. Gibbon's "Decline and Fall of the Roman Empire" pages 528, 529—Vol. v

He further described how those who resisted these decrees and acts of persecution conducted themselves, "On the approach of Catholic priests and soldiers, they grasped with alacrity the crown of martyrdom." Page 529, Vol. IV.

Gibbon then proceeds to relate how the church was drenched in the blood of the persecutions instigated by Justinian. Surely our two witnesses were then testifying in sackcloth. By A.D. 531, four years after his ascension to the Eastern throne, Justinian issued a decree which subjected the whole of Christiandom to the Roman pope.

D'Aubigne's Reformation, Vol. 1, page 42 informs us that in A.D. 533, Justinian bestowed upon the Roman pope for the first time, the title of Rector Ecclesiae," or Lord of the churches.

Surely Paul's 'man of sin' mentioned in II Thess. 2:3, has now been fully exposed to view and revealed to all history. The papacy, the mystery of iniquity, working from the days of the apostles, after centuries of struggle has come to the full bloom of ecclesiastical power.

The secular power has finally placed its stamp of approval upon the supremacy of the papacy and supported this royal sanction by inflicting persecution upon all who failed to bow the knee to papal Rome. The climax has now been reached in the long series of ecclesiastical encroachments upon the supremacy of Christ and the autonomy of the local church. The word of God is superceded by the word of papal Rome and the two witnesses begin their long period of testifying in the mourning of sackcloth.

At this time Daniel's little horn has risen above its fellow sovereigns, the holy city, the true church begins to be trodden under the feet of Gentile government, both physical and spiritual. The true church is driven into the wilderness of hiding.

Now shall we continue our scriptural unfolding, or uncovering of the experiences of our two witnesses.

vs. 8 "And their dead bodies shall be in the streets of the great city, which spiritually is called Sodom and Egypt, where also our Lord was crucified."

vs. 9 "And they of the people, and kindreds, and tongues, and nations, shall see their dead bodies three days and a half and shall not suffer their dead bodies to be put in graves.

In other words the death of these two witnesses will be such a conspicuous event that all nations shall take note of it and perceive it, and this event will bring rejoicing just as the angel says:

vs. 10 "And they that dwell upon the earth shall rejoice, over them, and make merry, and shall send gifts one to another, because these two prophets *tormented* them that dwell on the earth."

These witnesses prophesied, or taught the will of God and their warnings, exhortations, admonitions and denunciations against the apostacy tormented the dwellers of earth.

It has ever been so. The word of these two witnesses, the Old and New Testaments have always been tormenting to the wicked, morally or spiritually speaking.

The Bible may be a 'little Book,' and those who proclaim it, few in number and of lowly mein, yet it is as Paul declares:

"For the weapons of our warfare are not carnal, but *mighty through God* to the pulling down of strongholds) casting down imaginations, and every high thing that *exalteth itself against the knowledge of God* and bringing into captivity every thought to the *obedience* of *Christ*." (II Cor. 10:4-5)

Now shall we take up the thread of history again. Going back to the date 533 A.D. when the "man of sin" was fully revealed in the ascension of the pope by secular decree to the Lord of the church, instead of Christ as head, we add 1260 years. This brings us up to the year A.D. 1793. Shall we let history tell us what notable event happened in that year. Did the testimony of the two witnesses suffer death at that time?

The church had become so apostatized and corrupt that the world swung like a pendulum to the other extreme, to skepticism, agnostician and outright infidelity. There came the age of free thinking and infidelity.

There were Voltaire and Rousseau in France; Frederick the great in Germany: Tom Paine, Hume, Bolingbroke and Gibbon in Britain, and Thomas Jefferson and Paine in America.

The head of all this infidelity centered in France. Voltaire predicted that in one hundred years the Bible would become extant. The crest of the storm broke in France. The nation arose in a mighty movement that became a crusade, the object of which was to abolish religion and enthrone atheism. France the mightiest nation on earth at the time, for the first and only time in history, by legislative enactment abolished all religion. The convention met and by law abolished not only the Bible, but God. Not even Russia, with all her infidelity has gone to this legislative extreme.

They abolished the old calendar and inaugurated a new one, the seven day week was suppressed, each month being divided into three periods of ten days each called 'decades' and each day into ten parts. On Nov. 7, 1793 the revolutionists proceeded to abolish Christianity. They had dethroned the kings of earth; they proceeded to dethrone the King of heaven. The guillotine surplanted the cross. On Nov. 10, 1793 this madness culminated in the inauguration of the worship of reason. A mayor, or some popular leader, upon every tenth day would mount the altar and harangue the people concerning the achievements of the revolution and the privilege of living in the new era when no one was oppressed, either by the kings of earth or the King of heaven.

This convention began on Sept. 20, 1792 and ran for three years, to Oct. 26, 1795 or 749 days, to be followed by the "Reign of Terror."

Gradually, saner heads began to take hold of the helm of state. One of the great movers to saner thinking was a deputy of the Third Estate, by the name of Robespierre. He "wished to sweep away christianity as a superstition, but he would stop at deism."

He did not believe a state could be established on atheism. He declared, "If God did not exist it would behoove man to invent him." Shall we hear Myers at this juncture:

"In a remarkable address before the convention on May 7, 1794, Robespierre eloquently defended the doctrines of God and immortality, and then closed his speech by offering for adoption this decree.

(1) The French people recognize the existence of the Supreme Being and the immortality of the soul.

(2) They recognize that the worship most worthy of the Supreme Being is the practice of the duties of man——"

192

The convention adapted the resolution with the utmost enthusiasm.

The two witnesses were to lie unburied for three days and a half, or three years and a half, since a day prophetically stands for a year. The enthronement of atheism lasted appproximately three years and a half, when the French nation began to recover from its satanic madness. The atheistic decrees were repealed and Christianity acknowledged.

vs. 11 "And after three days and a half the Spirit of life from God entered into them and they stood upon their feet; and great fear fell upon all them that saw them.

This signifies that the two witnesses regain their power and influence to testify. The witnesses were in sackcloth no longer. The age of religious toleration set in.

Summary

Thus we see that the man of sin was fully revealed in A.D. 533, when the pope became Lord of the church, dethroning, as it were the Christ. 1260 years later, the two witnesses were killed by the same legislative power which enthroned the Bishop of Rome as Rector Ecclesiae. "But three years and a half later these atheistic enactments were repealed and an age was inaugerated which gave the two witness freer reign and activity than ever before.

The Bible began to be circulated around the globe. With the nineteenth century began a mighty movement to circumnavigate the globe with the Scriptures, until today they are translated into nearly eleven hundred languages and dialects. And the very house where Voltaire lived, who predicted the Bible would be an unknown book in one hundred years, became a printing house to print the Bible itself! This lends light to our next verse:

vs. 12 "And they heard a great voice from heaven saying unto them, come up higher, and they ascended up to heaven in a cloud; and their enemies beheld them."

This is still in the realm of symbolism. To be exalted up to heaven, symbolically, means to experience new power, influence and prosperity. An example of this usage is found in Christ's statement concerning Capernaum:

"And thou Capernaum, which art *exalted into heaven,* shall be brought down to hell." (Matt. 11:23)

And truly the enemies of the two witnesses have had ample opportunity to behold the exaltation of the two witnesses in the world wide circulation of the Bible throughout all the nations under heaven. Even the soldiers of the armies of the nations are furnished with copies of the Bible and that by the millions in number! Bible Societies date from this period which also marks the era of modern missionary endeavor.

No wonder the next verse follows naturally and logically.

vs. 13 "And the same hour was there a great earthquake, and the tenth part of the city fell, and in the earthquake were slain of men seven thousand; and the remnant were affrighted, and gave glory to the God of heaven."

Remembering always that the great city referred to is the apostate church in contradistinction to the holy city the true church, we also remember that the Roman Empire in its downfall divided into ten horns, or, kingdoms, of which France was one of the ten. So a tenth part of the city fell from papal domination and inaugerated the age of religious freedom and toleration.

"And the same hour was there a great earthquake." An earthquake symbolized a great change. From a monarchy France changed to a republic. Says Myers:

"The revolution having accomplished its work in France, having there destroyed Royal despotism and abolished class privilege, now set itself about fulfilling its early promise of giving liberty to all peoples. In a word, the Revolution became what has been called "an armed propaganda"—She would make all Europe like herself. Herself a republic, she would make all nations republic."

Myers "Medieval and Modern History page 586

Myers further relates:

"From the coronation of Napoleon in 1804 until his downfall in 1815 the tremendous struggle went on almost without intermission. It was the war of the giants. Europe was shaken from end to end with such armies as the world had not seen since the days of Xerxes."

Myers. Medieval and Modern History page 553.

Then there was another earth shaking event. France's soldiers excited an insurrection in Rome, made the pope a prisoner and proclaimed the Roman Tiberine Republic. Napoleon declared the pope "was no longer a secular prince" and took possession of his domains. Pope pius straightway excommunicated the Emperor, who thereupon arrested him, and for three years held him a state prisoner. He further removed the college of cardinals to Paris. His ambition was that Paris would become the capital of Christendom and he would govern the religious as well as the poltical world.

At the same time the two wintesses were exalted in the new birth of freedom, an *earth quake* was shaking Europe. This was a religious and political earthquake.

The slaying of seven thousand men may well represent the wholesale destruction of royalty, of rank and nobility in France. The guillotine speaks eloquently here how thousands fell in the days of the Reign of Terror. Kings, Queens, Dukes-all fell. Paris became hardened to the sound of carts lumbering through the streets, carrying distinguished and insignificant people to the knife.

Around the guillotine gathered the terrible "knitting. woman" of whom Dickens tells in his book "The Tale of Two Cities." These knitters stopped in their counting of stitches only long enough to check the heads as they fell from the descending knife.

vs. 14 "The second woe is past; and behold the third woe cometh quickly."

The Seventh Trumpet Sounds

vs. 15 "And the seventh angel sounded; and there were great voices in heaven, saying, The Kingdoms of this world are become the Kingdoms of our Lord, and of his Christ; and he shall reign for ever and ever."

This is the seventh trumpet of the seventh seal, which brings the final victory and consumation of the age. Here is the last great triumph. It is the brightness of Zion's glad morning, which ushers in the reign of Christ and the instrumentality by which this final victory is brought about is the exaltation of the two witnesses, or the world-wide conquest of God's Word.

The heavenly citizens join in the paen of praise.

vs. 16 "The four and twenty elders, which sat before God on their seats, fell on their faces, and worshipped God."

This is the first we have beheld these princes of heaven since the opening of this great vision of the seven seals and the seven trumpets with its parenthetical interludes. And what is their song? Hear them:

vs. 17 "We give thee thanks, O Lord God Almighty, which art, and wast and art to come, because thou hast taken to thee thy great power and has reigned."

They sing of the eternality of Christ, the great I AM—the self-existant One. While it may have seemed to the Saints that Christ was not reigning during this long period from Pentecost, when Christ sat down at the right hand of God, to the end of the gospel age, yet he was reigning and was able to bring to pass his will in the end. And now John reveals the distress of the nations at the time of judgment, and the reward of the saints.

vs. 18 "And the nations were angry and thy wrath is come, and the time of the dead, that they should be judged."

This is a vision of the judgment day. He continues:

"And that thou shouldest give reward unto thy servants the prophets, and to the saints, and them that fear thy name, small and great:"

This the reward for which the saints waited who had cried "How long O Lord, Holy and true, dost thou not judge and avenge our blood on them that dwell on the earth?"

They are now blessed with the eternal reward while those who persecuted them also received the reward of God's revenge. They are destroyed.

"And shouldest destroy them which should destroy the earth."

The nineteenth verse begins a new series of visions which belongs to our next consideration. We have now studied two series of visions given to John.

The First was of the seven church periods as he was in the Spirit on the Lord's Day.

(Rev. 1:10) the history of the spiritual welfare of the church is given, covering her life from Pentecost to the end.

The Second was of the political development of the Roman Empire as it effected the church. This is the period of the seven seals and seven trumpets, which also runs from Christ's enthronement on the right hand of God, as proclaimed by Peter on Pentecost, to the blast of the seventh trumpet "and the time of the dead," or the resurrection of the dead for judgment. Paul referred to this last trump when he spoke of the resurrection. He saw there the resurrection of the righteous:

> "Behold, I show you a mystery; we shall not all sleep, but we shall all be changed, in a moment, in the twinkling of an eye, at the last *trump;* for the *trumpet* shall sound, and the dead shall be raised incorruptable, and we shall be changed." (I Cor. 15:51-52)

So we see that our first two visions begin at the same starting point—Pentecost, and ends at the same point of time—The Judgment.

PART III

THE TWO SIGNS IN HEAVEN

CHAPTER XII

Text (11:19—12:17)

19 And there was opened the temple of God that is in heaven; and there was seen in his temple the ark of his covenant; and there followed lightnings, and voices, and thunders, and an earthquake, and great hail.

1 And a great sign was seen in heaven: a woman arrayed with the sun, and the moon under her feet, and upon her head a crown of twelve stars; 2 and she was with child; and she crieth out, travailing in birth, and in pain to be delivered. 3 And there was seen another sign in heaven: and behold, a great red dragon, having seven heads and ten horns, and upon his heads seven diadems. 4 And his tail draweth the third part of the stars of heaven, and did cast them to the earth: and the dragon standeth before the woman that is about to be delivered, that when she is delivered, he may devour her child. 5 And she was delivered of a son, a man child, who is to rule all the nations with a rod of iron: and her child was caught up unto God, and unto his throne. 6 And the woman fled into the wilderness, where she hath a place prepared of God, that there they may nourish a thousand two hundred and threescore days.

7 And there was war in heaven: Michael and his angels going forth to war with the dragon; and the dragon warred and his angels; 8 and they prevailed not, neither was their place found any more in heaven. 9 And the great dragon was cast down, the old serpent, he that is called the Devil and Satan, the deceiver of the whole world; he was cast down to the earth, and his angels were cast down with him. 10 And I heard a great voice in heaven, saying, Now is come the salvation, and the power, and the kingdom of our God, and the authority of his Christ: for the accuser of our brethren is cast down, who accuseth them before our God day and night. 11 And they overcame him because of the blood of the Lamb, and because of the word of their testimony; and they loved not their life even unto death. 12 Therefore rejoice, O heavens, and ye that dwell in them. Woe for the earth and for the sea: because the devil is gone down unto you, having great wrath, knowing that he hath but a short time.

13 And when the dragon saw that he was cast down to the earth, he persecuted the woman that brought forth the man child. 14 And there were given to the woman the two wings of the great eagle, that she might fly into the wilderness unto her place, where she is nourished for a time, and times, and half a time, from the face of the serpent. 15 And the serpent cast out of his mouth after the woman water as a river, that he might cause her to be carried away by the stream. 16 And the earth helped the woman, and the earth opened her mouth and swallowed up the river which the dragon cast out of his mouth. 17 And the dragon waxed wroth with the woman, and went away to make war with the rest of her seed, that keep the commandments of God, and hold the testimony of Jesus.

INTRODUCTION

We have considered two series of visions; namely, the Seven Churches, and the vision of the seven seals, with their accompanying seven trumpets.

In each of these series John is caught up out of the flesh. Before the unfolding of the first series—the Seven Churches—he is "in the Spirit on the Lord's Day. Before the second vision—the Seven Seals and Seven Trumpets, he says "immediately I was in the spirit." Obviously between the two visions he was again in the flesh, else he would not have been called by the voice, as of a trumpet calling him to come up higher, whereupon he was again "immediately in the spirit."

We are about to begin the unfolding of a new series of visions, as evidenced by the language of Rev. 11:19, which, in passing we must say, should belong to the twelfth chapter. This division of the book into Chapters and verses, as well as the punctuation is a modern method introduced to facilitate easy reading and ready reference to the different passages. Early manuscripts of the Bible were written in continuous rows of capital letters, without spaces between the words and sentences. The early manuscripts had no stops at all. Revelation 12:1 would have appeared in this fashion:

WOMAN CLOTHED WITH THE SUN

The earliest example of separated words is found in a manuscript of the ninth century and it was not until about this time that punctuation marks came into existence. The same is true of the employment of verses and chapters. Therefore, the division between the eleventh and twelfth chapters here is purely artificial and does violence to the division of the visions of *Revelation*.

Properly the blowing of the seventh trumpet closes that vision. It naturally follows that 11:19 begins a new vision. The very language indicates a new starting point. Note its similarity in wording to that of the opening of the second series of visions—the seals and trumpets. There it reads:

> "After this I looked and behold, *a door was opened in heaven*" Rev. 4:1

Here it reads:

> "*And the temple of God was opened in heaven*" and there was seen in his temple the ark of his testament: and there were

lightnings, and voices and thunderings, and an earthquake, and great hail."

While John seemed to have returned to the flesh between the first and second series, here there is no mention of that experience, rather indicating that he continued "in the spirit," but the similarity of words with those of Rev. 4:1, indicates that a new vision is being presented.

The language also makes it clear by its likeness to the former vision, which we found to have its starting point at Pentecost, that the same starting point begins that new series of visions. As we study this chapter we shall find this to be true.

Since this is still the language of symbolism in a book of sign-i-fied visions, the symbol here is called heaven because it is a spiritual warfare about to start.

The ark of the Convenant in the Holy of Holies is brought to view. There are to be events "uncovered" which have to do with the temple of God. Since we are the temple of God, (I Cor. 3:16), then, the trials and vicissitudes of the church are to be presented in the language of symbolism.

This refers not to the Jeiwsh temple, which had been destroyed some twenty-five years earlier by Titus, but to the spiritual temple, the Church of Christ. Its door is opened and its history foretold. The vision following will "uncover" the fortunes, sorrows, trials, persecutions and triumphs of the church. Its history will be traced until it is glorified by Christ, the husband.

The Church's heavenly destiny is symbolized by the fact that the Holy of Holies, the type of her final destiny is seen.

The thunders and lightnings and earthquakes symbolize and foreshadow the commotions, earth shaking events, revolutions and judgments which shall take place in the fulfillment of the symbols of this new vision.

Now we are ready to begin the study of the two wonders, or more properly, signs of chapter twelve—I say more properly "signs," for while the text reads "wonders," in the margin the translation is "sign."

These two "signs" are diametrically opposed to each other, both as to character and their war with each other. Shall we consider their interpretation as they apppear in the verses. Rev. 12:1 "And there appeared a great wonder (sign or symbol) in heaven: a woman clothed with the sun, and the moon under her feet, and upon her head a crown of twelve stars."

In all God's references to his chosen, redeemed people, he likens them to a woman, whether the language was typical, prophetic or that of fulfilment. A woman is employed many times in the scripture as a symbol of the church.

"Say to the daughter of Zion, behold thy salvation cometh" (Isa. 62:11). This is a prophecy of the church to come.

"Ye are not the children of the bond woman, but of the free." (Gal. 4:31). The free woman here is the church.

God took the first pair to typify Christ and His church.

Paul said "Nevertheless death reigned from Adam to Moses, even over them that had not sinned after the similitude of Adam's transgression, who is a figure of him that was to come." (Romans 5:14)

Here he says Adam was a figure or type of Christ, so much so that in (I Cor. 15:45) Christ is called the last Adam, for we read: "And so it is written, the first Adam was made a living soul, the last Adam was made a quickening spirit."

If Adam then was a type of Christ, Adam's wife would be a type of the bride of Christ—the church, for Christ is the bridegroom as Christ claimed for himself in (Matthew 9:15).

"And Jesus said unto them, can the children of the bridechamber mourn, as long as the *bridegroom* is with them? but the days will come when the bridegroom shall be taken away from them, and then shall they fast."

Paul, in (Eph. 5:21-31), likens the relationship between the husband and wife to that between Christ and his wife, and closes with these words: "This is a great mystery, but I speak concerning Christ and the church." (Eph. 5:32)

Adam was indeed a type of Christ, because:

1. He was single awhile; so was Christ for he had no wife, the church, until he purchased her with his own blood. (Acts 20:28)
2. He went down into a deep sleep; so did Christ in the sleep of death.
3. His side was pierced in his deep sleep; so was Christ's by the spear of the Roman soldier. (John 19:34)
4. Out of his side was taken his bride; so Christ purchased his wife by the blood that flowed from his side.
5. Adam said, "This is now bone of my bone, and flesh of my

flesh;" and Paul said the same of Christ's bride the church: "For we are members of his flesh, and of his bones." (Eph. 5:30)

6. Adam called her "woman," because she was taken out of the "Man," and the church here in Revelation is called a "woman" because she was taken out of the "Man," as Pilate called Jesus, in being purchased by Christ's death upon the cross.

7. Adam and his wife wore the same name, for we read: "Male and female created he them; and blessed them, and called their name *Adam,* in the day when they were created." (Genesis 5:2). And the church wears Christ's name collectively in being called the "Church of Christ." How wrong it is then to wear a denominational name which dishonors Christ! And individually his redeemed ones are called "Christians," which means "belonging to Christ". (Acts 11:25, 26).

8. Adam called his wife "Eve," meaning the 'mother of all creation,' and the church is the spiritual mother of the re-creation. In (Gal. 4:26) Paul said: "But Jerusalem, which is above is free, which is the mother of us all."

So the woman here is a sign or symbol (and so called in the margin) of the church. We must get our symbolism right in order to progress truthfully and scripturally.

So we have amply identified the woman here as the church, and of her we read that she was "clothed with the sun, and the moon under her feet, and upon her head a crown of twelve stars."

Naturally, she should be clothed with the sun, because Christ, the Son of Righteousness gives her light. Jesus said: "Ye are the light of the world." Said Paul: "For God, who commanded the light to shine out of darkness, hath *shined in our hearts* to give the light of the knowledge of the glory of God in the face of Jesus Christ." (II Cor. 4:6)

Take Christ out of the life of the church, then she, who is fair as the moon and clear as the sun, would walk in darkness.

But she stands on the moon! The Old Testament has been called the moonlight age-typically reflecting the glorious light of the New Testament fulfillment. So in a very definite sense she does stand on the moon, not as a foundation (for other foundation can no man lay than that is laid, which is Christ), but she stands in the sense of following in succession of fulfillment.

A diadem of twelve stars rests upon her brow, which undoubtedly refers to the twelve apostles, under whose teaching she dispenses light to the world. Christ filled the twelve apostles with the Holy Spirit to inspire the church to know His mind and will until the true church can say: "We have the mind of Christ." Having identified the first sign, we will pass over the second verse for the time being to consider the second sign, for before we proceed farther we must understand the other sign, or wonder contained in this chapter.

Rev. 12:3 "And there appeared another sign in heaven, and behold a great red dragon." The latter part of this verse will await a little while for clarification.

For the third time in this book of Revelation we find the book itself "uncovering" its own symbolism. The first and second instances were in the case of the stars and candlesticks in Rev. 1:20. In almost all of the symbolism we have had to turn elsewhere for interpretation. Not so here, however, for the ninth verse explains this second sign. "And the great *dragon* was cast out, that old *serpent* called the *devil, and Satan,* which deceiveth the whole world, he was cast out into the earth, and his angels were cast out with him."

Our understanding of him is made crystal clear. It would seem that God made a special effort here to so definitely identify the dragon that there would never be the least doubt. This is the same serpent—that old serpent which met the first woman, wife of the first Adam in the garden, and for a purpose typical of this appearing of him before the woman here, or the church.

In the garden he made his appearance to deceive the woman with subtility. Surely, he is as old as creation, for in the garden he began his age-long career as a deceiver of mankind.

Then began the age-old conflict inaugurated by the divine dictum: "And I will put enmity between thee (the serpent) and the woman, and between thy seed and her seed; it shall bruise thy head, and thou shall bruise his heel." (Genesis 3:15)

And just as he ever tried to destroy the seed line and finally "the seed of the woman" when the Son of God, become flesh, in the butcher of the infants of Bethlehem and the attempt to "take" his life during his ministry, so here we see a similar attempt to "devour" the seed of the woman as soon as he was born.

The purpose of the dictum was to put enmity between them, and the accomplishment of God's purpose involved the overthrow of the devil, and the supreme purpose of the devil has ever been to *"devour"* the woman's seed, as soon as she brings him forth to the world.

So we have interpreted both signs and are ready to begin our study of the chapter. We will go back to the verse we purposely skipped to complete the unfolding of the two signs. Rev. 12:2: And she, being with child, travailing in birth, and pained to be delivered."

John here calls our attention to the condition of the woman. She is about to become a mother. Evidently great significance is attached to this, because of the attention called to her condition. Shall we interpret the symbol of childbirth. In Isaiah 66:8, we read: "As soon as Zion *travaileth* she brought forth *children."* The travail of Zion caused an increase.

Shall we turn now to the New Testament. Paul, speaking of the church said: "Wherefore, my brethren, ye also are become dead to the law by the body of Chirst; that ye should be married to another, even to him who is raised from the dead, *that ye should bring forth* fruit unto God." (Rom. 7:4)

The law that bound these Jewish brethren to God, to whom they were married (Jer. 3:14) had been nailed to the cross and now being baptized into Christ they were married to Christ. And this spiritual marriage relationship was for the purpose of "bringing forth fruit into God."

With this shall we hear Peter: "If these things be in you, and abound, they make you that ye shall neither be *barren* nor *unfruitful* in the knowledge of our Lord Jesus Christ." (II Peter 1:8)

Just as husband and wife reproduce after their kind, so the church is to bring forth after her kind, or make other Christians. Here the church is pictured bringing forth Christ to the world in great travail of birth. From Pentecost forward she has, in travail of sorrow, affliction, persecution and opposition, brought Christ to the world. She is symbolized here as crying, "travailing in birth and *pained to be delivered."*

203

That "this manchild who was to rule the nations with a rod of iron" which she brought forth, is the Christ is so obvious as to hardly need elaboration. There is no other way by which Christ can be brought forth to the world except by the church. Remember this is the language of spiritual symbolism.

But if any proof is needed, the fact that this "manchild was to rule the nations with a rod of iron" carries our minds back to the Messianic second psalm.

> "The Lord hath said unto me, Thou art my son; this day have I begotten thee. Ask me, and I shall give thee the heathen for thine inheritance, and the uttermost parts of the earth for thy possession. *Thou shall break them with a rod of iron.*" (Psa. 2:7-9)

And if there were not enough proof, then hear Christ himself, for he takes this very perogative to himself alone, "And he shall rule them with a rod of iron." (Rev. 2:27). Also see Rev. 19:15.

And this conflict has a globe encircling aspect. Sun, moon and stars also are indicative of dominion. This is a stupendous conflict. The woman, the church and her manchild Christ are contending with the devil for stakes no less than the dominion of the world.

This is emphasized by Christ's battle, while yet in the flesh with the devil in the wilderness. Matthew said: "Again the devil taketh him up into an exceeding high mountain, and sheweth him all the *kindgoms of the world,* and the glory of them. And saith unto Him, All these things will I give thee, if thou wilt fall down and worship me." (Matt. 4:8, 9)

But before He shall rule the world with a rod of iron, before the kingdoms of this world become the Kingdoms of our Lord and his Christ, Child—the manchild has ascended into heaven to sit on the right hand of God until the last enemy is destroyed. This symbolism is not chronologically presented here in the order of his ascension and his being brought forth to the world by the church.

We have had to travel back and forth in this chapter, leaving out some symbolism, in order to establish the meaning of the two great wonders or signs, and the interpretation of this birth of the manchild.

vs. 3 Now we must return to finish the "uncovering" of the symbol of the dragon as he is described in Verse 3. We have been told by the Book itself that the dragon is that old serpent the devil, called Satan. Four titles are assigned to him. Four is the numerical symbol of the entire compass of the earth. We have already seen four angels standing on the four corners of the earth, and there are four points of the compass to cover all directions on the earth.

Remembering always the devil is contending with Christ and the church for the possession of all the world, it is altogether fitting that this symbolism should represent him as having seven heads, expressive of the fullness of his assumed royalty and the ten horns symbolizing the world wide character of his rule and dominion.

Since he works through a world power, and we know by subsequent history that he used a world power, Pagan Rome in his attempt to devour the manchild wherever the church travailed in birth to bring Him forth, the symbolism is perfect. We shall develop this move fully later in this book, but suffice to say here, that Pagan Rome, after her downfall divided into two kingdoms. A horn is a scriptural symbol of a kingdom as Daniel in the seventh chapter makes clear.

Here is portrayed the death struggle between the Kingdom of Christ and the kingdom of the world under the sway of the dragon. Rev. 12:4 "And his tail drew the third part of the stars of heaven."
In agreement with the stars being angels later in this chapter (verse 7) we read of "how the dragon fought and his angels." In our study of the Saracen scorpions we found that their sting was *in their tails*. In Isaiah 9:15 we found that "the prophet that speaketh lies, he is the tail."

Putting this Biblical interpretation with our present verse under consideration that "his tail drew the third part of the stars of heaven," and also recalling that the devil, or dragon "is a liar and the father of it"—the lie (John 8:44) we arrive at the meaning of it all. It was through falsehood or lies that the devil drew these angels after him, even as by a lie he deceived the first woman, or Eve in the beginning of creation.

Shall we recall a startling statement, in this connection, made by Paul: "And again, when he bringeth in the first begotten into the

205

world, he saith, And let all the angels of God worship him." (Heb. 1:6)

Here there seems to be quite a group who refuse to worship him but became subject to the devil. This also recalls Pauls declaration "For we wrestle not against flesh and blood, but against principalities, against powers, against rulers of the darkness of this world, against spiritual wickedness in high places." (Eph. 6:12)

So the church, in bringing forth the non resurrected and ascended Christ, to the world faces the devil, his angels and world kingdoms. Surely she can only do this through Christ who keeps on pouring strength into her. Now we are ready to advance in the chapter.

vs. 6 "And the woman fled into the wilderness, where she hath a place prepared of God, that they should feed her a thousand and two-hundred and three score days."

For the true church the whole world is a wilderness, a place where there are no spiritual sources of nourishment. So God providently cared for her. But more when we come to verse 14, where her fleeing into the wilderness is again mentioned.

The War in Heaven

vs. 7 "And there was war in heaven. Michael and his angels fought against the dragon, and the dragon fought and his angels."

At first we would be tempted to fix the arena of this battle in the place usually indicated by the word "heaven," but in as much as this is a book of symbolism, heaven as we usually understand that connotation to mean, cannot be the place of conflict.

Particularly is this so when we anticipate the weapons used, and the results which follow in this warfare as enumerated in verse eleven. The overcoming was accomplished "by the blood of the Lamb, and by the word of their testimony, and they *loved not their lives unto death*."

Certainly there is no dying in heaven as we usually understand by that term, Heaven has no cemeteries. Death is an experience of this earth life only. But we will not say more on this verse until we come to it in its logical order. We have merely quoted it to show that this warfare was not in heaven itself. We have quoted it to establish the place of conflict.

Heaven, here, is a symbol of the arena of conflict. The church and the devil fight in the spiritual arena, which only the term "heaven" could properly represent. The devil fights here in this world. Peter said: 'Your adversary, the devil, as a roaring lion, walketh about seeking whom he may *devour*" (I Peter 5:8). Notice the word "devour." Peter uses the same word as John in Revelation.

This walking about of the devil mentioned by Peter reminds us of another instance recorded in the Book of Job:

"Now there was a day when the sons of God came to present themselves before the Lord, and *Satan* came also among them. And the Lord said unto Satan, Whence comest thou? Then Satan answered the Lord, and said, "From going to and fro in the earth, and from walking up and down in it." (Job 1:6, 7)

How perfectly in agreement are these passages with the Revelation description of the arena of warfare began at Pentecost—the point of beginning of this vision and has continued ever since. We have already quoted page after page of history in the first two series of visions how Satan fought with the saints with bloody persecutions from the very setting up of the church. This casting out of the devil took place beginning at Pentecost and he is still being cast out "into the earth" or from things heavenly. We have already, under the brief discussion of the seven heads and horns, referred to a similar prophecy of Daniel. In Daniel we find that Michael is *the great prince that standeth up* for the children of thy people." (Daniel 12:1). So it is completely in keeping that we should find this same Michael standing up for the saints in this vision of Revelation.

Another insight to all this is that neither is the instance recorded in Daniel, nor this one in Revelation the only times Michael and the devil met in combat. In Jude 9 we read:

"Yet *Michael* the *archangel*, when, contending with the devil, he disputed about the body of Moses, durst not bring against him a railing accusation, but said, "the Lord rebuke thee."

So this archangel must be of very great power because when the dead in Christ shall arise at the Lord's descent from heaven, he is to come with the voice of the archangel. (I Thess. 4:16). It is this mighty archangel which leads the angelic forces against the devil and his angels.

What encouragement this ought to give the saints to know how unseen forces fight on their side against the adversary of their souls.

A notable instance of unseen forces fighting for a servant of God, even Elisha, is found in II Kings 6:15-17:

"And his servant said unto him, Alas, my Master! how shall we do? And he answered, Fear not: for they that be with us are more than they that be with them (the Syrians).

And Elisha prayed and said, Lord, I pray thee, open his eyes, that he may see. And the Lord opened the eyes of the young man; and he saw: and, behold, the mountain was full of horses and chariots of fire round about Elisha."

We now come to the result of this great conflict.

vs. 12:8,9 "And (that is the devil and his angels) prevailed not; neither was their place found any more in heaven. And the great dragon was cast out, that old serpent, called the devil, and Satan, which deceiveth the whole world: he was cast out into the earth, and his angels were cast out with him."

This symbolism makes clear that the devil was defeated in his attempt. He was not only vanquished and defeated, but humiliated, or "cast down." That this was to be accomplished by preaching is declared by Christ himself, as he commended his disciples upon their return from preaching. "And he said unto them, I beheld Satan as lightning *fall from heaven.*" (Luke 10:18)

Christ said, anticipating his death upon the cross, which death would overcome sin and its wages, "Now is the judgment of this world, now shall the prince of this world be *cast out.*" (John 12:31) This was a crushing defeat because not only is the devil cast out, but his power to kill by death was ended in Christ's victory.

"For as much then as the children are partakers of flesh and blood, he also himself partook of the same; that through death he might destroy him who had the power of death, that is the devil." (Heb. 2:14)

Then comes the song of triumph:

vs. 10 "And I heard a loud voice from heaven saying, Now is come salvation, and strength, and the Kingdom of our God, and the power of his Christ: for the accuser of our brethren is cast down, which accused them before our God day and night."

These declarations of this poem of praise again give us added information on the time of the beginning of this series. This victory came about when salvation came, and when strength from heaven came (ye shall receive power), "and the Kingdom of our God," which we know Peter proclaimed at Pentecost when he preached the first gospel sermon, using the "Keys" to open the door of entrance into the Kingdom. This he did by the power of Christ who sent the energizer—the Holy Spirit on that day. It was a power which Christ said "had been given him in heaven and earth." (Matthew 28:18).

The words of this song are a fulfillment, almost item by item, of the promise Christ gave his apostles just ten days before Pentecost. He had been with them forty days, "speaking of things *pertaining to the Kingdom of God.*" (Acts 1:3) He further said: *"But ye shall receive power* (the power of our Christ) after that the Holy Spirit is come upon you, and ye shall be witnesses unto me both in Jerusalem, and in all Judea, and in Samaria, and unto the uttermost parts of the earth." (Acts 1:8). Now we behold the weapons of their warfare, which Paul said are not carnal, but mighty through God to the pulling down of strongholds.

(II Cor. 10:4) Shall we read the list:

vs. 11 "And they overcame him by the blood of the Lamb."

That was by preaching the atonement and teaching all men to be baptized unto the death of Christ that the blood might be applied for in His death he shed His blood for the remission of sins. (Rom. 6:3-6)

"And by the word of their testimony." This was done on this earth the arena of the spiritual conflict, because John, the author of this very book was in the isle of Patmos for the word of God and for the *testimony* of Jesus Christ. (Rev. 1:9)

"And they loved not their lives unto death."

There is no death in the heaven above. This action transpired here because men died as martyrs by untold thousands in the death struggle with the devil and his angels.

Surley, this one verse removes all question as to the time and arena of these events. Pagan Rome, the political power through which the dragon or the devil worked, was vanquished and Christianity triumphed.

vs. 12 "Therefore rejoice, ye heavens, and ye that dwell in them. Woe to the inhabiters of the earth and the sea! for the devil is come down unto you, having great wrath, because he knoweth that he hath but a short time."

This verse is a call for those who as overcomers dwell in the heavenlies, spoken of here as "ye heavens and ye that dwell in them." This is not addressed to the angels, neither to the martyred dead, nor to the heaven, as usually understood by that term, because this call is like a door swinging on a hinge. "Therefore" in this case is the hinge, the door-post is the eleventh verse. Those of the eleventh verse are those who overcame him by the blood of the Lamb and the word of their testimony.

According to the New Testament conception of things, the people of God, living here, are viewed as now dwelling in heaven, since their citizenship is there. The Christian is taught to consider himself a stranger and a pilgrim in the earth. Paul said:

"Blessed be the God and Father of our Lord Jesus Christ, who hath blessed us with all spiritual blessings in *heavenly places* in Christ." (Eph. 1:3). Again
And hath raised us up together, and made us sit together in *heavenly places* in Christ Jesus." (Eph. 2:6) Yet again:
"To the intent that now unto the principalities and powers in

heavenly places might be known by the church the manifold wisdom of God." (Eph. 3:10)

Paul also says that here and now we have already "come to Mount Zion, and unto the city of the living God, the heavenly Jerusalem." (Heb. 12:22)

So near to heaven is the church that Paul adds these words in that same verse, "and to the innumerable company of angels." Why shouldn't this be so when we remember that he said of the angels "are they not all ministering spirits sent forth to minister for them who shall be heirs of salvation?" (Heb. 1:14)

Thus we see that the saints are spoken of as they "that dwell in the heavens" in contrast to those who are spoken of as "the inhabiters of the earth and of the sea," upon whom a woe is pronounced because "the devil is come down to them, having great wrath because he knoweth he hath but a short time."

Defeated, humiliated, cast out by overcoming Christians he heaps the spleen of his anger upon the inhabiters of the earth, who are of the earth earthly.

The Persecution of the Church by the Devil

We see how the first great struggle between the woman and the dragon ended in ignominious defeat for the devil and a glorious triumph for the church. But the struggle is renewed. He now tries persecution. This is the exact order of the devils work and the experience of the church as depicted in the first series of visions. After the Ephesian period came the Smyrian period of the martyrs. So here we read:

vs. 13 "And when the dragon saw that he was cast unto the earth, he *persecuted* the woman which brought forth the man child."

This completely agrees with what history tells us of the work of the devil during the second and third centuries of the church.

From Nero in A.D. 70 to Diocletian in A.D. 303 to 313 the church went through ten major persecutions. Of course Pagan Rome was the instrument of persecution, but the guiding genius was the devil himself.

The object of this malignant and venomous persecution was the "woman which brought forth the man child," or the church bringing Christ to the pagan world. So God's people are the object of hatred of the devil and they ever bear the reproach of Christ.

Persecution, as a portion of the Saints dates from the last part of the Ephesian period and reaches its height in the days of Diocletian who inaugurated the longest and severest, as well as the last pagan persecution against the church. The devil learned that persecutions did not accomplish his purpose to blot out the name "Christian" from the earth, but rather the reverse. As far as he was concerned, he wisely changed his tactics, but as the church's welfare was involved, the change of attack proved her downfall. Compromise was substituted for crucifixion. But more anon of this change of method.

> *vs. 14* "And to the woman were given two wings of a great eagle, that she might fly into the wilderness, into her place, where she is nourished for a time, and times and half a time from the face of the serpent."

Between verse 6 and verse 14, we have as it were a parenthesis thrown in, in order to reveal the contestants, the method and weapons of warfare, and the triumph of the saints. The events described embrace both sides of the veil, some of which are heavenly and others on the earthly side of things.

Now verse 14 takes up where the narrative of "unfolding" was abruptly cut off or interrupted at verse 6.

There is given in verse 6 a description of how the woman fled into the wilderness to a place prepared of God where she was to dwell 1260 days, or years. Here she goes to "her place," and was to continue there a time, or a year, times, two years and half a time, one half year, or in other words three and one half years, or 1260 days, which in prophetic history is 1260 years. Therefore the periods are of the same length and both refer to the same segment of time.

But here is added a new symbol. The woman, or church is "given

212

two wings of a great eagle" to facilitate her flight into hiding. This signifies divine aid given the saints to assist them in their escape from Satan while they still dwell in this world-the enemy territory. (John 14:30). The meaning and significance of eagle's wings becomes manifest by turning to a couple of Old Testament passages. The first is in Exodus 19:4 where God said to Moses:

"Ye have seen what I did into the Egyptians, and how I bore you on eagle's wings, and brought you unto myself."

These people of the Old Covenant were a type of the saints of the New Covenant and their deliverance foreshadowed the escape of the people of God of the New Testament.

Here the deliverance of the latter is described by the same symbol "eagles' wings" as the former.

The second passage is found in Deut. 32:10-12:

"And found him (Jacob) in a desert land, and in the waste in the howling wilderness; he led him about, he instructed him, he kept his as the apple of his eye.
    As an eagle stirreth up her nest, fluttereth over her young, spreadeth abroad her wings, taketh them, heareth them on her wings; so the Lord alone did lead him and there was no strange God with him."

Eagles wings then are a symbol of divine strength supplied and applied with energy and swiftness.

We said earlier that there was indicated a change in tactics on the part of the wily serpent, the dragon or the devil. The next verse enlarges on this change.

vs. 15 "And the serpent cast out of his mouth water as a flood after the woman, that he might cause her to be carried away of the flood."

So when the devil failed to accomplish his design to destroy the saints and their witness, through violent persecution, he resorted to a new method of attack.

Here we meet with a new symbol, that of a "flood." The symbol of a "flood" is employed in the Word of God to represent some overpowering and overwhelming agency of destruction.

"Let not the waterflood overflow me." (Psa. 69:15)
"Thou carriest them away as with a flood." (Psa. 90:5)
"The enemy shall come in like a flood." (Isa. 59:19)
"And the end thereof shall be with a flood." (Dan. 9:26)
"Behold waters rise up out of the north, and shall be an overflowing flood." (Jer. 47:2)

This symbol is a most suitable one. None other could be employed which would so well picture the stupendous effort put forth by the devil to carry the church away and drown her testimony by the means of a flood of half truth, comprising alliances, false doctrines, pagan philosophies and practices, blended with the gospel.

Since the true teaching comes from the mouth of the witnesses so here the flood pours from the mouth of the devil. This indicates false doctrines proceeding from the dragon's mouth. And this is just what happened! After persecuting Diocletian came Constantine, who though a pagan embraced Christianity because he had won the battle of Milvian Bridge and he proceeded to corrupt the church with a flood of blended pagan philosophy and Christian doctrine. Thus we see the Smyrnan period of persecution fading out of the symbolic picture and the Pergamos period of compromise coming on the stage of church history.

To save the church God carries her into hiding. And how long was she there? How long was she to be in the wilderness? 1260 years. We found in the second series of visions, consisting of the seven seals and the seven trumpets that this period began with the elevation of a man as "Rector Ecclesiae," Lord of the church and ran until 1793, when the two witnesses were slain in the streets of that great city— the papal empire of Rome—the apostate city in contradiction to the holy city. Much of this time corresponds to the Thyatira period or the Catholic church period.

vs. 16 "And the earth helped the woman, and the earth opened her mouth, and swallowed up the flood which the dragon cast out of his mouth."

214

To exactly what providential deliverance from this flood the incident refers, it is most difficult to say, but a suggestion or two might help.

Many of the heretical teachings of the early centuries disappeared, although it must be honestly admitted that others arose to take their places. But they were swallowed up, as if buried in the earth.

Again: and this seems more likely, while apostate and pagan doctrines were flooding the religio-politico empire church with spiritual and doctrinal corruption, the truth of God was kept by a comparatively faithful few. These being unable to contend with the almost universal defection, contented themselves to dwell in obscurity or hiding.

The Roman Church, which, was most certainly of the earth, swallowed up the flood of false teaching that poured out of the devil's mouth.

vs. 17 "And the dragon was wroth with the woman and went to make war with the remnant of her seed, which keep the commandments of God, and have the testimony of Jesus Christ."

God has always preserved to himself a remnant. In the days of Old Testament Israels worst defection God told Elijah:
> "Yet I have left me seven thousand in Israel, all the knees which have not bowed unto Baal, and every mouth which hath not kissed him." (I Kings 19:18)

That has been the case through all dispensations. It was true during the Thyatira, or Catholic period of church history. The Albigerses, the following of Huss, the Hugenots and others are but a few of the larger groups that bear out this truth, to say nothing of the countless little groups of faithful saints who kept the torch of truth aflame.

Though not visible to the eye of the historians during this period of the dark ages, intellectually, doctrinally and spiritually, yet the true church fed and nourished by God, survived in the hearts of hidden saints.

215

Then followed the age of awakening, when the Bible was translated into the common vernacular, and the Sardis, or reformation period appeared on the stage of action. This in turn was followed by the Philadelphia, or Restoration period in which the church of the First Century reappeared, speaking where the Bible speaks, and keeping silence where the Bible is silent.

Summary

In this chapter we have presented to us a very rapid survey of the progress of the divine decree "I will put enmity between thee, (the devil) and the woman, but magnified in the enmity between the devil and the church, symbolized as a woman in Revelation.

The design of the vision of the twelfth chapter of Revelation is to carry us forward with the rapidity of bold, symbolic strokes to portray the early and middle stages of this great conflict; until we arrive at the last stage as "uncovered" under the vision of the two wild beasts of Chapter thirteen. For whereas the events of the twelfth chapter are described with extreme brevity, with long periods of time compressed into a few words, in the thirteenth chapter the "uncovering" becomes more detailed and definite.

CHAPTER XIII

THE VISION OF THE TWO BEASTS

Text (13:1-18)

INTRODUCTION

1 and he stood upon the sand of the sea.
And I saw a beast coming up out of the sea, having ten horns and seven heads, and on his horns ten diadems, and upon his heads names of blasphemy. 2 And the beast which I saw was like unto a leopard, and his feet were as the feet of a bear, and his mouth as the mouth of a lion: and the dragon gave him his power, and his throne, and great authority. 3 And I saw one of his heads as though it had been smitten unto death; and his death-stroke was healed: and the whole earth wondered after the beast; 4 and they worshipped the dragon, because he gave his authority unto the beast; and they worshipped the beast, saying, Who is like unto the beast? and who is able to war with him? 5 and there was given to him a mouth speaking great things and blasphemies; and there was given to him

authority to continue forty and two months. 6 And he opened
his mouth for blasphemies against God, to blaspheme his name,
and his tabernacle, even them that dwell in the heaven. 7 And it was
given unto him to make war with the saints, and to overcome them:
and there was given to him authority over every tribe and people
and tongue and nation. 8 And all that dwell on the earth shall worship him, every one whose name hath not been written from the
foundation of the world in the book of life of the Lamb that hath
been slain. 9 If any man hath an ear, let him hear. 10 If any man
is for captivity, into captivity he goeth: if any man shall kill with the
sword, with the sword must he be killed. Here is the patience and
the faith of the saints.

11 And I saw another beast coming up out of the earth; and he
had two horns like unto a lamb, and he spake as a dragon. 12 And
he exerciseth all the authority of the first beast in his sight. And he
maketh the earth and them that dwell therein to worship the first
beast, whose death-stroke was healed. 13 And he doeth great signs,
that he should even make fire to come down out of heaven upon the
earth in the sight of men. 14 And he deceiveth them that dwell on
the earth by reason of the signs which it was given him to do in
the sight of the beast; saying to them that dwell on the earth,
that they should make an image to the beast who hath the stroke
of the sword and lived. 15 And it was given unto him to give
breath to it, even to the image of the beast, that the image of
the beast should both speak, and cause that as many as should
not worship the image of the beast should be killed. 16 And he
causeth all, the small and the great, and the rich and the poor, and
the free and the bond, that there be given them a mark on their
right hand, or upon their forehead; 17 and that no man should
be able to buy or to sell, save he that hath the mark, even the name
of the beast or the number of his name. 18 Here is wisdom. He that
hath understanding, let him count the number of the beast; for it
is the number of a man: and his number is Six hundred and sixty
and six.

In the twelfth chapter, we, as it were, were taken back stage, to
behold the real personality behind the church's persecution. Under
the symbolism of a dragon, we found the arch villian to be none
other than "that old serpent, that is called the devil and Satan."

But as Christ must have human instrumentality to present Him to
the world, so, likewise, the devil must employ some human instrument to carry on his nefarious work.

The thirteenth chapter is devoted to the "uncovering" of the
agents employed by Satan. They are two in number:

1. First, the seven-headed, ten-horned beast coming up out of
   the sea. 13:1

2. Second, the two-horned beast, like a lamb, coming up out of
   the earth. 13:11

Taking them under consideration in the order in which they are
presented, we begin with the first.

217

The First Beast

vs. 1, 2 "And I stood upon the sand of the sea, and saw a beast rise up out of the sea, having seven heads and ten horns, and upon his horns ten crowns, and upon his heads the name of blasphemy. And the beast which I saw was like a leopard, and his feet were as the feet of a bear, and his mouth as the mouth of a lion: and this dragon gave him his power and his seat, and great authority."

This first beast appears again in 17:3 and undoubtedly, the beast mentioned in the nineteenth chapter in relation to the false prophet is the same as this first beast.

From this we are given to understand that the record of these two beasts extends into the nineteenth chapter, where both are "cast alive into the lake of fire burning with brimstone."

Our first symbol, then, to be unfathomed is that of the "beast." Daniel stands ready to help us with this, as he had a wonderful experience with beasts, of the very same nature. In the seventh chapter, Daniel tells us of four beasts which he saw. The first was like a lion, the second was like a bear, the third was like a leopard, and the fourth was a nondescript beast, dreadful and terrible, strong exceedingly, with ten horns. He was grieved in spirit concerning them and was told by "one of them that stood by," who made Daniel know the interpretation of the things:

"These great beasts, which are four are four Kings which shall arise out of the earth" (Daniel 7:17) Later in the same chapter and verse 23 we read:

"The fourth beast shall be the fourth Kingdom upon the earth, which shall be diverse from all Kingdoms, and shall devour the whole earth, and break it in pieces.

If the fourth beast is the fourth Kingdom, then it naturally and logically follows that the third beast is the third Kingdom upon the earth; the second beast is the second Kingdom and the first beast is the first great world empire.

There have only been four world empires in all history. In their order they are: The Babylonian, or the lion world empire, the Media-Persian, the bear empire, the Grecian, symbolized by the leopard, and last, the Roman Empire, the non-descript beast.

Daniel not only informs us that the "beast" is a symbol of a world empire, but further informs us that the last great world-empire, the greatest and most dreadful of them all, is the Roman. Also he tells us that the Roman empire is to have ten horns. These ten horns, he tells us in (Dan. 7:24) are ten Kings.

As the four great beasts were said to be four Kings, which later we are told are four world empires, by the same token the ten horns being called ten Kings, are also ten Kingdoms, but lesser ones than the great parent empire.

History records that the Roman Empire was broken up into ten smaller Kingdoms. So, we have identified the "beast" as the Roman Empire and the "horns" as smaller Kingdoms.

Another matter we should notice here is that in Daniel, the seventh chapter, the plurality of world empires is presented by a "succession" of different beasts, each beast representing a succeeding empire, but in Revelation, only one beast appears in this part of the vision, but combining all the properties of all the beasts of Daniel's vision.

The beast John saw combines the feline cruelty and dexterity of "a leopard," the tremendous strength of "a bear" and the terrifying roar of "a lion."

The succession of world empires, one succeeding the other, could not be symbolized by a succession of beasts in this vision, because the Roman Empire possessing the characteristics of all the preceeding beasts, as a whole is pictured here by a single beast of composite character. Since no beast in the natural world possesses all such characteristics, this last one is presented as a *nondescript*-literally "not able to be described in the realm of nature."

We notice something else interesting to behold. In John's vision the beasts going to make up the composite symbol of the beast coming up out of the sea are enumerated in the reverse order as given in Daniel. In Daniel, the ten-horned beast, or Rome, was the *last* of the four, but in John's vision, it is the *first,* then as named the leopard, or Greece, then the bear, or Meda-Persia, and last the lion, or Babylon, which in Daniel's vision is *first*.

A simple explanation of this reversal of order is that Daniel, in the days of the Lion, or Babylon, was looking forward from the time of that first great world empire. John, on the other hand, lived in the days of the nondescript beast, or Roman Empire and was looking backward. Looking backward, the order of the beasts to him, then, would be the leopard, the bear, and the lion. Daniel looking forward would see them in the reverse order, the lion, the bear, the leopard and the nondescript beast.

The beast nearest to Daniel was the farthest from John, and the beast nearest to John was the farthest from Daniel.

How appropriate to symbolize a worldly empire by a "beast." While man is an "uplooking" creature, the beast takes a "downward" look. So an earthly Kingdom ever looks downward because it takes an earthly view of things. While the Kingdom of Christ ever looks upward because its affections are "set on things above and not on things on the earth." (Col. 3:2)

We are now ready to consider yet another symbol, that of the "sea." John saw this beast come up out of the sea. The restless ocean is a symbol of commotion. Revelation used the term "sea" as a symbol of "peoples, multitudes and nations."

"The waters which thou sawest, where the whore sitteth, are peoples, and multitudes, and nations and tongues." (Rev. 17:15) Knowing that the beast John saw is the Roman Empire, how fitting that it is said to come up out of the "sea". The Roman legions conquered all the then known world and thereby was composed of many kinds of peoples, nations and tongues—together constituting multitudes.

The symbol of the "sea" not only represents peoples, nations, multitudes, tongues but also their perpetual *unrest*. Let Isaiah speak here: "But the wicked are like the *troubled sea*, when it cannot rest, whose waters cast up mire and dirt. There is no peace, saith my God to the wicked." (Isaiah 57:20, 21)

We must not fail to note what part of the body of this beast was likened to a "lion." It was the mouth! Since the lion, in Daniel's vision was Babylon—a word that means "babel" or "confusion," the beast of John's vision which is the Roman empire speaks confusion to the world. This will be enlarged upon when we consider the second beast of this chapter.

The Heads Considered

We have thus far passed over the interpretation of the symbol of the "Heads." In 17:10 we read: "But the seven heads are also seven Kings. We found in Daniel that a King represented a Kingdom, or government. Since these seven heads, or governments belonged to the one and same beast empire, or Rome, we must look for the explanation in the form of government of the Roman empire. In all her long history Rome had seven forms of government, as follows: 1. Kings, 2. Consuls, 3. Dictators, 4. Tribunes, 5. Decemvirs, 6. Emperors, and 7. Military governors.

While John sees these seven heads all at the same time, even as the parts of Nebuchadrezzar's image was seen all at once, but represented four Kingdoms, one following and displacing another, so here these heads symbolize seven succeeding forms of government, one following and displacing another.

Again we read: "And upon his heads the name of blasphemy." we must interpret the term "blasphemy." By blasphemy is meant the claiming of divine prerogatives. Upon one occasion Jesus said,: "I and my Father are one, then the Jews took up stones again to stone Him. Jesus answered them: "Many good works have I shewed you from my Father; for which of those works do ye stone me?

The Jews answered him saying, For a good work we stone thee not; but for blasphemy; and because thou being a man, makest thyself God. (John 10:30-33)

Did the King and emperors of Rome blaspheme? Yes, they claimed to be divine and required their subjects to worship them. The Roman emperors made the worship of themselves compulsory and was enforced under penalty of torture and death.

Alexander claimed to be the son of Jupiter Ammon, and the Roman Emperors claimed divine honors and required men to worship their statutes and to offer them sacrifices. "And the dragon gave him his power, and his seat, and great authority."

Here is revealed who manipulates the reins of the pagan Roman government, or all ungodly governments for that matter. The twelfth chapter revealed the devil under the symbol of a dragon. So the devil was behind the vile Roman Government. The devil gave the beast his seat or throne. We read in the vision of the seven churches: "Where Satan's seat is." Also, the devil gave the Pagan Roman Empire its great authority. No other world empire ever enjoyed such great and sweeping dominion. Rev. 13:3 "And I saw one of his heads as it were wounded to death, and his deadly wound was healed, and all the world wondered after the beast."

Literally the phrase "wounded to death" means "as slain to death." And we should remember that whatever hurts the beast or Roman Empire is a direct blow to the dragon, or the devil, which gave the political government its power. This wounding of the head is a phase of the bruising of the head of Satan, or the devil. (Genesis 3:15)

But shall we proceed to the identification of the head that was bruised. We have already found the seven heads to represent the seven forms of government through which the beast-political Rome-went in all its history. The woman, or the church began to bring forth Christ to the world in the days of the fifth form, or fifth head, namely the Emperors. Did the days of the Empire receive a "wound unto death?" Most certainly it did as we learned in the story of the vision of the trumpets. The first four covered the wounding of the western half of the Empire and the next two the slaying of the eastern half, culminating with the fall of Constantinople, the then existing capitol after the Fall of Rome.

The imperial head was wounded unto death in A.D. 476 when Odoacer hurled the last of the Roman emperors from the throne. Gauging our conclusion from the experience of all past history, we would expect this to be the end of the empire.

Ninevah fell to rise no more. Babylon succomed to the armies of Cyrus and became and it still is an abode of doleful creatures as prophesied by Isaiah: "And Babylon, the glory of Kingdoms, the beauty of the Chaldees" excellency shall be as when God overthrew Sodom and Gomorrah.

It shall not be inhabited, neither shall it be dwelt in from generation to generation: neither shall the Arabian pitch tent there; neither shall the shepherd make their føld there. But wild beasts of the desert shall lie there: and their houses shall be full of doleful creatures; and owls shall dwell there, and satyrs shall dance there." (Isaiah 13:19-21)

Tyre fell and on the bare rock, which once was the site of that great city became a place where fishermen spread their nets.

Therefore thus saith the Lord God: behold I am against thee, O Tyrus, and will cause many nations to come up against thee, as the sea causeth his waves to come up. I will make her like the top of a rock. It shall be a place for the spreading of nets in the midst of the sea." (Ezek. 26:3-5)

Carthage, the great rival of Rome, fell and Caius Marius, seven times lifted to the consulship, but banished to Africa a century after the fall of that great African City, as he sat among its ruins, musing upon the fickleness of the fortunes of empire, said to the Roman officers who came to him, "Go tell your masters that they have seen Marius sitting among the ruins of Carthage!"

This was a subtle but pointed warning that Rome would meet the same fate as Carthage. Marius did see the coming of the wounding of the head, but he could not know that the deadly wound would be healed. He understood not the satonic power behind the Roman Empire, symbolized by the first beast depicted here.

Mysteriously, slain Rome arose out of her ashes. Something new under the sun transpired. Conquered by the northern hordes of Goths,

Vandals, Huns and Heruli, the vanquished overpowered the victors by converting them to a religion, which was a mixture of paganism and Christianity. Constantine had, by royal edict, made whole armies Christian. There was no regeneration in the hearts of those soldiers, so instead of Christianizing his soldiers, great masses of unconverted heathen paganized the church. How easy it was for the pagan conquering hordes out of the north to embrace such a half pagan religion. And all the time mysteriously, wondrously the wounded head of the period of the emperors was being healed by this religious state arising in the midst of the political arena. Hear Myers, on this. I quote only a few exerps because the whole statement is too long for this space alloted.

"Long before the fall of Rome there had begun to grow up within the Roman Empire an ecclesiastical state, which in its constitution and its administrative system was shaping itself upon the emperial models. This spiritual empire like the secular empire, possessed a hierarchy of officers, of which deacons, priests or presbyters, and bishops were the most important.

These bishops collectively formed what is known as the episcopate. There were four grades of bishops, namely: country bishops, city bishops, metropolitans or arch bishops, and patriarchs.

At the end of the fourth century, there were five patriarchates, that is regions ruled by patriarchs. These centered in the great cities of Rome, Constantinople, Alexandria, Antioch and Jerusalem.

Among the patriarchs, the patriarchs of Rome were accorded almost universally a precedence in honor and dignity.

Before the close of the eighth century, there was firmly established over a great part of Christendom what we may call an ecclesiastical monarchy.

The removal, by the acts of Diocletion and Constantine, of the chief seat of the government to the east, instead of diminishing the power and dignity of the Roman bishops, tended greatly to promote their claims and authority. It left the pontiff the foremost personage in Rome.

Upon the surrender of the sovereignity of the West into the hands of the Emperor of the East, the bishops of Rome became the most important personages in the Western Europe. A dispute about the use of images in worship, known in church history as the "War of the Iconoclasts," which broke out between the

Greek Churches of the East and the Latin Churches of the West, drew after it far-reaching consequences as respects the growing power of the Roman pontiffs.

In this quarrel with the Eastern emperors, the Roman bishops formed an alliance with the Frankish princes of the Carolingian house. The popes consecrated the Frankish Chieftains as Kings and emperors, the grateful Frankish kings defended the popes. Such a broad outline was the way in which grew up the Papacy, an institution which, far beyond all others, was destined to mould the fortunes and direct the activities of western Christendom throughout the medieval times."—Myers' Ancient History pages 582, 583, 584, 585, 586.

Thus we see how one of the heads was "wounded, as it were to death," and how "his deadly wound was healed."

In the Pergamos period of Church History, as visioned in that of the Seven church periods, which corresponds to the time when Constantine united church and state, thus compromising the truth with Paganism, we read these words: "I know thy words, and where thou dwellest, even where Satan's seat is."

The papacy could never have healed the wounedd head of the pagan empire of Rome had she not occupied the seven-hilled city, where Satan's seat has ever been.

We have taken some time, and quoted to some length from history, though only a fragment which could be given, but it has provided us with a comprehensive picture of the head wounded unto death and how the wound was healed.

"The sway of Rome under the papal system of government became in spite of her downfall, mightier and more extensive than her sway under the Caesars, because she had power over both body and soul.

We are ready now to proceed in this chapter: Rev. 13:5, "And there was given unto him a mouth speaking great things and blasphemies and power was given unto him to continue forty and two months."

From the revised pagan Rome, went out great pronouncements, Blasphemy is not merely profanity, but the claim to divine perogatives by human beings. Did the pontiffs claim divine perogatives?

The popes claim to be the vicegerent of Christ. He calls himself the vicar of Christ. A vicar is defined "as one who is authorized to act in place of another." Whom did Christ authorize to act in His stead. Hear Him:

"How when he, the Spirit of truth, is come, he will guide you into all truth: for he shall not speak of himself; but whatsoever he shall hear, that shall he speak: and he shall show you things to come. He shall glorify me: for he shall receive of mine, and shall show it unto you." (John 16:13, 14) Christ's authority is absolute, in heaven and in earth (Matt. 28:18) and he has never delegated it to any human being. The apostles only spoke "as moved by the Holy Spirit (Acts 2:4). Therefore no man has the right to claim to be the Vicar of Christ. To do so is the heighth and depth of blasphemy.

The heighth of this blasphemy was reached in 1870 when it was decreed that the pope sitting as God in the temple of God, spoke with an infallible voice. How the world needs to keep in mind what Paul wrote in AD. 54: "Let no man deceive you by any means: for that day (as that the day of Christ is at hand Verse 2) shall not come except there come a falling away first, and that man of sin be revealed, the son of perdition, who opposeth and exalteth himself above all that is called God, or that is worshipped, so that he is as God sitteth in the temple of God, showing himself that he is God." (II Thess. 2:3, 4)

"And power was given unto him to continue forty and two months."

That is, power was given pagan Rome, rising out of the ashes of a slain head, the emperors and the empire, to continue through the rise of the Papacy.

Again this period of forty and two months, 1260 days or years is mentioned. We have found that the holy city, or the true church of Christ was to be trodden down by the Gentiles for forty and two months; the two witnesses prophesied in sack cloth for one thousand two hundred and three-score days; the woman, or the true church, was driven by the dragon (the devil) into the wilderness for twelve hundred and sixty days, where she was nourished for the entire time, called a "time and time and half a time;" and now the beast-political Rome is given power to continue for forty and two months. All refer to the same length of time and all refer to the same period of time.

All these events begin and end at the same time. Each mention only presents different phases of the persecution of the Church for that span of years. They are different parts of the same history.

225

We have already, in our study of the two Witnesses, found this period designated ended in 1793 A.D.

At the end of that time-period, there is an exaltation of the two witnesses in the printing and distribution of the Bible on a worldwide scale, the Church of the Philadelphian period (the Restored Church) comes out of the wilderness and the old imperial Rome, revised in the power of the Papacy, receives a mortal blow. Ecclesiastical Rome, through its alliance with the Frankish princes of the Carolingian house, united church and state, and the descendants of these same Frankish princes, the modern French nation, dealt a death blow to the papal imperial duality, bringing it to an end.

Napoleon Bonaparte conquered Italy, carried the pope to France and forced him to crown himself (Napoleon) as emperor of France. The coronation took place in the cathedral of Notre Dame in Paris Dec. 2, 1804.

"In less than a year after Napoleon's coronation the subservient French clergy were teaching the youth of France, "The Emperor is the minister and power of God, and his image on earth," ran the new catechism;" "to honor and serve him is to honor and serve God." Myers Mediaeval & Modern History, page 552. Blasphemy? Yes. The heart is still "speaking great things" and "opening his mouth in blasphemy against God."

Thus did this bring about the complete breakdown of the ancient empire. So did the Holy Roman Empire, the longest lived of human institutions, come to an end. And the end was 1260 years after the Pope was declared "Lord of the Church." So again as always, we see history corroborating the Bible. We must ever carry the book of Revelation, and its symbolism, in one hand and a book of history in the other. Things are come to pass and do come to pass as it was sent and sign-i-fied to the apostle John.

While the pope still attempts to take a hand in politics, his influence from that fateful day when the Holy Roman Empire came to a sudden end, has steadily waned. Shorn of his sceptre as a temporal ruler, he now presides over a mock Vatican state with a railroad only six hundred feet in length!

vs. 7 "And it was given unto him to make war with the saints, and to overcome them: and power was given him over all kindreds, and tongues and nations."

And did political Rome make war with the Saints? From Justinian, when Gibbon said, "Catholic soldiers burned the conventicles with their 'congregations' down through the centuries, political Rome, motivated by papal intrigue has reddened her domains with blood."

To name the murdering of the Waldenses, Albigerses, the Carnisards, the massacre of Bartholomew's day, and the slaughter of life in the Spanish Inquisition, besides the host of unnamed massacres, only serves to attest the truth, that "It was given unto Him to make war against the saints." Truly, political and papal Rome was made drunk with the blood of the saints. And surely "it was given him to overcome the saints." And also power was given him "over all kindreds and tongues and nations."

vs. 8 "And all that dwell upon the earth shall worship him, whose names are not written in the book of the Lamb slain from the foundation of the world."

All worship this beast-government, namely, render fealty to this government, whose names are not written in the book of Life of the Lamb slain from the foundation of the world.

A book of life is a registry of the lawful citizens of a place. By the same token, the Lamb's book of life must then be the registry of the names of the true citizens of the Kingdom of God, or the Church of Christ.

All who by faith and obedience to the required scriptural terms are rightful citizens. In the first church is described in the New Testament, all who entered into the Kingdom of Christ were first preached to or taught. So Christ, the law-giver commanded in His commission: "Go ye therefore, and *teach* all nations." Matthew 28: 19. "Go ye into all the world, and *preach* the gospel to every creature." Mark 16:15

This then first required *"hearing"*. But during the days when the beast held sway, babies who could not hear were admitted to the Kingdom.

*Second*s All in the beginning were required to believe. They were taught so that they might believe. "Faith cometh by hearing and hearing by the Word of God." (Rom. 10:17)

"Go ye into all the world and preach the gospel, he that believeth." (Mark 16:16)

But under this beast government babies were admitted into the Kingdom without faith.

Third: In the New Testament Church, all who heard, by being taught or preached to, were buried by baptism, or immersion into Christ.

"Baptizing them in the name of the Father, and of the Son and of the Holy Spirit." (Matt. 28:19)

"He that believeth and is baptized shall be saved." (Mark 16:16)

But under the beast government an unbeliever was sprinkled in order to become a citizen of that government. Hear Cardinal Gibbons the late Catholic Cardinal to the United States:

"For several centuries after the establishment of Christianity, baptism was usually conferred by immersion, but since the twelfth century, the practice of baptizing by affusion (*sprinkling*, italics ours) has prevailed in the Catholic Church, as this manner is attended by less *inconvenience* than baptism by immersion. (*Faith of Our Fathers*, page 266)

Much, much more might be included here to illustrate the point but sufficeth to say, all who seek citizenship in the Kingdom of God in the divinely prescribed manner have their names written in this book of life of the Lamb, and by this act reject the authority and claim of the beast.

The beast government, or the papacy, which revived the dying head of the beast, prescribed naturalization laws not found in the New Testament, and claimed all who conformed to these laws were citizens of the Kingdom, while the Lamb's Book of Life contains only the names of those who have been *born again,* according to Scriptural requirements.

But a deceived world worshipped the beast. Never must it be forgotten, that the one who gave this beast such power that required the worship of all men was that old deceiver, which deceiveth the whole world, the dragon, or the devil.

vs. 9 "If any man have an ear, let him hear."

This is the eighth time this admonition occurs in Revelation, the other seven times are found in the vision of the seven churches. This is a characteristic saying of the Lord. Since He was the speaker who uttered the other seven like admonitions, we logically must infer that He is, likewise, the spokesman here. No one else makes use of it, and He always employs it in connection with certain of His utterances in order to impress upon us their peculiar and special importance.

How significant its use here, in connection with stressing of the divine difference between citizenship in the kingdom of the dragon (devil) energized beast kingdom of papal Rome, and the citizenship of those of Christ's Kingdom, whose names are written in the Lamb's Book of Life!

How ill becomes the denominational world to practice the same Satan-inspired citizenship requirements of the beast government! How needful to heed the call to come out of this spiritual Babylon! Such a call is given in Rev. 18:4:

"And I heard another voice from heaven, saying, Come out of her, my people, that ye be not partakers of her sins, and that ye receive not her plagues."

vs. 10 "He that leadeth into captivity shall go into captivity: he that killeth with the sword must be killed with the sword. Here is the patience and faith of the saints."

While not the same wording, how very similar in thought to the statement following the call to come out of Babylon, as we have just quoted from the 18th Chapter.
"Reward her even as she rewarded you, and double unto her double according to her works: in the cup which she has filled fill to her double." (Rev. 18:6)

If the beast and his adherents lead the worshippers of her government captive, the beast shall finally and eventually be made captive: as the beast has slain with the sword, so it shall be likewise slain with the sword-a strong intimation that the last great war will cut off the head and not merely wound it. "They that take up the sword shall perish by the sword." (Matt. 26:52)

Here is the patience and faith of the saints. The true saints then, "with patience shall wait for it." Wait for what? During the centuries of oppression, misrule, arrogant false claims and oppositions to God's will, the patience of the saints will be maintained by their faith in the prophecies concerning the doom of Satan and his beast government which oppressed the true church.

229

The Second Beast

Thus far we have followed the career or the first, or seven headed, ten-horned beast. The first ten verses of the chapter have dealt with this first beast, the remainder of the chapter describes another beast, different, yet allied to the first one.

The very fact that the first beast had to do with a world government, wounded to death, but resurrected in a religio-political temporal government, gives us strong reasons for understanding that the second beast symbolizes something of like nature, for the *symbol being* the same, the thing symbolized must be the same.

How startlingly significant! As in the creation, the water was first and the dry land, or earth came out of the water (Gen. 1:9), so out of the sea, or waters, (signifying peoples, nations and tongues in great commotion), came the earth from whence arose the second beast.

It is subsidiary to the first and arises in order to continue the existence of the first. Shall we read the record:

> *vs. 11, 12* "And I beheld another beast coming up out of the earth; and he had two horns like a lamb, and he spoke as a dragon. And he exerciseth all the power of the first beast before him, and causeth the earth and them that dwell therein to worship the first beast, whose deadly wound was healed."

We have already learned that the "earth" to John meant the Roman Empire in its political aspects. John here sees this second beast rising up out of the Roman Empire, the *ordered part of the world*.

While the first beast, or political Rome had ten horns with crowns, this second beast had two horns like a lamb, this presenting similitude like the Lamb of God, which presents it as a beast with a religious aspect. It professes to be Christian, or Chirst-like in character.

No symbol could more fittingly represent the real character of a religious organization exercising all the power of the first beast (political Rome) before him. Such a religious organization would claim to represent the Lamb of God, but really its voice is the voice of the devil—"he spake as a dragon."

Has there ever arisen anything "out of the earth" (or the Roman Empire, as John understood the "earth" to mean) while the empire continued to exist after one of its heads (the imperial form) was wounded? Has there arisen a beast government, lamb-like in appearance out of political Rome, intimately aligned with that government which continues even to this day? If so, does it resemble this symbolism given in Revelation?

Only a cursory acquaintance with history will call to our remembrance such a system which has been known for fifteen centuries as Romanism, or the Roman Catholic church. It arose out of the earth,—political Rome and is a system religious in character and political in aim. It was closely associated with the temporal empire and is still identified with the nations which are off-springs of the old universal empire.

We digress here for a space to present a picture of the three great systems which have arisen at different times and under diverse circumstances, each of which have been religious in character, but political in aim. All have opposed the true church. Since Pentecost, the birthday of the church, there have been three great adversaries which have arisen to oppose the New Testament Church. They have perpetuated the time-long struggle between the serpent and the seed of the woman-Christ.

All these, religio-political systems, have had one supreme purpose-the opposition of God's declared purpose to bring everything under the dominion, sway and sovereignty of Christ. All three systems were energized by the devil.

It was a contest over the kingdoms of the world embodied in the battle between Christ and the devil in the wilderness of temptation (Matt. 4:1-11). Shall we deal with them in their order.

The Three Great Adversaries

1. *First:* The first adversary against the church was Judaism, which first opposed Christ in his life time and would not rest until he was crucified. This is not fanciful interpretation. Hear Christ, himself, declare that these were of the devil.

> "Ye are of *your father* the devil, and the lusts of your father will ye do. Because I tell you the truth, ye believe not." (John 8:44, 45)

The nation, though until 1949, without national life, has miraculously maintained its national character, and throughout the centuries, and, even now, when they have set up a government in Palestine, are bitterly opposed to the Church of Christ and the seed of the woman, which the church brings to the world. Judiasm has never changed in nature. Its aim still is supremacy over the Gentiles and the rejection of Christ as her Messiah. She has never withdrawn from the field of battle.

2. *Second:* The second great adversary, or next of these great religious systems, having as its aim domination of the world and the overthrow of Christ's Kingdom is Islam, or Mohammedanism.

Islam, you remember was a movement that came up out of the bottomless pit, the devil's domain. It was led by a false prophet Mohammed, who based his teaching upon a false book, the Koran. At one time it almost conquered the world and to this very second is opposed to the true Church and the Christ himself. This system, too, has never withdrawn from the field of conflict.

3. *Third:* The third great adversary, or third of the three great religious systems having uncompromising purpose of world dominion, and the destruction of the true church is Romanism. This system, like the two preceding, is also religious in character, but political in aim. This system is the most formidable of all three. Like the other two, its purpose is to seize dominion of the world, the exact aim of the dragon himself, or the devil.

While all three are Satanic systems with a common character and purpose, the last of the three is different from the others in its method of opposition. Its manner of opposition is infinitely more subtle.

Judiasm and Mohammedanism were *openly* opposed to Christ and his Kingdom, Catholicism presents itself in a Lamb-like characterization, or as the embodiment of Christianity itself. No wonder, then, it was revealed in the Thyatira period of church history, that "the depths of Satan" had been reached. (Rev. 2:24)

What an exact symbol, then, is this second beast of this third system!

Such a remarkable difference is presented to us, because Romanism did not come into existence as an open and outright opponent to the true church, but *claiming* to be *the* true church. She has always had a close and a Siamese-like connection with political Rome. In the truest sense Siamese twins of church history. To sever one from the other would mean death for both. While the first beast-political Rome-arose out of the tumultuous and restless *sea* of a multitude of nations; papal Rome arose out of the earth-the Roman Empire.

This second beast rose up out of the earth in the guise of a two-horned lamb, being both political and religious, speaking as the dragon, or proclaiming devil doctrine in the cloak of religiosity, and exercising all the power of the first beast, or political Rome. Shall we quote Myers on this. Under the heading "The Two World Powers," he says:

" 'The two great ideas, 'says James Bryce,' which expiring antiquity bequeathed to the ages that followed were those of a world *monarchy* and a world religion.'

We have seen how out of one of these ideas, under the favoring circumstances of the earlier Mediaeval Centuries, was developed the *Empire,* and out of the other the Papacy. The history of these two powers, of their relations to the rulers and the peoples of Europe, and of their struggle with each other for supremacy, makes up a large part of the history of the Mediaeval Centuries."—Myers. 'Mediaeval and Modern History.' Page 111.

Hear Myers again, same book, page 112:

"As God has set in the heavens two lights, the sun and the moon, so has he established on earth two powers, the spiritual and the temporal; but as the moon is inferior to the sun and receives its light from it, so is the Emperor inferior to the pope and receives all power from him."

Myers inserts a footnote here. Quoting:

"Dante, maintaining the rights of the Emperor, ruined the force of this comparison by pointing out that, while the moon often eclipses the sun, the sun never eclipses the moon."

We now quote a similar statement from another source:

"Like the two great luminaries fixed by the Creator in the firmament of the heaven to give light to His creatures, so also hath He ordained two great powers on earth, by which all are to be governed and preserved from error. Those powers are the *pontifical* and the *royal*; but the former is the *greater,* the latter the *lesser.* Yet under *both,* the religion of Christ is so ordered that, by God's assistance the *apostolical power* shall govern the *royal.*"

Henderson's Select Historical Documents of the Middle Ages. Bohn's edition, 1896.

We quote from yet a third source in which Dr. Green in his history on page 468 describes the inauguration of Boniface VIII.

"At his inauguration two kings held his stirrups. He proclaimed a jubilee for the year 1300. He appeared before the multitude on one day in his pontificals, on another day with sword, crown and sceptre, exclaiming, 'I am Caesar! I am Emperor!' This same Boniface issued a famous bull (Unam Sanctum) in

233

which with marvelous exegesis, he quoted (Luke 22:38): ("And they said, behold, here are two swords. And he said unto them, It is enough," insertion mine) saying: 'Both swords, the spiritual and the temporal are in the power of the church.' That bull further explicitly declares that 'there is one holy Catholic and apostolic church, outside of which there is no salvation or remission of sins. We declare, announce and define, that it is altogether necessary to salvation for every human creature *to be subject* to the Roman pontiff'."

"He exerciseth all the power of the first beast before him." With what infinite brevity is here described how the papal power would exercise the powers of the state. The papacy was for centuries the "power behind the throne."

Shall we also note that he exercised not only the same power-political, but he exercised that same power, from *the same place,* the seat of the Roman Empire and the *seat* of *the depths of Satan,* the imperial city of Rome, where Christ tells us: "Satan's seat is." (Rev. 2:13)

vs. 13 "And he doeth great wonders, so that he maketh fire come down from heaven on the earth in the sight of men." We are still in the realm of symbolism and must constantly remind ourselves of that fact.

The alleged miracles of papal Rome are inumerable. Rome has claimed the power to perform miracles throughout the ages. In the Breviary are recorded such miracles as: Francis Xavier turning sufficient salt water into fresh to save five hundred travelers. St. Raymond laid his cloak upon the sea and sailed upon it. The statue of the Virgin Mary is made to weep. At Naples a reddish solid in a vial, said to be the blood of St. Januarius turns to liquid. At the grotto of Lourdes, the Virgin Mary appears frequently. I now quote from "The Externals of the Catholic Church," second edition, 1918, revised to conform to the new code of Canon Law. On pages 226, 227 we read:

"The Miraculous Medal." There is a widely used medal known by this title because it takes its origin from a vision. It is a medal of the Blessed Virgin. This beautiful medal has a remarkable history. It was given to the world through a vision which was vouchsafed to a holy servant of God, Sister Catherine, a French Sister of Charity, known to the world as Zoe Laboure.'

On November 27, 1830 and on several occasions, the Blessed

Virgin appeared to her as depicted on the medal, and commanded the saintly nun to cause the medal to be made. This was done, with the sanction of the Archbishop of Paris, within two years; and the use of the medal of the 'Immaculate Conception' spread rapidly throughout the world.

Many and great indulgences have been given to its wearers." And do not for a moment entertain the thought that all these miracles are spurious. To John was revealed the fact that this second beast was given power "to do great wonders":

vs. 14 And the object of the performance of these miracles is given in Verse 14:

"And deceiveth them that dwell upon the earth by the means of those miracles which he had power to do in the sight of the beast."

Not only had this second beast (Papal Rome) the voice of the dragon, for "he spake as a dragon," but he deceived the world like the dragon, for the devil is "that old serpent and satan, which deceiveth the whole world." (Rev. 12:9)

Again quoting:

"Saying to them that dwell on the earth, that they should make an image to the beast which has the wound by a sword and did live."

The word "image" means something like another thing. The first beast represented a world-wide political power and the Roman Catholic Church is fashioned after the old political Rome in her governmental functions, even to making the seat of her government in Rome, even as did Imperial Rome make that her capital.

The Roman Catholic Church ever calls her head, the pope, after the fashion of old Imperial Rome. Hear Myers at this point:

"The College of the Pontiffs was so called probably because one of the duties of its members was to keep in repair a certain bridge (pons) over the Tiber. This guild was the most important of all the religious institutions of the Romans; for to the Pontiffs belonged the superintendence of all religious matters. The head of the College was called *"Pontifex Maximus,* or "Chief Bridge Builder," which title was assumed by the *Roman Emperors,* and after them by the Christian *bishops of Rome*; and thus the name has come down to our times."— Myers Ancient History—page 365.

Not to see in all this symbolism the union of church and state,

235

the union of political and papal Rome is to be utterly spiritually blind.

"In whom the god of this world hath *blinded* the *minds* of *them which believe not,* lest the light of the glorious gospel of Christ, who is the *image of God,* (not the beast), should shine unto them." (II Cor. 4:4)

vs. 15 "And he had power to give life unto the image of the beast, that the image of the beast should both speak, and cause as many as would not worship the image of the beast to be killed."

This image was not a mere likeness of political Rome; this image had life. Papal Rome gave life to the ecclesiastical government fashioned after the temporal. The spiritual power converted the restored temporal power of Rome into a terrible reality. The pronouncements of interdicts, bulls and anathemas eminating from Rome through the centuries, even to the late pronouncement of the Assumption of Mary, December 1950, attest to the truth that the image was given power to speak.

And as to the power given the image to kill again, we refer you to history. Witness the Albigenses of the southern Alps; the wars carried on against the Waldinses, who, persecuted by Pope Greogry IX, because they believed men should interpret the Bible in their own way, as against church pronouncements; the wars waged against the Huguenots; the slaughter of 18,000 victims in the Acquisition of the Netherlands; the terrible wars pursued against the Protestants in Europe, the persecution by "bloody Mary" of England, and the massacre of St. Bartholomew's, August 24, 1572.

vs. 16, 17 "And he causeth all, both small and great, rich and poor, free and bond, to receive a mark in their right hand, or in their foreheads: and that no man might buy or sell, save he that had the mark, or the name of the beast, or the number of his name."

This, doubtless, is a figurative way of expressing object servitude to the image of the beast, but there is more detail revealed.

A brand or a mark upon a person is a symbol or badge signifying complete ownership of the one so marked, or branded by him whose mark he bears. Slaves used to be branded. Even one who sold himself to another, as recorded in the Scriptures were branded.

"And if thy brother, an Hebrew man, or an Hebrew women, be sold unto thee, and serve thee six years; then in the seventh year thou shalt let him go free from thee.

And it shall be, if he say unto thee, I will not go away from thee, then shalt thou take an aul and thrust it through his ear, and he shall be thy servant forever." (Deut. 15:12, 16, 17)

Coming back to our passage under consideration, then, to bear the mark of the beast is to be his servant and the right hand is the servants instrument of action in that servitude. We found out earlier that the right hand also signifies strength, so the servant of the image of the beast also serves with his strength, giving that strength unto that image.

That, not only the strength was given to the image of the beast, but also the mind is indicated by the mark being received on the forehead.

"And these words which I command thee this day, shall be in thine heart. And thou shalt teach them diligently to thy children . . . and thou shalt bind them for a sign upon *thine hand,* and they shall be as frontless *between* thine eyes." (Deut. 6:6-8)

Here, we see these two members are mentioned together in relation to one's belief or faith. Do we find that multitudes gave their entire allegiance of hand and mind to the image of the beast, or religio-political Rome? Most certainly this is amply fulfilled in Romanism.

A mark in the hand represents the practice, whereas a mark in the forehead indicates a profession of belief. It can not be merely an accident or coincidence that a mark on the forehead inducts a person into the Roman Church and the making of a mark evidences his faithful subservance.

And the mark? It is the sign of a cross with water in the sprinkling ceremony. Without this mark there is no salvation. And it is the Roman Catholic Church-the image of the beast-which instituted this mark.

vs. 17 "And no man might buy or sell, save he that had the mark, or the name of the beast, or the number of his name."

It has been a common practice for Catholics to patronize Catholics and to hire only Catholics in business and institutions wherever possible. The councils of Tours, Constance, and the Laterans forbad business dealings with heretics.

And Romanism is ever associated with the Latin people and language. Rome was the ancient capital of the Latins. The Romans spoke the Latin language. The Roman Catholic church has always been known as the Latin church, as against the eastern church, being known as the Greek Orthodox church. The Roman sacred books are written in Latin, the masses are conducted in Latin, regardless of the country in which the church is established. The councils of the Roman church conduct their sessions in Latin. In the earliest history of Italy the inhabitants dwelt in the central section known as Latium and the reputed founder of this Latin race was Latinus or as the Greeks, who preceded the Romans as a world empire, spelled the name LATEINOS. Which leads us to the last verse:

vs. 18 "Here is Wisdom. Let him that hath understanding count the number of the beast: for it is the number of a *man,* and his number is six hundred three-score and six."

Thus Revelation declares this number. Remember it is the "number of the beast," the "number of his name," and the "number of a man," and the number of all three are the same-666.

Now the figures 666 are the Arabic characters for the numbers, but they were unknown for several hundred years after John wrote. John wrote in the Greek language for readers who understood that tongue. So the numbers, naturally, would be expressed in Greek characters. Now the Greeks did not indicate their numbers by figures but by letters, just as the Romans did. The number symbols of the Latin language are as follows:

I,   V,   X,   L,   C,   D,   M
1   5   10   50   100 500 1,000.

Latinus was the reputed founder of the Latin Race. The New Testament was penned in Greek. The Greeks spelled the name "Latinus" as "L-A-T-E-I-N-O-S." Greek letters had a numerical quality, like the Latin language did. The word "Lateinos" adds up as follows: L=30, a=1, t=300, e=5, i=10, n=50, o=70, s=200. Adding 30 plus 1 plus 300 plus 5 plus 10 plus 50 plus 70 plus 200 equals *666.*

So the name is the number of the beast and that name, Latinos, the number of the man, is 666. Thus Christ has left us with no room for the faintest shadow of a doubt as to the identity of the beast. Indeed, here *is* wisdom!

Having so identified the beast, we still must not improverish our understanding, but rather enrich it by a further understanding of the spiritual meaning of the number 666.

666 stands as the sum total of all human achievement, spiritually speaking. That "number of man" is six, repeated three times to call our attention to the incompleteness of the Roman church. It is a human church, founded on a claimed foundation of a human

being "Peter." It has a human at its head-the pope. Its doctrines are human pronouncements. Its foundation and superstructure are homogeneous-both human.

But over against this number of incompleteness, God's doings reach seven, the symbol of perfection and completeness. Man never gets, in human achievements, or religious practice, beyond six. He has never attained the seven of perfection.

When God completed the six days of creative acting, the six days were a "finished" work-a perfected work. But God did not stop at six. He went on to completion. God rested on the seventh day.

Yet another thought. Only one other time does the number 666 occur in the Scriptures. It is found once in the New Testament, and once in the Old Testament. The Old Testament reference is Ezra 2:13 and one that has to do with numbering, also:

"The children of Adonikam, six hundred sixty six." The word Adonikam, according to Young's Concordance, means "My Lord has risen." The head of the Roman church called himself, "Rector Ecclesaei" or "Lord of the Church." He rises up to make himself Lord, though only human. How logical that he should be given a number of six thrice repeated, to reveal to us his utter humanness, heading a two beast institution, which is political and papal Rome, speaking like a dragon, or the devil!

CHAPTER XIV
PARENTHETICAL VISION OF THE TIME OF THE END
Text (14:1-20)

1 And I saw, and behold, the Lamb standing on the mount Zion, and with him a hundred and forty and four thousand, having his name, and the name of his Father, written on their foreheads. 2 And I heard a voice from heaven, as the voice of many waters, and as the voice of a great thunder: and the voice which I heard was as the voice of harpers harping with their harps: 3 and they sing as it were a new song before the throne, and before the four living creatures and the elders: and no man could learn the song save the hundred and forty and four thousand, even they that had been purchased out of the earth. 4 These are they that were not defiled with women; for they are virgins. These are they that follow the Lamb whithersoever he goeth. These were purchased from among men, to be the firstfruits unto God and unto the Lamb. 5 And in their mouth was found no lie: they are without blemish.

6 And I saw another angel flying in mid heaven, having eternal good tidings to proclaim unto them that dwell on the earth, and unto every nation and tribe and tongue and people; 7 and he saith with a

great voice, Fear God, and give him glory; for the hour of his judgment is come: and worship him that made the heaven and the earth and sea and fountains of waters.

8 And another, a second angel, followed, saying, Fallen, fallen is Babylon the great, that hath made all the nations to drink of the wine of the wrath of her fornication.

9 And another angel, a third, followed them, saying with a great voice. If any man worshippeth the beast and his image, and receiveth a mark on his forehead, or upon his hand, 10 he also shall drink of the wine of the wrath of God, which is prepared unmixed in the cup of his anger; and he shall be tormented with fire and brimstone in the presence of the holy angels, and in the presence of the Lamb: 11 and the smoke of their torment goeth up for ever and ever; and they have no rest day and night, they that worship the beast and his image, and whoso receiveth the mark of his name. 12 Here is the patience of the saints, they that keep the commandments of God, and the faith of Jesus.

13 And I heard a voice from heaven saying, Write, Blessed are the dead who die in the Lord from henceforth: yea, saith the Spirit, that they may rest from their labors; for their works follow with them.

14 And I saw, and behold, a white cloud; and on the cloud I saw, one sitting like unto a son of man, having on his head a golden crown, and in his hand a sharp sickle. 15 And another angel came out from the temple, crying with a great voice to him that sat on the cloud, Send forth thy sickle, and reap: for the hour to reap is come; for the harvest of the earth is ripe. 16 And he that sat on the cloud cast his sickle upon the earth; and the earth was reaped.

17 And another angel came out from the temple which is in heaven, he also having a sharp sickle. 18 And another angel came out from the altar, he that hath power over fire; and he called with a great voice to him that had the sharp sickle, saying, Send forth thy sharp sickle, and gather the clusters of the vine of the earth; for her grapes are fully ripe. 19 And the angel cast his sickle into the earth, and gathered the vintage of the earth, and cast it into the winepress, the great winepress, of the wrath of God. 20 And the winepress was trodden without the city, and there came out blood from the winepress, even unto the bridles of the horses, as far as a thousand and six hundred furlongs.

The Vision of the Harvest

In the thirteenth chapter we studied about the two beasts, namely political and papal Rome. These two agencies were given power for a period of 1260 years to wage war upon the Chruch of Christ. The weapons used were both temporal and spiritual. The arm of the state and the false, deceitful and miraculous powers of the apostate church worked together as one.

It was a dark picture, well designed to plant fear and despair in the hearts of true Christians.

Therefore, a parenthesis of encouragement is inserted at this point to strengthen the saints. A like parenthesis of consolation was inserted between the sixth and seventh seals and the sixth and seventh trumpets. This present parenthesis, the third one, resembles the first parenthesis in character, but harmonizes and coincides with the second in point of time.

So here we witness the history of the two beasts being interrupted at the end of the thirteenth chapter, to be resumed and completed in future visions incorporated in the 15th, 16th, 17th 18th and 19th chapters.

By this definite harmony with the parenthesis between the sixth and seventh trumpets, we are able to get a bench mark reading of our location in respect of time.

Taking a perspective view of the whole chapter, it portrays to us a culmination of all things ending with the judgment. The chapter stands related to the days between the sixth and seventh trumpet in the same manner as the sealing of the 144,000 in the seventh chapter is related to the encouragement of the saints before the seventh seal.

Briefly, this chapter, first, gives encouragement to the saints, reveals a glorious revival of gospel preaching, announces the fall of Babylon, gives a warning against worshipping the beast, then hurdles time and presents the coming of the Son of Man, sitting upon the clouds of heaven and finally describes two reapings in the harvest of the earth, one of the elect and the other of the wicked. Shall we now proceed to a more detailed study of this Chapter:

> *vs. 1-5* "And I looked, and lo, a Lamb stood on the Mount Zion and with him an hundred forty and four thousand having His fathers name written in their foreheads.
>
> And I heard a voice from heaven as the voice of many waters, and as the voice of a great thunder: and I heard the voice of harpers harping with their harps.
>
> And they sing as it were a new song before the throne, and before the four beasts and the elders, and no man could learn that song but the hundred and forty and four thousand which were redeemed from the earth.
>
> These are they which were not defiled with women; for they are virgins. These are they which follow the Lamb whithersoever he goeth. These were redeemed from among men, being the first fruits unto God, and to the Lamb.
>
> And in their mouth was found no guile: for they are without fault before the throne of God."

What a vivid contrast is this scene to the one of the terrible beasts of the last chapter! Mount Sion is a symbol of the church. Paul said:

> "We are come unto Mount Sion, and unto the City of the Living God, the heavenly Jerusalem, and to an innumerable company of angels, and to the general assembly and church of the first born." (Heb. 12:22, 23)

And Peter declares Christ to be the chief corner stone in Sion:

> "Wherefore also it is contained in the Scriptures, Behold, I lay in Sion a chief corner stone, elect, precious: and he that believeth on Him shall not be confounded. (I Pet. 2:6)

So Sion is a symbol of the true church. And these, whom John saw, had His Fathers name upon their foreheads, in contrast to those of the thirteenth chapter, who had the mark of the beast on their foreheads.

This vision, vouchsafed to John, lifts the veil so that the redeemed may see what they could not see with physical eyes.

John heard a voice from heaven, as the voice of many waters. This voice though tremendous, nevertheless, melodiously blends with the singing of the 144,000 redeemed saints. And all sung to the accompaniment of instrumental music—"harpers harping with their harps."

This scene reminds us of the great Oratorio of Redemption, sung by the solo voices, the four living creatures the four and twenty elders, the myriads of angels and the redeemed of every kindred, and tongue and people and nation, which is described in the fifth chapter of Revelation.

The 144,000 doubltess is symbolical and not intended to represent an exact number. They are the first fruits to God and the Lamb. As, in the Old Testament economy, the first fruits devoted to God were representative of the whole harvest to follow, so these seem to stand forth as symbolical of the whole harvest of souls to follow.

A description of these who were "redeemed from among men," follows:

First, they are described as those "which were not defiled with women, for they are virgins." All obedient believers are classed as virgins and are presented to the Lamb of God as such. Said Paul: "For I am jealous over you with godly jealously: for I have espoused you to one husband, that I may present you as a *chaste virgin* to Christ. (II Cor. 11:2)

Second, "they follow the Lamb whithersoever He goeth." They are sheep that hear and heed the Shepherd's voice. Christ, in the days of His flesh, said, "My sheep hear my voice, and I know them, and they follow me." (John 10:27)

Third, they are described as "the first fruits unto God and to the Lamb."

They were, as James said of those God had begotten with the word of truth: "Of His own will begat he us with the word of truth that we should be a kind of first fruits of his creatures." (James 1:18)

In the despensation of the Mosaic law, the firstfruits were that which was set apart as God's portion of the productivity of the earth. So in the despensation of the gospel these 144,000 are God's portion from the hosts of men. And are representive of the whole harvest.

Fourth, they are described as "those in whose mouths was found no guile, for they are without fault before God."

In contrast to the beast whose mouth spoke great things and was full of blasphemies, the mouths of the saints were without guile, for they spoke the truth. And being baptized in Christ, wherein they came under the blood of Christ, they were made faultless.

They had put on the righteousness of Christ as Paul declared, "But of Him are ye in Christ Jesus, who of God is made unto us wisdom and *righteousness* and sanctification and redemption." (I Cor. 1:30)

And in his righteousness, we are to be presented faultless before the presence of God.

"And now unto Him that is able to keep you from falling, and to present you faultless before the presence of His glory with exceeding joy, to the only wise God our Savior, be glory and majesty, dominion and power both now and forever. Amen. (Jude 24, 25)

The next scene logically follows, for as the first fruits were rendered faultless before God by the truth of God's word, all the remaining harvest of souls must also hear the one, simple, and only gospel of Christ. Hence, there follows a scene in which the fervent, missionary church proclaims the glorious and everlasting gospel of Christ.

vs. 6, 7 "And I saw another angel in the midst of heaven, having the everlasting gospel to preach to them that dwell on the earth, and to every nation, and kindred, and tongue, and people, saying with a loud voice, Fear God, and give glory to him; for the hour of his judgment is come: and worship him that made heaven, and earth, and the sea, and the fountains of waters."

There is a startling similarity between the angelology of the three interludes, or parentheses.

In the first parenthesis between the sixth and seventh seals an angel with a loud voice speaks: "And I saw another angel having the seal of God, and he cried with a loud voice to the four angels." (Rev. 7:2)

Again in the second parenthesis, between the sixth and seventh trumpets, we read: "And I saw another mighty angel come down from heaven clothed with a cloud." (Rev. 10:1)

In the first, second, and third parenthesis these angels are different from the other angels mentioned in their respective settings.

Here in this chapter six other angels are mentioned. Four messages and two commands concerning the harvest are given by these six angels.

The First Angel and His Message. This angel is seen flying in the midst of heaven. He has the everlasting gospel. It is the same gospel that Paul preached and of which the apostle said, "But though we or an *angel from heaven* preach any other gospel unto you than that which we have preached unto you let him be accursed." (Gal. 1:18)

So this is an eternal or unchangeable gospel which was to be preached "unto them that dwell on the earth, and to every nation, and kindred, and tongue and people."

Christ said, "The field is the world." So this angel "flying" speaks celerity, and since an angel excells in strength, this symbolism portrays a season of vigorous and rapid evangelism of all the world.

This angel flys rapidly across the heavens with the Blessed Message, the old Jerusalem gospel-the gospel of Pentecost, Caesarea Philippi and other New Testament places.

Here the revived church, full of zeal, with a sublime missionary spirit goes everywhere preaching the word.

That definitely identifies the point of time of this vision. After the "Little book" was given, world-wide evangelism began.

That this movement will be world-wide is made clear in that the angel addresses all races.

The message is a call to fear God (rather than papal power). And to give God glory and worship Him, because the hour of his judgment is come. This brings us to the message of the second angel.

The Second Angel and His Message.

vs. 8 "And there followed another angel saying, Babylon is fallen, is fallen, that great city, because she made all nations drink of the wine of the wrath of her fornication."

The message of this angel is closely linked with the first angel and his message. In the closing statement of the first angel's message the hour of God's judgment was announced, and in this second angel's message the proclamation is made "Babylon is fallen, is fallen."

Doubtless "Babylon" is used here, because the Babylon of antiquity with all its vileness, as well as granduer, was a type of the great Babylon of the Apocalypse.

John could not have referred to the ancient city of Babylon of the Old Testament, for it fell centuries before John wrote. It has never been rebuilt, even to this day. John then refers to some great city or power, unseen while John lived on Patmos, but would be revealed in due process of time.

Perhaps a careful consideration of that ancient Babylon—a type of this future Babylon—will help us in the latter's identity.

First: Before the erection of ancient Babylon all men were of one language and one family. On this site occurred the confusion of tongues and the dividing of the nations. The name "Babylon," itself, means, "confusion," derived from "babel." We still speak of a polyglot of noises as a "babel" of confusion.

Second: This old Babylon lead the old Israel of God into captivity and destroyed their temple in Jerusalem.

Third: It was the first great universal empire, as described in Daniel.

As this was a type, the New Testament Babylon must correspond.

Before the beasts, political and Papal Rome, jointly ruled on the seven-Palatine Hills, the church spoke the same language, taking the Bible, or the "Little Book" for all authority. They spoke where the Bible spoke and were silent where it was silent.

There was unity of belief and practice. But with the coming of the apostate church to power, human decrees, dogmas, papal pronouncements and findings of church councils were substituted for the one Biblical language, and confusion resulted.

Satan was back of the rearing of the first tower of Babel, as, likewise, he was the one who spoke through political and papel Rome, as a spiritual tower of Babel was raised.

The new Babylon lead the world into spiritual captivity. In the preceeding chapter, verse 10, we have a parallel prophesy of the fall of this spiritual Babylon: "He that leadeth into captivity shall go into captivity: he that killeth with the sword must be killed with the sword."

As the Babylon on the Euphrates was a powerful and universal Empire, so did the spiritual and political Babylon on the Tiber, hold universal sway over, both the bodies and souls of men.

The ancient, literal Babylon was the subject of prophesy concerning drunkenness, to be followed by a prediction of her downfall. "Babylon hath been made a golden cup in the Lord's hand, that *made all the earth drunken:* The *nations have drunken of her wine;* wherefore the nations are mad." (Jeremiah 51:7)

The comes the prophesy of her downfall: "Babylon is suddenly fallen, and destroyed." (Jeremiah 51:8)

Just so antitypical, or spiritual Babylon is to come to a sudden end.

The literal Babylon of the Old Testament made the nations drunk in a physical way; the spiritual Babylon makes the nations drunk of the wine of spiritual fornication, or unchasteness toward Christ.

As a man drunken with "spirits," has an addled, or confused brain, mentally, so a man drunk with "evil spirits," also has a spiritually addled mind, confused by false doctrine and practice.

The announcement is made by anticipation as on the eve of the accomplishment. Just as Joseph said to Pharaoh: "And for that the dream was doubled unto Pharaoh twice; it is because the thing is *established,* and God will *shortly* bring to it pass," (Genesis 41:32) so the pronouncement of Babylon's doom is doubled, "Babylon is fallen, is fallen." In another vision of the same event the repetition of the announcement is also given double: (Rev. 18:2): "And he cried mightily with a strong voice, saying, Babylon the great, is fallen, is fallen."

What assurance is given the saints that this unholy institution, hoary with age will surely fall! This truly *is* the patience (or reward) of the saints. *The Third Angel and His Message.*

Just as the second angel's message (that of the destruction of Babylon) was linked with the message of the first angel (that the hour of judgment is come), so the message of this third angel is linked with that of the second one.

This third angel declares that those who *drink* of the wine of the wrath of Babylon's fornication shall also drink of the wine of the wrath of God. We read:

vs. *9-11* "And the third angel followed them, saying, if any

246

man worship the beast and his image, and receive his mark in his forehead, or in his hand, the same shall drink of the wine of the wrath of God which is poured out without mixture into the cup of His indignation; and he shall be tormented with fire and brimstone in the presence of the holy angels, and in the presence of the Lamb: and the smoke of their torment ascendeth up forever and ever and they have no rest day or night, who worship the beast and his image, and whosoever receiveth the mark of his name.

The first thing to which we would call attention is the associating of Babylon with the beast" and "the image of the beast," and, the receiving the mark of the beast in the forehead and upon the hand and having the mark of his name. This proves beyond the least shadow of a doubt that "Babylon" and the beast and its image are one and the same institutions. Therefore, a declaration that "Babylon is fallen, is fallen" is an assurance to the true Church of Christ that both political and papal Rome, with its image—the Roman Catholic Church, will fall. And when it comes it will be very sudden. When the fullness of God's wrath has come, that apostate church will fall with a suddenness that will shock the whole world.

The awful punishment which will befall those who worship the beast and his image, and have his mark in the forehead, or in his hand, will be two-fold:

First: They shall drink of the wine of the wrath of God and it will be without mixture—not diluted, or mixed with mercy, hope or love. The cup of God's indignation not only will be full, but full of unadulterated divine wrath.

Second: They are to be tormented forever and ever. There are many today who laugh at and jeer at the idea of an everlasting hell of punishment for the wicked. Many verbal thrusts are made at the "preachers of fire and brimstone." But none other than a great and mighty angel from heaven proclaimed this fact, and with a *"loud"* voice. Whose word shall we believe and accept before it is eternally too late—God's angel, or man's wishful thinking and human opinion?

vs. 12, 13 "Here is the patience of the saints: here are they that keep the commandments of God."

This is the reward of the saints, that they shall be spared such a fate. And who are the saints? Those "that keep the commandments of God."

The devotees of papal pronouncements and denomination mimickings, will find their worship vain. This makes no difference whether a papal power commands other than the scriptural requirements, or whether it be a denominational bishop or preacher who teaches the doctrines of men, namely doctrines without divine authority. Did not Christ say: "But in vain they do worship me, teaching for doctrines the *commandments* of men?" (Matthew 15:9)

In God's sight there is no difference between a Roman priest sprinkling a person on the forehead, and a protestant preacher doing the same act. Both are teaching doctrines of men and putting the same into obedient practice.

Again there comes ringing the challenge of Christ: "And why call ye me Lord, Lord, and do not the things which I say?" (Luke 6:46) Rev. 14:13, "And I heard a voice from heaven saying unto me, write, Blessed are the dead which die in the Lord from henceforth: yea saith the Spirit, that they may rest from their labors: and their works do follow them."

When a matter of great and outstanding importance is to be considered we meet with the word "write." With the exception of John being forbidden to write what the voices of the seven thunders uttered, we do not run across this word since the time John was told to write the messages to the seven churches. The same is true of the mention of the Spirit speaking. Not since the admonitions of the Spirit to the seven churches, "Let him that hath an ear hear what the Spirit saith to the churches," does the Spirit speak until this present verse under consideration and he does not speak again until Rev. 22:17. Here then is the comfort of the saints and the Spirit confirms it.

So John is commanded to "write." because a matter of great importance is the subject matter. Since this time roughly corresponds to the period of the Reformation and, subsequent Restoration, the saints would be those who had heard and believed the "Little Book," and having obeyed the commands of entrance, and faithful continuance in the Kingdom of God's dear Son, were *in the Lord.*

There is an infinite difference between those who die in the Lord and those who die in their sins. "There is therefore now *no condemnation to them which are in Christ Jesus.*" (Rom. 8:1) Again: "The Lord shall descend from heaven with a shout, with the voice of the archangel, and with the trump of God: and *the dead in Christ shall rise first.*" (I Thess. 4:16)

But to die out of Christ, with the "Little Book" printed and published throughout the world—and not to have obeyed its commands, to get into and remain in Christ—will be eternally tragic. Of such Jesus said, "Ye shall die in your sins." (John 8:21)

"Henceforth" is a precious word. Having scripturally become a Christian, death offers blessedness. "For me to die is gain." (Phil. 1:21)

Those from henceforth do rest from their labors. The realm of departed spirits is not some sort of purgatory where labors on both sides of the veil must be entered into in order to complete salvation, but the Spirit, after a long silence—since the first chapter, speaks up to say, "that they may *rest* from their *labors*."

How timely this message after the long Thyatira period of Catholicism! In this period arose, and flowered to fullness, the diabolical dogma that the departed must reside in Purgatory and are only released through much labor and purchasing of many masses *to secure rest for them*. If such a dogma is true, how would one on this side of the veil know when sufficient masses had been said to complete the transaction? No, the Scripture declares plainly that they are already at rest.

The words, "Their works do follow them," promises a reward awaiting the saints *there* for their works done *here*. Paul said: "For as much as ye know that your labor is not vain *in the Lord*." (I Cor. 15:58)

The character the true saint acquired, the influence for truth exerted, the results of transformed souls attained—all follow him into the presence of Christ.

The Vision of the Harvest

Proclamation has now gone forth that the hour of judgment has come, that Babylon has fallen, that the damnation of beast-marked worshippers is at hand, that "the dead in Christ rest in their labors." We now are given a vision of the reaping of the harvest. First, the righteous are reaped, followed by the reaping of the "grapes of wrath."

> *vs. 14-16* "And I looked and behold a white cloud, and upon the cloud one sat like unto the Son of man, having on his head a golden crown, and in His hand a sharp sickle. And another angel came out of the temple, crying with a loud voice to him that sat on the cloud. Thrust in thy sickle, and reap: for the time is come for Thee to reap; for the harvest of the earth is ripe. And he that sat on the cloud thrust in His sickle on the earth; and the earth was reaped."

A work of separation takes place between the sixth and seventh trumpet. (Rev. 11:1, 2). Here, in Rev. 14:14-16 the separation of the good and bad again appears prominently.

The Son of man, as seen in this vision, has a golden crown on his head, showing that he comes back as a *King*.

John said, "I saw, and behold a white cloud." The cloud is a signal of the second advent of the Lord Jesus Christ. When He ascended, "A cloud received him out of their sight;" and at the same time two men stood by the apostles and said, "This same Jesus, which is taken up from you into heaven, shall so come *in like manner* as ye have seen him go into heaven." (Acts 1:10-11)

The cloud took him up and the cloud will bring Him back. Luke said, "They shall see the *Son of man* coming *in a cloud* with power and with great glory." (Luke 21:27)

Let the Master, himself, clarify this dual harvest. In Matt. 13:24-30, he speaks a parable concerning the sowing of the good seed of the Kingdom and the harvest thereof:

> "Another parable put He forth unto them, saying, The Kingdom of heaven is likened unto a man which sowed good seed in his field."

Then he proceeds to show what this Kingdom is to be like, down to the time of the harvest. It was to be a mixture of tares and wheat together. He, seed of the woman, Himself, the Christ sows good seed—the children of the Kingdom; the tares are sowed by the devil and are the "children of the wicked one."

When his disciples asked for the interpretation, He thus explained the good and bad seed and then proceeds to explain how the wheat and the tares will be separated at the time of the harvest. The discription coincides in the finest way and parallels the order of gathering the harvest as protrayed in the fourteenth chapter of Revelation. Hear him: "The harvest is the end of the world; and the reapers are the angels. As therefore the tares are gathered and burned in the fire; so shall it be in the end of this world."

"The Son of man," (same title as found in Rev. 14:14) shall send forth his angels, and they shall gather out of his Kingdom all things that offend, and and them which do iniquity, and shall cast them into a furnace of fire: "there shall be wailing and gnashing of teeth." (Matt. 13:39-42).

In (Mark 4:26-29) he said:

> "And he said, so is the Kingdom of God, as if a man should cast seed into the ground, and should sleep, and rise night and

day, and the seed should spring and grow up, he knoweth not how, for the earth bringeth forth fruit of herself; first the blade, then the ear, after that the full corn in the ear. But when the fruit is brought forth, immediately he putteth in the *sickle* because the harvest is come."

So we see the evil has its harvest as well as the good.

The setting of Christ on the cloud was to inaugurate the harvest and to this end, this gold-crowned King holds in his hand a sharp sickle.

Seeing Him with this harvest-sickle in his hand caused another angel to cry with a loud voice: "Thrust in thy sickle, and reap for the time is come for thee to reap, for the harvest of the earth is ripe." This is another angel, other than to those mentioned in verses 6, 8 and 9. Even the angel seems to cry out for speedy vengeance.

"And He that sat on the cloud thrust in His sickle on the earth; and the earth was reaped." What awesome words! What an experience in the wind up human affairs, and with what brevity! Nothing but inspiration could have confined itself to such narrow limits of recording an event, a mere human being would have required volumes to relate.

But this is only one phase of the reaping. After the *grain* harvest comes the *grape* harvest. So we read: Rev. 14:17, "And another angel (this is the fifth thus far mentioned) came out of the temple which is in heaven, he also had a sharp sickle."

Whereas the angel in verse 15, (the fourth angel mentioned in this chapter) came from the temple—not the temple which is in heaven, but evidently the spiritual temple as made up of those who keep his commandments, this angel in the 17th verse came out of the temple which is in heaven. This angel comes from the holy place not made with hands. It is in this heavenly temple that Christ is now appearing in the presence of God for us as our great High Priest. And it is from that temple He is to come when He returns the second time.

vs. 17 Again we come to a parallel. Just as when Christ was seen coming on a cloud with a sickle in His hand (Verse 14), and the fourth angel in (Verse 15) cried with a loud voice, "Thrust in thy sickle," so here, as the fifth angel in verse 17, came out of the temple which is in heaven, having a sharp sickle in his hand, another angel, the sixth introduced in this chapter, came out from the altar and also cried with a loud voice saying, "Thrust in thy sickle." Shall we read the account:

251

vs. 18 "And another angel came out from the altar, which had power over fire; and cried with a loud cry to him that had the sharp sickle, saying, Thrust in they sharp sickle, and gather the clusters of the vine of the earth; for her grapes are fully ripe."

This last angel, one who has power over fire, comes forth from the altar where the fire was kept burning, or the altar of burnt offering.

Fire is an emblem of judgment and punishment.

John, the Immerser, referred to this scene when he said, "I indeed baptize you in water unto repentence: but he that cometh after me is mightier than I, he shall baptize you with the Holy Spirit and with fire." (Matt. 3:11). The "fire" here refers to the final judgment, and John continues to so apply it: "Whose fan is in his hand, and he will thoroughly purge his floor, and gather his wheat into the garner; but he will burn up the chaff with unquenchable fire."

This angel of the altar-fires is so outraged by the awful vintage of the wickedness of the earth that he cries with a loud voice for the angel to thrust in his sickle.

vs. 19 "And the angel thrust in his sickle into the earth, and gathered the vine of the earth, and cast it into the great winepress of the wrath of God."

Here we observe that "the vine of the earth" is set over against "the vine of heaven." The true vine is Christ and Christians are the branches, as Christ himself declared: "I am the true vine," (John 15:1) Ye are the branches." (John 15:5)

The grapes of the vine of the earth are the fully matured children of the wicked one, They are "fully ripe".

Into this mass of "vines of the earth" the sickle was thrust. The vine of the earth is cast into the great winepress of the wrath of God. The judgment is final and complete.

vs. 20 "And the winepress was trodden without the city, and blood came out of the winepress, even unto the horses bridles, by the space of a thousand and six hundred furlongs."

The winepress is said to be trodden "without the city." First, this would mean that it was without the church, for in the apocalypse, the city, unless a wicked city is under consideration, refers to that institution. And, second, it would mean the Holy City of the future. There will be nothing unclean or defiling in that city. Speaking of that future city, John said, "For without are dogs" etc. (Rev. 22:15)

And who will do this treading of the wine press without the city?

None other than an outraged Christ himself. In a definite prophesy of the Christ, Isaiah said:

"I have *trodden* the winepress alone; and of the people there was none with me; for I will *tread* them in my anger, and *trample* them in my fury; and their blood shall be sprinkled upon my garments. For the day of vengence is in mine heart, and the year of my *redeemed* is come." (Isaiah 63:3, 4).

And what a horrible flow of blood follows! From the trodden vintage there flows a stream of such magnitude that it rose to the horses bridles to the distance of 1600 stadia, or furlongs. What an appalling result!

Since this is a symbol in a book which is, of all the books of the Bible, preeminently symbolic, this doubtless symbolizes the terrible final destruction of the hosts of wickedness. A symbol of a river of human blood, one hundred and sixty miles in length, to the depths of the horses mouths, tells the tragic story.

The very mention of horses bridles here causes our minds to leap forward to the nineteenth chapter where Christ is pictured mounted upon a white horse, followed by the armies of heaven, also mounted on horses. (Rev. 19:11-16)

The whole seems to be symbolic of the awful carnage in the punishment of the wicked in that day. The figures 40 times 40 equals 1600, or 4 times 4 multiplied by 10 times 10 is a symbol of the completeness of the final judgment.

Four seems to be the apocalyptic symbol of the earth as there are said to be four corners, four winds, or four directions and four quarters of the earth. The earth 4 times 4 times 100 implies the completeness of the Divine Judgment.

CHAPTER XV

Text (15:1-8)

1 And I saw another sign in heaven, great and marvellous, seven angels having seven plagues, which are the last, for in them is finished the wrath of God.

2 And I saw as it were a sea of glass mingle with fire; and them that come off victorious from the beast, and from his image, and from the number of his name, standing by the sea of glass, having harps of God. 3 And they sing the song of Moses the servant of God, and the song of the Lamb, saying,

Great and marvellous are thy works, O Lord God, the Almighty; righteous and true are thy ways, thou King of the ages. 4 Who shall not fear, O Lord, and glorify thy name? for thou only art holy; for all the nations shall come and worship before thee; for thy righteous acts have been made manifest.

5 And after these things I saw, and the temple of the tabernacle of the testimony in heaven was opened: 6 and there came out from the temple the seven angels that had the seven plagues, arrayed with precious stone, pure and bright, and girt about their breasts with golden girdles. 7 And one of the four living creatures gave unto the seven angels seven golden bowls full of the wrath of God, who liveth for ever and ever. 8 And the temple was filled with smoke from the glory of God, and from his power; and none was able to enter into the temple, till the seven plagues of the seven angels should be finished.

This chapter takes up a detailed account of the final judgments poured out upon the beast, the image of the beast and those who have his mark.

The preceeding chapter simply gives a preview or a summary of events that lie in the future; the fifteenth, sixteenth, seventeenth, eighteenth and nineteenth chapters cover the same territory but give a more detailed account.

Throughout these above mentioned chapters the theme is the destruction of spiritual Babylon. Looking back, the seven seals recount the history and overthrow of Roman paganism. The seven trumpets carry us through the overthrow of the Roman Empire of the west by the Goths, Vandals, Huns and Heruli and the ruin of the Eastern portion of the empire by the Saracens and Turks. The seventh trumpet terminates with the trump of the archangel. The seven vials, or bowls, give the history of an epoch and like each series of sevens before it, carry us to the end of that epoch. Particularly do the events of the seventh seal refer to the ecclesiastical or spiritual Rome, called the papacy. The seven seals have as their object, the overthrow of Roman paganism. The seven trumpets have as their design the overthrow of the Roman Empire. The seven vials have as their goal the overthrow of the blasphemous power, the papacy which is spiritually called Babylon.

This is not the ancient capital on the Euphrates, nor the Roman imperial city situated on the Tiber, but Rome as a spiritual symbol.

The last chapter closed with the two harvests, one of the wheat and the other of the grapes; now we would naturally expect the presentation of the new heaven and the new earth. But again there is a new series of judgments. John reviews, recapitulates and enlarges upon the scenes sketched in the fourteenth chapter. He does this under the symbolism of the emptying of seven vials; or seven golden bowls full of the wrath of God.

Here in the fifteenth chapter we encounter the third and last of the three great *signs in heaven* given by John. In Revelation, the 12th chapter, the word "wonder" in the first and third verses, we have found to be *signs*.

The first *sign* in heaven was the *woman* clothed with the sun, or the Church of Christ. The second *sign in heaven* was the great red dragon, or the devil, or Satan. It is the sign of "the mystery of iniquity" spoken of by the apostle Paul. The third *sign in heaven* which is now before us, is the vision of the seven last plagues. This sign is described by John as "great and marvelous." Hear him:

vs. 1 "And I saw another sign in heaven, great and marvelous, seven angels having the seven last plagues; for in them is filled up the wrath of God."

The seven angels and their vials do not begin their work until we reach the sixteenth chapter. But the emphasis in the fifteenth chapter is that these are the seven *last* plagues and that by them the purpose of God will be fully and finally accomplished, because God's wrath will be "filled up."

The word "plagues," not used in reference to the trumpet judgments, is evidently intended to refer us back in the Scriptures to a parallel case of God's deliverance of His persecuted people in Egypt. The plagues of Egypt were ten in number to symbolize fullness of Divine visitations; here they are seven in number to symbolize completeness and finality.

vs. 2 "And I saw as it were a sea of glass mingled with fire; and them that had gotten the victory over the beast, and over his image, and over his mark and over the number of his name, stand on the sea of glass, having the harps of God."

John here sees the victory gained by the saints over the beast. There is a sea as of glass mingled with fire." It was the sea that overwhelmed the Egyptians in the ten plagues visited upon them. But the people of God passed safely through it. Here is a greater victory. They *stand* upon the sea. The fire with which this symbolic sea is intermingled represented the judgments of God fully and finally accomplished. The saints are *standing on this sea*. They are represented as above, or beyond the reach of the sea of judgment.

They have the harps of God to sing the song of Moses and the Lamb. It is very worthy of note that in these visions of the triumphant saints, they are ever pictured as singing to the tune of instrumental music.

vs. 3 "And they sing the song of Moses the servant of God, and

255

the song of the Lamb, saying, "great and marvelous are Thy works, Lord God Almighty; just and true are Thy ways, thou king of saints."

They sing in a higher key and in a more glorious diapason the old "song of Moses" which the ancient Israel of God sang on the shore of the Red Sea on the morning of their deliverance. (Exodus 15th Chapter) Now into the old redemption song mingles a new and loftier strain the song of completed redemption. Shall we listen to this song of the Lamb as it reaches its grand crescendo:

vs. 4 "Who shall not fear thee, O Lord, and glorify thy name? for thou art holy: for all nations shall come and worship before thee for thy judgments are made manifest."

Whereas the worshipers of the beast glorified "the number of the name of the beast," these true worshipers glorify "the name of the Lord." They sing in ecstacy of spirit because the judgments of God are made manifest.

The truth and righteousness of God's judgments are revealed in that Christ manifests himself as the King of the true saints of all nations.

As the strains of praise sink into sacred silence the apostle's attention is turned again to the agents of divine judgments. He sees the temple of the tabernacle of the testimony in heaven.

The fifth verse of the fifteenth chapter resumes the thread of thought dropped in Revelation 11:19 which reads, "and the temple of God was opened in heaven, and there was seen in his temple the ark of his testament." So after the great interruption in which were given the three celestial signs in heaven—the woman, the dragon and the sign of the seven angels with the seven last plagues, John now returns to his starting point of the opened temple.

vs. 5, 6 "And after these things" (the celestial signs and other visions Rev. 12:1 to Rev. 15:1-4) "I saw and the tabernacle of the testimony in heaven was opened: and there came out from the temple the seven angels having the seven plagues, clothed in pure and white linen, and having their breasts girded with golden girdles."

The garb is royal and priestly. Their ministry is priestly although involving duties marked by severity of punishment. Now they are empowered to perform and execute their tasks.

vs. 7 "And one of the four beasts (or four living creature) gave unto the seven angels seven golden bowls full of the wrath of God, who liveth forever and ever."

This living creature,—one of the four,—we found in the study of the fourth chapter to be one of the cherubim. In Ezekial 10:20 Ezekial said, "I knew they were cherubim."

So, one of the cherubim who appears again and again in Revelation, gave the seven bowls full of God's wrath, to the seven angels.

vs. 8 "And the temple was filled with smoke from the glory of God, and his power; and no man was able to enter the temple, till the seven plagues of the seven angels were fulfilled."

So it was of old. Smoke covered Mount Sinai when God spoke the "ten words." (Exodus 19:18) The cloud filled the house, when the erection of the tabernacle was finished. "And it came to pass, when the priests were come out of the holy place that cloud filled the house of the Lord, so that the priest could not stand to minister because of the cloud for the glory of the Lord had filled the house of the Lord." (I Kings 8:10, 11)

We also find that "the house was filled with smoke" when Isaiah was granted his vision as described in (Isaiah 6:4).

"And the posts of the door moved as the voice of him cried, and the house was filled with smoke."

All this imagery symbolized divine majesty. Here, in Revelation, the smoke proceeds "from the glory of God, and from His power."

And no one was able to enter into the temple until the seven plagues of the seven angels were fulfilled."

This does not mean that no one can enter the church until after the seventh plague has been poured out. The door of the church was opened at Pentecost and no man can shut that door until the final judgment. But here the meaning seems to be that the true saint of God cannot enter the final place of eternal reward until after these plagues.

Christ, in his life, said, "I go to *prepare a place for you*" (John 14:2) To do this, Paul said, "He ascended far above all heavens that he might fill all things." (Ephesians 4:10) And in Revelation 21:2 we read:

"I John saw the Holy City, New Jerusalem, coming down from God out of heaven, *prepared* as a bride adorned for her husband."

Until the place Christ went to prepare is finished, which certainly will be after the time of the seven plagues, no one could enter therein.

257

CHAPTER XVI

Text (16:1-21)

INTRODUCTION

1 And I heard a great voice out of the temple, saying to the seven angels, Go ye, and pour out the seven bowls of the wrath of God into the earth.
2 And the first went, and poured out his bowl into the earth; and it became a noisome and grievous sore upon the men that had the mark of the beast, and that worshipped his image.
3 And the second poured out his bowl into the sea; and it became blood as of a dead man; and every living soul died, even the things that were in the sea.
4 And the third poured out his bowl into the rivers and the fountains of the waters; and it became blood. 5 And I heard the angel of the waters saying, Righteous art thou who art and who wast, thou Holy One, because thou didst thus judge: 6 for they poured out the blood of saints and prophets, and blood hast thou given them to drink: they are worthy. 7 And I heard the altar saying, Yea, O Lord God, the Almighty, true and righteous are thy judgments.
8 And the fourth poured out his bowl upon the sun; and it was given unto it to scorch men with fire. 9 And men were scorched with great heat: and they blasphemed the name of God who hath the power over these plagues; and they repented not to give him glory.
10 And the fifth poured out his bowl upon the throne of the beast; and his kingdom was darkened; and they gnawed their tongues for pain, 11 and they blasphemed the God of heaven because of their pains and their sores; and they repented not of their works.
12 And the sixth poured out his bowl upon the great river, the river Euphrates; and the water thereof was dried up, that the way might be made ready for the kings that come from the sunrising. 13 And I saw coming out of the mouth of the beast, and out of the mouth of the false prophet, three unclean spirits, as it were frogs: 14 for they are spirits of demons, working signs; which go forth unto the kings of the whole world, to gather them together unto the war of the great day of God, the Almighty. 15 (Behold, I come as a thief. Blessed is he that watcheth, and keepeth his garments, lest he walk naked, and they see his shame.) 16 And they gathered them together into the place which is called in Hebrew Har-Magedon.
17 And the seventh poured out his bowl upon the air; and there came forth a great voice out of the temple, from the throne, saying, It is done: 18 and there were lightnings, and voices, and thunders; and there was a great earthquake, such as was not since there were men upon the earth, so great an earthquake, so mighty. 19 And the great city was divided into three parts, and the cities of the nations fell: and Babylon the great was remembered in the sight of God, to give unto her the cup of the wine of the fierceness of his wrath. 20 And every island fled away, and the mountains were not found. 21 And great hail, every stone about the weight of a talent, cometh down out of heaven upon men: and men blasphemed God because of the plague of the hail; for the plague thereof is exceeding great.

The sixteenth chapter describes the pouring out of the plagues from the seven vials, or bowls. These are the final judgments visited upon the Roman Empire. One finds himself confronted with confusion unless he keeps in mind that the major theme of the book of Revelation is the unfolding of the history of the church as that institution relates to the Roman Empire, whether it be pagan, political or papal Rome.

Shall we briefly review the path over which we have come in the "series of sevens" we have studied.

The seven seals carried us to the triumph of Christianity over paganism, or pagan Rome. The seven trumpets brought us to the overthrow of the western half of the empire by the Goths, Vandals, Huns and Suevi, and the collapse of the eastern half of political Rome under the onslaught of the Parocens and Turks. Those, trumpets, in the main, reveal the fall of political Rome.

Thus we see that each of these three "series of Sevens" had a distinct purpose. Briefly again: The seven seals fulfilled a definite purpose, the overthrow of Roman paganism. The seven trumpets had as their purpose, the overthrow of the Roman Empire, politically. The seven vials also have a definite design, the overthrow of that blasphemous religious institution variously described as, a beast which had two horns like a lamb, the city of fornication, a scarlet adulteress and "that great city Babylon."

While we are still on the subject of the "series of Sevens," we note, as in the case of the seven seals and the seven trumpets, there was an interruption, or a parenthesis between the sixth and seventh seals and trumpets, respectively, (see Rev. 7:1-17 and Rev. 10:1-11, 11:1-14). So, here between the pouring out of the sixth and seventh bowls, there occurs a brief parenthesis, or interlude.

Furthermore, we should take cognizance of the fact that while the fifteenth chapter introduces the seven vials in immediate connection with those who *have overcome* the beast, his image mark and number of his name, here in this chapter as the first vial is poured out, its wrath falls upon the men *who have* the mark of the beast and worshipped his image. The second bowl of wrath is emptied upon those who had "Poured out the blood of saints and prophets. The fifth vial is poured out upon the seat, or throne of the beast. The sixth vial is poured out upon the river Euphrates, and, like stirring as a snakes nest, three unclean Spirits like frogs come out of the mouth of the dragon, of the beast and of the false prophet.

The emptying of the seventh bowl is upon the great city Babylon, spiritually speaking.

All these considerations help us to identify the arena of activity portrayed by the seven last plagues. The definite purpose of these plagues is the destruction of spiritual Babylon, or papal Rome.

The symbols of this "series of sevens," in a great measure are drawn from the record of the plagues of Egypt, and, while there are differences, they do have a close correspondence to the ten plagues.

The term "plagues" applied to this "vial, or bowl series" recalls God's punishments visited upon the Eygptians. How natural it is that "plagues" should also be applied to the punishments visited upon papal Rome, for in Rev. 11:8, we found that apostate Christendom is also called Egypt, spiritually speaking. "And their dead bodies shall be in the street of the great city, which spiritually is called Sodom and Egypt, when also our Lord was crucified."

Having determined the purpose of pouring these bowls of wrath and the object on which they are to be poured, we are ready to take up their historical fulfillment. We must ever remember that John was to write, "the things he had seen, the things that are, and the things which shall come to pass hereafter." This being true, we are not to spiritualize these symbols away, but to treat them as prophetic symbols of historic events to come to pass.

So the seven angels begin to empty their vials.

The First Vial Poured Out

vs. 1, 2 "And I heard a great voice out of the temple, saying to the seven angels, go your ways, and pour out the vials of the wrath of God upon the earth."

As the plagues of physical Egypt were designed to destroy the oppressor of the Israel of God, in the Old Testament economy, and to bring about the deliverance of God's chosen, so this vial and its companions are for the destruction of the oppressor of the Israel of God of the New Testament, and to bring about their deliverance from spiritual oppression.

The time of the pouring of this vial and its following bowls without doubt, follow the 1260 year period when the apostate church, or papal Rome was in full flower. This time period we have found to be that time when the bishop of Rome was first blasphemously called "the Lord of the church," and continued until 1793 when he was humiliated. Then the time of these vials must follow that termination of the 1260 year period.

In 1793, exactly at the close of the 1260 years, there broke out in France a moral ulcer which had been festering for a long while. The church had become so corrupt and the royalty, acting as the temporal arm of the church so rotten, that the pendulum swung to the opposite extreme and the "age of Reason," dawned upon the world.

Hear Myers on the terrible condition of the church of that time:

"The upper clergy formed a decayed feudal hierarchy. A third of the lands of France was in their hands, and this immense property was almost wholly exempt from taxation. The bishops and abbots were usually drawn from the ranks of the nobility, being attracted to the service of the church rather by its enormous revenues and social destinction, than by the inducements of piety. They spent their princely incomes in luxurious life at court. . . .

Though there were noble exceptions, the most of these dignitaries were narrow-minded and self-seeking, and many of them so shamelessly immoral that as a class they had lost all credit and authority with the people. They had brought the church into disrepute. The hatred of the people felt toward them was transferred to the religion which they so unworthily represented."

Myers Mediaeval and Modern History, pages 502, 503.

Under these was what was called the Third Estate or Tiers Etal. This embraced all the nation aside form the nobility and clergy.

Hear Myers again page 503:

The peasants constituted the majority of the Third Estate. The condition of most of them could hardly have been worse. Their only recognized use in the state was "to pay fuedal services to the lords, tithes to the priests, and imports to the King."

La Bruyére, in Les Caractires, wrote of human slaves:

"One sees certain fierce animals, male and female, scattered through the fields; they are black, livid and burned by the sun, and attached to the soil, which they dig up and stir 'with indomitable industry; they have what is like an articulate voice, and when they rise to their feet they show a human face,— in truth they are human beings. They retire at night into dens, where they live on black bread and water and roots; they save other men the trouble of sowing and delving and harvesting."

No wonder, then, when the mob cried for bread and they were contemptuously told 'to eat cake," that the match was struck to the fagots of the revolution, in which the King, Marie Antonette, the girondins and thousands of lessor lights were executed. This inaugurated the Reign of Terror in which the enslaved masses, maddened to fury, sent the Catholic King, royal families, nobles and priests to the guillotine, by the tens of thousands. The nation declared itself atheistic, inaugurated a new calendar, and forever unshackled the world from the tyranny of papal Rome.

As a result of this breaking out of grevious sore upon those who worshipped the beast and his image, the mightest Catholic nation of that time was plunged into Civil war and as a result Europe was deluged in blood.

The Reign of Terror resulted in the pouring out of the first vial or bowl.

The Second Vial Poured Out

vs. 3 "And the second angel poured out his vial upon the sea; and it became as the blood of a dead man; and every living soul died in the sea."

How fitting that this second vial was emptied on the sea. The revolution in France unsettled all Europe. Keeping in mind that the destruction of papal Rome is the prime object of this pouring out of the vials, shall we proceed to the historical fulfilment of this vial. In some way it will affect the fortunes of spiritual Babylon.

There is a noticible parallel here in the vial series with the Trumpet series. Under the second trumpet a great and burning mountain was cast into the sea. And historically the Vandals swept the Mediterranean, to drive the Roman navy from its waters. Likewise from the sea, under the second vial, papal Rome was weakened.

France, a Catholic power was evenly matched with England. At the time of this vial began a death struggle for the mastery of the seas. This contest lasted for twenty years.

France, after the revolution, again became Catholic, by reason of Napoleon's concordat with the papacy. She rallied other Catholic nations, namely, Spain, Italy and Portugal—all great maritime powers of that day, to battle with Protestant England, another great sea power.

From the Indian Ocean to the Carribean, from the North Sea to the Nile, over the Atlantic and Pacific, their navies fought. And the Catholic flag was lowered everywhere. We can only grasp the significance of this by a review of hisotry.

Upon the return of Columbus from his successful expedition to the new world, Pope Alexander 6th, with a view to adjusting the conflicting claims of Spain and Portugal, issued a bull wherein he drew from pole to pole a line of demarcation through the Atlantic, one hundred leagues west of the Azores, and gave the Spanish sovereigns all pagan lands, not already in possession of Catholic princes, that their subjects might find west of this line, and to the Portuguese, all unclaimed pagan lands discovered by Portuguese navigators east of the designated meridian.

How the mighty had fallen! Catholic power had been swept from the oceans. Spain, the discoverer of the new world and once the greatest naval power of the world, Portugal, great in naval equipment, France, long the rival of England on the seas, did not have a ship left to hoist their flags to the salty breeze.

"On Oct. 21, 1805, Lord Nelson, having, near Cape Trafalgar on the coast of Spain, the combined French and Spanish Fleets, almost completely destroyed the combined armaments. This decisive battle gave England the control of the sea. The "wet ditch," as Napolen was wont to call the English Channel, was hence forth an impossible gulf. He might rule the continent, but the sovereignty of the ocean and its islands was denied him."

Myers, Mediaeval and Modern History, page 557.

So we behold the maritime power which supported Rome, swept from the seven seas. Truly a terrible blow to papal power, prestige and pride!

The Third Vial Poured Out

vs. 4-7 "And the third angel poured out his vial upon the rivers and fountains of waters; and they became blood, and I heard the angel of the waters say, Thou art righteous, O Lord, which art, and wast and shall be, because thou hast judged thus. For they have shed the blood of saints and prophets, and thou hast given them blood to drink; for they are worthy. And I heard another out of the altar say, Even so, Lord God Almighty, true and righteous are thy judgments."

Never does the divine chronicler permit us to forget the object of these bowl judgments. Interpreters have gone far afield in applying these vial punishments to fanciful objects like, "humanism," commercialism and atheism, but we are ever told that the object of this 'bowl series' is the apostate church which "has shed the blood of saints and prophets."

This oft reminder keeps us in line on the time, place and object in the circle of Revelation's visions.

This third angel pours out his vial upon the rivers and their sources. This is understandable when we remember that papal Rome had for years wrecked her vengence upon the dwellers of the Piedmont, source of Italy's river system, because they dared to resist the Pontiff's pronouncements.

This very region was the home of the Albigenses and the Waldenses, against which the papacy hurled its legions generation after generation. The blood of the Protestants of the Alps had oft flowed, until Oliver Cromwell informed the Pope that unless he called off his wolves from preying on the flock in the Piedmont, the cannon of his army would teach him mercy around the castle of St. Angelo. The river system of Italy was the center of papal persecution and in the time of the third vial, became the arena of war.

One glance at a map of Northern Italy and one will be abundantly convinced that this is a region of rivers and fountain of waters.

And one of the results of the French Revolution was the invasion of Northern Italy, the gage of battle being fought on the Rhone, the Po and their tributaries. It is a remarkable corroborating bit of history. The French fought the battles, that punished papal Rome, upon the Rhone, the Po, the Adda, the A'dege and Bromida.

Myers mentions among the noted engagements of Napoleon's campaign, the battles of Lodi (May 10, 1896), Castiglione (Aug. 5, 1796), Arcola (Nov. 15-17, 1796), Rivoli (Jan. 14, 15, 1797), and the siege of Mantua (July 1796-Feb. 1797)

In Student's France, we read:

"The French crossed the *Po* at Piacenza and drove back Beaulieu upon the line of the *Adda;* the strongly fortified bridge of *Lodi* was carried after a severe struggle, and the enemy retreated upon the line of the river Mincio. Page 581.

Marching secretly from Verona, the French descended the *Adige* river . . . on Nov. 14th, they made a furious attack upon the bridge (over the Adige) of Arcole. Page 583.

From the theater of their triumphs upon the *Adige* and *Mincio* rivers, Bonaparte led his armies into the territory of the *Pope,* against whom the Directory had resolved to proceed to extremities. Page 584.

Bonaparte took up a position with his whole army upon the great plain of Marengo, being separated by the river *Bromida* from the enemies lines. Page 598.

A convention was signed the day after the battle by which the Austrains agreed to retire beyond the river *Mincio.*" Page 598.

So at the hand of two witnesses a thing is firmly established. The persecution of the saints centered for generations upon this river system and the fountains, or source of rivers. And here also the third vial was poured out upon those who, "shed the blood of saints and prophets."

We can almost hear the Albigenses and Waldenses joining with the angel in saying, "Righteous are thou, who art and wast and shalt be, because thou hast judged thus. Thou hast given them blood to drink; for they are worthy!

While it is entirely aside from our present consideration of Revelation, it is interesting to notice that angels are employed about such regulations as the flow of rivers and streams. It was the angel of the waters who spoke here. John writing by inspiration said: "Now there is at Jerusalem, by the sheep market a pool, which is called in the Hebrew tongue Bethesda, having five porches. In these lay a great multitude of impotent folk, of blind, halt, withered, waiting for the *moving of the water*. For an *angel* went down at a certain season into the pool and troubled the water." (John 5:2-4).

Throughout the Scriptures we find the angels performing many and varied tasks, and it doubtless will be quite an eye-opener on the other side to learn just how intimately they are connected with the activities of mankind.

This brings us to the pouring out of the fourth vial:

The Fourth Vial Poured Out

vs. 8, 9 "And the fourth angel poured out his vial upon the sun and power was given unto him to scorch men with fire. And men were scorched with great heat, and blasphemed the name of God, which hath power over these plagues; and they repented not to give Him glory."

We have already found that the "sun" is a symbol of a great ruler or King. Anyone who attains great prominence may be so designated. Joseph, in his dream is likened to a sun, with his father Jacob and his brothers bowing in obeisence to him. Christ is called the Sun of Righteousness.

In this fourth vial period, the contents are poured upon the sun, and power is given it to scorch men with fire. Remembering always we are walking in the realm of symbolism, we recall that at this particular time in history, Napoleon was elevated from a Corsican Corporal, to first Consul and ruler of France. Then in 1802, was elected and made Consul for life. Thus did he move a step higher, nearer the imperial throne. Following a royal custom, Napoleon, from that time on, used only his first name. In 1804, the Senate conferred upon him the title of Emperor of the French. The coronation took place in Paris, on Dec. 2, 1804. Napoleon had forced the Pope to come to Rome to crown him, because it was the little Corsican's design, to have himself regarded, not only as the successor of the Bourbons, but, also, as the successor of Charlemagne and the Caesars. Hear Myers at this juncture:

"The pope poured the holy oil upon the head of the kneeling Emperor and girded him with the imperial scepter; but when he would have placed the crown upon his head, Napoleon checked him, and, taking the diadem from the pope, crowned himself with his own hands. What portion of the spirit of the old divine-right monarchies entered into the new French Empire, may be inferred from the doctrines which in less than a year after Napoleon's coronation, the subservient French clergy were teaching the youth of France. "The Emperor is the minister and the power of God, and his image on earth," ran the new cateclism; "to honor and serve him is to honor and serve God." Myers, Mediaeval and Modern History—pages 551, 552.

Thus we see the sun of the fourth vial given power to scorch men. And scorch men, Napoleon did. No such scorching sun had risen on the political horizon for more than a thousand years. He conquered Italy and invaded Egypt and as he sat his horse in the shadow of the Pyramids, inspired his soldiers with a now historic challenge, "Soldiers," he exclaimed, pointing to the Pyramids, "forty centuries are looking down upon you." Austria, Germany, Prussia, Portugal, Spain, Holland, fell in rapid succession to this "scorching sun."

"The empire which this soldier of fortune had built up stretched from Lubech to beyond Rome, embracing France proper, the Netherlands, part of western and northwestern Germany, all western Italy as far south as the Kingdom of Naples, together with the Illyrian Provinces and the Ionian Islands.

He, himself, was King of the Kingdom of Italy, Protector of the Confideration of the Rhine and Mediator of Switzerland. Austria and Prussia were completely subject to his will . . . Not since the time of the Caesars had one man's will swayed so much of the civilized world." Myers Mediaeval and Modern History, page 569.

And we read that under the scorching heat of this "sun," men blasphemed the name of God. The sweep of atheism over France in Napoleon's day surely fulfils this phase of the prophetic symbolism of the fourth vial.

And in spite of it all, we read that, "men repented not to give Him (God) glory."

We now, advance to the pouring out of the fifth vial of wrath.

The Fifth Vial Poured Out

vs. 10, 11 "And the fifth angel poured out his vial upon the seat of the beast; and his Kingdom was full of darkness; and they gnawed their tongues for pain, and blasphemed the God of heaven because of their pains and their sores, and repented not of their deeds."

Thus far the four vials, or golden bowls have followed the sequence of the first four trumpets. The first trumpet and the first vial affect the earth, the second trumpet and vial, the sea; the third trumpet and vial, the rivers and fountain of waters; and the fourth trumpet and vial, the sun. Now a departure is made, and the fifth vial's scene of action is entirely different from the fifth trumpet.

The explanation lies in the fact that the trumpet series followed the history of the fall of political Rome, whereas the vial series described the fall of religio-political papal Rome.

The only similarity between the fifth vial and fifth trumpet is the prominence of darkness in each case. Under the fifth trumpet, the darkness was occasioned by a dense smoke coming up out of the bottomless pit. There, we found, the smoke was a symbol of the spiritual force of Mohammedanism which brought darkness to the earth.

By the same token, since this activity is concerned with the seat or throne of the beast, or religio-political papal Rome, the darkness here is a spiritual one, brought on by apostacy. Surely, the Kingdom of the beast is full of darkness.

Rome was the seat, or throne of the papal power of this period indicated by the fifth vial, so naturally we look to the "seat of Satan," or Rome, for the fulfilment of the events symbolized. In our study of the Thyatira period, we found that the church of this period, now known as the Catholic Church, reached "the depths of Satan." (Rev. 2:24)

Therefore, the scenes of the fifth vial will be, Italy and Rome, for this had been the seat of the beast for thirteen centuries. The very seat, or throne of the beast is to receive the blow that will cause great dismay and anguish, to where men will gnaw their tongues in pain—an expression sybolical of terrible suffering and anguish of heart.

We found under the fourth vial that Napoleon, as the scorching sun, converted the whole of Europe—the ten horn Kingdoms succeeding the beast, or political Rome—into an armed camp. Every nation was torn with war and crimsoned with blood-shed. It is estimated that his wars, from 1796 to 1815, too the lives of two million soldiers, besides civilians who perished from attendant causes.

But this scorching sun exerted its most baleful power upon the papacy. We know, by history, that Napoleon and his armies invaded the papal provinces in 1797, and took the city of Rome, the seat of the beast, imposing a forced peace upon papal Rome in which the pope paid a rich tribute. In 1798, Pope Pius 6th was carried, a prisoner, to France, where he died. His successor was elected not in Rome, but in Venice. I take time to quote from Allison's History of Europe, Vol. I—page 546:

"Immediately after the entry of the French troops commenced the regular and systematic pillage of the city. Not only the churches and the convents, but the palaces of the cardinals and of the nobility were laid waste . . . Not only the palaces of the Vatican, and the Monte Cavallo, but those of Castel Gandolfo, on the margin of lban Lae, the villa Ablani, and others, in the environs of Rome, were plundered of every article of value. The whole sacerdotal habits of the pope and cardinals were burned, in order to collect from the flames the gold with which they were adorned. The Vatican was stripped to its naked walls. A contribution of four millions in money, two millions in provisions, and three thousand horses, was imposed upon a city already exhausted. . . .

Nor were the exactions of the French confined to the plunder of palaces and churches. Eight cardinals were arrested and sent to Civita Castellona, while enormous contributions were levied on the papal territory. At the same time, the ample territorial possessions of the church and the monasteries were confiscated, and declared national property, a measure which, by drying up, at once, the whole resources of the affluent classes, precipitated into the extreme of misery, the numerous poor who were maintained by their expenditure or fed by their bounty."

No wonder, under the fifth vail it was said they should "gnaw their tongues for pain!"

While this was going on in Italy, the same procedure obtained in France. Hear Myers on this:

"One of the most important of its (the National Assembly) measures, and one far reaching in its effects was the confiscation of the property of the church. Altogether, property consisting largely of lands, and worth, it is estimated, over a billion francs, was by decree, made the property of the nation." Myers, Midiaeval and Modern History—page 518.

Note: This decree was made Nov. 2, 1789.

In 1808, Pius 7th, was dragged from his palace, as his predecessor Pius 6th had been, and taken as a prisoner to France. His states of the church were confiscated and the pope was left without temporal possessions. The pope was forced to sign an agreemnt by which he gave up the power of appointing bishops, in the French Empire, to Napoleon.

The length of these vial outpourings is not stated, but the contents of the fifth vial continued to be poured until 1848.

In that year, the citizens of Rome rose in rebellion to papal authority and drove Pius 9th into exile. He was later restored to his throne by the French army—France now being in alliance with the Vatican. But in 1870, France was compelled to withdraw her troops to defend her own soil from German invasion.

Hear Myers on this:

"This sharp, quick war between France and Prussia gave the coveted capital to the Italian government. Upon the overthrow of the French Empire and the establishment of the Republic, Victor Emmanuel was informed that France would no longer sustain the papal power. The Italian government, at once gave notice to the pope that Rome would henceforth be considered a portion of the Kingdom of Italy and forthwith an Italian army entered the city, which by a vote of almost one hundred to one (Exactly 133, 681 to 1507) resolved to cast its lot with that of the Italian nation.

This marked the end of the temporal power of the pope, and the end of an ecclesiastical state, the last in Europe, which long before Charlemagne, had held a place among the temporal powers of Europe, and all that time had been a potent factor in the political affairs, not only of Italy, but of almost the whole continent." Myers Midiaeval and Modern History—pages 629, 630.

Albert Barnes quotes an old writer by the name of Robert Fleming, who in 1701, wrote and published a work called, "Apocalytic Key." On the fifth vial, or bowl, this author said: "The fifth vial which is to be poured out on the seat of the beast, or the dominions which belong more immediately to, and depend upon, the Roman see; that I say this judgment will begin about AD 1794 and expire about A.D. 1848."

And looking now upon history, Napoleon invaded Italy in 1796 and in 1848, the citizens of Rome arose in rebellion against papal authority and drove Pius 9th into exile. And, to think Robert Fleming writing two and one-half centuries ago, and one full century before the begining of events he predicted and one and one half centuries before the culmination of these same events, saw it all so clearly!

The popes have steadfastly refused to recognize the legitimacy of the act which stripped them of their temporal power, maintaining there can be no settlement of the Roman question save through the restoration of the pope to his former status, as an independent temporal sovereign. Thus it is true, as the concluding words of the fifth vial declares, "They repented not of their deeds."

As for blaspheming God, in 1870, the pope declared himself infallible and made it a canon law of the church to which, all, who have the mark of the beast, and the number of his name, must subscribe, under penalty of excommunication.

But, in spite of all this the power of the papacy is forever broken to the extent that the church can no longer resort to forceful means in suppressing non-conformist teaching, or rebellion against her spiritual despotism. We now come to the sixth vial.

The Sixth Vial Poured Out

vs. 12 "And the sixth angel poured out his vial upon the great river Euphrates; and the water thereof dried up, that the way of the Kings of the east might be prepared."

The Euphrates was always regarded by the Roman world as its furthermost eastern boundry and it served as a barrier against the invasion of hostile tribes living east of that river. We will recall how in the sounding of the sixth trumpet, four angels were loosed, who set in motion the hords of Turkish soldiers.

Here the pouring out of the sixth vial dries up, or removes the Euphrates as a barrier, thus foreshadowing the fall of the Turkoman. The symbol "drying up," does not indicate a sudden calamity, but a gradual decay. This indicates extinction by slow degrees, and this is just what is taking place in the case of Turkey, the modern descendant of the ancient Turkoman Empire.

The Turko-Egyptian fleet was destroyed by the combined fleets of England, France, and Russia, in the Bay of Navarino in 1827. In 1828, Nicholas declared war against the Ottoman Porte. The Russian troops crossed the Balkans without serious opposition, and were marching upon Constantinople when the Sultan sued for peace. The Treaty of Adrianople (1829) bought the war to a close. Hear Myers again:

> "Tsar Nicholas held some provinces in Asia which gave him control of the eastern shore of the Euxine. The Turkish provinces of Moldavia (now Roumania) and Wallachia, were rendered virtually independent of the Sultan. All Greece, south of Thessaly and Epirus, was liberated, and along with most of the islands of the Aegian, was formed into an independent Kingdom, under the guardianship of England, France and Russia. Myers, Mediaeval and Modern History—page 655.

In 1849 Mohamet Ali revolted in Egypt. Since that time Egypt has been independent of Turkey.

Then came the Crimean War (1853-1856). We again quote the very reliable historian, Myers:

> "A celebrated parable employed by the Tsar Nicholas in conversation with the English minister at St. Petersburg, throws a great deal of light upon the circumstances that led to the Crimean War. "We have on our hands," said the Tsar, "A sick man—and very sick man; it would be a great misfortune if he should give us the slip some of these days, especially if it happened before all the necessary arrangements were made." Nicholas had cultivated friendly relations with the English government, and he now proposed that England and Russia should divide the estate of the 'sick man,' by which phrase Turkey, of course, was meant. England was to be allowed to take Egypt and Crete, while the Turkish provinces in Europe were to be taken under the protection of the Tsar, which meant, of course, in the complete absorption, in due time, of all Southeastern Europe into the Russian Empire." Myers Mediaeval and Modern History.—page 656.

In 1876, Herzeovina revolted along with Montenegro. The war of 1877 resulted in the loss of the greater part of the Turkish possessions in Europe, as well as a part of Armenia, to Russia. Today the

Turkish Empire, once so great, is a very sick nation, and only manages to keep alive because greater nations preserve her as a barrier between them. The Eurphrates is surely drying up. And for what reason? That the way of the Kings of the east may be prepared.

No further hint is given who these Kings of the east will be, but the prophecy implies that when this obstacle is entirely removed, the way of the inhabitants of the east shall be opened. The drying up of the Euphrates is still going on. Before the final destruction of this Mohammedan power it seems destined to receive help which will aid it in its last struggle which undoubtedly will end in utter ruin. John proceeds to describe this future gathering of the Kings of the whole world:

> vs. 13-16 "And I saw three unclean spirits like frogs come out of the mouth of the dragon, and out of the mouth of the beast, and out of the mouth of the false prophets. For they are the spirits of devils, working miracles, which go forth unto the kings of the earth and of the whole world to gather them to the battle of that great day of God Almighty. Behold, I come as a thief. Blessed is he that watcheth, and keepeth his garments, lest he walk naked, and they see his shame. And he gathered them together in a place called in the Hebrew tongue, Armangeddon."

Just as in the case of the seven seals and the seven trumpets, there was an interlude between the sixth and the seventh of each series, so here between the pouring out of the sixth and seventh bowls, there occurs a brief parenthetical interruption.

In this interlude we are given the process, the purpose and the place of the gathering of the Kings of the whole world. First, the process:

These Kings are gathered through the Satanic influence of the three great enemies of Christ and his church. All three have appeared before in our study in Revelation. They are a monstrous trinity of evil in contradistinction to the blessed trinity of good in the Godhead, namely, the Father, the Son and Holy Spirit. This evil trinity consists of the dragon, the beast and the false prophet.

The first of this trinity, the dragon, is called "the old serpent, the devil and satan." (Rev. 12:9). He it is who has animated the age-long opposition to the church.

But he has as his agents, the last two of this unholy trinity, the beast and the false prophet. The beast, we have found to be, political Rome, which John saw coming up out of the sea (Rev. 13:1), "unto whom it was given to make war with the saints," and "to

hold authority over every tribe and people and tongue and nation."
(Rev. 13:17)

The false prophet is, beyond all question, the second beast which
John saw, "coming up out of the earth," or papal Rome, as we have
found him to represent. This is the apostate religion-political church
which "exercised all the power of the first beast before him" and
"to worship the first beast, whose deadly wound was healed." (Rev.
13:11, 12)

These three, the devil, political and papal Rome exercise their
influence by means of three unclean spirits, as they were frogs. From
the mouth of each one of these goes forth one such spirit. The mouth
is ever the instrument which the devil has used to persuade people
by falsehood. "When he speaketh a lie, he speaketh of his own: for
he is a liar, and the father of it," said Christ. (John 8:44)

In Christ called Satan the father of lies, and he did; then the
first beast, political Rome would stand in the place of the Son,
who had all power, and the false prophet, or papal Rome would
occupy, in this unholy trinity, the place of the Holy Spirit. As
the Holy Spirit animated the life of the true church, so the papacy
animated the life of the apostate church. And isn't it more than a
coincidence that the pope calls himself, the Vicar of Christ?

Christ said, the Holy Spirit would speak for Him, so the pope tries
to take the place of the Holy Spirit, by claiming himself to be the
Vicar of Christ.

To the mind of John the frogs represented uncleanness. So, were
they considered in the plagues of frogs in Egypt. Thus, we see here
Satan's promptings, political lust and malice, and religious fanaticism unite to percipitate a war involving the whole world.

Already, we see this allignment coming about. The way of the
Kings of the east is being prepared and all the Kings of the whole
world being "gathered together unto the war of the great day of God
Almighty."

We have now considered the "process" and the "purpose" of this
gathering; we now would logically consider the "place" of gathering.
But just as we are ready to do so, John breaks the sequence of
thought by inserting a message intended to emphasize the nearness
of that final gathering, and the need for watchfulness on the part of
the true saints. It is as though Christ were himself speaking, for the
words are his very own: "Behold, I come as a thief. Blessed is he that
watcheth and keepeth his garments, lest he walk naked, and they
see his shame."

To come "as a thief," means to come suddenly and unannounced and these words are unmistakably those of Christ. "But know this, that if the good man of the house had known in what watch the thief would come, he would have watched. Therefore, be ye also ready: for in such an hour as ye think not the Son of Man cometh. (Matt. 24:43, 44)

To the church in Sardis, Christ also said: "If therefore thou shalt not watch, I will come on thee *as a thief.*" (Rev. 3:3)

To this, Peter by inspiration, adds his testimony, "But the day of the Lord will come as a *thief in the night.*" (II Pet. 3:10)

Two things are to be kept in mind by the true Christians. They are to watch and they are to keep his garments, dressed, ready. Wakeful attitude and proper raiment will ever guarantee his readiness for Christ's sudden return.

And "Blessed" is such a one. This is the third of the seven beautitudes of the Apocalypse.

To the mind of the Lord, his triumphant return at the time of the final conflict, were very near in the period of the sixth vial.

Now we are ready to return to the consideration of the "place" of this gathering of all the Kings of the East and of the whole world. The Kings of the whole world are to be there.

The place of this final struggle is described by a striking symbol, freighted with deep meaning. "And he gathered them together in a place called in the Hebrew tongue (Har-Magedon) Armageddon."

The name denotes "the hill of Megiddo." Jackson's Dictionary of Scriptural names gives the meaning, "The Hill of Slaughter." This battlefield is in the plain of Esdraelon, the depression between Judea and Galilee. Armies passing through the country from north to south, or from south to north, always sought the advantage of this pla'n.

This famous valley eight miles southeast of Mount Carmel is one of the most fought over spots of earth. Here, Barak defeated Sisera. In this valley Josiah fought at Megiddo with Pharaoh-Necho. Here, Gideon and his three hundred men routed the Midianites in the beginning of the middle watch. Near here Saul and Jonathan fell on Mount Gilboa. Here, the Crusaders fought the Moslems. Here, Napoleon battled with the Turks. Here, the British army, under Allenby, fought the Turks of his day. And here, the Kings of the East and the Kings of the whole earth are to be gathered, at the Hill of Megiddo, the Hill of Slaughter, in the plain of Esdraelon.

And they are gathered there by the lying mouths of the Infernal

Trinity. This reminds us of an Old Testament illustration, how a lying spirit can lead one to certain death:

"The Lord said: who shall persuade Ahab, that he may go up and fall at Ramoth-Gilead? And one said on this manner, and another said on that manner. And there came forth a spirit, and stood before the Lord, and said: I will persuade him. And the Lord said unto him, where-with? And he said: I will go forth, and I will be a *lying spirit in the mouth of all his prophets.* And He said: Thou shalt persuade him, and prevail also; go forth and do so . . . the Lord put a lying spirit in the *mouth* of these thy prophets." (I Kings 22:20, 23)

The result was that Ahab was deceived by the lying spirit and went up and fell at Ramoth-Gilead.

So here the devil, the father of lies, uses the mouth of the beast and the mouth of the false prophet to deceive the Kings of the East and the Kings of all the world to gather for the Battle of Armageddon and there perish.

With the gathering of the Kings of all the world and their armies to this place of Armageddon, this sixth bowl ends. It breaks off suddenly, because it simply brings things into readiness for the final catastrophe, which only the seventh vial, or bowl can bring forth.

The Seventh Vial Poured Out

vs. 17-21 "And the seventh angel poured out his vial into the air; and there came a great voice out of the temple of heaven, from the throne, saying, It is done.

And there were voices, and thunders, and lightnings, and there was a great earthquake, such as was not since men were upon the earth, so mighty an earthquake, and so great.

And the great city was divided into three parts, and the cities of the nations fell: and great Babylon came in remembrance before God, to give unto her cup of the wine of the fierceness of his wrath.

And every island fled away, and the mountains were not found. And there fell upon men a great hail out of heaven, every stone about the weight of a talent: and men blasphemed God because of the plague of the hail; for the plague thereof was exceeding great."

This seventh vial, which completes the perfect number, symbolizes the consummating catastrophes to fall upon Papal Rome. As

275

the seven seals covered the events which brought about the downfall of Pagan Rome; and the seven trumpets described the historical happenings which terminated in the destruction of Political Rome; these seven vials delineate the events which bring about the utter wiping out of Papal Rome.

This seventh vial is poured out upon the air. Two applications might be made here.

First, the air, or atmosphere which all must breathe is affected, by which health and life are endangered. Since this is the time of the end, we are able to see this first application very readily. The nations airy navies battle with increasing ferocity as greater wars follow one after the other. Bomb, atomic and chemical warfare fulfil the physical aspects of this plague. But, *Second,* if the air visited with this bowl is spiritual, the sense in which Paul once used it in (Eph. 6:12), then this vial seems to refer to the spiritual warfare between principalities against powers, against the rulers of the darkness of this world and against spiritual wickedness in high places.

When the vial was poured there came forth a voice from the throne, saying, "It is done." Literally, in the Greek, there is just one word, "Done!" The work of visitation of judgments was done, even as Christ, in completing the work of sacrifice for our redemption, cried from the cross, "It is finished!"

The result was the usual symbolic manifestations of divine judgments in a demonstration of voices, thunderings, lightnings. Then follows a great earthquake, such as was not since there were men upon the earth.

These features are attendant to the tremendous movements of the divine will and purpose. In the closing period of the history of the church, society is to experience an unheaval that will shake it to it's very foundations. This being near the time of Christ's return, Haggai's prophecy in (Hag. 2:6-7), is most fitting:

"For thus saith the Lord of hosts, yet once, it is a little while and I will shake the heavens, and the earth, and the sea, and the dry land; and I will *shake all nations,* and the *desire of all nations shall come* and I will fill this house with glory, saith the Lord of Hosts."

Of course, Christ is "the desire of all nations" whose coming is predicted. But before his coming there shall be a marvelous shaking of all the nations of the world.

This seventh vial must be upon us, for never have all nations, the world over, been so shaken economically, idiologically, politically, religiously and even physically.

This Old Testament prediction re-echoes in the New Testament, for we read in Heb. 12:25-29:

"See that ye refuse not him that speaketh. For if they escaped not who refused him that spake on earth, much more shall not we escape, if we turn away from him that speaketh from heaven. Whose voice then shook the earth: but now he hath promised, saying Yet once more I shake not the earth only, but also heaven.

And this word, yet once more, signifieth the removing of those things that are shaken, as of things that are made, and those things which cannot be shaken may remain.

Wherefore we receiving a Kingdom that cannot be moved, let us have grace whereby we may serve God acceptably with reverence and Godly fear. For our God is a consuming fire."

The dividing of the city into three parts is most difficult to explain, since that event lies in the future, but we have found out that "the great city," refers to religio-political Rome. The proof will be even more clinching in the next chapter which we are approaching.

But it would seem that all that is embraced in the phrase, papal Rome, will be divided into three parts, It is to be broken asunder and shaken to pieces.

And with her fall, the cities of the nations fall. What a cataclysm awaits the end of this age!

And Babylon, another name for that city, the city, the confuser of spiritual tongues, is brought up in remembrance before God. A fuller description of her fate is given in the eighteenth chapter.

Babylon which is at the base of the pyramid of rebellion and sin against God, Christ and His church, is made to drink the bitterest draught of all. God gives to her the "cup of the wine of the fierceness of His anger."

Furthermore, the islands and mountains fled away at the climax of the seventh plague. Islands and mountains denote earthly powers. He does not say that islands ceased to be, or that no mountains are to remain or exist after this mighty shaking, but there is to be a recession of the islands from their present places and the mountains were not found.

In other words, great portions of the earth, with its present national standings will be drastically altered, as to their boundaries and relations to one another, and particularly to that "great city" called Babylon, or Papal Rome. It would seem that old lines between states and nations are to be obliverated and pass away.

Three quarters of a century ago, Loxely Hall seemed to have dipped his poetic pen into the ink of inspiration, to write of this very prediction contained in the events of the seventh vial:

> "For I dipped into the future, far as human eye
> could see
> Saw the vision of the world, and all the wonders
> that would be;
> Saw the heavens filled with commerce,
> Argosies of magic sails,
> Pilots of the purple twilight, dropping down
> with costly bales;
> Heard the heavens filled with shouting, and
> there reigned a ghostly dew,
> From the nation's airy navies, grappling in the
> central blue;
> Far along the world-wide whisper of the
> south wind rushing warm,
> With the standards of the peoples, plunging
> through the thunder storm;
> Till the war-drums throbbed no longer, and the
> battle flags were furled,
> In the Parliment of man, the Federation
> of the World!"

The grand climax of the plague is marked by the dropping of hail stones. The symbolism of these vials have followed, in many respects, that of the ten plagues of Egypt, in which one of the plagues was one of hail.

Hail is a symbol of Divine judgment and hail stones of such weight signify terrible judgments. One might see in these hailstones the falling of bombs, but we have studiously steered our course away from the treacherous shoals of speculation.

"And men blasphemed God because of the plague of hail; for the plague thereof was exceeding great."

We who now live in the days of the seventh vial, have never ceased to marvel that, in spite of a rising tempo of wars, men have not been driven back to God and the church, but, rather, go on in their sins, blaspheming God!

With each war there have arisen the false prophets who declared, "with the end of this war, men will go back to the church and seek God." But men have gone their wilful way, little heeding the pious pronouncements of the pink tea prophets!

Here the seventh vial discussion draws to a close, not an end. The symbolism here indicates only a mere outline of what is set forth in more detail in the visions of the eighteenth and nineteenth chapters.

The kings of the east and the Kings of the whole world have been summoned to the battle of Armageddon. Babylon has come into remembrance "in the sight of God." An outline has been given of the changing picture of national upheaval and a description is given of continued ungodliness, in spite of the awful visitations of Divine judgment.

We are now ready to "uncover" the closing scenes of awful grandeur and the glories of the new heaven and the new earth wherein will dwell righteousness.

CHAPTER XVII

MYSTERIOUS BABYLON SITTING
UPON THE BEASTS

Text (17:1-18)

1 And there came one of the seven angels that had the seven bowls, and spake with me, saying, Come hither, I will show thee the judgment of the great harlot that sitteth upon many waters; 2 with whom the kings of the earth commited fornication, and they that dwell in the earth were made drunken with the wine of her fornication. 3 And he carried me away in the Spirit into a wilderness: and I saw a woman sitting upon a scarlet-colored beast, full of names of blasphemy, having seven heads and ten horns. 4 And the woman was arrayed in purple and scarlet, and decked with gold and precious stone and pearls, having in her hand a golden cup full of abominations, even the unclean things of her fornication, 5 and upon her forehead a name written, MYSTERY, BABYLON THE GREAT, THE MOTHER OF THE HARLOTS AND OF THE ABOMINATIONS OF THE EARTH. 6 And I saw the woman drunken with the blood of the saints, and with the blood of the martyrs of Jesus. And when I saw her, I wondered with a great wonder. 7 And the angel said unto me, Wherefore didst thou wonder? I will tell thee the mystery of the woman, and of the beast that carrieth her, which hath the seven heads and the ten horns. 8 The beast that thou sawest was, and is not; and is about to come up out of the abyss, and to go into perdition. And they that dwell on the earth shall wonder, they whose name hath not been written in the book of life from the foundation of the

279

world, when they behold the beast, how that he was, and is not, and shall come. 9 Here is the mind that hath wisdom. The seven heads are seven mountains, on which the woman sitteth: 10 and they are seven kings; the five are fallen, the one is, the other is not yet come; and when he cometh, he must continue a little while. 11 And the beast that was, and is not, is himself also an eighth, and is of the seven; and he goeth into perdition. 12 And the ten horns that thou sawest are ten kings, who have received no kingdom as yet; but they receive authority as kings, with the beast, for one hour. 13 These have one mind, and they give their power and authority unto the beast. 14 These shall war against the Lamb, and the Lamb shall overcome them, for he is Lord of lords, and King of kings; and they also shall overcome that are with him, called and chosen and faithful. 15 And he saith unto me, The waters which thou sawest, where the harlot sitteth, are peoples, and multitudes, and nations, and tongues. 16 And the ten horns which thou sawest, and the beast, these shall hate the harlot, and shall make her desolate and naked, and shall eat her flesh, and shall burn her utterly with fire. 17 For God did put in their hearts to do his mind, and to come to one mind, and to give their kingdom unto the beast, until the words of God should be accomplished. 18 And the woman whom thou sawest is the great city, which reigneth over the kings of the earth.

INTRODUCTION

Beginning with the Vision of the Three Signs, namely, the Women (Rev. 12th chapter), the Two Beasts (Rev. 13th chapter) and the Seven Vials (Rev. 15th and 16th Chapters), we have found that the woman (or the true church of Christ) has had three great adversaries.

These three were the Dragon, or the Devil and Satan, political Rome, the beast coming up out of the sea and papal Rome, the beast coming up out of the earth and later called the false prophet in (Rev. 16th chapter). In this chapter, in which we now enter, papal Rome is called "Mystery, Babylon, the Great, the Mother of Harlots, and the abominations of the earth."

It is altogether fitting that as we reach the climax of the "uncovering" of her idenity, she should be so designated in the chapter upon whose threshold we now stand.

The introduction, of this new revelation of the apostate church, is linked to the judgments visited upon her under the Seven Vials, by the declaration:

vs. 1 "And there came one of the seven angels that had the seven vials, and talked with me, saying unto me, come hither; I will show unto thee the judgment of the great whore that sitteth upon many waters."

The seven "vial" angels had given a sweeping account, of the overthrow of this spiritual Babylon, by the pouring out of their vials. This one of the seven angels will present to John, Babylon's overthrow in greater detail. This, and the two following chapters, relate to her final fate.

Twice before, in chapters 14:8, and 16:19, this Babylon has been named and her fall foretold, yet in neither mentioning has she been described, nor has her identity been disclosed. Here the mystery of her is to be "uncovered," or revealed.

There is a second definite linking of this description with the Babylon of the Seven Vials. Under the third vial, we read: "They have shed the blood of saints," In this present chapter and the sixth verse, this Babylon, characterized as a woman, "is drunken with the blood of saints, and with the blood of the martyrs of Jesus."

This repeating of "unfoldings" of revelation, in a seres of visions is proof positive that the Apocalypse is divided into a series of approaches, in which there is a constant returning in later visions to territory, that has already been covered, either for a fresh start, or to show a vision in greater detail.

The seventeenth chapter is expressly an "uncovering" of the judgment of the "great harlot"—the apostate church.

This great harlot is described as sitting upon *many waters*. Here again, we meet with one of the few times in Revelation *when the book itself, interprets the symbol given*. The symbol of "waters," is explained in the fifteenth verse of this same chapter, "And he saith unto me, the waters which thou sawest, where the whore sitteth, are peoples, and multitudes, and nations and tongues." These waters, then, are symbolic of the many nations and races that support the whore.

The papal church calls herself the "Catholic" church, meaning, the universal church. It is a church, here in Revelation, under the characterization of a harlot, which sits upon, or has dominion over peoples and nations and races, the world over. The very name "Catholic," even if no other identification were given, is enough to prove she is the harlot depicted here in Revelation. How unwittingly has this apostate church revealed herself by the very name she wears, as the Babylon of the Apocalypse! By her very name she presents the student of the Bible, not with mere circumstantial evidence, but with positive, incontrovertible, direct evidence.

God works in a mysterious way his wonders to perform. He not only will not allow a church to wear a scriptural name, which observes unscriptural practices and follows unbiblical doctrine, but He brings it about that every church that so departs from the truth *wears a name in keeping with that departure.* We continue to read:

vs. 2 "With whom the kings of the earth have committed fornication, and the inhabitants of the earth have been made drunk with the wine of her fornication."

In the first verse she is called a whore or harlot, and in this verse, the participants with her in her harlotry, are disclosed.

For centuries past the kings of the earth, or earthly governments have had unholy relations with this Jezebel. Since she if a religio-political institution, she has enticed the governments of the world to support and sustain her unholy ambitions, by secret, as well as open alliances. History breathes in the record of her political and religious concordats with the rulers and governments of the earth.

"And the inhabitants have been made *drunk* with the wine of her fornication."

Fornication, in the Scripture, spiritually speaking, refers to false worship, and disloyalty to Christ and His word. Judged by this stand, the Roman Church stands self condemned. When she endeavors to obtain mercy and redemption through Mary as Mediatrix, rather than through Christ, directly, she is untrue to Him. When she teaches doctrines of men, rather than a "thus saith the Lord," she is guilty of spiritual fornication.

The Scripture here says, "They are drunk with the wine of her fornication. Intoxication addles the brain, and affects the muscles so the intoxicated cannot walk straight. The wine of spiritual fornication also addles the mind so the one drunk cannot think God's thoughts after Him, and their walk is crooked. Not according to the straight and narrow way of New Testament truth. A drunk thinks himself sober; likewise, the deluded think themselves right and everyone else wrong. Hence, you hear the apostate church declaring, "The Catholic Church is the only true church."

vs. 3 "And he carried me away in the Spirit into the wilderness."

The true church fled into the wilderness, where she had a place prepared of God. (Rev. 12:6), but here it is a place of the apostate church's own preparing. Her growth and development was so obscure and unnoticed, until her true nature was revealed, that she was like one living hidden in a wilderness. John had to be carried away in the spirit to clearly see her true nature and only those with God-opened eyes can spiritually see this great apostasy and departure from the truth.

vs. 3 "And I saw a woman sit upon a scarlet colored beast, full of names of blasphemy, having seven heads and ten horns."

We have already learned in Rev. 13th chapter, that the beast was political Rome, one of those heads was wounded as to death, but whose deadly wound was healed. We learned from history how the old political Rome fell during the seven trumpets, but how, simultaneously, the papal, political state arose to heal the head of government and cause it to continue to live.

So, here, the woman rides upon political Rome, or a secular power. It was a scarlet colored beast, a color symbolical of bloodshed. Both old imperial Rome, and later papal Rome, that arose from the ashes of the destruction of the former, were guilty of sheding the blood of the saints.

John saw the heads of the beast full of names of blasphemy. Blasphemy is the sin of claiming the attributes of God. Because Christ claimed that he was the Son of God, the high priest accused him of blasphemy. (Matt. 26:63-65)

We shall find, presently, that these heads represented forms of government. Did the Roman rulers claim deity, and in so doing become guilty of blasphemy? Let history speak for itself, on this point.

Alexander, reading Homer, found that the ancient heroes were sons of gods, so he, also, claimed and received divine honors, reserved for a god.

The infamous Antioches Epiphanes was assigned a place among the holy gods. We read, in the Scriptures that, Herod, with all his vileness, was hailed as a god.

"And upon a set day, Herod, arrayed in royal apparel, sat upon his throne, and made an ovation unto them.

And the people gave a shout, saying, it *is the voice of a god, and not of a man.*" (Acts 12:21, 22)

Caius Marius (about 156 to 86 B.C.), seven times elected to the consulship of Rome, was classed with the gods, by the people of Rome.

Julius Caesar was worshipped as a god, and after his death many temples were built and frequented in order to worship him.

Trajan worshipped Nerva and honored him with chief priests, with altars and with scared gifts.

Plury, the younger, in turn, honored Trajan as a god.

The vile Caligula claimed to be a god, calling himself by names of the diety. He boasted that every nation, except the Jews, worshipped him.

The King of Parthis, kneeling before Nero, said to him: "You are my God, and I am come to adore you as I adore the sun."

Domitian filled the earth with his statues, to which sacrifices were offered, and required that all letters written, or published in his name should begin with, "Our Lord and god commands."

One of the underlying reasons for the martyrdom of the early Christians, was that they would not worship, nor sacrifice to the Emperors, as gods.

And the woman herself, patterned after old imperial Rome, in that she was an eccleseastical state springing up out of the old empire, also is full of names of blasphemy.

The pope claims to be the vicar of Christ, or the representative of Christ on earth; but Christ declared that he sent the Holy Spirit to speak for him on earth. (John 16:12-14) He also claims to be the head of the Church, but Paul's words come to us across the centuries saying that God "hath put all things under his feet, and gave him to be *the head* over *all things* to the church, which is his body." (Eph. 1:22, 23)

Some of these blasphemous names come to light in the Mariolatry, or worship of Mary of the apostate church.

Some of these names have been spoken so often by this institution of blasphemy that they no longer shock the world whose spiritual sences have been dulled and deadened. Listen to a few of them as we hear Mary called: "Mother of God," "Queen of Heaven," "Mary, the Immaculate." And listen to those pronouncements of blasphemy: "There is one mediator between Christ and men, "the Holy Mother, Mary." How blasphemous this sounds when read along beside I Timothy 2:25: "For there is one God, and *one mediator between God and men, the man Christ Jesus.*"

Or listen to this blasphemy, "Mary is the way, the Truth and the Life, no man cometh to Jesus, but by Mary," in comparison with Christ's own words, "I am the Way, the Truth, and the Life; no man cometh unto the Father, but by me." (John 14:6)

The Psalter of Bonaventure, reads: "We praise thee, O Mary! We acknowledge thee to be the Virgin. All the earth doth worship thee, spouse of the Eternal. To thee angels and archangels cry, Holy, Holy, Holy, art thou, Mary, Mother of God."

Archbishop Vachon, of Ottawa, who sponsored the Marian Congress, (June 1947), in his pastorial letter, given in the Canadian

Register (Feb. 8, 1947), quoted the encyclical of Leo 13th (Sept. 22, 1891). "No portion whatsoever of the immense treasury of graces accumilated by the Savior, is bestowed upon us except through Mary, such is the will of God . . . no heavenly gift comes to men which does not pass through her virginal hands."

The canonized saint, Liguori, in his work, "The glories of Mary," says, "this good Mother, for the love she bore us, wished also to help the cause of our salvation with the merits of her sufferings, which she offered for us on Calvary." (Vol. 2, page 19)

Again same author, Volume I, page 409:

"The wills of Christ and of Mary were then united, so that both offered the same holocaust; she thereby producing, with him the one effect, the salvation of the world. At the death of Jesus, Mary united her will to that of her Son; so much so, that both offered one and the same sacrifice."

No wonder Cardinal Gibbons, in his book, "Faith of Our Fathers," page 215, 38th Edition, attempted to escape the accusation of Mariolatry, by saying, "And yet the admirers of Mary's exalted virtues can scarcely celebrate her praises without being accused in certain quarters of Mariolatry."

Then, there is the familiar claim of the power to forgive sins, which only Christ has the power to do. Truly, both imperial Rome and religio-political papal Rome are full of names of blasphemy!

We also note that papal Rome, or the apostate church, here is presented under the symbolism of a "woman." The very circumstance that this woman is seen *in the wilderness,* places her in contrast to the other woman of the twelveth chapter of Revelation who, as the true church, was forced to flee *into the wilderness,* where she had a place prepared of God.

Since the woman of the twelvth chapter, represented the true church, this woman in the seventeenth chapter, being a harlot, symbolizes the false or apostate church.

This is further substantiated by turning to the twenty-first chapter of Revelation. Just as one of the seven angels which had the seven vials, had revealed to John, in the seventeenth chapter, the apostate church, here, in this chapter, one of the seven angels, also, shows John the true church, the Lamb's wife:

"And there came unto me one of the seven angels which had the seven vials full of the seven last plauges, and talked with me, saying, come hither, I will show thee the bride, the Lamb's wife.

And he carried me away in the Spirit, (Just as in Rev. 17:3)
to a great and high mountain, and showed me that great city,
the Holy Jerusalem, decending out of heaven from God."

Here the Lamb's wife is called a city, just as the harlot woman is
also called a city, "And the woman which thou sawest is that great
city, which reigneth over the Kings of the earth." (Rev. 17:18)

Further, the harlot woman of the seventeenth chapter is identified
with the earthly city of Babylon, or the city of confusion and instead
of being the immaculate bride of Christ, she is one with whom
the kings of the earth have committed fornication.

This, beyond a scintilla of a doubt. is the false church, which
came into being in the Pergamos Period, characterized by the doctrine of Baalam, or the doctrine of compromise, and the doctrine of
the Nicolaitanes or the doctrine of overlordship. This is the apostate
church which came to full flower in the Thyatira church period,
when the church reached "the depths of Satan." Removing all
symbolism the false church is known, in history, as the Roman
Catholic Church.

The only symbolism left in this verse yet to be considered
the seven heads and the ten horns—will be taken up in the more
logical place where they are mentioned later in this chapter. Shall
we proceed with the description of the woman.

vs. 4 "And the woman was arrayed in purple and scarlet color,
and decked with gold and precious stones and pearls."

Purple is the color of royalty. She has ever claimed temporal and
spiritual sovereignty, hence the mention of this color. As for scarlet,
her cardinals wear the color scarlet with their red hats. Her altars
throughout the world are decorated with gold and precious stones.
These colors, purple and scarlet are characteristic of the vestments
of the Roman hierarchy, scarlet being particularly identified with the
cardinals, who are called, "princes of the church." The red color
also identifies this church with the great red dragon or the devil and
satan.

The gold and precious stones and pearls are truly representative
of the earthly gorgeousness and magnifigance of the embellishments
with which the Roman church adorns her altars, temples, rites and
ceremonies.

Over against the showy attire of the harlot church, Paul speaks
of the true church as follows:

"Whose adorning, let it not be that outward adorning of plait-
ing of hair, and wearing of gold, or of putting on of apparel;

but let it be the hidden man of the heart, in that which is not corruptible, even the ornament of a meek and quiet spirit, which is in the sight of God of great price." (I Peter 3:3, 4)

Even the pope is reported using a solid gold telephone and has a car in which to ride on six hundred feet of track in the Vatican grounds. And that car is covered within and without with pure gold.

Besides all this, this apostate church is the richest institution in all the world, that is materially, though not spirtually. The papal church has enriched herself at the expense of peoples, multitudes and nations (many waters), upon which she has fastened her tenacles. Her treasures are fabulous beyond the knowledge of men. Her revenues are enormous. Her land, factory and building values run into astronomical figures, much of which is non-taxable, though oftimes competing with legimate business, which must bear a staggering tax burden. Never in history, was there ever a more flagrant example of contempt for and regard of Christ's pronouncement, "Lay not up for yourselves treasures on the earth." (Matt. 6:19)

Continuing this verse, we read: "Having a golden cup in her hand, full of abominations and filthiness of her fornication."

This harlot woman, the apostate church, had in her hand the means of conveying the truth—a golden cup; but instead she filled it with her own abominations and filthiness of false teaching, called fornication.

Later this woman is called, "Babylon," which, in connection with the mentioning of a cup in her hand, brings to our mind a statement made concerning the Babylon, of the Old Testament, which was a type of this spiritual Babylon: "Babylon hath been a golden cup in the Lord's hand, that made all the earth drunken: the nations have drunken of her wine, therefore the nations are mad." (Jeremiah 51:7)

Shall we note also, that the cup is one. In all the varied systems of religion, whether Roman Catholic, the degenerate catholicism of the Byzantine church, or the false teachings and worship of denominationalism—all have the essence of the old harlotry of Babylon.

Shall we continue to the next verse.

vs. 5 "And upon her forehead was a name written, *Mystery*."

Of all the institutions of the world, whether secular or spiritual, there has never been one so mysterious as the apostate church. Her rising out of the ashes of the old Roman empire, her hold upon the souls of men, as well as the life of nations, her political machinations, her age-long ability to seduce men to subscribe to her half-pagan ritualism, her power to demand an unquestioning blind following of her devotees, her seductive influence to induce men to substitute the worship of Mary, in the place of Christ, her strong hold of slavish fear over the hearts and minds of men—all combine to make her the most mysterious religio-ecclesiastical-political organization in all history.

But there is even more hidden in this word, "Mystery." It is entirely fitting that this name should be written upon her forehead —the seat of all false thinking and teaching. Paul, looking down through the corridors of time, saw this coming, whose beginning was manifest, even in his day:

"For the *mystery* of iniquity doth already work; only he who letteth will let until he be taken out of the way: and then shall that Wicked be revealed, whom the Lord shall consume with the spirit of his mouth, and shall destroy with the brightness of his coming." (II Thess. 2:7, 8)

This church that went into the wilderness of error, superstition and false teaching, yea even humanism became the monstrous mystery Babylon.

The second name by which she is called is *Babylon the Great*.

Here we come to one of the deepest symbols. In the tenth and eleventh chapters of Genesis—the book of beginnings, we have in these two chapters the record of the beginning of various nations. These chapters may rightfully be called, "the chapters of origins." In this catalog of nations, we are given the origin of the Kingdom of Nimrod, the grandson of Ham. This kingdom is called Bab-el or Babylon, in the land of Shinar.

Nimrod, we read was a mighty hunter before the Lord. The Targum of Jonathan renders this, "a mighty rebel before the Lord, the mightiest rebel before the Lord that ever was on earth."

The apostate church, or New Testament Babylon is likewise, the greatest rebel before God, scripturally and spritually speaking.

As Nimrod was such a brazen offender, who hesitated not to withstand God, Himself, so the Roman church is the world's worst offender in God's sight, because she wilfully rejects God's authorative pronouncements.

"Bab-el," means, "the gate of God." The Catholic Church teaches no one can come to God but by that particular church, thus claiming she is "the gate of God."

"Bab-el," or Babylon, means, "confusion," because there began the confusion of tongues. The apostacy, by its false teaching, has confused the religious world.

The people, in the days of the erection of the tower of Babel, did it to make a name for themselves. (Genesis 11:4) Literally it is, "make a sem," meaning token, sign, banner, name or mark, "lest we be scattered abroad upon the face of the earth." (Genesis 11:4)

That name, "sem or "sema," was a mark of their greatness. In the language of that day, a "sema-rama." From this we derive the name, "semiramis," the dove-goddess, the ensign of all Assyrian princes. This mark, or name figures prominently in the national lives of the pagan nations. It came to be the name of a woman closely resembling the Virgin Mary of the Roman Church. In ancient Babylon, she was Semiranii, in Assyria, she was Astarte; in Egypt, Isis, in Greece, Aphrodite, in Rome, Venus. Hesiod, one of the earliest Greek writers, described her as, "the mother of the gods. Catholics call her, "mother of God."

The symbol of such a mark came to take the place of a god and became the holy mother, the great heavenly protectress.

She is called, Babylon the Great. She is the *great* church that ruled over the kingdoms of earth. History substantiates this with an abundant flood of proof.

She is called, "The mother of harlots." The Catholic Church habitually calls herself, "the Mother Church," and ever urges her children—the churches who broke away from her—to return to the fold.

Revelation not only calls her a harlot, but the "Mother of Harlots."

This church is pictured as the mother of a family of churches. Since she is a harlot and a church, then her children, being harlots, are likewise churches. How necessary for each person to examine with extreme care the donimimation to which he belongs, to see whether it may not be like its mother, holding a cup full of humanisms and doctrines of men, rather than a "thus saith the Lord." The apostate church surely has a numerous and growing family of daughters. And ever this "Mother Church" longs to gather her daughters to her ample arms.

She is also called the mother of "abominations of the earth." How astonished the entire world will be when "that Wicked shall be revealed!" The more one studies the harlotry and abominations of this apostate church, the more utterly amazed he becomes that he never realized before her hideousness in God's sight, and, also, that the world is so blind to the true character of this God-hated institution.

And speaking of how abominable she is in God's sight. One of the, if not the most characteristic features of this woman is her *harlotry*. Harlotry is the standing symbol, in the Scriptures, for a system of debauched worship, idolatry, and false teaching.

The Scriptures call it adultery, whoredom and fornication.

Harlotry uniformly symbolizes the apostacy of God's church. The word, "harlot," is used at least fifty times to describe spiritual fornication. In eighteen out of twenty occurances of this figure of speech, the import is that God's church and people have forsaken Him. There are only three times in the entire Bible where the figure is applied to heathen cities or nations, twice to Tyre and once to Nineveh. So she is a harlot and the Mother of Harlots, or other false churches which have followed in her footsteps.

vs. 6 "And I saw her drunken with blood of saints, and with the blood of the martyrs of Jesus. And when I saw her, I wondered with great admiration."

She not only made "the inhabitants drunk with the wine of her fornication" (Rev. 17:2), but she herself has become drunk with the blood of saints and martyrs.

The word "drunken" expresses the state of being glutted or surfeited with blood, although, judging by her persecution and slaughter of the saints, her thirst is insatiable.

There have been harlot daughters who have also engaged in persecution, but there is only one church who could be styled, "drunk with the blood of the saints." And, note she was drunken with the blood of the martyrs of Jesus. That identifies her as an institution this side of the time Jesus walked on the earth, was crucified, died, was buried and rose again.

Her blood-drunken state made the Apostle to wonder with great wonderment.

vs. 7 "And the angel said unto me, wherefore didst thou marvel? I will tell thee the mystery of the woman and the beast that carrieth her, which hath the seven heads and ten horns.

290

The beast that thou sawest was, and is not; and shall ascend out of the bottomless pit, and go into perdition."

We have found this beast to represent a government, and in this case Imperial Rome, which perished during the seven trumpets, but arose from the ashes of destruction, as the papal hierchy restored the government, but in another form. And this restored government, ascended out of the bottomless pit, the final abode of the devil. In other words, it was devil born and satan inspired.

vs. 8 "And they that swell on the earth shall wonder, "whose names were not written in the book of life from the foundation of the world," when they behold the beast that was, and is not, and yet is."

vs. 9, 10 "And here is the mind which hath wisdom." Of course, this refers to spiritual wisdom for, "the natural man (the unrenewed man through the new birth) receiveth not the things of the Spirit of God, for they are foolishness unto him; neither can he know them, because they are spiritually discerned."

"The seven heads are seven (I Cor. 1:14) mountains, on which the woman sitteth."

While there is a much deeper meaning hidden here, Rome has always been recognized as the "seven-hilled city," from the seven hills on which she stood. They were Mt. Aventine, Mt. Capitaline, Mt. Palatine, Mt. Esquiline, the Caelian Mount, the Quirinal and Viminal. Ovid, Horace, Levy, the early church fathers, Tertullian, as well as Jerome, all called Rome the seven-hilled city.

Jerome, born 342 A.D., wrote a letter to a certain Christian lady urging her to "read what is written in the apocalypse of the seven hills."

But there is a deeper meaning. A mountain, in symbolism, represents a government of some form or nature. The seven heads are also seven kings, or kingdoms, or governments, for the original term may signify either of the three. Rev. 17:10, "And there are seven kings: five are fallen, and one is, and the other is yet to come; and when he is come, he must continue a short space."

Rome, in all her political history, had seven forms of government, as follows:

1. The *first* form was *Kingly*. The first king was Romulus; the last, Torquin, the Proud. There were seven kings in all.
2. The *second* form, that of Consulers. Two consuls were elected annually.
3. The *third* form was that of *Dictators*. In this form one man was invested with dictatorial power.
4. The *fourth* form was that of *Tribunes*. Under this form, the chief magistrates were the Tribunes of the people.
5. The *fifth* form was that of *Decemvirs*. Under this system absolute government was invested in ten men who were superior to all laws.

These first five forms had come and gone before John's day, because "five are fallen." The sixth form was in existence at the time, for we are here told that "one is." We know from earlier studies, that the system of government, at the time of the revelation given to John, was that of Emperors. John had been banished to Patmos by the Emperor, Domitian. The form was that of an Imperial government.

So, now we have found six of the heads to be, (1) Kings, (2) Consuls, (3) Dictators, (4) Tribunes, (5) Decemvirs and (6) Emperors.

But we are informed that "one is to come." We have already discovered this seventh form in our study of the "Seal Series." Following the overthrow of the Emperors, there followed a period in which Rome was ruled by Military Governors. Under this form, the Roman Legions set up their own Generals as Military Governors. Of this form, John said, "And when he cometh, he must continue a short space." This seventh form was to give way for an eighth. Shall we read about it:

vs. 11, 12 "And the beast that was, and is not, even he is the eighth, and is of the seven, and goeth into perdition."

In the light of our already gained knowledge, we know with the fall of Rome, a new form of government had already begun to rise, like an empire within an empire. Long before the fall of Rome, there had begun to grow up within the secular state, an ecclesiastical state, which in its constitution and administrative system, was shaping itself upon the imperial model, with finally the pope becoming temporal sovereign, with the states of the church, its domain.

This eighth form then, was an image of the old secular government, yet with something distinctly new added—the merging of church and state. The eighth form was, then, a religio-political form.

This is the reason why the woman is said to be seated on the beast. The secular system supported the papal form. The temporal form carried the religious system.

It is worthy of note that it is never said of the other seven forms that they should go into perdition. It is only of this eighth form —that of religion and politics combined, that it is said "And goeth into perdition." This is the Babylon of the seventh vial (Rev. 16:19) that "came into remembrance before God to give her the cup of the wine of fierceness of His wrath."

Now, we are ready to advance to the next verse. Rev. 17:12, "And the ten horns which thou sawest are ten kings, which have received no Kingdoms as yet, but receive power as Kings one hour with the beast."

We have, earlier in this study, learned that a horn represents power, espceially a Kingdom, not necessarily a world power. When John wrote, those Kingdoms did not yet exist.

After the fall of Rome, the dominion of the Caesars divided into ten smaller states. Sir Isaac Newton traced this ten as follows:
1. Kingdom of the Vandals in Spain and Africa.
2. Kingdom of the Visigoths.
3. Kingdom of the Suevi.
4. Kingdom of the Alans in France.
5. Kingdom of the Burgundians.
6. Kingdom of the Franks.
7. Kingdom of the Britons.
8. Kingdom of the Huns.
9. Kingdom of the Lombards.
10. Kingdom of the Revenna.

So the Roman Empire broke up into ten lesser nations, but all the ten carried or supported the Papacy. They are not to exist very long as ten, for a part of them soon passed away.

vs. 14 "These shall make war with the Lamb, and the Lamb shall overcome them: for He is Lord of Lords, and Kings of Kings: And they that are with him are called and chosen, and faithful."

These are evidently mentioned again in (Rev. 19:19) when the Kings of the earth and their armies come forth to battle the Lamb.

vs. 15 "And he saith unto me. The waters which thou sawest, where the whore sitteth are peoples, and multitudes, and nations, and tongues."

This verse is one of the few in Revelation that seems to be included in that book to give us an interpretation of some symbol. We will recall that the verses mentioning seven candlesticks, the seven stars, and the one explaining that the dragon was the devil and satan, are verses employed as interpreters of symbols.

Rome, in the Papal form, or eighth governmental system, held vast sway of the power over peoples and nations and tongues.

vs. 17 "And the ten horns which thou sawest upon the beast, these shall hate the whore, and shall make her desolate and naked, and shall eat her flesh, and burn her with fire."

We have already shown how France, one of the ten horn Kingdoms, conquered the Papal states and humiliated the pope by taking him a prisoner to France. With the action of France, we read of how "a tenth part of the city (or papal Rome) fell. As nations threw off the Roman yoke, they made the Harlot on the Tiber, desolate, and naked, by stripping her of her treasuries, her power and her temporal states. The seven vials recounted how these made war on religion-political Rome. And how did it happen that they were of one mind to do this? Judging from the historical viewpoint, we would say they did this because of oppression and through a desire to throw off the papal yoke.

But John was permitted to step in behind the scenes, and see the hand back of it all, "For God hath put in their hearts to fulfil his will, and *to agree* and give their Kingdom unto the beast, until the Word of God shall be fulfilled."

He caused them to agree and used these ten agencies to carry out His divine will.

First, they unitedly gave their support to the woman, or the apostate church, until God's word was accomplished; then they turned on the woman or ecclesiastical Rome to destroy her.

vs. 18 "And the woman which thou sawest is that great city, which reigneth over the Kings of the earth."

There is but one church that ever ruled over the Kingdoms of this earth, the City of Babylon, spiritually speaking, or the Roman Catholic Church.

This entire seventeenth chapter seems to have been dedicated to to the task of leaving the world without the faintest doubt as to what the beast is, as to what Babylon is, what the Mother of Harlots is, and what church, in God's sight, is the abomination of the earth. Mystery, Babylon the great, has now been fully revealed so that all who runs may read.

CHAPTER XVIII

BABYLON IS FALLEN

Text (18:1-24)

1 After these things I saw another angel coming down out of heaven, having great authority; and the earth was lightened with his glory. 2 And he cried with a mighty voice, saying, Fallen, fallen is Babylon the great, and is become a habitation of demons, and a hold of every unclean spirit, and a hold of every unclean and hateful bird. 3 For by the wine of the wrath of her fornication all the nations are fallen; and the kings of the earth committed fornication with her, and the merchants of the earth waxed rich by the power of her wantonness.

4 And I heard another voice from heaven, saying, Come forth, my people, out of her, that ye have no fellowship with her sins, and that ye receive not of her plagues: 5 for her sins have reached even unto heaven, and God hath remembered her iniquities. 6 Render unto her even as she rendered, and double unto her the double according to her works: in the cup which she mingled, mingle unto her double. 7 How much soever she glorified herself, and waxed wanton, so much give her of torment and mourning: for she saith in her heart, I sit a queen, and am no widow, and shall in no wise see mourning. 8 Therefore in one day shall her plagues come, death, and mourning, and famine; and she shall be utterly burned with fire; for strong is the

Lord God who judged her. 9 And the kings of the earth, who committed fornication and lived wantonly with her, shall weep and wail over her, when they look upon the smoke of her burning, 10 standing afar off for the fear of her torment, saying, Woe, woe, the great city, Babylon, the strong city! for in one hour is thy judgment come. 11 And the merchants of the earth weep and mourn over her, for no man buyeth their merchandise any more; 12 merchandise of gold, and silver, and precious stone, and pearls, and fine linen, and purple, and silk, and scarlet; and all thyine wood, and every vessel of ivory, and every vessel made of most precious wood, and of brass, and iron, and marble; 13 and cinamon, and spice, and incense, and ointment, and frankincense, and wine, and oil, and fine flour, and wheat, and cattle, and sheep; and merchandise of horses and chariots and slaves; and souls of men. 14 And the fruits which thy soul lusted after are gone from thee, and all things that were dainty and sumptuous are perished from thee, and men shall find them no more at all. 15 The merchants of these things, who were made rich by her, shall stand afar off for the fear of her torment, weeping and mourning; 16 saying, Woe, woe, the great city, she that was arrayed in fine linen and purple and scarlet, and decked with gold and precious stone and pearl! 17 for in one hour so great riches is made desolate. And every shipmaster, and every one that saileth any whither, and mariners, and as many as gain their living by sea, stood afar off, 18 and cried as they looked upon the smoke of her burning, saying, What city is like the great city? 19 And they cast dust on their heads, and cried, weeping and mourning, saying, Woe, woe, the great city, wherein all that had their ships in the sea were made rich by reason of her costliness! for in one hour is she made desolate. 20 Rejoice over her, thou heaven, and ye saints, and ye apostles, and ye prophets; for God hath judged your judgment on her.

21 And a strong angel took up a stone as it were a great millstone and cast it into the sea, saying, Thus with a mighty fall shall Babylon, the great city, be cast down, and shall be found no more at all. 22 And the voice of harpers and minstrels and flute-players and trumpeters shall be heard no more at all in thee; and no craftsman, of whatsoever craft, shall be found any more at all in thee; and the voice of a mill shall be heard no more at all in thee; 23 and the light of a lamp shall shine no more at all in thee; and the voice of the bridegroom and of the bride shall be heard no more at all in thee: for thy merchants were the princes of the earth; for with thy sorcey were all the nations deceived. 24 And in her was found the blood of prophets and of saints, and of all that have been slain upon the earth.

vs. 1 "And after these things."

After the descriptions given us in the seventeenth chapter to reveal to us the identity of that great city of Spiritual Babylon, or papal Rome which rules over the kings of earth, we now come to the consideration of her downfall.

"I saw another angel come down from heaven, having great power, and the earth was lightened with his glory." (Rev. 18:1)

The introduction of such a mighty angel at this juncture emphasizes the importance of the subject matter of this vision before us. This is another angel than one of the seven angels which had the seven vials who talked with John in the seventeenth chapter.

To this present angel was given great power or authority because of the world-shattering events introduced in this chapter. The earth was lightened with his glory, because he came with a revelation of great enlightment concerning the final destruction of that great city Babylon which had darkened the earth doctrinally, spiritually, politically and economically.

vs 2 "And he cried mightily with a strong voice, saying, Babylon is fallen, is fallen, and is become the habitation of devils, and the hold of every foul spirit, and a cage of every unclean and hateful bird."

Here this angel repeats a former angelic pronouncement recorded in (Rev. 14:8), "Babylon is fallen is fallen." By referring back to that setting we find that this first pronouncement falls into the time of the seventh vial, because in the pouring out of his seventh plague "great Babylon came in remembrance before God, to give unto her the cup of the wine of the fierceness of His wrath." (Rev. 16:19)

The repetition of this announcement of Babylon's fall calls our attention to the importance of this climactic event of history's consummation. Again the emphasis becomes apparent in the double declaration "is fallen is fallen."

When Joseph explained to Pharoah why his dream was "doubled," he said: "And for that the dream was *doubled* unto Pharoah *twice*; it is because the thing is *established*, and God will shortly bring it to pass." (Genesis 41:32)

For the same evident reason the word "fallen" is repeated twice, even *doubled* unto us *twice*,—one *double* in 14:8 and the second double in 18:2.

The importance of all this is readily seen when we realize that all the activities of men, all their religious or business enterprises,

297

eventuate in that condition of a godless civilization as typified by the literal Babylon of antiquity and the spiritual Babylon symbolzed under that name in Revelation.

The confusion that obtains in religion, education, economics, finance, industry, government, politics and morality—all is traced back to that great city that rules over the Kings of the earth the "Mystery, Babylon the Great, the Mother of Harlots and abominations of the earth." This Babylon we have proved by the testimony of Scripture and History alike to be the religio-political heirarchal system known to the world as the papacy and the apostate church.

With a false church dominating the world, it follows, as naturally as daylight comes after dark, that men would have false conceptions of right and wrong in the moral, spiritual, intellectual, financial, economic and political realms of activity.

Our present state of civilization is the harvest. Rome sowed the wind and the closing period of this age is reaping the whirlwind.

The angel describes this present age of which the world is so blindly proud, as a habitation of devils, a hold for every foul spirit, a cage for every unclean and hateful bird.

Of course to the spiritually deluded and the worldling this all sounds absurd. They point to the grandeur of the Roman church, her multitudes of earnest devotees, her pronouncements on peace, her denunciation of intellectual evils, etc. This generation boasts of its material accomplishments in the way of scientific research and inventive genius, but they do not see all this through God's eyes.

Surely, the world, in its evaluation of things, needs to hark back to the declaration God made to Samuel who was trying to select a king to be annointed. Samuel was one of the noblest men of history, yet even this fine man illustrates how far wrong a good man can be in property evaluation. Hear God's council to him:

> "And the Lord said to Samuel; Look not on his countenance, or on the height of his stature: because I have refused him: for the Lord *seeth not as man seeth;* for man looketh on the outward appearance, but the Lord looketh on the heart." (I Samuel 16:7)

This twice repeated expression "is fallen is fallen" describes a twin falling action. Babylon, as a system of false teaching and worship in an apostate church, and, Babylon as a system of commercialism resulting from a scriptural departure in doctrine and practice, falls.

Twin falls are thus portrayed. Both Mother and child, both spiritual and carnal, both cause and effect are included in this repeated expression, "is fallen is fallen."

And the reason by both fall together is given in the very next verse:

vs. 3 "For all nations have drunk of the wine of the wrath of her fornication and the kings of the earth have committed fornication with her and the merchants of the earth are waxed rich through the abundance of her delicacies."

Then John hears a call for God's people to come out of this Babylonish nightmare: *vs. 4* "And I heard another voice from heaven, saying, Come out of her my people, that ye be not partakers of her sins, and that ye receive not her plagues."

This call to come out of this spiritual Babylon, producer of all the evils of our present civilization, is not the first time such a call has been heard. The call to flee from either physical or spiritual Babylon has been issued seven times in all the scriptures. The call occurs five times in the Old Testament. They are: (Isaiah 48:20; 52:4-11) (Jeremiah 50:8, 9; 51:6, 8) (Zechariah 2:6, 7)

In the New Testament there are two calls. Although in the first of the two the name "Babylon" is not actually mentioned, but is implied by the confusion caused by the mixing of believers and unbelievers. The two instances are: (2 Cor. 6:17, 18) (Rev. 18:4)

The seven-fold, or fullest possible measure of calling, for the people of God to flee this great Babylon is impressive indeed.

However, we should recall that whereas God brought His people out of Egypt in a body, with a strong hand and with an outstretched arm, in the case of this call to flee Babylon is an individual one.

Again his people were forced to flee out of Egypt, but here only those who have a mind to come out may do so.

It will not be a mass evacuation, but rather an individual and voluntary leave of this world-wide institution of confusion and apostacy.

vs. 5 Regardless of man's human judgment her sins are enormous, for we read: "For her sins have reached unto heaven, and God hath remembered her iniquities."

While the promise to the obedient believer is "Their sins and their iniquities I will remember no more" (Hebrew 8:12), the sins of Babylon are remembered and unforgiven by God, because we read:

vs. 6 "Reward her even as she rewarded you, and double unto her double according to her works: in the cup which she hath filled fill to her double."

Contemptous flaunting and defiance of the word of God is the essence of the sin of Babylon. If Revelation did not here declare it so plainly we would know it applied to our age in which we live.

Rome's disregard for the Scriptures and the authority of Christ's word has caused the world to hate what they know as the church. They have falsely and mistakenly judged the church of Christ by what they have beheld in the Catholic church. The result has been that men have turned away from God's word, the church and drifted into utter indifference, agnosticism, skepticism, free-thinking and out right infidelity. We live, as a result of Babylons heaven reaching sins, in this age of humanism.

God's principle of judgment is that every individual, as well as every institution, is to be rewarded according to his or its work. What is sown must be harvested. This Thyatira church as "given space to repent of her fornication and she repented not." (Rev. 2:21)

He further adds, "Behold, I will cast her into a bed, and them that commit adultery with her into great tribulation except they repent of their deeds." (Rev. 2:22)

But an added measure of punishment is revealed here. Babylon, or Rome shall be rewarded *double*.

Not only was she and still is unrepentant, but she is the most arrogant institution in all the world. Hear the angel describe her haughty attitude: "How much hath she glorified herself, and lived deliciously, so much torment and sorrow give her."

vs. 7 "This recalls the case of the rich man and Lazarus: "There was a certain rich man, which was clothed in purple and fine linen, and fared sumptuously every day," but at the end, in hell a far different scene is presented: "But Abraham said, Son, remember that thou in thy life time receivedst thy good things, and likewise Lazarus evil things; but now he is comforted and thou art tormented. (Luke 16:19, 25)

Likewise, she who lived deliciously shall be meted out torment and sorrow.

But her boasting continues: "for she saith in her heart, I sit a queen, and am no widow, and shall see no sorrow."

What a strange statement of the angel concerning Babylon—the papal church! The holy word of God, says Christ is the bridegroom and the repentant baptized believers are his bride. But inform a member of this apostate church of his condition and he will immeidately declare, "the Roman Catholic church is the only and true church." It is the voice of the apostacy crying "I sit as a queen, and am no widow, and shall see no sorrow."

And as for this ungodly and unregenerate civilization she has produced, if you tell them of the impending danger of living in sin until Christ comes, they if not in substance, at least in their actions will reply, "Where is the promise of His coming? for since the fathers fell asleep, all things continue as they were from the beginning of the creation (2 Pet. 3;4). But Christ said of these last days,

"As it was in the days of Noah, so shall it be also in the days of the Son of man. They did eat, they drank, they married wives, they were given in marriage, until the day that Noah entered the ark, and the flood came, and destroyed them all. Even so shall it be when the Son of man is revealed." (Luke. 17:26, 27, 30)

So shall the plagues of Babylon come suddenly:

vs. 7 "Therefore shall her plagues come in one day, death and mourning, and famine; and she shall be utterly burned with fire: for strong is the Lord who judgeth her."

Man's disbelief that God will punish, notwithstanding, God will destroy her suddenly.

Like the saints under the fifth seal the true saints of this day, cry out, "How long, O Lord, holy and true, dost thou not judge and avenge our blood on them that dwell on the earth?"

I know all who have perused the contents of this book are crying out, How long? When will Babylon fall? In answer will say that such time has never been revealed. There is the highest authority for such a reply, even Christ himself:

"But of that day and hour knoweth no man, no, not the angels of heaven, but my Father." (Matt. 24:36)

Christ continued after this declaration "But as the days of Noah were, so shall also the coming of the Son of Man be." (Matt. 24:37)

So even the angel who here announced the suddenness of Babylon's destruction knew not the hour, so could not tell us when the destruction shall be."

vs. 9-11 And the kings of the earth, who have committed fornication and lived deliciously with her, shall bewail her, and lament for her, when they shall see the smoke of her burning. Standing afar off for the fear of her torment, saying, Alas, alas, that great city Babylon, that mighty city! for in one hour is thy judgment come.

And the merchants of the earth shall weep and mourn over her; for no man buyeth their merchandise any more:"

The follows an enumeration of the articles in which they made traffic.

vs. 12, 13 "The merchandise of gold, and silver, and precious stones, and of pearls, and fine linen, and purple and silk, and scarlet, and all thyine wood, and all manner vessels of ivory, and all manner vessels of most precious wood, and of brass, and iron, and marble.

And cinnamon, and odors, and ointments, and frankincense, and wine, and oil, and fine flour, and wheat, and beasts, and sheep, and horses, and chariots, and slaves and souls of men."

In this lamentation over the sudden fall of Babylon, the merchants of earth and king's of earth join in their voices.

Probably not until God himself reveals all things to us will we begin to realize how this spiritual Babylon has her hand in business and politics—as symbolized by the lament of merchants and kings.

For a book of such brevity as the apocalypse to devote so much space and divulge so many articles of traffic as here confronts us, it must be that the angel wanted to make plain to a startled world how vast are the ramifactions of Rome's activities in all the affairs of men.

The whole world is conscious of the political activities of this apostate church which maintains embassies and sends ambassadors to almost every nation on earth, but it may come as a complete surprise to learn of her commercial activities.

But the last statement of these verses is the most startling—a revelation of her traffic in the "slaves and souls of men." Literally, the word "slaves" should read, "bodies." Thus the Greek reads.

Here it is that men and women barter their souls and bodies. There are multitudes of Esaus who will barter their spiritual birthright for a mess of this world's pottage.

How pertinent are Christ's words about the conditions of the near approach of His return.

303

"For what is a man profited if he shall gain the whole world, and lose his own soul, or what shall a man give in exchange for his soul? For the Son of Man shall come in the glory of his Father with his angels; and then he shall reward every man according to his works." (Matt. 16:26, 27)

The spiritual Babylon has with business made traffic of the bodies and souls of men. And when we recall the masses for the dead which are said by the priesthood of Papal Rome, in which the devotees pay to have their loved ones prayed out of Purgatory, surely there has been a long and lively traffic in the souls of men.

But the things for which Babylon longed are gone forever at the time of her fall.

vs. 14-19 "And the fruits that thy soul lusteth after are departed from thee, and all the things that were dainty and goodly are departed from thee, and thou shall find them no more at all.

The merchants of these things which were made rich by her, shall stand afar off for the fear of her torment, weeping and wailing, and saying, Alas, alas, that great city, that was clothed in fine linen, and purple and scarlet, and decked with gold, and precious stones and pearls!

For in one hour so great riches is come to nought. And every ship-master, and all the company in ships, and sailors, and as many as trade by sea, stood afar off, and cried when they saw the smoke of her burning, saying, What city is like unto this great city! And cast dust on their heads, and cried, weeping and wailing, saying, Alas, alas that great city, wherein were made rich all that had ships in the sea by reason of her costliness! for in one hour is she made desolate!"

Thus we see merchants, kings and shipmaster with their sailors lamenting the fall of Babylon. In other words, business, politics and transportation were under the denomination of and blessed by a false religious system that fostered their respective ungodly world-systems.

And three times we hear the cry, Alas. alas! Once it comes from the kings of the earth, or the political realm; once it is uttered by the merchants, or the commercial realm; and once from the ship-masters and sailor, or the transportation realm. It is a triple voice, each part of which is double. It is that evil number six complete.

The repeated Alas, alas! is striking. The word is the same as that of the angel in Rev. 8:13, when he cried, "Woe, woe, woe, to the inhabiters of the earth by reason of the other voices of the trumpet of the three angels, which are yet to sound."

The casting of dust on the head is a symbolic act of one who thus expresses his utter hopelessness and despair. Because of the sin of Achan which brought defeat to Israel we read:

"And Joshua rent his clothes, and fell on the earth upon his face before the ark of the Lord until the eventide, he and the elders of Israel, and put *dust upon their heads*." (Joshua 7:6)

Again this recurrence of the word "woe" or "alas" (verses 10, 16, and 19) helps us to identify the time of the fall of Babylon as being in the period of the third and last woe. (Rev. 11:14)

We have had symbolized to us the suddenness of Babylon's downfall in the expressions: "in one day" Verse 8, "in one hour" verses 17 and 19. Now we are informed as to the violence of the downfall.

vs. 20 "And a mighty angel took up a stone like a great mill-stone, and cast it into the sea, saying, Thus with violence shall that great city Babylon be thrown down, and shall be found no more."

This symbolic action of the mighty angel as portrayed in this verse is an intensified picture of a typical act which Jeremiah commanded Seraiah to perform when he came to that Babylon on antiquity:

"And Jeremiah said to Seraiah, when thou comest to Babylon, and shalt see, and shalt read all these words, . . . and it shall be, when thou hast made an end of reading this book, that thou shalt bind a stone to it and cast it into the midst of Euphrates. And thou shalt say. Thus shall Babylon sink and shall not rise from the evil that I will bring upon her." (Jeremiah 51:61, 63, 64)

Thus we see that the destruction of ancient Babylon was typical of the destruction of spiritual Babylon.

Thus we see that the fall of mysterious Babylon, that Romish church; that great Harlot woman; the Mother of Harlots and abominations of the earth; is one of the, if not the most outstanding and marvelous events of all time. More is said about Babylon in the Scriptures than any other great religious and secular occurrence.

But the rejoicings of heaven, and those whose affections are set on things above and not on things on the earth (Col. 3:2), are now set forth in exact contrast with the lamentations of the kings, merchants and shipmasters and all their peoples they represent.

vs. 21 "Rejoice over her, thou heaven, and ye holy apostles and prophets; for God hath avenged you on her."

While earth rings with the chorus of lamentation, dissappointment and despair, a grand jubulation fills the heaven. While the world cries, Woe, woe over the fall of this religio-political system, the citizens of heaven pour out of their mighty halleluias.

The angel then announces:

vs. 22 "And the voice of harpers, and musicians, and of pipers, and trumpeters, shall be heard no more at all in thee, and no craftsman, of whatsoever craft he be, shall be found any more in thee; and the sound of a millstone shall be herd no more at all in thee.

And the light of a candle shall shine no more at all in thee; and the voice of the bridegroom and of the bride shall be heard no more at all in thee: for thy merchants were the great men of earth; for by thy sorceries were all nations deceived.

And in her was found the blood of prophets, and of saints, and of all that were slain upon the earth."

It will be an event unbelievable to the world. The world has become so accustomed to seeing the Roman church, her priesthood and religious processions and pronouncements played up with such righteousness in the press, magazines and periodicals; propagated in the movies, on the radio and television screen; eulogized in song, poetry and story; kowtowed to by politician, merchant, transportation interests, advertisers, rulers and common citizens that the fall of such a church with such suddenness and violence will be shock that will shake the whole earth.

And it will be the immediate act of God. No earthy power or agency could bring to an end an institution so hoary with age and deeply intrenched in every activity of man.

And to think that all of this could have been avoided!. If there had been the New Testament church, with Christ as head and supreme authority upon the earth since Pentecost there would have been no spiritual Babylon to confuse the world religiously, currupt political governments, compromise truth and morals, and finally to condemn the world to eternal destruction and damnation.

CHAPTER XIX

THE HALLELUJAH CHORUS AND
FINAL JUDGMENT

Text (19:1-21)

1 After these things I heard as it were a great voice of a great multitude in heaven, saying, Hallelujah; Salvation, and glory, and power, belong to our God: 2 for true and righteous are his judgments; for he hath judged the great harlot, her that corrupted the earth with her fornication, and he hath avenged the blood of his servants at her hand.
3 And a second time they say, Hallelujah. And her smoke goeth up for ever and ever. 4 And the four and twenty elders and the four living creatures fell down and worshipped God that sitteth on the throne, saying, Amen; Hallelujah. 5 And a voice came forth from the throne, saying, Give praise to our God, all ye his servants, ye that fear him, the small and the great.
6 And I heard as it were the voice of a great multitude, and as the voice of many waters, and as the voice of mighty thunders, saying, Hallelujah: for the Lord our God, the Almighty, reigneth. 7 Let us rejoice and be exceeding glad, and let us give the glory unto him: for the marriage of the Lamb is come, and his wife hath made herself ready. 8 And it was given unto her that she should array herself in fine linen, bright and pure: for the fine linen is the righteous acts of th saints.
9 And he saith unto me, Write, Blessed are they that are bidden to the marriage supper of the Lamb. And he saith unto me, These are true words of God. 10 And I fell down before his feet to worship him. And he saith unto me, See thou do it not: I am a follow-servant with thee and with thy brethren that hold the testimony of Jesus: worship God: for the testimony of Jesus is the spirit of prophecy.

11 And I saw the heaven opened; and behold, a white horse, and he that sat thereon called Faithful and True; and in righteousness he doth judge and make war. 12 And his eyes are a flame of fire, and upon his head are many diadems; and he hath a name written which no one knoweth but he himself. 13 And he is arrayed in a garment sprinkled with blood: and his name is called The Word of God. 14 And the armies which are in heaven followed him upon white horses, clothed in fine linen, white and pure. 15 And out of his mouth proceedeth a sharp sword, that with it he should smite the nations: and he shall rule them with a rod of iron: and he treadeth the winepress of the fierceness of the wrath of God, the Almighty. 16 And he hath on his garment and on his thigh a name written, KING OF KINGS, AND LORD OF LORDS.

17 And I saw an angel standing in the sun; and he cried with a loud voice, saying to all the birds that fly in mid heaven, Come and be gathered together unto the great supper of God; 18 that ye may eat the flesh of kings, and the flesh of captains, and the flesh of mighty men, and the flesh of horses and of them that sit thereon, and the flesh of all men, both free and bond, and small and great.

19 And I saw the beast, and the kings of the earth, and their armies, gathered together to make war against him that sat upon the horse, and against his army. 20 And the beast was taken, and with him the false prophet that wrought the signs in his sight, wherewith he deceived them that had received the mark of the beast and them that worshipped his image: they two were cast alive into the lake of fire that burneth with brimstone: 21 and the rest were killed with the sword of him that sat upon the horse, even the sword which came forth out of his mouth: and all the birds were filled with their flesh.

vs. 1 "After these things."

Following the stirring scenes pertaining to the fall of Babylon, John hears these songs of rejoicing and thanksgiving. Such anthems are heard whenever some great triumph or blessing is about to come.

In the twentieth verse of the eighteenth chapter there was a call to heaven and the holy apostles and prophets to rejoice over the downfall of Babylon. Here we have the response to that call. John said:

vs. 19:1-18.

"I heard a great voice of much people in heaven, saying Alleluia; salvation and glory, and honor, and power, unto the Lord our God. For true and righteous are His judgments: for He hath judged the great whore, which did corrupt the earth with her fornication, and hath avenged the blood of his servants at her hand. And again they said, Alleluia. And her smoke rose up for ever and ever. And the four and twenty elders and the four

308

beasts fell down and worshipped God that sat on the throne, saying, Amen; Alleluia."

"And a voice came out of the throne, saying, Praise our God, all ye servants, and ye that fear him both small and great.

And I heard as it were the voice of a great multitude, and as the voice of many waters, and as the voice of mighty thunderings, saying, Alleluia; for the Lord God omnipotent reigneth.

Let us be glad and rejoice, and give honor to him; for the marriage of the Lamb is come, and His wife hath made herself ready. And to her it was granted that she should be arrayed in fine linen, clean and white: for the fine linen is the righteousness of saints."

This has been a lengthy quotation, but it includes the verses which present this great Alleluia Chorus. This Hallelujah Chorus contains the only Hallelujahs of all the New Testament. It would seem as if these Hallelujahs were reserved for this wonderful victory in the downfall of spiritual Babylon.

These first verses of this chapter are an interlude between the fall of Babylon, Chapter 18, and the fall of the beast (Rev. 19:11-21). This is the fifth parenthesis thus far in the book of Revelation. These interludes are thus familiar features throughout the book. This parenthesis consists of a fourfold chorus and each chorus has the same theme: "Hallelujah." We note that the music and singing of heaven has been heard often throughout the "uncovering" of the mysteries of God, but not until now has the "Hallelujah Chorus" sounded.

The Hallelujahs are four in number. Perhaps this points the divine finger to God's victory over the powers of the earth, because four seems to be the numerical symbol of the earth—four corners, four winds, four directions.

The first two Hallelujahs celebrate the fall and utter destruction of Babylon, the harlot. John hears the "voice of a great multitude, saying, "Hallelujah: Salvation, and glory, and power, belong to our God: for true and righteous are his judgments; for he hath judged the great harlot." (Rev. 19:2).

"And, again (second time) they say, Hallelujah, and her smoke goeth up for ever and ever." (Rev. 19:3).

The third Hallelujah is uttered by the twenty-four elders (we found them to be heavenly princes) and the four living creatures (we found them to be Cherubim).

Then a voice came forth from the throne, as it were the voice of a heavenly director or conductor, saying, "Give praise to our God, all ye his servants, ye that fear Him, both small and great."

Then this majestic chorus is heard in answer to the voices bidding. The chorus is like "the voice of a great multitude," and like "the "the voice of many waters," and like "the voice of mighty thunders," saying,

"Hallelujah: for the Lord God omnipotent reigneth: for the marriage of the Lamb is come, and his wife hath made herself ready."

As the majestic heavenly chorus comes to its grand finale John hears a voice commanding him to open the fourth of the seven beatitudes of the apocalypse.

"Write, Blessed are they which are called unto the marriage supper of the Lamb."

A solemn confirmation of this beatitude follows: "And he saith unto me, These are the true sayings of God." (Rev. 19:9).

What a contrast is this with that of the eighteenth Chapter! There we read "And the voice of the Bridegroom and of the bride shall be heard no more at all in thee" (Babylon); here is pictured the approaching marriage of the Lamb. This vision brings us only to the announcement of the coming marriage of the Lamb. The subject will be taken up again in the twenty-first chapter.

So deeply impressed was John and so overwhelmed by such a glorious revelation from this voice that came out of the throne that he fell at the feet of the messenger to worship him.

vs. 10 "And he said unto me, See thou do it not; I am thy fellow-servant, and of all thy brethren, that have the testimony of

Jesus: worship God: for the testimony of Jesus is the spirit of prophecy."

While the apostate church worshipped saints, Mary and the angels, members of the true church are forbidden thus to do so. This ought to be sufficient warning to the devotees of such a false worship.

In this verse and also in Rev. 22:7, 8, the apostle, John, offered to worship the angel and in each instance the prohibition is instantaneous.

Another comparison between the two instances is enlightening. Here the angel says: "See thou do it not; for I am thy fellow-servant, and of thy brethren." In Rev. 22:9 he adds, "of thy brethren, the prophets." Here the explanation is added, "The testimony of Jesus is the spirit of prophecy."

In testifying of Jesus the angel seems to present himself as becoming one of the prophets. This spirit of prophecy is the witness to Jesus of His being the Messiah, the Son of God, the Redeemer, the Lamb that was slain, the Bridegroom and the King of the Kingdom, when the kingdoms of this world shall become the Kingdom of our Lord and His Christ.

Now we seem to come to the opening of a new vision, because of the similarity of the wording to that used at the beginning of other new visions.

In Rev. 4:1, where the vision of the throne, the slain Lamb and the seven seals began, we read:

"After this I looked, and behold, a door was opened in heaven."

"In Rev. 11:19, another beginning, we read: "And the temple of God was opened in heaven."

And here in Rev. 19:11-16 we read: "And I saw heaven opened, and behold a white horse and he that sat upon him was called Faithful and True, and in righteousness He doth judge and make war. His eyes were as a flame of fire, and on his head were many crowns; and he had a name written, that no man knew but He himself. And

311

He was clothed with a vesture dipped in blood: and His name is called The Word of God and the armies which were in heaven followed Him upon white horses, clothed in fine linen, white and clean.

And out of His mouth goeth a sharp sword, that with it He should smite the nations: And He shall rule them with a rod of iron; and He treadeth the winepress of the fierceness and wrath of Almighty God. And He hath on His vesture and on His thigh a name written, *KING OF KINGS, AND LORD OF LORDS.*"

All this is symbolism at its highest and best. Some have called this the Battle of Armageddon and thereby made such statements literal. We shall never see a white horse with a sword projecting out of the mouth of its rider. Truly, and without doubt this is a spiritual presentation of symbolism. And how logical and natural should this follow the Hallelujah Chorus.

Up to this point the false apostate church has been under consideration. Now we see the triumphant church with presentations of conditions that would have obtained had it not been for the departure from the truth.

Here we get a glimpse of what can, and will obtain when Babylon is burned. Shall we briefly consider some of the characterizations here, remembering always that we are walking in the realm of symbolism.

First: He rides upon a white horse. This is the first time Christ has appeared since a door was opened in heaven in Rev. 4:1 and a vision was given of God sitting upon His throne and Christ standing like a Lamb as it had been slain. There he was portrayed in His mediatorial work, now he is presented as a conqueror. We have already found that a horse is an emblem of war, and a white one as a symbol of victory.

As the King of the Jews he rode, in his entry into Jerusalem, upon an ass, a colt the foal of an ass. There he was meek and lowly, but here he rides a martial charger, as the King of the entire world.

Second: He is called Faithful and True. This presents Him in sharp contrast to the previous visions, where the Harlot church is unfaithful and the dragon, or the devil, is a deceiver.

Third: "In Righteousness He doth judge and make war."

In the last church period, the Laodicean period, corresponding to the time element of this present chapter, Christ is called "the Faithful and True Witness," (Rev. 3:14). Chirst is here presented in a dual role, namely, Judge and avenger, or executioner, but in both, Jesus Christ the righteous."

Fourth: "His eyes were as a flame of fire."

To be able to judge justly he has eyes that seeth all things, hence this flaming vision.

Fifth: "And on His head were many crowns."

This presents Him as a victorious King, whereas, heretofore he was the Lamb slain. The many crowns are significant.

When Ptolemy entered Antioch, he wore two crowns on his head (1 Macc. 11:13). When the popes put on their headgear it is a triple crown, emblematic of three sovereignities in one. The dragon or the devil had seven crowns on his seven heads. The beast, or political Rome, had ten diadems on his ten heads, signifying the union of ten sovereignties. In all these instances, the accumulation of diadems symbolized accumulated victories and increased dominion.

Christ is crowned with many diadems, symbolical of His complete dominion over heaven and earth.

Sixth: "He was clothed with a vesture dipped in blood."

If it were not immediately said "and His name was called the Word of God" we would still know by his blood-stained garments that he was the Christ, "the Lamb of God that taketh away the sins of the world," by virtue of His shed blood.

Seventh: "And out of his mouth goeth a sharp sword that with it he should smite the nations."

Already we have found this symbol stands for the word of God (Heb. 4:12). This would certainly indicate that this whole action is spiritual.

Eight: "And He shall rule them with a rod of iron." Literally, it means "He shall shepherdize them with a rod of iron." In other words, His rule is to be firm yet at the same time in the spirit of a shepherd.

All this is highly symbolic. The armies which follow him in heaven are also portrayed riding on white horses—a symbol of triumphant warfare—and clothed in fine linen, white and clean, which symbolizes the righteousness of saints.

These wear no armor and we notice that they are not the executors of this vengeance. The victory belongs to Chirst alone. He bears the only weapon, the sword, or the word of God. He treadeth the winepress alone. Those who accompany Him need no weapons for the victory is represented as already won. Therefore, the sword of the Captain of their salvation is sufficient. They merely follow up the achievements of the sword he wields.

This is according to (I John 3:8).

"For this purpose the Son of God was manifested, that he might destory the works of the devil."

Here is being fulfilled the prophetic utterance of the Psalmist concerning Christ's great triumph to be followed by a description of His glorious wife:

"Thou art fairer than the children of men: grace is poured into thy lips . . . gird on thy sword upon thy thigh, O Most Mighty, with thy glory and thy majesty. And in thy majesty ride prosperously because of the truth and meekness and righteousness; and thy right hand shall teach thee terrible things . . .

Thy throne O God is forever and ever, the scepter of thy Kingdom is a righteous scepter . . .

Kings' daughters were among thy honorable women, upon thy right hand did stand the queen in gold of Ophir." (Psalms 45:2-9).

The name used here is not "Jesus," one who saves, but is the "word of God" as the destroyer of His enemies.

The "Word of God" is all powerful, because it was "the Word of God" who in the beginning made all things (John 14:1-3). Therefore, none can stand before Him as He comes in the might of that name.

That the victory is certain is further emphasized by the verses that follow:

vs. 17, 18 "And I saw an angel standing in the sun; and he cried with a loud voice, saying to all the fowls that fly in the midst of heaven, Come and gather yourselves together unto the supper of the great God;

That ye may eat the flesh of kings, and the flesh of mighty men, and the flesh of horses, and of them that sit on them, and the flesh of all men, both free and bond, both small and great."

Thus the call to the great supper of God. What a startling contrast between this great supper of God, and that of the marriage supper of the Lamb.

This passage carries our minds back to Ezekial 39:17, 18.

"Speak unto every feathered fowl, and to every bird of the field, Assemble yourselves, and come; gather yourselves on every side to my sacrifice that I do sacrifice for you.

You shall eat the flesh of the mighty, and drink the blood of the princes of the earth."

vs. 19-21 "And I saw the beast, and the Kings of the earth, and their armies gathered together to make war against Him that sat on the horse, and against His army. And the beast was taken, and with him the false prophet that wrought miracles before him, with which he decieved them that had received the mark of the beast, and them that worshipped his image.

These both were cast alive into a lake of fire burning with brimstone. And the remnant were slain with the sword of Him that sat upon the horse, which sword proceeded out of His mouth; and all the fowls were filled with their flesh."

There is deep symbolism employed here and a different type of warfare conducted so that the whole struggle is wrapped in mystery, which doubtless will only be fully understood when the fulfillment comes.

The description of this great battle in which the Kingdoms of this world become the Kingdom of our Lord and his Christ is as strange in its weapon of warfare as it is brief in detail. Its very brevity amazes us. But the result is decisive.

The beast, representative of all political despotism and tyranny and the false prophet, the embodiment of false religion are taken, are seized and thrown alive into the lake of fire and brimstone.

And their followers alike are dispatched. Again the strange weapon that destroys them is the sword which proceedeth out of His mouth— that spiritual weapon of irresistible might.

Such a strange warfare and such a feast of death has never before been witnessed. Thus is terminated the present order of things as we know it. Only the dragon's, or the devil's fate remains to be uncovered.

Truly, more we would like to know, but we must not speculate. Neither dare we read in human opinions or theories. It is still true, "The secret things belong unto the Lord our God, but those things which are revealed belong unto us and to our children forever." (Deut. 29:29).

We dare not be wise above that which is written.

CHAPTER XX

THE THOUSAND YEARS

Text (20:1-15)

INTRODUCTION

1 And I saw an angel coming down out of heaven, having the key of the abyss and a great chain in his hand. 2 And he laid hold on the dragon, the old serpent, which is the Devil and Satan, and bound

him for a thousand years, 3 and cast him into the abyss, and shut
it, and sealed it over him, that he should deceive the nations no
more, until the thousand years should be finished: after this he
must be loosed for a little time.

4 And I saw thrones, and they sat upon them, and judgment was
given unto them: and I saw the souls of them that had been beheaded for the testimony of Jesus, and for the word of God, and such
as worshipped not the beast, neither his image, and received not the
mark upon their forehead and upon their hand; and they lived, and
reigned with Christ a thousand years. 5 The rest of the dead lived
not until the thousand years should be finished. This is the first resurrection. 6 Blessed and holy is he that hath part in the first resurrection: over these the second death hath no power; but they shall be
priests of God and of Christ, and shall reign with him a thousand
years.

7 And when the thousand years are finished, Satan shall be loosed
out of his prison, 8 and shall come forth to deceive the nations which
are in the four corners of the earth, Gog and Magog, to gather them
toegther to the war: the number of whom is as the sand of the
sea. 9 And they went up over the breadth of the earth, and compassed the camp of the saints about, and the beloved city: and fire
came down out of heaven, and devoured them. 10 And the devil
that deceived them was cast into the lake of fire and brimstone, where
are also the beast and the false prophet; and they shall be tormented
day and night for ever and ever.

11 And I saw a great white throne, and him that sat upon it,
from whose face the earth and heaven fled away; and there was
found no place for them. 12 And I saw the dead, the great and
the small, standing before the throne; and books were opened:
and another book was opened, which is the book of life: and the
dead were judged out of the things which were written in the books,
according to their works. 13 And the sea gave up the dead that were
in it; and death and Hades gave up the dead that were in them: and
they were judged every man according to their works. 14 And death
and Hades were cast into the lake of fire. This is the second death,
even the lake of fire. 15 And if any was not found written in the
book of life, he was cast into the lake of fire.

Shall we take a very brief parting look at the preceding chapter,
before taking up the consideration of the one before us.

The portrayal of Christ coming seated on a white horse, followed
by his armies, also on white horses, has been interpreted by
some, who are advocates of His visible return before the Millennium,
as substantiation for their theory called "Pre-millennialism."

They maintain this description as given in Revelation 19:11-
16, pictures a personal coming visible to all eyes, and is the second
advent often referred to in the Scriptures. Such advocates need to
consider some very serious objections before accepting such a theory
with too much enthusiasm, or spiritual fervor. Only a few objections are listed here:

First, The language here is in the realm of symbolism.

Second, That this being so, how can they interpret this as a visible return at this particular time, without including a literal sword protruding out of his mouth?

Third, Then, this must be an actual horse and he must have eyes from which flash a flame of fire.

Fourth, He must actually be clothed in a vesture dipped in blood.

Fifth, His armies must be real men with literal bodies (and that before the resurrection of the body) riding upon real horses.

That there is to be a literal, personal return of Christ is a well-established truth in the Scriptures, but in this instance to make His return literal and personal when the language is purely symbolical leads to confusion. Logic demands that if this is His personal and literal return, then that return is accompanied by literal horses and all other manifestations attendant to this description here must be considered literal.

All this false, unscriptural and misleading concept has come about by those who advocate the doctrine known as "Pre-millennialism."

The term "pre-millennialism" is no where to be found in all the Scriptures. Then, does not reason, logic and love for God's "thus saith the Lord" prompt, yea compel us "to be silent where the Scriptures are silent?" All who believe in the divine inspiration of God's Word recognize the truth that "we must speak where the Bible speaks." Ought not there be as reverent a recognition of the necessity of "being silent where the Bible is silent?"

Never once did Christ mention "Pre-millennialism." Was it because He had not the time in his brief ministry to refer to it? Or is it as John said, "There are also many other things which Jesus did, the which if they should be written every one, I suppose that even the world itself could not contain the books that should be written?" (John 21:25)

Of all that has been written in God's inspired Word, not once is the expression "pre-millenialism" included. Yet, today, perhaps no word is used so much or heard so frequently as this one, even by those who pride themselves as being fundamentalists—another unscriptural term, by the way.

Upon another occasion Christ said to His apostles, and, in his farewell conversation when every word was freighted with sublime meaning:

"I have yet many things to say unto you, but ye cannot hear them now" (John 16:12)

Was the term "pre-millennialism" to be among the things yet to be revealed? He promised that further revelation (all things) should be completed after the Spirit should come, even to the giving of new prophecies—"He will show you things to come." His words to them are:

"Howbeit when he, the Spirit of truth is come, he will guide you into all truth: for he shall not speak of himself; but whatsoever he shall hear, that shall he speak and he will show you things to come." (John 16:13)

Yet those same apostles who were all filled with the Holy Spirit on the day of Pentecost spoke, even with other tongues as the spirit gave them utterance (Acts 1:26); (2:1-4) never in all their labors ever so much as once let fall from their lips this oft heard word of the present day—"Pre-millennialism."

It could not be because their memories failed them, for the spirit was *to bring them remembrance all things* Christ had said to them. Said Christ on this matter of remembrance:

"But the Comforter, which is the Holy Spirit, whom the Father will send in my name, he shall *teach you all things,* and *bring all things* to your remembrance, whatsoever I have said unto you." (John 14:26)

Then we are forced to one of two, or even both conclusions.

First, Christ did teach "pre-millennialism" and sent the Holy Spirit to remind his apostles of all things, among which would be this doctrine, if its advocates are right, and that the Holy Spirit failed to remind, not one, but all the apostles, including Paul chosen out of due season, to mention this doctrine by the name used so frequently today.

Or *second,* the Holy Spirit did remind them and they failed to speak as the Holy Spirit was to give them utterance.

Either conclusion is utterly untenable and preposterous, even sacreligious.

There is only one logical, ethical and scriptural decision left us. The term "pre-millennialism" never once crossed Christ's lips, therefore the Holy Spirit did not have this word to bring to their remembrance. Pre-millennialism was never among "all things to be remembered."

Furthermore, it was not among the many things Christ had yet to say unto them, which they yet were not able to hear.

319

It was not among the things the Holy Spirit was to hear of Christ, neither was it among the things of which it was said, "He *shall show you things to come.*"

It was not among the "all truth" into which the Holy Spirit was to guide them.

There is a truism recognized by every close student of divine truth, a self-evident fact, requiring no demonstration, a sound accepted principle.

"If *anything*, be it a matter of belief or practice, is called by an unscriptural name, it is axiomatic that the thing which the name represents, *is also unscriptural.*

Applying this self-evident truth to the usage of the term "pre-millennialism," since the name is unscriptural, then it follows that the belief in it is also unscriptural.

Then this nomenclature must be dropped, or we are not being "silent where the Scriptures are silent."

But coming back to the verses we have had under observation, namely Revelation 19:11-16, not only is the language here symbolic, but the description is not in harmony with Christ's own account of His personal return. Shall we review a few of his declarations concerning the manner of His return:

"And then shall appear the sign of the Son of man in heaven: and then shall all the tribes of the earth mourn, and they shall see power and great glory.

And He shall send His angels with a great sound of a trumpet, and they shall gather together his elect from the four winds, from one end of heaven to the other." (Matthew 24:30, 31)

Again "when the Son of man shall come in His glory, and all the holy angels with Him, then shall he sit upon the throne of His glory:

And before Him shall be gathered all nations: and He shall separate them one from another, as a shepherd divideth his sheep from the goats," (Matt. 25:31, 32)

To this may be added Paul's description of Christ's return: "For the Lord himself shall descend from heaven with a shout, with the voice of the archangel, and with the trump of God: and the dead in Christ shall rise first. Then we which are alive and remain shall be caught up together with them in the clouds, to meet the Lord in the air: and so shall we ever be with the Lord." (I Thess. 4:16, 17)

Thus we see that (Rev. 9:11-16) does not rightly describe Christ's return, as some have interpreted these verses in order to substantiate their teaching that he returns before the millennium.

Shall we now proceed with the unfolding of this chapter before us.

The Dragon Bound for a Thousand Years

vs. 1 "And I saw an angel come down from heaven, having the key to the bottomless pit and a great chain in his hand."

There has been considerable discussion as to who this angel is, but the point is of no great consequence. We remember that it was Michael, the archangel, who fought against the dragon and his angels, as recorded in chapter twelve.

There it was a forensic foray; here it is the seizing, binding, and casting of him into prison. Certainly, Michael could be a victor in either contest, but, of course, the name and rank of the angel are not given here.

This angel possesses the key to the bottomless pit, or the abyss. This key is mentioned once before in Revelation in relation to the bottomless pit. It is first referred to in Revelation 9:1. There we read:

"I saw a star fall from heaven unto the earth and *to him* (a star is an angel Rev. 1:20) was given the *key* to the bottomless pit."

The bottomless pit, or abyss is mentioned in (Rev. 9:1, 9:11; 11:7; 17:8; 20:1, and 20:3). This comes from the greek "Abusoos," meaning "a very deep place," sometimes translated the "Abyss." This is not the same place into which the beast and the false prophet were thrown. That was "the lake of fire that burneth with brimstone." After a thousand years the devil is to join them there. Here he is cast into the "abyss," or a very deep place, from where the beast ascended to go into perdition. (Rev. 17:8)

And what is the difference between these two places? Briefly, the "lake of fire" is the final hell; the "abyss" is a very deep place, a prison in which the dragon and evil spirits are retained prior to the final judgment.

A homely comparison would be like that of a county jail where a criminal is incarcerated prior to his sentence, and the Lake of fire is like the state penitentiary where he is confined for final punishment.

"Having a great chain in his hand." Some have been troubled about the nature of that chain. Was it of iron or brass? If so how could such a chain bind a spirit being, like the dragon? The book does not declare it is a chain made of any earthly material. This, we must remember, is a book of symbolism. The chain is the symbol of some binding agent of Divine construction. It is a chain of such a nature that spirits and angels can be bound by it. Jude speaks of such a chain, which is actually binding rebellious angels *right now.* Hear Jude:

"And the angels which kept not their first estate, but left their own habitation, he hath received in *everlasting chains* under darkness unto the judgment of the great day." (Jude 6)

What they are made of or how they are able to bind spirit beings is beyond our knowledge now.

vs. 2 "And he laid hold on the dragon, that old serpent, which is the devil and satan and bound him a thousand years."

Here we find the arch enemy of Christ and the church called by four names, the same names assigned to him in Rev. 12:9.

And interesting parallel presents itself here. Christ, the rider on the white horse in the nineteenth chapter also had four names, namely, "Faithful and True," "a name written, that no man knew but Himself," "The Word of God" and "King of Kings and Lord of Lords."

But back to the four names of the Dragon, the enemy of the woman's seed. Shall we briefly consider these four names.

First, He called "the Dragon." This is the name given him with especial reference to his connection with political and spiritual powers, particularly that of Imperial and papal Rome.

Since these have by this time already been cast into the lake of fire and brimstone, when this evil spirit comes up out of the bottomless pit, or the abyss, at the end of the thousand years, he comes with only two of his former four names, viz. "Satan," and "the devil."

Second, he is called "the old serpent."

The "old" has reference to his existence since the beginning of man on the earth.

The "serpent" has reference to his subtlety, his deceiving ways, his deadly poison. It was the serpent that deceived Eve. It is as the serpent that brought in the false doctrine which corrupted the church. This name draws our attention to the subtlety of his temptations.

It does not appear from the symbolism employed here that he ever comes, after his being chained, in the capacity of a serpent. He is the same evil spirit when he is loosed for a short season but he induces God and Magog to "compass the camp of the saints," in the role of "the devil" and "Satan."

Third, he is spoken of as the "devil." This word means, a slanderer and a malignant liar. To this angel of his nature Christ referred when He said, "He was a murderer from the beginning, and abode not in the truth; when he speaketh a lie, he speaketh of his own; for he is a liar, and the father of it." (John 8:44)

Evidently, in his deepest malignity he is a liar. As a liar he will deceive the nations at the end of the thousand years.

Fourth, he is called "Satan," which means "The adversary," "the accuser." It really is a Hebrew word transferred and means "a hater."

As an accuser he charged God with a lie in the beginning when he said to the woman, "ye shall not surely die." in reply to Eve's statement "God hath said, Ye shall not eat of it, neither shall ye touch it, lest ye die." (Genesis 3:3)

He was Christ's great adversary when he made the attempt to snuff out His life in the murder of the babes of Bethlehem, through the temptation in the wilderness, in the casting of doubt upon Christ's diety, even to the struggle to make the gates of Hades prevail against his rising again to prove his Sonship to God.

He has been the adversary to every human soul. As an adversary he appears again in the short season in which he is unchained following the thousand years.

But it was, in all four of these characterizations, that the angel laid hold upon him to bind him a thousand years. Reading further:

vs. 3 "And cast him into the bottomless pit, and shut him up, and set a seal upon him, that he should deceive the nations no more, 'till the thousand years should be fulfilled. And after that he was to be loosed for a little season.

He is cast into the abyss, and sealed there, from whence there is no escape, instead of into the lake of fire, the place of no return.

This arch adversary is dealt with in two different stages. First, as described, he is shut up and a seal put upon him "for a thousand years." After this period he is "loosed for a little season."

Judging by the books-without-end which have been written on the subject of the "millennium," it has been quite apparent that men have overcentered their thinking upon that subject, rather than the real theme here, which is the imprisonment of Satan, first in the abyss, and then this final destruction in the lake of fire and brimstone. In the vision of the previous chapter, the last two of the unholy trinity, the beast and the false prophet were disposed of; here the third of those three is dealt with.

Whatever is included in any mention of the thousand years, its mention seems decidedly incidental to the importance of the doom of the dragon—the principle subject of this vision. This passage, the modern millennialist notwithstanding, is concerned chiefly with a prediction of the overthrow of satan. By a series of bold strokes John is presenting to us first the restraining and then the final destruction of the age-old enemy of Christ, who must be destroyed before the City of God can descend out of heaven.

This verse declares that the dragon or satan must remain in the abyss "till the thousand years should be fulfilled; and after that he must be loosed a little season."

There is absolutely no reason given here why he must be loosed for this brief time. A reason is assigned why the devil was bound, "that he should deceive the nations no more 'til the thousand years should be fulfilled," but no reason is given why he is loosed after the thousand years.

Of course we might raise the question, "why was the devil put into the scheme of things from the very beginning? A brief answer is that when God said, "Let us make man in our image, after our likeness: and let him have dominion," He was launching out on an age-long process. Since God knew right and wrong and had volition, man made in God's image, must have volition. Therefore, he had to have both good and evil influences play upon him. Thus, the devil's place in the scheme of things is to provide man with the opposite influences; that he may be tested and tried and act under his own violition.

If God had placed man in the garden eastward in Eden and left him there millennium after millennium without a tempter, he would have been *innocent,* but perfect in nothing.

But through overcoming, by a divinely designed plan, he would be made in God's image and after His likeness.

By the same token perhaps the devil is loosed for a little season. This is a logical reason based upon analogy. It still remains a fact that God has here revealed no reason, so we must not be wise above that which is written.

So we advance to the next verse:

vs. 4, 5 "And I saw thrones, and they sat upon them, and judgment was given them. And I saw the souls of them that were beheaded for the witness of Jesus, and for the Word of God, and which had not worshipped the beast, neither his image, neither had received his mark upon their foreheads, or in their hands. And they lived and reigned with Christ a thousand years."

We have made a sincere and earnest attempt to move cautiously throughout "this wonder book of the Bible," letting the Holy Spirit lead all the way. But as carefully as we have moved thus far we wish to use the utmost caution at this point.

There has been so much written upon this subject of the thousand years that we want to move with extreme care.

This period of a thousand years is not mentioned anywhere else in the entire Bible and here in rapid succession it occurs six times in the space of seven verses.

Six mentions in so short a space would, at first thought, give us the impression of the importance of the thousand years, yet, on the other hand, its importance lies primarily in the interval of the binding and loosing of the dragon or devil. Three, or half of the mentionings, refer directly to the devil, two to the souls who had part in the reigning with Christ and the sixth mention relates itself to the rest of "the dead who lived not again until the thousand years were finished."

But the fact that this thousand year period is mentioned six times, is rather significant. "Six" is short of "seven" or perfection. Therefore it is not the new heaven and the new earth. It is not the eternal dwelling place of the redeemed.

This fact leads us to another startling truth. Since it is not the eternal home of the children of God, then Christ is not personally present during the thousand years for He was not to return until that place was prepared. Let Christ speak for Himself at this point. He said in his confidential conversation with His apostles at the Passover meal, and the communion which followed it:

"In my Father's house are many mansions: if it were not so, I would have told you. I go to prepare a place for you.

And *if I go to prepare a place* for you, I will come again, and receive you unto myself; that where I am there ye may be also."

Shall we carefully scrutinize this first intimation of the day of the coming of Christ. We learn from this that the Father's House of many mansions is a place already existing—"*are* many mansions."

325

Christ said, *"I got to prepare a place for you."* 'Paul tells us in Eph. 4:10, "He that descended is the same also that ascended up far above all heavens, that he might fill all things."

The father's house is the third heaven, as taught in the Scriptures. Christ ascended above all heavens to prepare a place for us.

Therefore, since this thousand year period, with all its blessings is not the eternal home, then Christ has not at that time returned, because He said, "I go to prepare a place for you and if I go to prepare a place for you, I will come again *to receive you unto myself, that where I am,* ye may be also. He never, himself, promised to return to dwell with the saints here personally and visibly, but He did promise to receive them unto Himself to be with Him where He is.

Truly, we must take exceeding care not to read into a passage that which is not there and particularly if it is contrary to what Christ promised He would do.

Judging by the outstanding importance which some have placed upon this passage in Revelation, would it not seem logical that somewhere Christ would say something about it?

If so notable an event as His coming to be here personally during the thousand years was to come to pass at that time does it not seem that Christ would have made some statement concerning it?

In the fourteenth chapter of John He does mention His return but only *to receive us unto Himself* that where He is we might be also. He is strangely silent here, where human beings have been so vociferous. Would it not be more becoming of the saints to keep silent where He has done so?

Not only was Christ silent about coming at the beginning of the thousand years, but so was John, the divine Revelator, silent. He mentions an angel coming down from heaven and binding Satan for a thousand years, but never a word about Christ also coming at the beginning of the thousand year period.

And not only was John utterly silent on this point, but so, also, were all the other apostles. Of the early church it was said: "They continued steadfastly in the apostles' doctrine" (Acts 2:42) but never once was the personal visible return of Christ during the thousand years mentioned as a part of the apostles' doctrine. The conclusion is, that such a teaching is not apostolic.

Paul charged Timothy "the things which thou hast heard of me among many witnesses, the same commit thou to faithful men, who shall be able to teach others also." (II Timothy 2:2)

So this teaching of Christ's personal return during the thousand years is not included in the same which Paul committed to faithful men. All this evidence is rather heart searching, to say the least.

Now just what did John say? "I saw thrones and *they* sat upon them, and judgment was given unto *them*."

Now who are the *"they?"* "The *souls of them* that were beheaded for the witness of Jesus and for the word of God . . . *they* lived and reigned with Christ a thousand years."

"They" had thrones but where is the mention of a throne for Christ to occupy? Where does John say that Christ was here sitting on a throne? He is strangely silent.

Shall we delve a little further into the antecedent of *"They."* Looking ahead in the sixth verse of this twentieth chapter this *"they"* occurs again, and of them we read, *"They* shall be priests of God and of Christ, and shall reign with Him a thousand years."

Where have we heard of the redeemed being *priests* and *reigning with Christ* before? Why, back in (Rev. 5:9). "They (that is the four beasts, or living creatures and the four and twenty elders) sang a new song, saying, "Thou art worthy to take the book, and open the seals thereof, for thou wast slain, and hast redeemed (not *us* as in the Authorized version) to God by thy blood out of every kindred, and tongue, and people and nation; and has made them (not us as in the common version) unto our God *kings and priests, and they shall reign upon the earth."*

In this reference the redeemed are called kings and priests; in Revelation 20:6 they are called priests of God and of Christ, and shall reign with Him a thousand years. Also John here in the twentieth chapter saw them sitting upon thrones in this reigning.

Now, going back to the fifth chapter again where was Christ while these kings and priests were reigning? Hear John: "And I beheld, and lo, in the midst of the throne and of the four beasts, and in the midst of the elders, stood a Lamb as it had been slain." (Rev. 5:6)

Here we find that God is sitting on the throne and Christ is at His right hand. Paul said, "When He had by Himself purged our sins, sat down on the right hand of the Majesty on hand" (Heb. 1.3)

While John saw the souls of the martyrs sitting on thrones and reigning over the earth he mentions no throne for Christ. Why? Because Christ, until His return is at the right hand of God.

Into what a maze of errors we fall when we read into a passage something which is not there! By what authority can we assert that

Christ will be on earth, simply because John said these martyrs live and reign with Him for a thousand years. Have we become so earthly minded that we can not conceive of Christ reigning in any place except upon His footstool, the earth?

Did not the Jews make the same mistake in the days of His flesh? They were looking for an earthly kingdom with a temporal throne and the Messiah sitting upon it. Because Christ declared His kingdom was not of this world (not one with a temporal throne, and material appointments) they rejected him.

Has not the Roman Catholic church made the same mistake, placing the pope on an earthly throne, himself crowned with a golden crown and maintaining ambassadors at the courts of temporal kingdoms?

That the Roman Catholic church considers itself a temporal, visible kingdom is further substantiated by their official explanation of the triple crown worn by the pope.

"Among his (the pope's) insignia are the *pallium*, which signifies his rank as a Primate, and the tiara or triple crown. In the early centuries the pope wore a simple mitre, like other bishops; but about the ninth century a crown was added to it, to denote the pontiff's *temporal* power as ruler of the states of the church. Later a second crown was added, and about the year 1365 a third—signifying, according to some, the supreme authority of the pope in spiritual things, his jurisdiction over the church considered as a human society, and his dominion as a *temporal* monarch. According to others, the triple crown typifies his threefold office as teacher, lawgiver and judge." Externals of the Catholic church—page 9.

How ill becoming, then, for those who renounce the authority of the pope and the claims of the Catholic church to temporal dominion, to fall into the same error of teaching that Christ will sit upon a temporal throne ruling over a visible and temporal kingdom during the thousand year period! Why should the pot call the kettle black?

There have been those who have taught that a literal, temporal kingdom of Israel is to be set up by God at the end. Constant reference is made to the Jews return to Palestine and the setting up of their national government.

While such a return is being witnessed by our eyes, yet how can one, by the greatest stretch of his prophetic imagination see God's hand in this, when there is no acceptance of Christ by these returning Jews after the flesh? We are witnessing a return as an escape from persecution and earthly desire to restore their national life, but these motives are no different in nature from those of the Jews who fought the wars of the Maccabees with the same objectives in mind, during the four hundred years preceeding Christ's incarnation.

Christ's crucifixion swept aside forever the entire Jewish ceremonial of the temple, the priesthood and the sacrifices. Thus the Scriptures make it utterly impossible for God to ever recognize Israel after the flesh, or to establish the Jewish ritual again. Even if the nation should revive its Old Testament ceremonies, God's hand will not be in it nor His blessing upon it.

The whole Jewish system was a fore-shadowing of better things to come, and like the old covenant, of which it was a part, is done away forever.

Reformed Judiasm is not looking for a *personal Messiah,* but teaches that the Messianic hope is the restoration of national life. They still reject Christ as the long-looked-for-Messiah.

The teaching of the restoration of the Jewish nation with its old covenant ceremonies, is an out right denial of the very work Christ accomplished upon the cross.

This whole system of modern day teaching of a certain school of the prophets is based upon the same fallicious and utterly carnal system of interpretation that caused the Jews of Christ's day to reject Him as the Messiah.

The only Israel recognized by God since Christ's first coming is a spiritual one—a kingdom that cometh without observation, a kingdom that is within the heart of the obedient, repentant, baptized believer.

And yet earnest, but nevertheless misguided souls, blithely talk of a temporal kingdom being set up during the thousand year period, with Christ personally and visibly reigning over it!

Thousands of so-called fundamentalists will stand before classes and condemn the Jew of Christ's day for rejecting their Messiah because they looked for a temporal ruler reigning over a temporal kingdom. Yet these same folk will piously and fervently pray for and preach that a temporal kingdom will be set up during the thousand years with Christ personally, visibly reigning over it.

Some Insurmountable Objections to a
Physical Resurrection

There are some insurmountable objections to physically resurrected saints living on the earth during the thousand years. Such would have bodies like the resurrected body of Christ.

He could instantly make Himself visible or invisible. He could immediately appear in a closed room without use of a door, and just as instantly vanish from sight.

How can advocates of a literal, physical resurrection during the thousand years keep a straight face. Imagine two kinds of beings existing on the earth simultaneously for that length of time!

Christ for a few days did so appear on the earth between His resurrection and His ascension, but for a definite purpose, viz., to provide indubitable proof of His resurrection and to teach His apostles that He was always with them whether visible or invisible.

But a thousand year condition with multitudes of martyrs living with other multitudes still restrained to human limitations raises so many insoluble problems as to render such a teaching impossible, if not rediculous.

A second objection, and perhaps the greater, to this fallacious teaching is that this text does not so state such a resurrection. John said:

> "I saw the *souls* of them that were beheaded for the witness of Jesus, etc. and they lived and reigned with Christ a thousand years."

John does not say one word about the bodies of the martyrs being resurrected. He is very particular to call our attention to what he actually saw. He saw the *souls* of the martyrs living and reigning with Christ.

How different the language here from the account of the resurrection of those who came forth out of their graves at the time Christ died upon the cross. There we read:

> "And many *bodies* of the saints which slept arose, and came out of their graves after His ressurection and went into the holy city and appeared unto many." (Matt. 27:52-53)

Here John saw no bodies raised; only the *souls* of the martyrs, who lived and reigned with Christ a thousand years.

These had been beheaded and put to death and had never ceased to exist. There is an indication that in some way they now have a different existence than they had before, but it certainly cannot mean that they had come to live, for they had never ceased to live.

Just what is the meaning here? Certainly it refers to spiritual resurrection, not a physical one. The glorious reign of Christ is so manifest at that time because the spirit of the martyrs is resurrected and pervades all who name Christ's name and that they are filled with the spirit of the ancient martyrs.

And let us not entertain for a single second that this is a forced interpretation.

When the Bohemian martyr, John Huss was about to die, he prophesied, "And I, awakening from among the dead, and rising so to speak, from my grave, shall leap with great joy."

One hundred years later when Luther was engaged in a life-and-death-struggle with the papacy and the Roman Catholic church, Pope Adrian sent a letter to the German Diet meeting in Nuremberg, containing the following words:

"The heretic's Huss and Jerome are now alive again in the person of Martin Luther."

No one understood such a statement to mean that Huss and Jerome had literally been raised and were dwelling again in their bodies long since returned to the dust.

But shall we turn to a Scriptural parallel. It was prophesied that Elias should come again before the Messiah's first advent. In Malachi 4:5 we read:

"Behold, I will send you Elijah the prophet before the coming of the great and terrible day of the Lord."

Did this refer to a literal and bodily resurrection of that old Testament prophet. No. Hear none other than Christ interpret this for us.

"For this is he, of whom it is written, Behold, I send my messenger before thy face, which shall prepare thy way before thee.

Verily, I say unto you, among them that are born of women there hath not risen a greater than John the Baptist; notwithstanding he that is least in the Kingdom of heaven is greater than he, for all the prophets and the law prophesied until John. And if ye will receive it, this is Elias, which was for to come. He that hath ears to hear, let him hear." (Matt. 11:10-11, 15)

There is that statement, "Let him that hath ears to hear, let him hear—a characteristic declaration of Christ when he wishes to call our attention pointedly to some truth he wishes us to especially understand.

Elias, or Elijah was not bodily resurrected, but he did come in spirit and power, not in person, but as the fearless, rugged reformer in the wilderness of Jordan.

In speaking of the return of the captive Jews from captivity to their own land, Ezekial said:

"*I will open your graves,* oh my people, and cause you *to come up out of your graves,* and bring you into the land of Israel." (Ezekiel 37:12-14)

God didn't bodily resurrect these Jews in Babylonian captivity, but the return of the Jews as a nation to their homeland is spoken of as a resurrection.

Oh we are conscious that some claim if the first ressurection is not literal and bodily, then the second cannot be literal either.

But such miss the point. The second resurrection is the calling up of the Spirits of all the dead for judgment. The bodily resurrection is for those who having been judged righteous are to have their bodies raised. Hear Paul:

"For we know that the whole creation groaneth and travaileth in pain together until now.

And not only they, but ourselves also, which have the first fruits of the Spirit, even we ourselves groan within ourselves, waiting for the adoption, to wit, the redemption of our bodies." (Rom. 8:22-23)

This redemption of our bodies comes after "the manifestation of the Sons of God" (Rom. 8:19) for which the whole creation waits. And the manifestation of the sons of God is not to be until after the Judgment.

Christ appears at the time of the Judgment and John said that is the time when the sons of God shall be made manifest.

"Beloved, now are we the sons of God, and it doth not yet appear what we shall be: but we know that when He shall appear, we shall be like Him, for we shall see Him as he is." (I John 3:2)

We do not have our bodies raised incorruptible until the last trump:

"Behold, I show you a mystery; we shall not all sleep, but we shall be changed, in a moment, in the twinkling of an eye, at the last trump, and the dead shall be raised incorruptible, and we shall be changed." For this corruptible must put on incor-

ruption, and this mortal must put on immortality." (I Cor.
15:51-53)

This is to occur at the last trump, but there is no trump sounded
at the beginning of the thousand year period. Therefore, the first
resurrection is not a physical and bodily one.

Oh how much confusion has been brought in by reading into a
passage that which it never declared. John simply said, "I saw the
souls of them that were beheaded for the witness of Jesus . . . and
they lived and reigned with Christ a thousand years."

But one writer pens such confusion, others read it and quote it to
others and confusion is added to confusion. One pulpiteer proclaims
such confusion and his hearers go out and quote that confusion.
Thus like a tidal wave, such unscriptural and unsound teaching
sweeps far and wide.

"Behold, how great a matter a little fire kindleth!"

Having considered the insurmountable objections to the bodily
resurrection of the martyrs during the thousand years, we turn now
to another such objection which pertains itself to Christ visibly and
personally reigning over a temporal Kingdom during that time.

We again are reminded that we must not read into this passage
more than it says. Earlier in this chapter we have found that John
did not *say,* nor ever hint at Christ sitting on a throne and reigning
during the thousand years.

We also proved that Christ remained at God's right hand while
the martyrs as priests reigned on thrones.

Now we take up the third objection. If Christ were reigning on
earth personally during the thousand year period we must admit His
temporary defeat when the devil is loosed for a short season.

When Christ was upon the earth the first time He was in His body
of humiliation. Therefore the devil had power. Christ, Himself, said,
"The prince of this world cometh and hath nothing in me." (John
14:30) Thus Christ freely acknowledged the devil's power, calling
him the prince of this world.

But Christ is never pictured as coming to this earth again except
in His ineffable glory and His unlimited power. Such demonstration
of His omnipotence would render the devil incapable of restored
power, even for a short season.

Christ gave the devil free reign during the days of His flesh because He came to perfect our redemption through His suffering and
humiliation upon the cross. But the devil will be forever powerless
when the glorified Christ comes at the judgment time.

"Then cometh the end (note: the thousand years period was not the end), when He shall have delivered up the kingdom of God, even the Father; when He shall have put down all rule and all authority and power."

"For He must reign, 'till He hath put all enemies under His feet. The last enemy that shall be destroyed is death." (I Cor. 15:24-26)

In this we learn that when He does return the second time, He shall deliver up the Kingdom to God, He shall have put down all rule and authority and power and He shall have put all enemies under His feet, and finally He shall destroy the last enemy, or death.

None of these things mentioned was done before the thousand year period but rather earthly kingdoms and power and authority and rule and enemies and even death are still existant until after the thousand years.

All this precludes Christ being present and reigning personally during that period because the conditions do not agree with those obtaining at His second coming.

To take any other position requires us to admit that a returned, glorified Christ is powerless before the devil, even for a short season. The devil might and did have power over the Christ in the humiliation of the days of His flesh, but never has he power against a glorified Christ as portrayed at His second coming.

To advocate a return of Christ personally at the beginning of the thousand years and again at the judgment makes him come a *second* and a *third time*. Such a position is Scripturally untenable. Hear Paul on this:

"So Christ was once offered to bear the sins of many: and unto them that look for Him shall He appear the *second time* without sin unto salvation." (Heb. 9:28)

He was offered once at His *first* coming and He is to appear *a second time* without sin unto salvation. There will be no third coming.

The Scriptures only recognize *one visible* return of Christ and that does not take place until after the thousand years. Chapter 19:11-16 describes a coming in power, the power of the word, but not a visible coming.

This leads us forward to the consideration of what will be happeing at His *second coming,* or appearing.

First: The second coming of Christ and the glorification of Christians will occur at the same time.

334

"When Christ, who is our life shall appear, then shall ye also appear with Him in glory." (Colossians 3:4)

Second: The second coming of Christ and the gathering of the elect from the four winds shall be simultaneous:

"And then shall they see the Son of man coming in the clouds with great power and glory. And then shall He send His angels, and shall gather together His elect from the four winds, from the uttermost part of the earth to the uttermost part of heaven." (Mark 13:26-27)

Only the souls of the martyrs were seen by John at the beginning and in duration of the thousand years.

Third: The second coming of Christ and the resurrection of both good and bad, will be at the same time.

"Marvel not at this; for the hour is coming in the which all that are in the graves shall hear His voice, and shall come forth; they that have done good, unto the resurrection of life; and they that have done evil, unto the resurrection of damnation." (John 5:28-29)

Fourth: The second coming of Christ and the resurrection of those who have fallen asleep, or are dead in Christ, and the translation of the living will be at the same time.

"For this we say unto you by the Word of the Lord, that we that are alive that are left unto the coming of the Lord, shall in no wise precede them that are fallen asleep. For the Lord himself shall descend from heaven with a shout, with the voice of the archangel, and with the trump of God and the dead in Christ shall rise first; then we that are alive, that are left, shall together with them be caught up in the clouds, to meet the Lord in the air: and so shall we ever be with the Lord." (I Thes. 4:15-17)

Paul here asserts that the living shall not go before the dead to meet the descending Lord. He further declares that Christ "Himself" will come personally at His second coming. This rules out all possibility of Christ's coming being at the beginning of the thousand year period because then John said, "I saw *an angel* come down from heaven." (Rev. 20:1) "Himself" in I Thes. 4:16, proves that Christ will not come by representative, but in person.

Paul enumerates three sounds accompanying Christ's second coming. There will be the *shout* of *Christ,* the *voice* of the archangel, and the *trump* of God.

How can otherwise sincere and earnest folk confuse this scene of the second coming of Christ with the beginning of the thousand year period? In the description of the beginning of this latter period only an angel, not archangel comes down from heaven and not a word is uttered by him.

There is no trump sounded at the beginning of the thousand years, but the trump of God sounds at the return of Christ after the thousand years, or at the end.

Again how can sincere folk teach two resurrections, one for the righteous (the first resurrection) and one for the wicked (the second resurrection?) Shall we quote John W. McGarvey on this. It is so clear and fine and logical and scriptural and sound that it ought to be incorporated into every book upon this vital subject:

"Of course such a doctrine is abhorrent to the idea of a single hour of judgment, with the saved on the right hand and the lost upon the left. Those who hold this theory appeal to this passage (Rev. 20:4-5) in proof of it, reading it thus: 'The dead in Christ shall rise first, and the dead out of Christ shall rise second.'

But in order to make it read thus they have *supplied* a correlative clause which is totally foreign to the context, and which crowds out the correlative which Paul himself has given; for "shall rise *first*" is correlative with "then shall be caught up."

The apostle has been drawing a comparison, not between the righteous dead and the unrighteous dead, but between the dead and the living at the hour of the advent. He began His comparison at verse fifteen and he here completes it by showing that the supposition that the living would precede the dead is so contrary to the facts that, on the contrary, the dead will be raised *before* any ascension is allowed the living, and *then* after the resurrection of the dead, the living and the dead shall be caught up together to meet the Lord.

That glorious change, wherein the mortal puts on the immortal, as indicated at I Cor. 15:51-55, will no doubt be simultaneous with the resurrection of the dead."

McGarvey's Commentary on I Thessalonians—pages 22 and 23.

Fifth: The descent of Christ with clouds at His second coming and the dead and living saints being caught up occur at the same time.

We are not to understand that we are caught up with clouds, but that we are to meet Him who comes in the clouds.

Daniel in (Dan. 7:13) said, "I saw in the night visions, and behold, one like the Son of man, *came with the clouds of heaven.*"

Matthew said in Matt. 24:30, "They shall see the Son of man *coming in the clouds of heaven* and with power and great glory."

John said in Rev. 1:7, "Behold He cometh *with clouds.*"

The Psalmist said, "Who maketh the clouds His chariots." (Psa. 104:3)

This coming of Christ with clouds is after the thousand years, because no clouds are mentioned at the ushering in of that period, neither is Christ's coming mentioned there; only the descent of an angel.

At this coming we are to be caught up in the air to ever be with the Lord (I Thes. 4:17) This corresponds with Christ's description of His return:

"And if I go to prepare a place for you I will come again and *receive* you unto myself; that where I am, there ye may be also." (John 14:3)

At no time is Christ ever said to stand upon the earth at His second coming. Of His first coming Job declared: "I know that my redeemer liveth, and that he shall stand at the latter day upon the earth." (Job 19:25)

But this is not said of Christ at His second coming. Rather:

Sixth: The second coming of Christ and the destruction of the world will be at the same time. How then could He stand upon the earth at His second coming? No wonder we must be *caught up to meet Him in the air.* And again we see why at His coming He descends *to receive* us unto Himself.

"But the day of the Lord will come as a thief in the night; in which the heavens shall pass away with a great noise, and the elements shall melt with fervent heat, the earth also and the works that are therein shall be burned up." (II Peter 3:10)

He further declares, "Seeing that all these things shall be dissolved," and again, "Wherein the heavens being on fire shall be dissolved, and the elements shall melt with fervent heat." (II Pet. 3:11-12)

Seventh: The second coming of Christ and the changing of our vile body will occur at the same time.

337

"For our conversation is in heaven; from whence we look for the Savior, the Lord Jesus Christ:

Who shall change our vile body, that it may be fashioned like unto His glorious body." (Phil. 3:20-21)

Eighth: At the second coming of Chirst then shall be the restitution of all things, and this restitution and His coming are at the same time.

"And He shall send Jesus Christ, which was before preached unto you. Whom the heaven must receive until the times of the restitution (Greek-restoration) of all things which God hath spoken by the mouth of all his holy prophets since the world began." (Acts 3:20-21)

Ninth: The second coming of Christ and the judgment will be at the same time.

"When the Son of man shall come in His glory and all the holy angels with Him, then shall He sit upon the throne of His glory.

And before Him shall be gathered all nations; and He shall separate them one from another, as the shepherd divideth his sheep from the goats." (Matt. 25:31-32)

While in Rev. 20:11 the scene of the judgment, nothing is said of the coming of Christ, it is said in Matt. 25:31, as quoted above, that when the Lord comes he shall be seated on the throne of judgment, while in (Rev. 20:11) John sees the throne and the Lord sitting thereon. John there does not describe His coming, as Matthew does, but shows Him *already come* and engaged in judgment.

Summary

Summing up our investigation we have found:

1. That the name "pre-millenialism" is unscriptural and the thing it represents is likewise unscriptural.
2. That neither Christ nor His apostles ever mentioned such a word or the system of belief the term signifies.
3. That the Holy Spirit never brought such a teaching to the remembrance of the apostles.
4. That in 'the things to come' which He was to show the apostles, the Holy Spirit did not mention pre-millenialism.
5. That Rev. 19:11-16 does not properly describe Christ's return as some have interpreted it to be, since this return was to be marked by coming with clouds, the voice of the archangel and the trump of God, and these verses describe no such scene.

6. That it was an angel who descended at the beginning of the thousand years and not Christ Himself.

7. That the principle theme here is the binding of Satan and not the thousand years reign of the martyrs with the Christ.

8. That it was in all four characterizations—the Dragon, the old serpent, the devil and Satan that the angel laid hold upon him and bound him for a thousand years.

9. That it is under the characterization of Satan, or accuser and liar that he is loosed for a little season.

10. That he was cast into the abyss, or deep place, not the lake of fire, for a thousand years.

11. That the mention of the thousand years period is not the primary theme but is incidental to the real subject under discussion, the binding of Satan.

12. That those sitting on thrones are the martyrs.

13. That Christ is not pictured sitting on a throne with the saint but is at the right hand of God.

14. That these thrones are not said to be upon the earth.

15. That this thousand year period is mentioned six times, just short of perfection, and Christ only returns when the place of perfection is completed, and then only to receive the righteous unto Himself.

16. That Christ mentioned His return, not to reign a thousand years on the earth, but to catch us up to be with Him.

17. That He never once said He, Himself would set foot upon the earth.

18. That there is no bodily resurrection mentioned here, but only a vision of the *souls* of the martyrs.

19. That the body is not to be raised until the consumation of all things.

20. That the incorruptable body is to be put on at the end of all things and not before the thousand year period.

21. That there is to be no setting up of a temporal Kingdom on the earth.

22. That a physical resurrection of the martyrs during the thousand years, would place two kinds of beings on the earth, one held to the limitation of the flesh, the other with a body which could become visible or invisible at will.

23. That the reigning of the martyrs with Christ is a spiritual rule. But some may ask the question, "How can the saints reign with Christ when He is not personally present? The

answer is so simple that we marvel men would even ask the question.

Jesus is reigning in the hearts of Christians *right now*. He does not require a temporal Kingdom, nor an earthly throne to be able to reign in this present age.

The King of England reigns over the great commonwealth of nations under the British flag without being personally present in each nation of that commonwealth. It is not absolutely necessary for an earthly king to be personally present with his subjects in order to reign over them. How much less it is necessary for Christ to have a temporal throne and be personally present in order to reign over the souls of the martyrs!

24. That the redemption of our bodies comes after "the manifestation of the sons of God, which is when God returns at the judgment.

25. That to have Christ come in His glory at the beginning of the thousand years and have the devil regain his power after that period would be acknowledging Christ's defeat.

26. That Christ is not to come until He has put down all rule, and power, and authority and destroyed the last enemy—death. This only occurs at the judgment time.

27. That to teach Christ returns before the thousand years and again at the judgment would make Him return twice, once in the beginning of the thousand years, and again at the judgment, whereas He is to return only once.

28. That the coming of Christ and the glorification of His saints are simultaneous.

29. That the coming of Christ and the resurrection of the good and bad are simultaneous.

30. That the second coming of Christ and the raising of the dead and translation of the righteous living are simultaneous.

31. That Christ's second coming and the catching up of the redeemed are simultaneous.

32. That Christ comes with clouds, and we are to be caught up into the air.

33. That Christ's second coming and the destruction of the world are simultaneous.

34. That the second coming of Christ and the changing of our vile bodies is simultaneous.

35. That the second coming of Christ and the restitution of all things are simultaneous.

36. That the second coming of Christ and the judgment are simultaneous.

37. That John never said a word about the tabernacle of God being with men during the thousand years. He would have mentioned this if Christ had been here personally; but it is not until after the thousand years and after the judgment that we read, "Behold, the tabernacle of God is with men."

38. That if Christ's second coming was to be at the beginning of the thousand year period, at which time Satan was to be bound, then it becomes manifest that this binding was in adequate and incomplete.

> *vs. 1* "And when the thousand years are expired, Satan shall be loosed out of his prison."

Why Satan is loosed, even for this short season is an enigma to the mortal mind, but for some reason, hidden in the secret councils of the Almighty, he is deliberately and by divine design loosed out of his prison.

> *vs. 8* "And shall go out to deceive the nations which are in the four quarters of the earth, Gog and Magog, to gather them together to battle; the numbers of whom is as the sand of the sea."

We have a gain come to the point where we must move with extreme caution. There are numerous explanations and interpretations many of the final battle of the earth. This battle has been referred to as the battle of Armageddon by some. Others believe the Armageddon to be the battle immediately preceding the thousand years. Still others maintain that the gathering of "the kings of the whole world" at Har-magedon of the sixth bowl (Rev. 16:14-16), and "the kings of the earth and their armies," destroyed with the beast in the vision of Rev. 19:19) may be the same as this gathering of the nations, Gog and Magog for the last struggle. (Rev. 20:7-10)

After careful research and prayerful looking to the Christ for guidance, the best answer seems to be that there is a twin phase to the culminating struggle of the last days.

The First Phase of the Battle

In Jeremiah 23:3, 5, 8 we read:

> "And I will gather the remnant of my flock out of all countries wither I have driven them, and will bring them again to their folds and they shall be fruitful and increase.

> "Behold, the days come, saith the Lord, that I will raise unto

David a righteous Branch, and a king shall reign and prosper, and shall execute judgment and justice in the earth.

In His days Judah shall be saved, and Israel shall dwell safely; and this is his name whereby he shall be called, *"The Lord Our Righteousness.*

Therefore, behold, the days come, saith the Lord, that they shall no more say, the Lord liveth, which brought up and which led the seed of the house of Israel out of the north country, and from all countries whither I had driven them; and they shall dwell in their own land."

This is a gathering from the world-wide dispersion which they have experienced through the centuries. Whereas, they have had no rest for the soul of their feet, they at this gathering *dwell in their own land.* And the righteous Branch shall not reign over their own land alone, but "shall execute judgment and justice in all the earth."

In Jeremiah the thirteenth chapter the first seven verses we have a description of great trial and tribulation through which Israel is to pass before his deliverance from captivity. We have not space to quote it all here but a few words will suffice, directing the reader to read them all in his Bible:

"For, lo, the days come, saith the Lord, that I will bring again the captivity of my people Israel and Judah, and I will cause them to return to the land I gave to their fathers and they shall possess it. . . .

"Alas! for that day is great, so that none is like it: it is even the time of Jacob's trouble, but he shall be saved out of it. . . .

"For I am with thee, saith the Lord, to save thee: though I make a full end of all nations whither I have scattered thee, yet will I not make a full end of thee."

Christ Himself said, while yet in the days of His flesh: that until the Gentile age comes to an end these promises will not be fulfilled.

"And they shall fall by the edge of the sword, and shall be led away captive into all nations: and Jerusalem shall be trodden down of the Gentiles *until* the times of the Gentiles be fulfilled." (Luke 21:24)

Thus we see the Jew shall not possss his own land which God gave him until Gentile domination shall come to an end.

But at the termination of the Gentile age the Jew will return to his own land to rebuild it and make it a treasure trove among the nations of earth.

This return is transpiring before our very eyes. During the first

World War 1914-1918, under the Balfour Declaration, England
went on record in favor of the setting up, in Palestine, a national
home for the Jewish people. On December 9, 1917 General Allenby
marched into Jerusalem at the head of his triumphant army. In
March 1918 the Jewish flag was unfurled from the tower of
David and the General proclaimed a Jewish state.

On May 24, 1920 the League of Nations officially granted to
England mandatory power over Palestine.

Then came the second World War and its terrible persecution of
the Jews in Germany and the increased migration of the Jew to his
homeland.

Finally, on May 14, 1948, the Jewish Nation officially came into
being under the designation of "Israeli." David Gurion became the
first President of the Jewish State.

This fulfilled the prophecy that at the end of the Gentile age the
Jew must be in possession of his homeland, because that land is
to be the scene of a great world conflict.

"The way of the Kings of the east is being prepared." "The kings
of the earth and of the whole world" are being gathered for the
battle of that great day of God Almighty.

The chemical wealth of Palestine and the oil field of Iran are
drawing the forces of the nations together for this first phase of the
conflict.

This battle, of course is not the final one, although it will be
terrible in its consequences. After the thousand years have passed will
come the last phase of the Battle of Armageddon.

Here in the twentieth chapter of Revelation we learn that the devil
is to be loosed for a brief time *after* the thousand years are completed.
Under his deception Gog and Magog take up the final struggle.

Thus we see if the Battle of Armageddon is to be the *last* battle,
it is plainly obvious that it cannot occur until *after* the thousand
years.

The first phase of this battle, which transpires *before* the thousand years, will occur in the invasion of Gog, the prince of Magog.
This angel of the struggle is portrayed in the 37, 38 and 39th chapters of Ezekial.

The first of those three chapters declares that the Jews will return
to Palestine. The second of the three predicts the invasion of the
restored homeland by Gog and Magog. The third of the three
chapters describes the defeat of the invaders.

As to who these invaders are, we pause to give a brief sketch of identification. Before proceeding with this identification we wish to review the setting. Before this tragedy comes to Israel she must be in her homeland. Ezekiel did prophecy the return of Israel after the Babylonain captivity, but the invasion of the restored land following that captivity was inflicted by the Romans. It was under Roman brutality that Israel was dispersed among the nations. It is from this Roman dispersion that Israel was to be gathered again, not a remnant this time and not from Babylon alone. This last "gathering" is to be from *all nations*. After this last mentioned return there shall be a concentration of wealth in Palestine and Gog will invade the land for the frank purpose of taking the spoils. He says, according to Ezekiel, "I will go up to take a spoil and to take a prey." Also Ezekiel declares, that when this invasion occurs the people will be living in a defenseless existence. They, evidently, will consider themselves secure because of the convenants the nations of earth have made with them to guarantee them an unmolested occupancy of the land of Palestine.

Now we shall proceed to a consideration of the nations which will constitute the invading forces.

The starting clue is the declaration that the alliance will be headed by Gog, who comes from Magog. Ezekiel declares that Gog is the chief prince of "Meshech and Tubal." Gog is to be the ruler and Magog is his domain.

The name 'Gog' is a proper name and occurs for the first time in the Bible in I Chron. 5:4. The name is given to a descendent of Reuben. The time is about sixteen centuries before Christ. The second occurance is in Ezekiel 38:2. In this last reference the name is applied to Gog the chief prince of Meshech and Tubal. This is a region anciently called Scythia, or Tartary.

This Gog is also the chief prince of Magog. Magog is first mentioned in Genesis 10:1-3 as the second son of Japheth. It reads:

> "Now these are the generations of the Sons of Noah, Shem, Ham and Japheth: and unto them were sons born after the flood.
>
> The sons of Japheth; Gomer and *Magog,* and Madai, and Javan, and *Tubal* and *Meshech* and *Tiras.*
>
> And the sons of Gomer, Ashkenaz, and Riphath, and Togarmah."

So here is the first occurance of the name Magog. Later the name was applied to his descendents, and still later to their land. The land also came to be called Scythia.

Herodotus, a Greek historian who lived about 484-424 B.C., who is called the "Father of History," declared that in his day the Scythians were savages, and that Scythia was a region of vast extent, lying north of the Black and Caspian Seas, and also north of the Caucasus mountains.

Josephus, the Jewish historian, who wrote the Jewish Antiquities, a history of his countrymen from the earliest period down to the close of Nero's reign—says that Magog represented the Scythians, a race spread over the country now occupied by southern Russia. This region has always been and now is the land of Russia.

But this Gog is represented as being the chief prince of Meshech. Referring to the famous Table of Nations in the 10th chapter of Genesis, we find that Meshech was also a son of Japheth (Gen. 10:2). His descendents came to be called "Mosche" from which comes the term "Muscovites." The name originally referred to those Russians who come from Moscow and its nearby territory. The name "Muscovites" is still applied to greater Russia. The region was first called "Muscovi" and finally "Moscow." But the identification has always been Russia.

Now we turn to the third link in our lengthening chain of identification. The fifth son of Japheth was *Tubal* and Ezekiel mentions Gog as the chief prince of Tubal. His ancient descendents are always linked with those of Meshech.

Josephus calls the children of "Tubal 'the Moschoi'." The historians of Mesopotamia called these people "Tobali" and Muski." So Tubal and Meshech are associated together historically. They lived north of the Black and Caspian seas, or Crimea, which again is southern Russia. There was a city in primitive Russia called Tubal.

So Gog of the land of Magog, the chief prince of the land of Meshech and Tubal, refers to Russia and none other. And Gog and Magog are to head the alliance which invades Palestine in the first phase of the battle against the land of Israel.

There remain other nations which Ezekiel associates with Gog and Magog in this first phase of the final battle against Palestine.

There is Gomer to be considered. Referring to ethnology again and the Table of Nations as recorded in the tenth chapter of Genesis, we find that Gomer was the first son of Japheth, which makes him of the same blood as Magog, Tubal and Meshech.

In the Assyrian records we find that Assyria fought in wars against the inhabitants of Gomer. These Assyrian records inform us that Gomer was a barbaric tribe of Aryans which came out of Russia through the Caucasian mountains. They overran Cappadocia and settled in the territory we know today as "the Balkans."

The Armenian name for Cappadocia is "Gamir," which comes from the ancient word "Gomer."

Russia and these people are kindred, being as we say today, of Slavonic blood.

Then Ezekiel (in Ezekiel 38:6) mentions "Togarmah of the North quarters". Genesis 10:3 declares that Togarmah was a son of Gomer and the grandson of Japheth.

Togarmah is now known as Armenia. It is so designated in the Assyrian records. Tacitus, a Roman historian, one of the greatest of all ages, who lived from about 55 A.D. to 120 (?) A.D., also declared that Togarmah was Armenia. Finally all Armenian literature allude to their land and its people as "The House of Togarmah." There is also Armenian tradition that they descend from the grandson of Japheth.

In Ezekiel 38:5 we have mentioned in rapid succession Persia, Ethiopia and Libya. These are also to be allies of Russia in this great battle before the thousand year period.

Persia, the first of the three has a long history reaching back into the dim shadows of antiquity. With Media she formed the second great world empire. Recently she assumed the ancient name of "Iran."

In recent years Persia, or Iran, has been the political battle-ground of Russian and British struggle for control of her fabulous oil fields. These fields contain one-fourth of the proven oil reserves of the world.

The other two nations mentioned by Ezekiel are Libya and Ethiopia. These are the modern names for the ancient countries called in the Hebrew language Phut and Kush.

The Egyptians called Libya by the word "Pessent," indicating that region of Africa directly west of Egypt lying on the coast of the Mediterranean.

The Persian record of Maqsh-i-Rusten applies the name "Kush" to Ethiopia.

In the Table of Nations in the tenth chapter of Genesis, Phut and Kush were the sons of Ham. The people of Kush occupied the country south of Egypt. Later they spread to include the territories of Nubia, Kordofan and Abyssinia. The Egyptians called the land "Kas," the Babylonians called it "Kusu" and the Hebrews called it "Kush."

All these countries, Gomer, or the Balkan states; Togarmah, or Armenia; Persia, or Iran; Lybia and the Egyptian countries are to be the allies of Magog, or Russia. This war is to be fought just preceding the thousand years and will bring to an end the "times of the Gentiles."

And where is this first battle to be fought? The one reference pertaining to it is in Rev. 16:16:

"And he gathered them together unto a place called in the Hebrew tongue, Armageddon." Armegeddon is the Greek: Har-Mageddon the Hebrew. The word means "The Hill of Megiddo. The Hill of Megiddo overlooks the plains of Esdraelon far north of Jerusalem.

So the storm of Ezekiel's vision is even now gathering, but at what hour it will break only God knows.

God, who knoweth the end of the matter from the beginning to the end has revealed to us this struggle. And the storm clouds of this great conflict, which Ezekiel saw gathering, will break, even as John saw the kings of the east being gathered to meet the kings of the earth and of all the world.

But after the thousand years there will come the final stage of the "Battle of Armageddon," because we read: "When the thousand years are expired, Satan shall be loosed out of prison and "Shall go forth to deceive the nations which are in the four quarters of earth, Gog and Magog, to gather them together to battle, the number of whom is as the sand of the sea."

But, whereas in the war before the thousand years a battle was to be engaged in by the nations involved, in this last struggle Gog and Magog, and the nations of the earth are to suffer divine punishment.

vs. 9 "And they went up on the breadth of the earth, and compassed the camp of the saints about, and the beloved city: and fire came down out of heaven, and devoured them."

One brief sentence tells the whole story: "There came down fire out of heaven, and devoured them." No one escapes.

Then follows the record of Satan's final destruction. He has before been imprisoned in the abyss, now he is cast into the lake of fire and brimstone. Hear John:

"And the devil that deceived them was cast into the lake of fire and brimstone, where the beast and the false prophet are, and shall be tormented day and night for ever and ever." Thus, Political and Papal Rome are joined by the devil. When Christ was on earth, He talked with His disciples about "the ever-lasting fire, prepared for the devil and his angels." (Matt. 25:41)

The Great White Throne

We now come to the last scene of the old, wicked and weary creation.

vs. 11 "And I saw a great white throne, and Him that sat on it, from whose face the earth and the heaven fled away; and there was found no more place for them."

This fulfills Peter's prophecy: "The day of the Lord will come as a thief in the night; in the which the heavens shall pass away with a great noise, and the elements shall melt with fervent heat, the earth also and the works that are therein shall be burned up." (II Pet. 3:10)

We now have come to the august day of divine judgment. Once before John, at the beginning of the second vision in Revelation, the fourth chapter, had beheld a throne and around that first throne were lesser thrones. Seven lamps, representing the seven spirits of God were before that first throne, manifesting the complete-ness of God's grace in the dispensation of mercy.

Here there is but one throne. There are no gracious seven lamps burning because the judgments meted out here are to be without grace and mercy.

In connection with the first throne there was joyous singing of redemption. There is no song, no voice of gladness for a word of triumph.

John is impressed by three things concerning this throne:

1. First, there was the greatness of this throne. This throne was great, not only because it is the final one of this sinful dis-pensation, but great because of the majesty of the occupant.

2. The second thing to impress John was the whiteness of that throne. White evidently portrays the glory of the judge.

3. Immeasurable power and invincible justice sit upon this throne, the Son, the Judge of all the earth. Christ had predicted His final judgment of the world: "The Father judgeth no man, but hath committed all judgment to the Son." (John 4:22)

John continues:

vs. 12 "And I saw the dead, small and great, stand before God: and the books were opened; and another book was opened, which is the book of life: and the dead were judged out of those things which were written in the books, according to their works."

vs. 13 We learn from the next verse that these dead are of every land of earth and sea and even Hades, the realm of departed spirits. "And the sea gave up the dead which were in it; and death and hell delivered up the dead which were in them and they judged every man according to his works."

The complete thought is that all the dead shall be judged.

The books that are opened contain the deeds of all men. The book of Life records the names of the saints. The overcomers are enrolled in the Book of Life:

"He that overcometh, the same shall be clothed in white raiment, and I will not blot out his name out of the book of life, but I will confess His name before my Father and before His angels." (Rev. 3:5)

The lost are not enrolled in this Book of Life. In Rev. 13:8 we read:

"All that dwell upon the earth shall worship him (the Dragon or devil), whose names are not written in the book of life of the Lamb slain from the foundation "of the world." (Rev. 13:8) And again we read, "And the earth shall wonder, whose names were not written in the book of life." (Rev. 17:8)

Christ while in the days of His flesh declared concerning those who obeyed His commandments, "that they should not come to judgment, but were passed out of death unto life. (John 5:24)

But to those whose names are not enrolled in the book of life, this is "the day when God shall judge the secrets of men."

The judgment of the dead according to those books is a judgment of condemnation.

The Codex Siniaticus, one of the best three manuscripts of the Bible reads:

"The sea gave the dead ones in it, and Death and Hades gave the dead ones in them, and they were condemned, every one, according to their deeds." It seems that not one was judged worthy of a place with the blessed dead.

vs. 14, 15 "And death and hell were cast into the lake of fire. This is the second death."

Thus we see that sentence is followed by immediate execution. When the beast and the false prophet were taken "they were cast into the lake of fire burning with brimstone." (Rev. 19:20)

A thousand years later Satan was cast into the lake of fire and brimstone" (Rev. 20:10) And into this lake of fire were cast the condemned ones. Some have asked, "Is this a lake of literal fire?" If it is not, and is but a symbol, we must keep in mind that the substance is always greater than the symbol. Revelation declares this is the eternal fate and destiny of those not written in the Lamb's Book of Life.

"This is the second death." Some have thought this means extinction, annihilation, but life continued after the first death. Likewise it would indicate continuation of life after the second death. The beast and the false prophet were in that death more than a thousand years and it is implied that they are still alive at the end of that time.

The fact that they shall be tormentd day and night forever seems pretty solid proof that this is not a state of extinction or annihilation.

The first death was a killing of the body, but not an extinction of it. The second death must needs be still more terrific and disastrous. "There the worm dieth not and the fire is not quenched." (Mark 9:44-48)

The torment is to be eternal, or literally "to the ages of the ages."

CHAPTER XXI

BEHOLD, I MAKE ALL THINGS NEW

Text (21:1-27)

INTRODUCTION

1 And I saw a new heaven and a new earth: for the first heaven and the first earth are passed away; and the sea is no more. 2 And I saw the holy city, new Jerusalem, coming down out of heaven from God, made ready as a bride adorned for her husband. 3 And I heard a great voice out of the throne saying, Behold, the tabernacle of God is with men, and he shall dwell with them, and they shall be his peoples, and God himself shall be with them, and be their God: 4 and he shall wipe away every tear from their eyes; and death shall be no more; neither shall there be mourning, nor crying, nor pain, any more: the first things are passed away. 5 And he that sitteth on the throne said, Behold, I make all things new. And he saith, Write: for these words are faithful and true. 6 And he said unto me, They are come to pass. I am the Alpha and the Omega, the beginning and the end. I will give unto him that is athirst of the fountain of the water of life freely. 7 He that overcometh shall inherit these things; and I will be his God, and he shall be my son.

8 But for the fearful, and unbelieving, and abominable, and murderers, and fornicators, and sorcerers, and idolaters, and all liars, their part shall be in the lake that burneth with fire and brimstone; which is the second death.

9 And there came one of the seven angels who had the seven bowls, who were laden with the seven last plagues; and he spake with me, saying, Come hither, I will show thee the bride, the wife of the Lamb. 10 And he carried me away in the Spirit to a mountain great and high, and showed me the holy city Jerusalem, coming down out of heaven from God, 11 having the glory of God: her light was like unto a stone most precious, as it were a jasper stone, clear as crystal: 12 having a wall great and high; having twelve gates, and at the gates twelve angels; and names written thereon, which are the names of the twelve tribes of the children of Israel: 13 on the east were three gates; and on the north three gates; and on the south three gates; and on the west three gates. 14 And the wall of the city had twelve foundations, and on them twelve names of the twelve apostles of the Lamb. 15 And he that spake with me had for a measure a golden reed to measure the city, and the gates thereof, and wall thereof. 16 And the city lieth foursquare, and the length thereof is as great as the breadth: and he measured the city with the reed, twelve thousand furlongs: the length and the breadth and the height thereof are equal. 17 And he measured the wall thereof, a hundred and forty and four cubits, according to the measure of a man, that is, of an angel. 18 And the building of the wall thereof was jasper: and the city was pure gold, like unto pure glass. 19 The foundations of the wall of the city were adorned with all manner of precious stones. The first foundation was jasper; the second, sapphire; the third, chalcedony; the fourth, emerald; 20 the fifth, sardonyx; the sixth, sardius; the seventh, chrysolite; the eighth, beryl; the ninth, topaz; the tenth, chrysoprase; the eleventh, jacinth; the twelfth, amethyst. 21 And the twelve gates were twelve pearls; each one of the several gates was of one pearl: and the street of the city was pure gold, as it were transparent glass. 22 And I saw no temple therein: for the Lord God the Almighty, and the Lamb, are the temple thereof. 23 And the city hath no need of the sun, neither of the moon, to shine upon it: for the glory of God did lighten it, and the lamp thereof is the Lamb. 24 And the nations shall walk amidst the light thereof: and the kings of the earth bring their glory into it. 25 And the gates thereof shall in no wise be shut by day (for there shall be no night there): 26 and they shall bring the glory and the honor of the nations into it: 27 and there shall in no wise enter into it anything unclean, or he that maketh a abomination and a lie: but only they that are written in the Lamb's book of life.

In the preceding chapter we beheld the final judgment of the dead, both small and great. In this present Chapter we are to behold that all things are made new. We Read:

vs. 1 "And I saw a new heaven and a new earth: for the first heaven and the first earth are passed away."

This "passing away" was first observed in the last Chapter we read:

"And I saw a great white throne, and Him that sat on it, from whose face the earth and the heaven *fled away;* and there was found no place for them." (Rev. 20:11)

Peter prophesied this cataclysmic change when he said:

"But the day of the Lord will come as a thief in the night; in the which the heavens shall pass away with a great noise, and the elements shall melt with fervent heat, the earth also and the works that are therein shall be burned up." (II Pet. 3:10)

He goes on to say, "All these things shall be dissolved."

All this seems to indicate a great change, not necessarily annihilation. When we come to think of it, nothing is really destroyed in the sense of ceasing to exist. Water brought to the boiling point turns into steam. It changes its form but does not pass out of existence. Wood burns and seems to be annihilated, but it has not ceased to exist. It has only been changed. It is turned into gas, which burning is transformed into energy.

Christ in His resurrected body had not ceased to exist. Mark said, "He appeared in another form." (Mark 16:12)

The same word "regeneration" is used here as was used to describe the changed condition of the man who has put off the old man and put on the new in the new birth.

In II Pet. 3:11, Peter said, "All things shall be *dissolved.*" This indicates a deliverance rather than a destruction. It is the same word used by Christ when He said of the colt: "*Loose* him," and, again, it is the same word employed by Christ at the tomb of Lazarus: "Loose him, and let him go."

This harmonizes with the scriptural teaching that the present world is in a state of captivity, or tied down, "Not willingly, but by reason of Him who hath subjected the same in hope." (Romans 8:20)

Creation and the recreated "shall be delivered from bondage of corruption into the glorious liberty of the children of God." (Romans 8:21)

Tremendous change in the whole physical set up of the earth and heaven is everywhere indicated, but not ceasation of existence or annihilation.

Evidently the earth is to undergo a renovation, a purification, a renewal to make it a fit place for the redeemed.

The old earth was sadly out of joint. Therefore, old things are to be surplanted by new things.

"And there was no more sea." Seas have always been barriers between peoples and nations. This condition has ceased to exist.

vs. 2 "And I John saw the holy city, New Jerusalem, coming down from God out of heaven, prepared as a bride for her husband."

Since this city is called the bride of Christ later in this Chapter, and since the Church is also called the bride of Christ in the New Testament, we logically conclude that this city is the glorified heavenly Church, prepared as a bride for the bridegroom. And the next voice that John hears is out of heaven:

vs. 3 "And I heard a great voice out of heaven saying "Behold, the tabernacle of God is with men, and He will dwell with them, and they shall be His people, and God Himself shall be with them, and be their God."

This restores the condition which obtained in the Garden of Eden when sinless man had immediate fellowship and companionship with God.

After man's fall, God withdrew Himself and made His presence known in the Shekinah glory of the tabernacle and temple. There He dwelt between the Cherubim. In the future state He will make His tabernacle and dwell in companionship with the redeemed.

And now John describes the blessedness of this companionship with God.

vs. 4 "And God shall wipe away all tears from their eyes, and there shall be no more death, neither sorrow, nor crying, neither shall there be any more pain: for the former things are passed away."

Someone has said that human hands are poor at drying tears. This because we can never completely and permanently dry the tears of sorrow. Only the hand of Him who made us can wipe away all tears by removing us from the cause of weeping.

"And there shall be no more death." The last enemy of our souls will have been destroyed, by Him who was able to destroy him who had power over death. "Death," then will have been swallowed up in victory."

"Neither shall there be any more sorrow, nor crying." Isaiah also spoke of this new heaven and this new earth and said: "And the voice of weeping shall be no more heard." (Isa. 65:19)

"Neither shall there be any more pain." Pain is a part and portion of this life of sin, although some try to delude themselves into thinking there is no pain here. There, with sin, and its penalty-death-removed, pain will be unknown.

The former things—sin, pain, sorrow, death—will have passed away.

vs. 5 "And He that sat upon the throne said, Behold, I make all things new." How could it be otherwise when there is a new heaven and a new earth and a new Jerusalem!

"And He said unto me, Write: for these words are true and faithful."

This is the third instance in the Book of Revelation, after the letters to the seven churches in Chapters Two and Three, that John is commanded to write. The other two instances are Rev. 14:13 and Rev. 19:9. And both of these two former occurrences a matter of great import is under consideration. The first of the two is a pronouncement of blessedness pronounced upon the dead who keep His commandments and die in the Lord, the second refers to the blessedness of those who are called to the wedding feast of the Lamb.

This third instance of the word "write" is to call our attention to the wondrous words that follow describing the eternal City of God.

vs. 6 "And He said unto me, It is done." All the details of the divine plan have been filled in. There is nothing left to be done. It is finished!

"I am Alpha and Omega. These words add force to his words "These words are faithful and true." They declare also that all things begin with God—He is the originating source and cause of all things. Also they proclaim that He is closing the drama of human history. These words show that Christ is the speaker here.

"I will give to him that is athirst of the fountain of the water of life freely."

The fountain of the water of life is now available. Here is fulfilled the inspired prophecy of Isaiah, "Ho, everyone that thirsteth, come ye to the waters; and he that hath no money; come ye buy, and eat; yea come buy wine and milk without money and without price." (Isa. 55:1).

The words point forward to the copious river flowing from the everlasting source—the throne of God and of the Lamb as described in (Rev. 22:1).

vs. 7 "He that overcometh shall inherit all things: and I will be his God and he shall be my son."

This is the first time, after the second of the seven letters to the seven churches, that we meet with the promise given to him who overcomes. This is the consummation of Paul's declaration:

All things are yours, whether Paul, or Apollos, or Cephas, or the world of life, or death, or things present, or things to come; All are yours; and ye are Christ's and Christ is God's. (I Cor. 3:21-23).

Now by way of contrast Christ presents the awful doom of the lost.

vs. 8 "But the fearful, and unbelieving and the abominable, and murderers, and whoremongers, and sorcerers and idolaters, and all liars, shall have their part in the lake which burneth with fire and brimstone; which is the second death."

Since there is no resurrection from the second death, these described in verse eight can never enter nor disturb the peace of the New Jerusalem. As the blackness of the storm cloud brings out the rainbow in sharp contrast, so these of the second death furnish a sharp contrasting backdrop to the glory of the redeemed.

vs. 9 "And there came unto me one of the seven angels which had the seven vials full of the seven last plagues, and talked with me, saying, come hither, I will show you the bride, the Lamb's wife."

These words are familiar to us. You will remember that one of the seven angels which had the seven last plagues called John's attention to Babylon, the harlot and Apostate Church which was also called a woman and a city and claimed to be no widow, but a bride.

"And there came one of the seven angels which had the seven vials, and talked with me saying unto me, come hither; I will show unto thee the judgment of the great whore that sitteth upon many waters." (Rev. 17:1).

This referred to the Roman Church, the apostate, Babylonish Church. The angel of Chapter Nineteen calls John's attention to the true church, the Lamb's bride. This vision is thus linked with the one in which John was carried away in the spirit into the wilderness that he might behold the judgment of Babylon. No one can fail to notice the parallelism of the two visions, each of a woman and a city.

vs. 10 And he carried me away in the spirit to a great and high mountain, "and showed me that great city, the holy Jerusalem, descending out of heaven from God.

To behold this celestial city John was again carried away in the spirit. He was in the Spirit on the Lord's Day to behold the vision of the seven churches. (Rev. 1:10.) He was in the spirit to behold the vision of the throne set in heaven. (Rev. 4:2). And here he is in the spirit to behold the Holy City.

What a vision burst upon his eyes! John could only get a clear view of it by being spiritually transported to the top of a great and high mountain. Rev. 21:11. "Having the glory of God: and her light was like unto a stone most precious, even like a jasperstone, clear as crystal." It is perfectly transparent. This recalls the appearance of Him who sat upon the throne. Rev. 21:12 "And had a wall great and high.

Verse 18 informs us that these walls were made of Jasper. Since this is a book of symbols, this speaks of the utter security of the happy inhabitants who live therein!

Isaiah in his vision of this city said:

"But thou shall call *thy walls salvation,* and thy gates, praise." (Isaiah 60:18)

"And had twelve gates, and at the gates twelve angels, and names written thereon, which are the names of the twelve tribes of Israel."

There were as many gates as there were tribes of Israel and had on the twelve gates the names of the twelve tribes. Doubtless, these were typical of the true Israel of God, according to the spirit and not the flesh. (Gal. 6:15, 16). And at the twelve gates were twelve angels as gate-keepers to guard the holy city.

Judging by Ezekiel's description of the new city, then the names on the gates were as follows:

On the three gates northward, Reuben, Judah and Levi; on the three gates eastward, Joseph, Benjamin and Dan; on the three gates southward, Simeon, Issachar and Zebulon; on the three gates westward, God, Asher and Napthali. (Ezekiel 48:31-34).

vs. 14 "And the wall of the city had twelve foundations, and in them the names of the twelve apostles of the Lamb."

How fitting, since the twelve apostles are the foundations of the church with Jesus Christ as the chief cornerstone!

vs. 15 "And he that talked with me had a golden reed to measure the city, and the gates thereof and the wall thereof."

The reed is the divine standard of measurement and the city conforms to the divine standard. We found in the eleventh Chapter, the first verse, that the Church was also measured with a reed. It seems that both the earthly and heavenly institutions must conform to the divine standard.

vs. 16 "And the city lieth foursquare, and the length is as large as the breadth. And he measured the city with the reed, twelve thousand furlongs: the length, and the breadth, and the height of it are equal." The city was a cube, picturing perfection.

The city is regular and symmetrical and its dimensions vast. He indicates the city is twelve thousand furlongs long, twelve thousand furlongs wide and twelve thousand furlongs high. A furlong is one-eighth of a mile, therefore, twelve thousand furlongs would be fifteen hundred miles. That would mean the city was fifteen hundred miles long, wide and high.

Whether these measurements are intended to reveal the exact size of the Holy City, or are but symbols in this Book of Symbolism, extreme vastness of the size of the New Jerusalem is portrayed.

. .*vs. 17* "And he measured the wall thereof, an hundred and forty and four cubets, according to the measure of a man, that is of the angel."

Again we meet with the number twelve, this time squared.

vs. 18 And the building of the wall of it was of jasper: and the city was pure gold, like unto clear glass.

And the foundations of the walls of the City were garnished with all manner of precious stones. The first foundation was jasper; the second, sapphire; the third, a chalcedony; the fourth, an emerald;

The fifth, sardonyx; the sixth, sardius; the seventh, chrysolite; the eighth, beryl; the ninth, a topas; the tenth, a chrysoprasus; the eleventh, jacinth; the twelfth, an amethyst."

This city well may be made literally of such precious stones. Again this is a book of majestic symbols and these precious stones may be symbols used to convey to our finite minds the wondrous beauty of that City. The costliest gems known to man are named in order to give us, at least a dim idea and conception of the glory of the Eternal City.

One cannot read these preceding verses without being struck by the oftrecurrence of the favorite Hebrew number—*twelve*. By counting twelve occurrences of that number are discoverable.

In Verse 12, we have *twelve* gates, *twelve* angels and *twelve* tribes, making *three* occurrences of the number twelve.

In Verse 14, we find *twelve* foundations and *twelve* apostles, making *two* occurrences of this number *twelve*.

In Verse 16, the length, breadth and height of the city are

twelve thousand furlongs each, making *three* more occurrences of the number *twelve.*

In Verse 17, the wall of the city is 144 furlongs, a multiple of *twelve,* making *one* occurrence.

In verses 19 and 20, there are *twelve* foundations described, making *one* occurrence.

In Verse 21, *twelve* gates and *twelve* pearls are mentioned, making *two* more occurrences of the number *twelve.*

This makes twelve occurrences in all. And the number *"twelve"* is closely associated with the Israel of God of both the Old and New Testaments. There were twelve tribes in the Old Testament Israel of God, and twelve apostles in the New Testament Israel of God.

The former twelve are associated with the gates of the Holy City and the latter twelve are associated with the foundations.

vs. 21 "And the twelve gates were twelve pearls; every several gate was of one pearl."

How significant that the gates—the means of entrance into the Holy City—were all made of pearl!

One of the most precious and beautiful gems in all the world is the pearl. Other gems are produced by chemical action, heat and pressure in inanimate nature, but pearls come from animate life.

The finest specimens command almost fabulous prices. The origin of the pearl found within the shell of the pearl oyster was, to the ancients, a matter of deepest mystery, but today we understand it.

We have learned that the pearl comes from irritation caused by some foreign substance, like a piece of sand, getting within the shell of the oyster, and results from the wonderful and mysterious power of the mollusk to obtain relief from things that irritate it by covering them with a secretion of pearl, until there is no longer any irritation.

What a beautiful symbolism and lesson here for the annoyances, irritations, and things that hurt and distrub us—to make pearls out of them instead of allowing them to go on hurting and vixing us!

And what a revelation is here that the entrance into the Celestial City is by the way of gate of pearl! Only those who are "overcomers," who have transformed their irritations, vexations, and trials into a pearl are able to enter that fair city.

Christ is the pearl of great price because he conquered as none other overcame and declared Himself to be the door by which we must enter. He is the way the truth and the life and no man cometh unto the Father but by Him. Therefore, we come into the Holy City, where God makes His dwelling place, by a gate of pearl.

While there is but one door of entrance, so there is but one foundation and Christ is both the door and the foundation.

But in this book which is written in divine sign-language the one door, or gate is represented as twelve gates, and the one foundation as twelve foundations. Earlier in this book of symbolism, and for the same reason, the one Spirit is represented as seven Spirits.

Completing the twenty-first verse, we read: "And the street of the city was pure gold, as it were transparent glass."

Now we know that gold is not transparent, but what is here stressed is the absolute purity of gold. Also transparency is a symbol of purity. Nothing could enter, nor walk upon the gold-paved streets of the Holy City that is impure.

. . vs. 22 "And I saw no temple therein; for the Lord God Almighty and the Lamb are the temple of it."

John seemed deeply impressed by this fact.

He had been accustomed to considering the glory of the earthly City of Jerusalem to be its magnificent temple. But one of the sublimest peculiarities of the Holy City was its lack of a temple.

A great and precious thought is contained herein. God is here revealed as bringing His saints into a closer relationship to Him than that of dwelling in a temple, however glorious, to worship Him therein. In that eternal city we are to be brought into a perfect union with the Father Himself. This recalls the Lord's own prayer:

> "That they may be one, even as we are one: I in them, and thou in me, that they may be made perfect in one." (John 17:22, 23).

When we remember that this city is the Bride, the Lamb's wife, a bride adorned for her husband (Rev. 21:1), then why there could be no distinct and separate temple. God and Christ and the saints *are one*. There is no need for an outward temple to commune with God, or to have fellowship with the Lamb. The worship there is immediate and direct. *Rev. 21:23*. "And the city had no need of the sun, neither the moon, to shine in it, for the glory of God did lighten it, and the Lamb is the light thereof."

As there was no need of a separate temple in which to worship, neither was there any need of some system of illumination. Evidently with the creating of a new heaven and a new earth, the starry sky and its pale moon passed away. They were physical systems of ministering to material organs of perception.

How well did Isaiah write, "the moon shall be ashamed and confounded"—ashamed because of the infinitely more glorious sh'ning of the light of God and of the Lamb, in whom there is no darkness at all.

vs. 24 "And the nations of them which are saved shall walk in the light of it: and the kings of the earth do bring their glory and honor into it."

The redeemed of all nations shall walk in the light of that brilliant city. For the first time in all ages there will be truly Christian nations living and walking in the ineffable light of God.

The kings of the earth are said to bring their glory and honor into it because the kings then will be Christ and his glorified saints, since we are to be Kings and Priests unto God.

We are not to understand by the word "Bring" that these nations mentioned are *without* the City, but rather within and are being illuminated by its light. At that time all nations are either in the New Jerusalem or in the lake of fire that burneth with brimstone. Symbolically, they *bring* their glory and honor into it, laying it at the feet of the Lamb.

vs. 25 "And the gates of the city shall not be shut at all by day; for there shall be no night there."

This is an emphatic way of saying that the gates will never be closed. Why should they be? Nothing that would defile can enter that Holy City.

vs. 26 "And they shall bring the glory and honor of the nations into it."

All nations as one man, shall bring all their reverence and devotion. Since this verse is almost identical with the latter part of the twenty-fourth verse, it would seem this repetition is made in order to emphasize an experience never known before in all history of man, in that all men shall be fully and completely devoted to God and the Lamb.

vs. 27 "And there shall in no wise enter into anything that defileth, neither whatsoever worketh abomination, or maketh a lie, but they which are written in the Lamb's book of Life."

Since the devil, the Father of all lies, the originator of all that defiles and is abominable, has been cast into the lake of fire, there can be only holiness and righteousness within this Holy City.

Did Jeremiah have such a thought in mind when he, describing the City beautiful, said, "And the name of the city from that day shall be, THE LORD IS THERE"?

God is righteousness and where God is there can be nothing that is unclean.

Only those may enter this city whose names are "written in the Lamb's book of life." This is the seventh time this book has been mentioned in the scriptures. The other references are: Psalms 69:29; Daniel 12:1; Philippians 4:3; Revelations 3:5; 13:8; 20:12.

Not to be enrolled in the Lamb's book of life means utter loss; to have our name written therein bestows upon us all that the infinite wealth of God can give.

CHAPTER XXII

THE NEW JERUSALEM AND ITS LIFE

Text (22:1-21)

1 And he showed me a river of water of life, bright as crystal, proceeding out of the throne of God and of the Lamb, 2 in the midst of the street thereof. And on this side of the river and on that was the tree of life, bearing twelve manner of fruits, yielding its fruit every month: and the leaves of the tree were for the healing of the nations. 3 And there shall be no curse any more: and the throne of God and of the Lamb shall be therein: and his servants shall serve him; 4 and they shall see his face; and his name shall be on their foreheads. 5 And there shall be night no more; and they need no light of lamp, neither light of sun; for the Lord God shall give them light: and they shall reign for ever and ever.

6 And he said unto me, These words are faithful and true: and the Lord, the God of the spirits of the prophets, sent his angel to show unto his servants the things which must shortly come to pass. 7 And behold, I come quickly. Blessed is he that keepeth the words of the prophecy of this book.

8 And I John am he that heard and saw these things. And when I heard and saw, I fell down to worship before the feet of the angel that showed me these things. 9 And he saith unto me, See thou do it not: I am a fellow-servant with thee and with thy brethren the prophets, and with them that keep the words of this book: worship God.

10 And he saith unto me, Seal not up the words of the prophecy of this book; for the time is at hand. 11 He that is unrighteous, let him do unrighteousness still: and he that is filthy, let him be made filthy still: and he that is righteous, let him do righteousness still: and he that is holy, let him be made holy still. 12 Behold, I come quickly; and my reward is with me, to render to each man accord-

ing as his work is. 13 I am the Alpha and the Omega, the first and the last, the beginning and the end. 14 Blessed are they that wash their robes, that they may have the right to come to the tree of life, and may enter in by the gates into the city. 15 Without are the dogs, and the sorcerers, and the fornicators, and the murderers, and the idolaters, and every one that loveth and maketh a lie.

16 I Jesus have sent mine angel to testify unto you these things for the churches. I am the root and the offspring of David, the bright, the morning star.

17 And the Spirit and the bride say, Come. And he that heareth, let him say, Come. And he that is athirst, let him come: he that will, let him take the water of life freely.

18 I testify unto every man that heareth the words of the prophecy of this book, If any man shall add unto them, God shall add unto him the plagues which are written in this book: 19 and if any man shall take away from the words of the book of this prophecy, God shall take away his part from the tree of life, and out of the holy city, which are written in this book.

20 He who testifieth these things saith, Yea: I come quickly. Amen: come, Lord Jesus.

21 The grace of the Lord Jesus be with the saints. Amen.

INTRODUCTION

The symbolic description of the City Celestial, as given in the preceeding chapter has prepared us for the bringing down of the prophetic curtain of Revelation.

In the chapter before us our attention is drawn from the description of Jerusalem's glorious structure and dimensions to the blessedness of the life that shall be lived in that radiant city.

Not only have we given us the unfolding of the manner of life lived there but the glory of that life is accentuated by reference to the class of people without that city.

Also the closing epilogue is given providing us with warnings, admonitions and gracious invitations. Reverently, now we turn to the "uncovering" of the closing words of the aposalypse.

vs. 1 "And he showed me a pure river of water of life, clear as crystal, proceeding out of the throne of God and of the Lamb."

Water has even been a symbol of eternal life. And this pure river of water of life flows from the source of all purity—the throne of God and of the Lamb. In this great book of Revelation, ever since John saw the vision of the open door in heaven, as described in the fourth chapter, God and the Lamb have been closely associated with reference to the throne.

Man in his innocence began his existance in a garden, eastward in Eden. There by pelucid ponds and translucent streams, he walked in intimate companionship with his God. Here at the close of the apocalypse, which brings down the curtain on all inspired revelation, redeemed man is again found in a new garden within the Holy city.

If the former banishment from the Garden of Eden was paradise lost, this living in the new Jerusalem, on a new earth, is paradise regained.

Here in this city celestial the pure river of life pours its crystal waters through the very middle of the street of gold, o'ershaded by the Tree of Life, for we read:

vs. 2 "In the midst of the street of it, and on either side of the river was there the tree of life, which bare twelve manner of fruits and yielded her fruit every month: and the leaves of the tree were for the healing of the nations."

In the first paradise man, after eating of the tree of the knowledge of good and of Evil, was banished from the garden lest he eat of the Tree of Life and live forever in sin.

"So the Lord God drove out the man, and he placed at the east of the Garden of Eden Cherubim, and a flaming sword which turned every way, to keep the way of the Tree of Life." (Genesis 3:24)

The cherubim there guarded the entrance of the garden to keep the man from reentering; the angels here stand guard at the gates to keep the redeemed *in* the Garden of God.

Truly the divinely inspired book, the Bible, is a perfect heavenly symphony. Just as a musical symphony begins and ends in the same key, so God's symphony of revelation begins and ends in the same key. Man was sinless in the first garden, and again in the second and last garden he is likewise sinless. The heavenly symphony begins with sinlessness and closes with sinlessness.

Which brings us to the central theme of this closing chapter. The theme is *Life*.

All the sin which resulted from the fall of man is swallowed up in the second death, when the devil, the dragon, the false prophet and all who were not found written in the Book of Life were cast into the Lake of fire.

The dominion of sin and death is gone forever. Now Life— abundant life—reigns everywhere.

Life here is presented as a glorious Triad. We have set before us:

1. The Book of Life.
2. The River of the Water of Life, and,
3. The Tree of Life.

363

And as if to place special emphasis upon this life-giving triad, each is mentioned twice. The Book of Life is mentioned in (Rev. 21:27) and (Rev. 22:19), the Water of Life is mentioned in (Rev. 22:1) and (Rev. 22:17), and the Tree of Life in (Rev. 22:2) and (Rev. 22:14).

Then as if wishing to again emphasize the theme of *Life,* there is an introversion to be found in these six mentionings. This will be readily seen by listing these references in the order in which they appear.

Rev. 21:27 Book
Rev. 22:1   Water
Rev. 22:2   Tree
Rev. 22:14 Tree
Rev. 22:17 Water
Rev. 22:19 Book

Again there is a divine pronouncement of the Glorious Trinity. The Book of that of the Lamb, or Christ; the water is a symbol of the Holy Spirit—so declared by Christ in John 7:38, 39, and the Tree is logically a symbol of God, the source of all life.

And inseparable associated with both triads is the thought of life—abundant life.

The tree bore twelve manner of fruits and yielded its fruit every month. Of course the primary thought is that the tree is ever fruitful, but we cannot escape the force of the divine declaration that God's year has always been and always will be divided into twelve months, the modern proponents of a revised calendar of thirteen months, notwithstanding.

The twelve manner of fruits will guarantee a complete, balanced and life-sustaining diet for the redeemed, in the city of Abundant Life.

Christ, after his resurrection ate, the psalmist said that man ate angel's food. (Psa. 78, 25). The angels ate of Sarah's cakes and Abraham's dressed calf (Gen. 18:6-8). Jesus said He, at His return would serve his saints when they sit down to meat, and here we are lead to believe that eating will be one of the joys of our life in that great City of Abundance.

Both river and tree supply all wants. The water quenches the thirst, namely, satisfies the desires of the ransomed. And what the river of water of life does for the thirsty, the tree does for the hungry. The one flows perennially, the other bears perennially.

But more than food is supplied by the Tree of Life; "the leaves of the tree were for the healing of the nations."

It hardly seems these were diseases to be healed, but rather the leaves were the means of the banishment of disease and death. The meaning seems to be not that there are maladies then existing needing to be removed, but rather the leaves were for the preservation of abundant health.

vs. 3 "And there shall be no more curse."

There shall be no more curse because no sin shall ever enter there. Truly, God has fulfilled His promise "to make all things new."

"And the throne of God and of the Lamb shall be in it; and his servants shall serve him."

It is because of the eternal permanency of the throne of God and of the Lamb and the absolute, yet benign reign of God and Christ over the redeemed, that there will never be any more curse. This is a picture of perfect rule and the state of perfection which follows as the natural covallary.

vs. 4 "And they shall see his face; and His name shall be on their foreheads."

This will be the fulfillment of Christ's predictive beattitude: "Blessed are the pure in heart: for they shall see God" (Matt. 5:8)

What a blessedness is this to enjoy the visible presence of the Lamb and to look upon the face of Him, which is as glorious that heaven and earth fled away from it.

"I saw a great white throne, and him that sat on it, from whose face the earth and the heaven fled away, and there was found no place for them." (Rev. 20:11)

Truly to see His face is to enjoy his favor. We "now see through a glass darkly, but then face to face."

But not only will the face of Him who is altogether lonely, be seen but "His name shall be on our foreheads."

"The Aaronic High Priest wore a plate of burnished gold upon his brow, on which was engraved the name of God Almighty. Likewise, the redeemed, as priests and Kings will wear the name of the Lamb of God in their foreheads forever witnessing that they are His.

vs. 5 "And there shall be no night there; and they need no candle, neither light of the sun; for the Lord God giveth them light: and they shall reign for ever and ever."

365

Thus again it is said (this truth was first declared in Rev. 21:25) there shall be no night. In Rev. 21:25, the absence of night indicated why the gates were never closed, because it will be one grand eternal day. In the present verse since His servants are serving Him, there will never be any interruption to that service, since there will be no night there.

How could night exist there when God and the Lamb, in whom is no darkness at all, shall be the eternal light.

The succession of day and night was necessary for sinful man, yes, even Adam in his innocence needed it for rest and sleep, but such a need will never arise in this glorious home of the redeemed.

Again the saints could not experience darkness of any sort because Daniel said:

"They shall shine as the brightness of the firemament, and as the stars forever and ever" (Daniel 12:3).

"And they shall reign forever and ever."

Not for a thousand years only. No such limitation could be compatible with things eternal. Literally, it reads: "reign to the ages of the ages." Christ said: "For in the resurrection they neither marry, nor are given in marriage, but are as the angels of God in heaven."

There will be no such thing as celestial marriages there, nor are men sealed to wives for time and eternity but in the glorified form, as angels, with marriage bond, shall reign forever and ever.

Such is the final and concluding picture presented to us in the "uncoverings" of the apocalypse. This closes the transendently glorious description of redeemed man's eternal destiny and home.

Thus ends the third division of the Apocalypse. Thus ends all the succession of prophecies. This book of Revelation began with a prologue. (Rev. 1:1-8), followed by Part I, extending from Rev. 1:9 to Rev. 3:22; then followed Part II, from Rev. 4:1 to Rev. 11:18; with Part III reaching through Rev. 22:5; and finally concluding with the epilogue beginning at Rev. 22:6.

The Apocalypse proper began at Rev. 1:9 and ended at Rev. 22:5. We are now to proceed with the study of the epilogue.

EPILOGUE

vs. 6 "And he said unto me, These sayings are faithful and true. The several visions of the apocalypse are now completed and the epilogue which follows is written to emphasize the great importance of the "sayings" of the Chapters that precede these closing words of the book.

Perhaps the stress that is here laid upon the importance of the "sayings" of this book is because there has been such a universal tendency to neglect this book due to its symbolic profoundity.

How significant that immediately following the description of the Holy City these admonitions are given, and particularly the assurance that "these sayings are faithful and true." A similar assurance was given in Rev. 21:5 which had reference to the creation of the new heaven and the new earth. And again a somewhat similar expression was found in Rev. 19:9 which referred to the destruction of Babylon and the marriage of the Lamb. The third use of this assurance is in the verse before us (Rev. 22:6) and has reference to the blessings promised to the dwellers in the New Jerusalem.

"And the Lord God of the holy prophets sent His angel to show unto His servants the things which must shortly be done."

This is a repitition, almost word-for-word of Rev. 1:1 where He "sent His angel to his servant John" for the purpose of giving him these revelations, and here at the conclusion of the book, we have it repeated that "the Lord God of the Holy prophets sent His angel to show unto His servants the things which must shortly be done."

A third similar repitition is found in (Rev. 22:16) when Christ himself adds special personal testimony, "I Jesus have sent mine angel to testify unto you these things in the churches."

Why this triple declaration? Undoubtedly it is to assure us that this book is divinely inspired and has the authority of the God of all inspiration.

Christ, looking down through the corridors of time, saw men either denying the inspiration of this book, or neglecting it because of its profound symbolism, thus this threefold declaration of its authoritative and inspired nature.

There is no other book in the entire Bible which Christ so personally and pointedly affirms as inspired, or more urgently presses upon us for our prayerful and devout study.

Then comes a repetition of the blessing promised in the prologue of the Book (Rev. 1:3). There it reads:

"Blessed is he that readeth, and they that hear the words of this prophecy, and keep those things which are written therein: for the time is at hand."

Here in *vs. 7.* 22:7 it reads: "Behold I come quickly: blessed is he that keepeth the sayings of the prophecy of this book."

When we recall that all this is in addition to the seven-fold repitition of the admonition, "He that hath an ear let him hear what the Spirit saith unto the churches," then we must conclude that there is no other book in the Sacred Canon which guarantees such blessings for reading and keeping of its words.

And how many folk become offended at the teaching of the prophecies of Revelation! How many otherwise earnest ministers and teachers ignore the book, or even ridicule and make light of its sayings! Oh that Christians might not despise or neglect this crowning book of God's Divine revelation! Surely, no other book is so difficult of understanding, nor so fruitful of its blessings.

Then John adds his own personal testimony that he saw and heard these things.

vs. 8 "And I John saw these things, and heard them."

The very directness and simplicity of this affirmation should convince any hesitant doubter that the sayings of this wonder book of the Bible are true and should be studiously heeded.

And to add to it all, John was so overwhelmed and overpowered by the wonder and sublimity of the things that he had seen and heard, that we read:

"And when I had heard and seen, I fell down to worship at the feet of the angel which showed me these things."

Once before in (Rev. 19:10) John had fallen at the feet of an angel to worship him, but was expressly forbidden to do so, but was commanded by the angel "to worship God."

Here in very similar words the angel declares:

vs. 9 "Then saith he unto me, See thou do it not: for I am thy fellow servant, and of thy brethren the prophets, and of them which keep the sayings of this book: worship God."

Had not Paul, long before the time of the writing of the apocalypse, warned, "Let no man beguile you of your reward in a voluntary humility and worshipping of angels, intruding into those things which he hath not seen?" (Colossians 2:18).

If man is not to worship an angel, a higher rank of created being than man, how utterly unscriptural and sinful it is for man to worship Mary, who gave birth to Jesus, and who had to look to Jesus for salvation the same as all other women have had to so look!

Jesus made this fact crystal clear in His third word from the cross. He said to her, "Woman, Behold thy son." (John 19:26)

Jesus was actually breaking the relationship of mother and son. He is saying, "From now on, not I, but John is your son!"

From that second on, Mary was no more to Jesus than any other woman. He is no longer any woman's son. From now on he is solely the only begotten Son of God.

By this third saying from the cross, Jesus was denying Mary any special position or privilege. He was deliberately placing her on the same plane of humanity with the rest of all those He loved.

Since she was the one person at the cross who might unwittingly steal the attention from the only Savior of the world, He took this drastic step to guard against the worship of Mary. She must not become His rival in His mediatorial reign. How ill-becoming for those of spiritual Babylon, the Roman church, not only to make Mary a rival of Christ, but actually to teach that God can more easily be approached through the heart of Mary than that of Christ. It is nothing short of blasphemy.

But it was not for Mary's benefit that Jesus uttered this third word. She already did, and had always, understood her relationship to Him. In her Magnificat, she declared:

"And Mary said, my soul doth magnify the Lord, and my spirit hath rejoiced in God *my savior*." (Luke 1:46, 47)

By her statement she gladly took her place among His devout worshippers.

By Jesus' declaration, she learned it was better to have Christ as her Savior and Lord than to be His mother. She, henceforth must look to Him for salvation, the same as all other human beings.

But as we have stated above, Jesus did not make this pronouncement for Mary's benefit; she needed no such word, for she already understood her relationship to Him. He said this for the benefit of those men who would unscripturally, even though done sincerely, make Mary a comediatrix with Christ.

If John was forbidden of the angel to worship him, but was enjoined emphatically to worship God only, then certainly there is no place for mariolatry, or the worship of Mary.

Furthermore, because the coming of Christ was regarded as near, the angel added:

vs. 10 "And he saith unto me, Seal not the sayings of the prophecy of this book: for the time is at hand."

To seal up the sayings would conceal them. But they are to be revealed and not hidden. These visions did not refer to some distant time and therefore to be kept secret for the present but belong to the present and must be given out, or unsealed, because the end of the age is not far distant.

Another reason for the urgent necessity of "uncovering" the sayings of this book is that there was such little time for obedience to the gospel of salvation which would enroll the obedient in the Lamb's book of Life.

The acceptance of the scriptural conditions of salvation would insure enrollment in the book of life; rejection would forever determine the unalterable fate of the disobedient. Hear the angel further:

> vs. 11 "He that is unjust, let him be unjust still: and he that is filthy, let him be filthy still: and he that is righteous, let him be righteous still: and he that is holy, let him be holy still."

What a warning. This is not to be construed as belonging to the category of a command; it is a dire warning that there comes a time when the course of free choice can not be altered. He that set his life in injustice and unrighteous will go on that way.

Well did Paul write to the Thessalonians:

> "And with all deceivableness of unrighteousness in them that perish; because they received not the love of the truth, that they might be saved.
>
> And for this cause God shall send them strong delusion, that they should believe a lie: that they all might be damned who believed not the truth, but had pleasure in unrighteousness."
> (II Thess. 2:10-12)

When, we by free choice pursue an unscriptural—and therefore an unrighteous course—God lets us, after due warning, to go our willful way. When we persist in following the way of delusion, though thinking our worship and actions right, He permits us to continue to believe a lie and support an untruth. There is nothing else He can do without interfering with our free-moral agency.

Men must be forewarned and forearmed, lest they be deceived and perish. Hence the absolute necessity of not sealing up "the sayings of the prophecy of this book."

However, there is joy unspeakable for those who have chosen to be righteous and holy by their obedience to the commandments of God.

> vs. 12 "And, behold, I come quickly; and my reward is with me, to give to every man according as his work shall be."

370

This is another compelling reason why the sayings of the prophecy of this book shall not be sealed. Its message is one of great urgency. The unrighteous and the filfthy, if they neglect its warnings, will just as surely suffer the judgments here foretold, as the righteous and the holy will luxurate in its promised reward. Because Christ is coming quickly to give to every man, in whichsoever class he may fall, according to his work.

This solemn pronouncement is made by none other than the Christ, who here announces Himself as:

vs. 13 "I am Alpha and Omega, the beginning and the end, the first and the last."

Here Christ in this epilogue employs the same terms as he used in the prologue. (Rev. 1:8)

In the prologue reference He adds, "the Almighty," thus claiming to be one with the Father. All begins with God and so here, since all ends with God, He rolls down the curtain on the drama of human history.

He now adds the seventh and final beatitude of the Book of Revelation.

vs. 14 "Blessed are they that do his commandments, that they may have right to the tree of Life, and may enter in through the gates of the city."

Man lost his access to the Tree of Life in the Garden of Eden by his disobedience. By his obedience to God's commandments he will have access to the Tree of Life in the Garden within the Holy City.

No wonder Jesus said, "If ye love me, keep my commandments" (John 14:15) and again, "And why call me, Lord, Lord, and do not the things which I say?" (Luke 6:46). And yet again:

> "He that rejecteth me, and receiveth not my words, hath one that judgeth him: the word that I have spoken, the same shall judge him in the last day." (John 12:48)

Over against this Christ declares of those who follow human creeds, confessions of faith, decrees of councils and doctrines of men:

> "But in *vain do they worship me, teaching* for *doctrines* the *commandments* of *men*." (Matt. 15:9)

An interesting added light shed on this passage is the literal translation as rendered by such authorities as the Codex Sinaiticus, Codex Alexandrinus the Vulgate and some Armenian copies:

> "Blessed they that wash their robes, that they may have

371

power over the tree of life, and enter into the gates into the city."

Rotherham translates it:

"Happy they who are washing their robes that their right (authority, license or permission) may be unto the tree of life and by the gates they enter into the city."

Thus we see the literal translation defines to "do His commandments" as equivalent to "they that wash their robes."

By this we see that washing or cleansing is a primary qualification to entering into the gates of the Holy City and to having access to the Tree of Life.

And how are we washed or cleansed? said Ananias to Saul, who became the apostle Paul: "And now why tarriest thou? Arise and be baptized, and *wash* away thy sins, calling on the name of the Lord." (Acts 22:16)

Paul in turn after he became a Christian and an inspired teacher of the commandments of Christ said: "Husbands, love your wives, even as Christ loved the church, and gave himself for it; that he might sanctify and cleanse it with the *washing of water* by the word. (Eph. 5:25,26)

Again Paul declared: "Not by works of righteousness which we have done, but according to his mercy he saved us, by the *washing of regeneration* and renewing of the Holy Spirit." (Titus 3:5)

Paul said: "Therefore, we are buried with him by baptism into death." (Rom. 6:4) This was predicated on his preceeding question, "Know ye not, that so many of us as were baptized into Jesus Christ were *baptized into His death*." (Rom. 6:3)

In Christ's death He shed His blood that remits sin, washing it away. That is why Peter on Pentecost said: "Repent and be baptized every one of you in the name of Jesus Christ *for the remission of your sins*." (Acts 2:38)

Blessed, then are those who through being buried with Him in baptism have access to the cleansing of Christ's blood, thus washing their robes that they may have their right to the Tree of Life and enter by the gates into the city.

Ones clothers are reckoned with himself; hence the scriptural figure of keeping one's garments and washing one's robes. And so he that hath not on the wedding garment is to be cast out and debared from sitting at the table of the Lamb. Thus in Rev. 16:15 we read, "Blessed is he that watcheth and *keepeth his garments*, lest he walk naked and they see his shame."

Nevertheless, this last beatitude of promise is followed by a forceable reminder of the status of those who by disobedience did not wash their garments and remain under the curse.

vs. 15 "For without are dogs, and sorcerers, and whoremongers, and murderers, and idolaters, and whosoever loveth and maketh a lie."

So not all may enter the Holy city. All can see and understand why the sorcerers and whoremongers and murderers and idolaters may not enter therein, but not many can see with equal clarity that those who make a lie may not enter there.

They are unable to see that to teach false doctrine contrary to the Scriptures, even though done in all sincerity, damns just as completely.

All such are *without,* even as those who have washed their garments by complying with Christ's commandments, are *within* the Holy city.

The completeness of this list of those without is revealed by the fact that seven classes of persons are listed, namely, dogs, representive of unclean animals, sorcerers, whoremongers, murderers, idolaters, whosoever loveth a lie and whosoever maketh a lie.

Now Christ now adds his further and emphatic attestation to the inspiration and authoritativeness of the book.

vs. 16 "I Jesus have sent mine angel to testify unto you these th'ngs in the churches."

This "I Jesus" stands in contradistinction the "I John" of Rev. 22:8. Christ declares He sent His angel to testify unto the churches the things that John affirms he had seen. Christ makes it forever clear that it is He who has given us these revelations.

John begins the book with "The Revelation of Jesus Christ" and here near its close Christ affirms that this is His revelation of things to the churches.

All the things contained in this book, its prophecies, revelations, promises, judgments, rest for their acceptance, not upon the word of a mere man, however honest and truthful, but upon Christ's own authoritative word.

Christ backs up this declaration by a glorious revelation of Himself in the last of His *"I am's."*

vs. 16b "I am the root and the offspring of David, and the bright and morning star."

Here Christ declares His diety and humanity, that He is both God and man." First, He is the *root,* or origination of David.

373

Second, He is the offspring of David, or David's son because He was, in His incarnation, born of the house and lineage of David.

By this surprisingly wonderful revelation of His dual nature, since His ascension and enthronement at the right hand of God, He makes known to us that He still retains the humanity, though now in a glorified form, which He assumed in His incarnation.

Since we are to be like Him, this is an earnest of our redemption that our humanity shall also be glorified, in our house not made with hands, eternal in the heavens.

Then follows an additional affirmation: "I am the bright and morning star."

Speaking of the "more sure word of prophecy," Peter said, "We have also a more sure word of prophecy, whereunto ye do well that ye take heed, as unto a light that shineth in a dark place, until the *day dawn,* and the *day star* arise in your hearts." (II Pet. 1:19)

Thus Christ promises to appear as the bright and morning star to those who accept the sayings of the prophecy of this book and look for His coming.

As the morning star shines more brightly just before the break of day, so He will shine all the brighter to His true followers before His return and the dawning of the radiant morn of eternity.

Stirred by the prospect of His return, the Spirit and the bride of the Lamb, the church extends the most gracious of all gracious invitations. Since Christ has sent His angel to testify these things in the churches, it now becomes the urgent responsibility of the churches to testify these things to others.

vs. 17 "And the Spirit and the bride say, Come." In verses 7 and 12 Christ has said He will come quickly, and here the Spirit and the bride respond to His promise by inviting Him to come. Their invitation is pressed into a single, but fervently potent word, "Come."

When Christ, before His departure, promised the coming of the Holy Spirit to comfort His apostles, He said, "He will guide you into all truth: and He will show you things to come." (John 16:13)

So throughout the existence of the church, the Holy Spirit has not only been teaching, comforting and energizing the church, but He has been showing the things to come. In all the operations of the Spirit there has been a constant looking for the consumation of all things in the coming of Christ, of whom He witnessed.

374

Therefore the Holy Spirit not only extends this invitation, but has inspired the church to join His importunings.

While the close association of the Spirit and the bride, the church is portrayed throughout the other New Testament books, this is the first instance in the book of Revelation that the joining together of the Spirit and the bride is mentioned.

After inviting Christ to come, the Spirit and the bride extend a second gracious invitation to all who have heard the gracious promise to join in the invitation and say, "Come." "And let him that heareth say, come. And let him that is athirst come. And whosoever will, let him take the water of life freely."

At the beginning of the apocalypse the church was portrayed as seven candelsticks, and the purpose of a candlestick is to give light, to shine as lights in the world, holding forth the world of life.

Christ, in the preceeding verse, had just said that he had sent His angel to testify these things in the churches. Now it becomes the responsibility of the churches to testify these things to others.

And if any one is athirst for the waters proffered, let him come —that is come into the fellowship of Christ, the Holy Spirit and the church.

"And whosoever will, let him take of the water of life freely." The *will* to come is the first essential in coming; the will not to come is the first step in the rejection of this gracious invitation. It has been well said, if said in a homely way, "In the end there will be only two classes of people, the whosoever wills and the whosoever won'ts."

That the accurate preservation of this book—the Wonder Book of the Bible—may be accomplished there follows a solemn warning is pronounced, the like of which is not associated with any other book of the sacred canon. A stern warning is issued against tampering with this last book either by adding to it or taking away from it.

> *vs. 18, 19* "For I testify unto every man that heareth the prophecy of this book, if any man shall add unto these things, God shall add unto him the plagues that arc written in this book:
>
> And if any man shall take away from the words of the book of this prophecy, God shall take away his part out of the book of life, and out of the Holy City, and from the things that are written in this book."

What a fearful thing it is to add to the living word! What a terrible thing it is to take from or stultify the word of God, and especially the words of the prophecy of this book.

For these reasons the author has prayed constantly that he might have the divine guidance of the Teacher of the church, the Holy Spirit, since He was to guide into all truth. Endeavoring to read nothing into this book, not contained therein, nor to delete from it anything it presents, these lines have been written. According to the grace and light given unto me I have written.

While there has been this solemn consciousness of condemnation for adding to or taking from the words of the prophecy of this book, there has been also an ever increasing realization of the seriousness of another injunction concerning this book. That sacred injunction reads:

"Blessed is he that readeth, and they that hear the words of this prophecy, and keep those things which are written therein." (Rev. 1:3)

If I have been in error I plead God's mercy and forgiveness; if I have spoken the truth in Christ—"I lie not, my conscience also bearing me witness in the Holy Spirit"—may God give his added blessing to my humble testimony.

In either eventuality may God further and hasten His eternal truth until it shall cover the earth as the waters cover the seas.

Weighing God's warnings at the end of this book, with the blessings promised at its beginning, deep conviction has moved the writing. Coupled with this consideration has been the deep and moving conviction that these things to be testified by the church are of extreme importance in the closing days of the present age.

In this stern pronouncement of the penalty for taking away from the words of the book of this prophecy, that "God shall take away his part out of the book of life, and out of the Holy City" there is also a grim warning on the danger of falling from grace.

Only those who were once in grace would have any part in the book of life or a portion in the Holy City. Such blessings could not apply to those who had never accepted God's mercy and washed their robes in the blood of the Lamb. For "whosoever was not found written in the book of life was cast into the lake of fire." (Rev. 20:15)

The warning is, that those who otherwise are enrolled in the book of life and are thus prospectively entitled to a part in the Holy City, may fall and forfeit such reward, by taking away from the words of the book of this prophecy. Such action could come about either by a deliberate taking away, or by thoughtless neglect.

As the book begins with the declaration "The Revelation of Jesus Christ," it closes with a parting pronouncement from the One who is herein revealed.

vs. 20 "He which testifieth these things saith, surely I come quickly."

We cannot fail to note the prominence of the word "Come" in the closing verses of this great book. Three times it occurs in verse 17. The Spirit and the bride say "come." He that hears, says, "come." He that is athirst, also, says, "come."

Now in this verse before us, Christ says, "Surely, I *come* quickly."

Finally, the apostle John here at the end of the book, bows his head and writes:

"Amen. Even so *come*, Lord Jesus."

And the word "come" is used so frequently in these closing words, because the coming of Christ runs like a scarlet thread throughout the New Testament scriptures. It is estimated that one out of every twenty-five words of the New Testament pertains to His coming. It is ever the abiding hope of the church.

But those under grace are not alone in holding this hope. Nature groans waiting His coming to rectify her grave disorders occasioned by the fall and its consequent curse visited upon the ground.

But grace, being more articulate, joins John in his supplication. "Amen," so be it. "Even so come, Lord Jesus."

Thus this book-the "Wonder Book of the Bible" comes to a close. We join in the apostolic benediction:

"The grace of the Lord Jesus Christ be with you all. Amen."

THE SEVENS OF REVELATION

1. *The Seven Churches* Rev. 1:4
2. *The Seven Eternalities*
   1. "Which is and which was and which is to come." Rev. 1:4
   2. "Which is and which was and is to come" Rev. 1:8
   3. 'I am He that liveth, and was dead, and I am alive" Rev. 1:18
   4. "The first and the last, which was dead and is alive" Rev. 2:8
   5. "Which was and is, and is to come" Rev. 4:8

6. "Which art, and wast, and art to come" Rev. 11:17
7. "Which art, and wast, and shalt be" Rev. 16:5
3. *The Seven Golden Candlesticks* Rev. 1:12
4. *The Seven Beatitudes*
   1. "Blessed is he that readeth" Rev. 1:3
   2. "Blessed are the dead that die in the Lord from henceforth" Rev. 14:13
   3. "Blessed is he that watcheth and keepeth his garments" Rev. 16:15
   4. "Blessed are they which are called unto the marriage supper of the Lamb" Rev. 19:9
   5. "Blessed and holy is he that hath part in the first resurrection" Rev. 20:6
   6. "Blessed is he that keepeth the sayings of the prophecy of this book" Rev. 22:7
   7. "Blessed are they that do His commandments" Rev. 22:15
5. *The Seven-fold description of Christ* Rev. 1:14-16
6. *The Seven Stars* Rev. 1:20
7. *The Seven Angels of the Churches* Rev. 1:20
8. *The Seven Letters to the Churches* Rev. 2:1-3:22
9. *The Seven-fold Arrangement of the Seven Letters* Rev. 2:1-3:22
   1. Salutation
   2. Declaration of works
   3. Commendation, or censure
   4. Reproof
   5. Exhortation
   6. Admonition
   7. Promise
10. *The Seven Declarations "I know thy works"* Rev. 2:1-3:22
11. *The Seven Admonitions "He that hath an ear, let him hear"* Rev. 2:1-3:22
12. *The Seven Lamps of fire* Rev. 4:5
13. *The Seven Seals of the Book* Rev. 5:1
14. *The Seven Horns of the Lamb* Rev. 5:6
15. *The Seven Eyes of Christ* Rev. 5:6
16. *The Seven things which Christ is worthy to receive* Rev. 5:12
17. *The Seven Seals* Rev. 6:1 to 8:1
18. *The Seven-fold Doxology* Rev. 7:2
19. *The Seven Trumpets* Rev. 8:2-11:19
20. *The Seven Angels which stand before God* Rev. 8:2

21. *The Seven Thunders* Rev. 10:3
22. *The Seven Heads of the Dragon* Rev. 12:3
23. *The Seven Crowns on the Seven Heads of the Dragon* Rev. 12:3
24. *The Seven Personages* Rev. 12:1-13:11
    1. Woman
    2. Satan
    3. Man-child
    4. Archangel
    5. Remnant of woman's seed
    6. The beast coming up out of the sea
    7. The beast coming up out of the earth.
25. *The Seven Angels having the Seven Last Plagues* Rev. 15:6
26. *The Seven Plagues* Rev. 15:6
27. *The Seven Golden Vials* Rev. 15:7
28. *The Seven Heads of the Scarlet Colored Beast* Rev. 17:3
29. *The Seven Mountains* Rev. 17:9
30. *The Seven Kings* Rev. 17:10
31. *The Seven Dooms*—The Doom of:
    1. Babylon
    2. The beast
    3. The false prophet
    4. The kings
    5. Gog and Magog
    6. Satan
    7. The unbelieving dead.
32. *The twenty-eight items of merchandise of Babylon,* or seven multiplied by four Rev. 18:12, 13
33. *The Seven New things* Rev. 21:1-22:1
    1. New Heaven
    2. New earth
    3. New creation
    4. New Jerusalem
    5. New temple
    6. New light
    7. New garden
34. *The Seven Visions of Revelation*
35. *The Seven calls to come out of Babylon*
36. *Seven mentions of the Book of Life*